In this new anthology a member of the American Oriental Society, Professor George L. Anderson, introduces the Western reader to an important and dynamic theater that has existed for thousands of years—

THE THEATER OF THE ORIENT.

Two Sanskrit plays, one by the famous classical writer Kālidāsa, the other an anonymous work attributed to a fourth-century dramatist, are dramas founded in the sacred scriptures of the Vedas, stories that combine the sensual and the spiritual in the style typical of Indian theater.

The evocative Japanese Nō plays are a ritualized form of poetry, music, and dance which probably originated in ceremonies centering about ancient shrine festivals. Other types of Japanese plays—the Jōruri and the Kabuki—deal with melodramatic and sentimental themes much like our western "soap operas." The first is a puppet theater, the second a drama performed by masked actors in symbolic stage settings.

The use of ritual, the downgrading of plot, the depicting of emotional nuance, are dramatic methods particular to Oriental theater—methods that have growing importance in contemporary Western drama.

Each group of plays is accompanied by Professor Anderson's introductory commentary and by extensive notes on the plays.

Other Mentor Anthologies of Outstanding Plays

THE GENIUS OF THE EARLY ENGLISH THEATER *edited by Sylvan Barnet, Morton Berman, and William Burto* (MQ438—75¢)

THE GENIUS OF THE FRENCH THEATER *edited by Albert Bermel* (MQ366—95¢)

THE GENIUS OF THE IRISH THEATER *edited by Sylvan Barnet, Morton Berman, and William Burto* (MT315—75¢)

THE GENIUS OF THE ITALIAN THEATER *edited by Eric Bentley* (MQ599—95¢)

THE GENIUS OF THE LATER ENGLISH THEATER *edited by Sylvan Barnet, Morton Berman, and William Burto* (MQ448—95¢)

THE GENIUS OF THE SCANDINAVIAN THEATER *edited by Evert Sprinchorn* (MQ600—95¢)

The Genius of the ORIENTAL THEATER

EDITED WITH INTRODUCTIONS AND NOTES BY

G. L. Anderson, 1920-

A MENTOR BOOK

Published by THE NEW AMERICAN LIBRARY,
New York and Toronto
THE NEW ENGLISH LIBRARY LIMITED, London

FIRST PRINTING, AUGUST, 1966

NOTE: Application for reproducing the plays and essays in this volume protected by copyright against any unauthorized performance or publication, in whole or in part, in any medium, should be made to the copyright holders, as indicated on the title page preceding each selection.

Library of Congress Catalog Card No. 66:22974

MENTOR TRADEMARK REG. U.S. PAT. OFF. AND FOREIGN COUNTRIES
REGISTERED TRADEMARK—MARCA REGISTRADA
HECHO EN CHICAGO, U.S.A.

MENTOR BOOKS are published *in the United States*
by The New American Library, Inc.
1301 Avenue of the Americas, New York, New York 10019,
in Canada by The New American Library of Canada Limited
295 King Street East, Toronto 2, Ontario,
in the United Kingdom by The New English Library Limited,
Barnard's Inn, Holborn, London, E.C. 1, England

PRINTED IN THE UNITED STATES OF AMERICA

Preface

Various kinds of drama and theatricals, almost all of them involving some form of dance, have been known in the Far East since early times. But only two of the great civilizations of the Oriental world have considered the drama as a major art form—India and Japan. Considerable drama exists elsewhere, but it has either remained in a popular or folk tradition or has not been regarded as a serious competitor to poetry in the world of literature. A large number of plays have come down to us from China, for instance, and a sophisticated drama existed there as far back as the thirteenth century. Nevertheless, the Chinese did not regard drama, either at its beginnings or since, as a major art form.

In India and Japan the situation has been quite different. Sanskrit drama in India goes back perhaps as early as the first centuries of the Christian era, has a long and vigorous history, and boasts half a dozen illustrious names, the chief one being Kālidāsa. In Japan, an aristocratic court drama of great poetry and beauty arose in the fourteenth century, the Nō drama, and in the seventeenth century a popular drama of considerable range and variety, the Kabuki (or Jōruri, if intended for the puppet stage), arose and continues to this day to draw crowds to the theaters of Tōkyō, Kyōto, and Ōsaka. The great masters of these forms—Zeami (or Seami) for the Nō and Chikamatsu for the Kabuki—are becoming and should become as well known in the West as Shakespeare is in the East.

It is for these reasons, and not to slight the fascinating drama of China and the puppet and shadow plays of Southeast Asia, that this volume, *The Genius of the Oriental Theater*, has been confined to India and Japan. The dramas included here or ones similar to them are still regularly performed and draw enthusiastic audiences; they are not of historical interest only. The editor has sat fascinated by plays like these in Tōkyō, in Kanazawa, and in New York, and is hopeful that a rising interest in Asian civilization will bring more of them to our local stage and cause more Americans to seek them out abroad.

I am indebted to all of the translators whose work appears

herein, but especially to Professor Donald Keene, whose translations of Chikamatsu make all earlier ones obsolete. This volume will, I trust, point the way to new readers to his large collection and be a gesture toward a decade of debts incurred by drawing on his advice in various matters, large and small. I am also indebted to Professor A. C. Scott and to the Hokuseido Press for expediting my use of his translation of *Kanjinchō,* that most typical Kabuki play. What has been borrowed from Professors Keene and Scott will be obvious; the distortions of it, where they occur, are my own.

The translations are printed, needless to say, without change, but I have everywhere adapted the original notes and added others, except for *The Courier for Hell,* for which Professor Keene prepared elaborate notes in his original edition. These are rendered verbatim.

Contents

Preface v

Part One: Indian Drama

Introduction to Indian Drama 9

Kālidāsa
Shakuntalā and the Ring of Recognition 16

Anonymous
The Little Clay Cart 124

Part Two: Japanese Drama—The Nō Play

Introduction to the Nō Play 281

Zeami
Haku Rokuten 289

Zembō Motoyasu
Atsumori at Ikuta 299
Early Snow 307

Zenchiku Ujinobu 313
Aoi no Uye 313

Hiyoshi Sa-ami Yasukiyo
Benkei on the Bridge 323

Miyamasu
The Hatmaker 331

Part Three: Japanese Drama—Kabuki and Jōruri Theater

Introduction to the Kabuki and Jōruri theater 343

Chikamatsu Monzaemon
The Courier for Hell 351

Namiki Gohei III
The Subscription List 391

Selected Bibliography 414

Part One

INDIAN DRAMA

Religion permeates every phase of Indian life even to this
ıy, and it is not surprising that despite the worldly sophis-
cation of Indian drama, its origins are traced to the *Vedas,*
ıe oldest and most sacred of the Indian scriptures. The god
rahma, the creative principle in Hindu religion, created
ıe drama as a source of pleasure for mankind and the other
ɔds, so the legend goes, by fashioning a fifth *veda,* which
as a sacred textbook of dramatic theory. From the *Rig-*
eda, which is the oldest and which is in part in dialogue
rm, came the element of dramatic dialogue. The *Sama-*
eda, a collection of hymns, provided the element of song.
he *Yajur-veda,* a manual setting forth the rituals of the
ırly church, describes the birth of mimetic art. And finally,
ıe *Atharva-veda,* a collection of incantations and spells,
ɔntributes the delineation of emotion or sentiments to the
rama, sentiments being the most important of all the com-
ɔnents of drama in Hindu theory, as we shall see. The leg-
ıd goes on to include the services of the other two gods of
ıe Hindu triad: Shiva, the god of time and death and de-
ruction, brought the dance into dramatic art; Vishnu "the
reserver," the third god, invented the four dramatic styles
classical drama. Delegated to do the work of actually
eating the first plays was the sage Bharata. He remains the
rst playwright, comparable to the Greek Thespis. A holy
eda for the drama, needless to say, does not survive, but
is said to be partially preserved in the *Nātyashāstra*
3ook of the Drama), which is attributed to Bharata. In
reek culture and in other cultures the divine origins of the
ama were attested to, and it is a natural process for the
ama to derive from religious pageantry and ritual; but the
dian tradition emphasizes as well the creation of a sacred

manual of dramaturgy. Certainly the *Nātyashāstra* ga birth to a series of detailed compendia of dramatic theo which in general have a far more exhaustive analysis of t components of the play than do similar Western works.

It is impossible to date with much certainty either t early plays or the theoretical texts written in Sanskrit, t classical language of India. It is possible the *Nātyashāst* dates back to the fourth century A.D. The three great nam in the early Sanskrit drama seem to cluster around the city Ujjayinī, which was located on the Siprā River in the mo ern state of Gwalior in north central India. There is today town called Ujjain near the site. A series of dynamic d nasties occupied this site from before the beginning of t Christian era. Perhaps during the reigns of the Gupta kin of the fourth century A.D. the drama reached its flower. Th dramatist Bhāsa survives, if the attributions are correct, in number of plays, one of which may be the source for *Th Little Clay Cart*. Certainly a sophisticated dramatic traditic was long established by the time of *The Little Clay Ca* and Kālidāsa, and we can imagine Ujjayinī as a rich ar worldly city of courtiers, wealthy merchants, and conside able intellectual attainments. Sūdraka, to whom is attril uted *The Little Clay Cart,* is probably mythical and is give superhuman attributes in accounts of him. The play itself ma date from the fourth century and is certainly after Bhās Little illumination is achieved by calling the author of th play "Pseudo-Sūdraka," as has been done. Kālidāsa's co siderable dramatic achievements come after *The Little Cla Cart*. Dramatic tradition by the time of all three of the writers was highly formalized and remained so for ce turies. This is not to say that later playwrights were n inventive—types of drama multiply and treatises on theo became increasingly complex—but a major tradition is e tablished early and remains *the* tradition. There is not th swift transition such as we have in English drama from Eliz bethan exuberance to Jacobean pessimism through Restor tion heroics to eighteenth-century sentimentalism. The da ing, therefore, of the Sanskrit plays that have survived far less important critically than it would be with Wester literary works.

The subject matter of Indian drama may be drawn eithe from the legends preserved in the great epics, the *Mah bhārata* and the *Rāmāyana,* or may be the invention c the author. If the former, we can presume that the entir body of legends was thoroughly known to the audience i the same way that the Greek audience knew as they sav *edipus Rex* that before the action of the play Oedipus' ther had been warned he would sire a murderer, that after e action of the play Oedipus would go on to Colonus, ıd that his twin sons would reign over Thebes and fall into ternecine strife. The Sanskrit drama, when it is derived om legend, perhaps even more than the Greek assumes an quaintance with a vast body of historical and religious gend—the *Mahābhārata* is almost four times the length the *Iliad* and *Odyssey* combined—and there is a greater nployment of divine and semi-divine figures. As with Greek ama, certain painful and unpleasant scenes were denied e stage in the name of propriety. Indian dramatic theory uts less emphasis on plot than did early Western theory, we shall see, and the total time for the action of a play ould cover years, but the single act was supposed to be conned to a day. Narrative prologues to the acts sometimes ıpply the links if a considerable amount of time was imaged to have elapsed between acts. The greatest literary fects of the plays are achieved in Sanskrit, the language of e upper classes (somewhat comparable to Latin in the Eupean tradition), but social castes are separated by the se of language: the hero speaks Sanskrit, as do kings, memers of the Brahman or priestly caste, and others of high ınk. Various colloquial dialects of Sanskirt called Prākrits are mployed by women and all men of the lower orders. Someıing comparable to this might be achieved in English by aving the hero of a drama speak Oxford English, his reiners cockney English, the queen with a southern drawl, e policemen Brooklynese, the court jester with a Texas vang, and the heroine French-Canadian English. This ould startle us to the extent that we would regard the play s a farce, but the differences in the Sanskrit drama are, in act, greater linguistically and significant in that they repesent caste levels. For comic effects, characters are somemes portrayed affecting a language form above their level.

The Hindu passion for elaborate classification permits the sting of many dramatic types, but there is nothing comarable to the stark tragedy of either Greek or modern Vestern drama. Joy and sorrow are mixed in the plays, but appy endings prevail. The hero's associate is frequently the *idūshaka* or court jester, and elements of farce are present. he hero himself is noble and self-controlled. He may be lightearted and suitable for the role of lover, or a person of reat strength and nobility, fit to govern an empire with firmess and wisdom but without egotism and vanity. This type of ero has affinities with certain too-perfect heroes of English and French drama of the neo-classical period. The hero heart is capacious enough to retain love and affection for wife or former love while he is occupied with a new lov Love is the subject, in fact, of many of the dramas, an *Shakuntalā* is typical in that the hero is a king who alread has several wives, but who is smitten with love for a beau teous maiden. The heroines of Indian drama have as man facets as the heroes and are elaborately classified. Wives ma be inexperienced, partly experienced, or fully experience and bold, and the heroine who is a lover has, according t the *Nātyashāstra,* one of no less than eight different poss ble relationships to her hero. The most ingenious of the class fication systems invents 128 possible types of heroines. Whi this type of logical *reductio ad absurdum* is not characte istic of Western approaches to the drama, the characters c the plays, in general, parallel the types we see in Elizabetha dramas of courts and kings, with porters and country bump kins at the bottom of the social hierarchy and ministers an magistrates at the top.

The most conspicuous difference between Sanskrit an Western drama is due to the Indian theory of *rasa* or "flavor, sometimes but less correctly translated as "sentiment." Supe ficially the structure of a Sanskrit play like *The Little Cla Cart* or *Shakuntalā* seems Western and Aristotelian. Thes plays seem, in fact, like loosely organized Western drama with an overabundance of fanciful or supernatural element and weak plots. Because Western literary critics since Shake speare's time have been attacking and defending his plot and debating the loosely structured mixtures of tragedy an comedy that are the Elizabethan drama, we may feel at hom with the Sanskrit plays and conclude that they are similar But the aesthetics of Sanskrit drama puts value on things othe than plot. The great influence of Aristotle's *Poetics* in th West has made plot predominate in our dramatic thinking To Aristotle, the poet (not only the dramatic poet) is first an foremost a maker of plots. The Indian emphasis is elsewhere

Sanskrit dramatic theory sees the play as a pageant o kaleidoscope of emotional moods or nuances which are varia tions of a predominant emotion or *rasa.* Thus the funda mental emotion of *Shakuntalā* is the erotic *rasa,* but end less variations are possible within it—jealousy, shyness, pas sion, melancholy, the pangs of separation, etc. Each act of a play, and each scene within each act, may be conceived o as having a dominating flavor. While no one would deny tha such an approach is possible for any Western drama, one would suspect that if such an analysis of a Western play were

ıade, it would be subjective and individual and that it would
e difficult to find critics who would agree on the precise
avor of a scene. But the Indian audience is cued to the
roper emotional response by traditional poetic devices in
he words of the play and by gestures on the stage. Thus
o one can mistake it that King Dushyanta has been struck
y love early in *Shakuntalā* because twitches of the eyelids
nd various other forms of "body English" indicate specific
ypes of good and bad omens. Furthermore, various natural
bjects—flowers, grass, weather—have their symbolic value.
n Western literature, too, of course, there are some con-
entional symbols that operate at least in our folklore: the
ose, perhaps, is a general symbol for beauty. But within the
ndividual literary work in the West the author is likely to
vork out his own code of symbols, and we do not object
o long as their meanings within the work are consistent. In
anskrit drama, however, we encounter a complicated struc-
ure of conventionalized poetic devices and stage gestures
vhich the audience learns and which it applies automatically
o the stage situation, somewhat in the way that the Western
pera-goer interprets minor and major themes as they occur
n an opera that he has listened to many times before.

The Sanskrit drama is, therefore, a series of depictions of
sychological states through words and stage business that
ngender appropriate emotions in the audience. Presumably if
he audience fails to be aroused with the proper emotion,
he play or the production is poor. If an individual member
f the audience is stimulated by an inappropriate emotion,
he fault lies with him—he is not in a receptive mood. This
s not to say that there are no ineffable and subjective re-
ctions in the audience. All art works permit us a degree
f entirely personal reaction. But the Indian audience is
dequately cued on what emotional state is intended to be
enerated by a given scene.

This emphasis on states of feeling rather than on plot en-
ourages the Sanskrit dramatist to write dramas that are pano-
amas of emotions. His forte is, if he is a good playwright,
he depiction of emotional nuances. His plot should be ade-
uate, of course, just as the depiction of emotion in a Western
rama must be adequate, but the Sanskrit playwright is less
oncerned with a compact plot. Greek tragedy, in comparison
vith Indian drama, puts a premium on tight plots and deep
nd intense but limited emotions. This is presumably the
pitome of Western drama. The Indian epic, incidentally, is
lso likely to cover an extended period of time (like our
nedieval romances), while Aristotle tells us that the epic

should have a single action and be about only part of tl
hero's life, not about his whole career. The Sanskrit dran
does generally confine its action within an act to the leng
of the action itself or of a day, but years may elapse durin
the intermissions.

The history of the early Indian theater is very obscur
We assume that dramas like *The Little Clay Cart* an
Shakuntalā were performed in palaces or in the homes
the wealthy, with little or no scenery except perhaps a cu
tain at the back through which the actors entered. It is likel
that costumes were both splendid and conventionalized s
that the audience knew at once that a king or a god wa
speaking. The origins of the drama are so closely involve
with those of the dance that we assume sophisticated actin
techniques did much to eliminate the need for props. An
one who has seen an Indian or Southeast Asian danc
imitate with his body or even with just his hands and arms
serpent or a tiger realizes that a stuffed animal or a ma
dressed in a skin and attempting a realistic imitation is fa
less effective.

Shakuntalā and the Ring of Recognition

(*ABHIJÑĀNA-ŚAKUNTALA*)

By Kālidāsa

Translated by Monier Williams. Second edition, Oxford, 1867.

Shakuntalā

Shakuntalā is the culmination of Kālidāsa's art, and happily it is possible to compare it not only with his other plays but with its source in the Indian epic, the *Mahābhārata*.[1] The erotic sentiment, which dominates *Shakuntalā*, makes the play a series of changes on love, sensual and spiritual. Shakuntalā is first transformed in the play from a shy and innocent maiden to a wronged mother, seeking just recognition for her lawfully born, noble son, and then to a woman purified by patience and fidelity and finally rewarded for virtue.

Working within a tradition that puts no premium on a tightly constructed plot, Kālidāsa is able to extend his drama over a long period of time and to provide his audience with a great variety of scenes. Many of them portray aspects of love, but others, like the complaints of the *vidūshaka,* or clown, about the rigors of the hunt or the interrogation of the fisherman by the police, are simple vignettes of human experience which are universal in appeal. The tone of the play is set by the piety and virtue of Dushyanta. His character requires him to be totally proper despite his love-at-first-sight infatuation with Shakuntalā. Given this premise, Shakuntalā's voluptuousness (echoed by the natural world around her in the hermitage) remains innocent even after the gibes of her handmaidens, and it is necessary for Kālidāsa to introduce the curse of the sage Durvāsas to give the play any plot at all. This rather arbitrary introducing

[1] The "Story of Shakuntalā" from the *Mahābhārata* is translated, along with another version of the play, by Arthur W. Ryder in *Shakuntala and Other Writings by Kālidāsa* (New York: Dutton Everyman Library, 1959).

of an element of conflict may disturb those used to Western plots, and the accidental resolving of the dilemma by the discovery of the ring may be equally disturbing. No faults exist in the character of the king, and the only fault that exists in Shakuntalā—her unintentional slighting of Durvāsas—is small and her punishment for it excessive.

The audience, not concerned with these matters, must have found the play an anthology of surefire dramatic devices and the proper mixture of the serious and comical. There are scenes of parting and reconciliation, of young love and maternal love, of the duties and pleasures of warriors—all of these set against a rich background of nature poetically depicted. The journey through the heavens on the chariot of Mātali in the final act was certainly a joy to the Hindu audience, however much a sudden shift into the world of the supernatural bothers us aesthetically today (in Greek tragedy perhaps as much as here).

Kālidāsa's poetic gifts are difficult to transmit across the language barrier.[2] His descriptions are complicated and yet vivid; he is both subtle and suggestive, and also simple and direct when the characterization demands it.

There are two chief recensions of the play, with considerable differences between them. The one translated here is the so-called Bengali or *devanāgari* version. The other one is from south India. Neither one is superior to the other.

[2] Keith provides some examples of poetic diction in his *Sanskrit Drama*, pp. 161–165 (see Bibliography).

CHARACTERS

DUSHYANTA, *King of India*
MĀDHAVYA, *a jester, companion of the king, the vidūshaka*
KANVA, *chief of the hermits, foster-father of Shakuntalā*
SHĀRNGARAVA } *two Brahman priests of the hermitage of*
SHĀRADVATA } *Kanva*
MITRĀVASU, *brother-in-law of the King and chief of police*
JĀNUKA } *policemen*
SŪCHAKA }
VĀTAYĀNA, *the chamberlain of the women's apartments*
SOMARĀTA, *a domestic priest*
KARABHAKA, *a messenger of the Queen*
RĀIVATAKA, *a doorkeeper*
MĀTALI, *charioteer of the god Indra*
SARVADAMANA (*afterwards* BHARATA), *a little boy, a son of the King by Shakuntalā*
KASHYAPA, *father of the gods*
SHAKUNTALĀ, *daughter of a sage and a divine nymph, foster-child of Kanva*
PRIYAMVADĀ } *companions of Shakuntalā*
ANASŪYĀ }
GAUTAMĪ, *hermit-mother of the hermitage*
VASUMATĪ, *King Dushyanta's queen*
SĀNUMATĪ, *a nymph, friend of Shakuntalā*
TĀRALIKĀ, *personal attendant of the King*
CHATURIKĀ, *personal attendant of the Queen*
VETRAVATĪ, *female doorkeeper*
PARABHARTIKĀ } *maidens in charge of the royal gardens*
MADHUKARIKĀ }
SUVRATĀ, *a nurse*
ADITI, *wife of Kashyapa and mother of the gods*
STAGE MANAGER *and* ACTRESS (*in the Prologue*)
FISHERMAN, HERMITS, COURT ATTENDANTS

Scenes: Acts I–IV, Kanva's hermitage. Acts V–VI, the King's Palace. Act VII, a celestial mountain,

The action takes place during a seven-year period.

Shakuntalā

PROLOGUE

Invocation

Isha preserve you! he who is revealed
In these eight forms by man perceptible—
Water, of all creation's works the first;
The fire that bears on high the sacrifice
Presented with solemnity to heaven;
The Priest, the holy offerer of gifts;
The Sun and Moon, those two majestic orbs,
Eternal marshalers of day and night;
The subtle Ether, vehicle of sound,
Diffused throughout the boundless universe;
The Earth, by sages called "The place of birth
Of all material essences and things";
And Air, which giveth life to all that breathe.[a]

Stage Manager (*after the recitation of the invocation, looking towards the tiring-room*). Lady, when you have finished attiring yourself, come this way.

Actress (*entering*). Here I am, Sir; what are your commands?

Stage Manager. We are here before the eyes of an audience of educated and discerning men; and have to represent in their presence a new drama composed by Kālidāsa, called, "Shakuntalā, or the Lost Ring." Let the whole company exert themselves to do justice to their several parts.

Actress. You, Sir, have so judiciously managed the cast of the characters, that nothing will be defective in the acting.

[a] Shiva the Destroyer, Vishnu the Preserver, and Brahma the Creator are the three chief Hindu gods. The various things enumerated in this invocation are manifestations of Shiva.

Stage Manager. Lady, I will tell you the exact state of the case.

No skill in acting can I deem complete,
Till from the wise the actor gain applause:
Know that the heart e'en of the truly skilful,
Shrinks from too boastful confidence in self.

Actress (*modestly*). You judge correctly. And now, what are your commands?

Stage Manager. What can you do better than engage the attention of the audience by some captivating melody?

Actress. Which among the seasons shall I select as the subject of my song?

Stage Manager. You surely ought to give the preference to the present Summer season that has but recently commenced, a season so rich in enjoyment. For now

Unceasing are the charms of halcyon days,
When the cool bath exhilarates the frame;
When sylvan gales are laden with the scent
Of fragrant Pātalas; when soothing sleep
Creeps softly on beneath the deepening shade;
And when, at last, the dulcet calm of eve
Entrancing steals o'er every yielding sense.

Actress. I will.

Fond maids, the chosen of their hearts to please,
Entwine their ears with sweet Shirīsha flowers,
Whose fragrant lips attract the kiss of bees
That softly murmur through the summer hours.

Stage Manager. Charmingly sung! The audience are motionless as statues, their souls riveted by the enchanting strain. What subject shall we select for representation, that we may insure a continuance of their favor?

Actress. Why not the same, Sir, announced by you at first? Let the drama called "Shakuntalā, or the Lost Ring," be the subject of our dramatic performance.

Stage Manager. Rightly reminded! For the moment I had forgotten it.

Your song's transporting melody decoyed
My thoughts, and rapt with ecstasy my soul;
As now the bounding antelope allures
The King Dushyanta on the chase intent. (*Exeunt.*)

ACT I

Scene—A forest

Enter King Dushyanta, *armed with a bow and arrow, in a chariot, chasing an antelope, attended by his* Charioteer.

Charioteer (*looking at the deer, and then at the* King).
Great Prince,
When on the antelope I bend my gaze,
And on your Majesty, whose mighty bow
Has its string firmly braced; before my eyes
The god that wields the trident seems revealed,
Chasing the deer that flies from him in vain.

King. Charioteer, this fleet antelope has drawn us far from my attendants. See! there he runs:—
Aye and anon his graceful neck he bends
To cast a glance at the pursuing car;
And dreading now the swift-descending shaft,
Contracts into itself his slender frame:
About his path, in scattered fragments strewn,
The half-chewed grass falls from his panting mouth;
See! in his airy bounds he seems to fly,
And leaves no trace upon th' elastic turf.

(*With astonishment.*)

How now! swift as is our pursuit, I scarce can see him.

Charioteer. Sire, the ground here is full of hollows; I have therefore drawn in the reins and checked the speed of the chariot. Hence the deer has somewhat gained upon us. Now that we are passing over level ground, we shall have no difficulty in overtaking him.

King. Loosen the reins, then.
Charioteer. The King is obeyed.

(*Drives the chariot at full speed.*)

Great Prince, see! see!
Responsive to the slackened rein, the steeds
Chafing with eager rivalry, career
With emulative fleetness o'er the plain;
Their necks outstretched, their waving plumes, that late
Fluttered above their brows, are motionless;
Their sprightly ears, but now erect, bent low;
Themselves unsullied by the circling dust,
That vainly follows on their rapid course.

King (*joyously*). In good sooth, the horses seem as if they would outstrip the steeds of Indra and the Sun.[b]
That which but now showed to my view minute
Quickly assumes dimension; that which seemed
A moment since disjoined in diverse parts,
Looks suddenly like one compacted whole;
That which is really crooked in its shape
In the far distance left, grows regular;
Wondrous the chariot's speed, that in a breath,
Makes the near distant and the distant near.
Now, Charioteer, see me kill the deer.

(*Takes aim.*)

A Voice (*behind the scenes*). Hold, O King! this deer belongs to our hermitage. Kill it not! kill it not!
Charioteer (*listening and looking*). Great King, some hermits have stationed themselves so as to screen the antelope at the very moment of its coming within range of your arrow.
King (*hastily*). Then stop the horses.
Charioteer. I obey.

(*Stops the chariot.*)

Enter a Hermit, *and two others with him.*

Hermit (*raising his hand*). This deer, O King, belongs to our hermitage. Kill it not! kill it not!

[b] Indra is the god of the atmosphere, and like Apollo, drives the chariot of the sun across the heavens.

Now heaven forbid this barbèd shaft descend
Upon the fragile body of a fawn,
Like fire upon a heap of tender flowers!
Can thy steel bolts no meeter quarry find
Than the warm life-blood of a harmless deer?
Restore, great Prince, thy weapon to its quiver;
More it becomes thy arms to shield the weak,
Than to bring anguish on the innocent.

King. 'Tis done.

(*Replaces the arrow in its quiver.*)

Hermit. Worthy is this action of a Prince, the light of Puru's race.
Well does this act befit a Prince like thee,
Right worthy is it of thine ancestry.
Thy guerdon be a son of peerless worth,
Whose wide dominion shall embrace the earth.

Both the other hermits (*raising their hands*). May heaven indeed grant thee a son, a sovereign of the earth from sea to sea!

King (*bowing*). I accept with gratitude a Brahman's[c] benediction.

Hermit. We came hither, mighty Prince, to collect sacrificial wood. Here on the banks of the Mālinī you may perceive the hermitage of the great sage Kanva. If other duties require not your presence, deign to enter and accept our hospitality.
When you behold our penitential rites
Performed without impediment by Saints
Rich only in devotion, then with pride
Will you reflect, Such are the holy men
Who call me Guardian; such the men for whom
To wield the bow I bare my nervous arm,
Scarred by the motion of the glancing string.

King. Is the Chief of your Society now at home?

Hermit. No; he has gone to Somatīrtha[d] to propitiate Destiny, which threatens his daughter Shakuntalā with some calamity; but he has commissioned her in his absence to entertain all guests with hospitality.

King. Good! I will pay her a visit. She will make me acquainted with the mighty sage's acts of penance and devotion.

[c] The highest and priestly caste.
[d] A shrine in West India on the Gujarat coast.

Hermit. And we will depart on our errand.
(*Exit with his companions.*)

King. Charioteer, urge on the horses. We will at least purify our souls by a sight of this hallowed retreat.

Charioteer. Your Majesty is obeyed.

(*Drives the chariot with great velocity.*)

King (*looking all about him*). Charioteer, even without being told, I should have known that these were the precincts of a grove consecrated to penitential rites.

Charioteer. How so?

King. Do not you observe?

Beneath the trees, whose hollow trunks afford
Secure retreat to many a nestling brood
Of parrots, scattered grains of rice lie strewn.
Lo! here and there are seen the polished slabs
That serve to bruise the fruit of Ingudī
The gentle roe-deer, taught to trust in man,
Unstartled hear our voices. On the paths
Appear the traces of bark-woven vests
Borne dripping from the limpid fount of waters.
And mark!
Laved are the roots of trees by deep canals,
Whose glassy waters tremble in the breeze;
The sprouting verdure of the leaves is dimmed
By dusky wreaths of upward curling smoke
From burnt oblations; and on new-mown lawns
Around our car graze leisurely the fawns.

Charioteer. I observe it all.

King (*advancing a little further*). The inhabitants of this sacred retreat must not be disturbed. Stay the chariot, that I may alight.

Charioteer. The reins are held in. Your Majesty may descend.

King (*alighting*). Charioteer, groves devoted to penance must be entered in humble attire. Take these ornaments. (*Delivers his ornaments and bow to the* Charioteer.) Charioteer, see that the horses are watered, and attend to them until I return from visiting the inhabitants of the hermitage.

Charioteer. I will. (*Exit.*)

King (*walking and looking about*). Here is the entrance to the hermitage. I will now go in.

(*Entering, he feels a throbbing sensation in his arm.*)

Serenest peace is in this calm retreat,
By passion's breath unruffled; what portends
My throbbing arm?[e] Why should it whisper here
Of happy love? Yet everywhere around us
Stand the closed portals of events unknown.

A Voice (*behind the scenes*). This way, my dear compan ions; this way.

King (*listening*). Hark! I hear voices to the right of yonde grove of trees. I will walk in that direction. (*Walking an looking about.*) Ah! here are the maidens of the hermitag coming this way to water the shrubs, carrying watering pots proportioned to their strength. (*Gazing at them.*) Ho graceful they look!
In palaces such charms are rarely ours;
The woodland plants outshine the garden flowers.
I will conceal myself in this shade and watch them.

(*Stands gazing at them.*)

Enter Shakuntalā, *with her two female companions, em ployed in the manner described.*

Shakuntalā. This way, my dear companions; this way.

Anasūyā. Dear Shakuntalā, one would think that Fath Kanva had more affection for the shrubs of the hermitag even than for you, seeing he assigns to you who are you self as delicate as the fresh-blown jasmine, the task filling with water the trenches which encircle their root

Shakuntalā. Dear Anasūyā, although I am charged by m good father with this duty, yet I cannot regard it as a tas I really feel a sisterly love for these plants.

(*Continues watering the shrubs.*)

King. Can this be the daughter of Kanva? The saintly ma though descended from the great Kashyapa,[f] must be ve deficient in judgment to habituate such a maiden to t life of a recluse.
The sage who would this form of artless grace
Inure to penance—thoughtlessly attempts
To cleave in twain the hard acacia's stem
With the soft edge of a blue lotus leaf.

[e] Throbbings and twitchings on the right side (for men) signi good omens: this is an omen of love.

[f] The father of the inferior gods, the animal world, demons, a mankind—by his various wives.

Well! concealed behind this tree, I will watch her without raising her suspicions.

Conceals himself.)

hakuntalā. Good. Anasūyā, Priyamvadā has drawn this bark-dress too tightly about my chest. I pray thee, loosen it a little.

nasūyā. I will.

Loosens it.)

riyamvadā (*smiling*). Why do you lay the blame on me? Blame rather your own blooming youthfulness which imparts fulness to your bosom.

ing. A most just observation!
This youthful form, whose bosom's swelling charms
By the bark's knotted tissue are concealed,
Like some fair bud close folded in its sheath,
Gives not to view the blooming of its beauty.
But what am I saying? In real truth, this bark-dress, though ill-suited to her figure, sets it off like an ornament.
The lotus with the Saivala entwined
Is not a whit less brilliant: dusky spots
Heighten the luster of the cold-rayed moon:
This lovely maiden in her dress of bark
Seems all the lovelier. E'en the meanest garb
Gives to true beauty fresh attractiveness.

hakuntalā (*looking before her*). Yon Keshara-tree beckons to me with its young shoots, which, as the breeze waves them to and fro, appear like slender figures. I will go and attend to it.

Walks towards it.)

riyamvadā. Dear Shakuntalā, prithee, rest in that attitude one moment.

hakuntalā. Why so?

riyamvadā. The Keshara-tree, whilst your graceful form bends about its stem, appears as if it were wedded to some lovely twining creeper.

hakuntalā. Ah! saucy girl, you are most appropriately named Priyamvadā ("Speaker of flattering things").

ing. What Priyamvadā says, though complimentary, is nevertheless true. Verily,
Her ruddy lip vies with the opening bud;

Her graceful arms are as the twining stalks;
And her whole form is radiant with the glow
Of youthful beauty, as the tree with bloom.

Anasūyā. See, dear Shakuntalā, here is the young jasmine which you named "the Moonlight of the Grove," the self-elected wife of the mango-tree. Have you forgotten it?

Shakuntalā. Rather will I forget myself. (*Approaching the plant and looking at it.*) How delightful is the season when the jasmine-creeper and the mango-tree seem thus to unite in mutual embraces! The fresh blossoms of the jasmine resemble the bloom of a young bride, and the newly-formed shoots of the mango appear to make it her natural protector.

(*Continues gazing at it.*)

Priyamvadā (*smiling*). Do you know, my Anasūyā, why Shakuntalā gazes so intently at the jasmine?

Anasūyā. No, indeed, I cannot imagine. I pray thee tell me.

Priyamvadā. She is wishing that as the jasmine is united to a suitable tree, so, in like manner, she may obtain a husband worthy of her.

Shakuntalā. Speak for yourself, girl; this is the thought in your own mind.

(*Continues watering the flowers.*)

King. Would that my union with her were permissible![g] and yet I hardly dare hope that the maiden is sprung from a caste different from that of the Head of the hermitage. But away with doubt:

That she is free to wed a warrior-king
My heart attests. For, in conflicting doubts,
The secret promptings of the good man's soul
Are an unerring index of the truth.

However, come what may, I will ascertain the fact.

Shakuntalā (*in a flurry*). Ah! a bee, disturbed by the sprinkling of the water, has left the young jasmine, and is trying to settle on my face.

(*Attempts to drive it away.*)

[g] Dushyanta is a pious man and knows he cannot marry Shakuntalā if she is of pure Brahman caste (he assumes Kanva is her father). He is of the next lower caste, the warriors. She turns out to be of mixed caste and acceptable.

King (*gazing at her ardently*). Beautiful! there is something charming even in her repulse.

Where'er the bee his eager onset plies,
Now here, now there, she darts her kindling eyes:
What love hath yet to teach, fear teaches now,
The furtive glances and the frowning brow.

(*In a tone of envy.*)

Ah happy bee! how boldly dost thou try
To steal the luster from her sparkling eye;
And in thy circling movements hover near,
To murmur tender secrets in her ear;
Or, as she coyly waves her hand, to sip
Voluptuous nectar from her lower lip!
While rising doubts my heart's fond hopes destroy,
Thou dost the fulness of her charms enjoy.

Shakuntalā. This impertinent bee will not rest quiet. I must move elsewhere. (*Moving a few steps off, and casting a glance around.*) How now! he is following me here. Help! my dear friends, help! deliver me from the attacks of this troublesome insect.

Priyamvadā and *Anasūyā.* How can we deliver you? Call Dushyanta to your aid. The sacred groves are under the king's special protection.

King. An excellent opportunity for me to show myself. Fear not—(*Checks himself when the words are half-uttered. Aside.*) But stay, if I introduce myself in this manner, they will know me to be the King. Be it so, I will accost them, nevertheless.

Shakuntalā (*moving a step or two further off*). What! it still persists in following me.

King (*advancing hastily*). When mighty Puru's offspring sways the earth,
And o'er the wayward holds his threatening rod,
Who dares molest the gentle maids that keep
Their holy vigils here in Kanva's grove?

(*All look at the* King, *and are embarrassed.*)

Anasūyā. Kind Sir, no outrage has been committed; only our dear friend here was teased by the attacks of a troublesome bee.

(*Points to* Shakuntalā.)

King (*turning to* Shakuntalā). I trust all is well with your devotional rites?

(Shakuntalā *stands confused and silent*.)

Anasūyā. All is well, indeed, now that we are honored by the reception of a distinguished guest. Dear Shakuntalā go, bring from the hermitage an offering of flowers, rice and fruit. This water that we have brought with us will serve to bathe our guest's feet.

King. The rites of hospitality[h] are already performed; your truly kind words are the best offering I can receive.

Priyamvadā. At least be good enough, gentle Sir, to sit down awhile, and rest yourself on this seat shaded by the leaves of the Saptaparna tree.

King. You, too, must all be fatigued by your employment.

Anasūyā. Dear Shakuntalā, there is no impropriety in our sitting by the side of our guest: come, let us sit down here.

(*All sit down together*.)

Shakuntalā (*aside*). How is it that the sight of this man has made me sensible of emotions inconsistent with religious vows?

King (*gazing at them all by turns*). How charmingly your friendship is in keeping with the equality of your ages and appearance!

Priyamvadā (*aside to* Anasūyā). Who can this person be whose lively yet dignified manner, and polite conversation bespeak him a man of high rank?

Anasūyā. I too, my dear, am very curious to know. I will ask him myself. (*Aloud*.) Your kind words, noble Sir, fill me with confidence, and prompt me to inquire of what regal family our noble guest is the ornament? what country is now mourning his absence? and what induced a person so delicately nurtured to expose himself to the fatigue of visiting this grove of penance?

Shakuntalā (*aside*). Be not troubled, O my heart, Anasūyā is giving utterance to thy thoughts.

King (*aside*). How now shall I reply? shall I make myself known, or shall I still disguise my real rank? I have it; I will answer her thus. (*Aloud*.) I am the person charged by his majesty, the descendant of Puru, with the administration of justice and religion; and am come to this

[h] Traditional rites of hospitality. They do not know who he is.

sacred grove to satisfy myself that the rites of the hermits are free from obstruction.

Anasūyā. The hermits, then, and all the members of our religious society have now a guardian.

(Shakuntalā *gazes bashfully at the* King.)

Priyamvadā and *Anasūyā* (*perceiving the state of her feelings, and of the* King's. *Aside to* Shakuntalā). Dear Shakuntalā, if father Kanva were but at home to-day—

Shakuntalā (*angrily*). What if he were?

Priyamvadā and *Anasūyā.* He would honor this our distinguished guest with an offering of the most precious of his possessions.

Shakuntalā. Go to! you have some silly idea in your minds. I will not listen to such remarks.

King. May I be allowed, in my turn, to ask you maidens a few particulars respecting your friend?

Priyamvadā and *Anasūyā.* Your request, Sir, is an honor.

King. The sage Kanva lives in the constant practice of austerities. How, then, can this friend of yours be called his daughter?

Anasūyā. I will explain to you, Sir. You have heard of an illustrious sage of regal caste, Vishvāmitra, whose family name is Kaūsika.

King. I have.

Anasūyā. Know that he is the real father of our friend. The venerable Kanva is only her reputed father. He it was who brought her up, when she was deserted by her mother.

King. "Deserted by her mother!" My curiosity is excited; pray let me hear the story from the beginning.

Anasūyā. You shall hear it, Sir. Some time since, this sage of regal caste, while performing a most severe penance on the banks of the river Godāvarī, excited the jealousy and alarm of the gods; insomuch that they despatched a lovely nymph named Menakā to interrupt his devotions.

King. The inferior gods, I am aware, are jealous of the power which the practice of excessive devotion confers on mortals.

Anasūyā. Well, then, it happened that Vishvāmitra, gazing on the bewitching beauty of that nymph at a season when, spring being in its glory—

(*Stops short, and appears confused.*)

King. The rest may be easily divined. Shakuntalā, then, is the offspring of the nymph.[1]

Anasūyā. Just so.

King. It is quite intelligible.

How could a mortal to such charms give birth?
The lightning's radiance flashes not from earth.

(Shakuntalā *remains modestly seated with downcast eyes. Aside.*) And so my desire has really scope for its indulgence. Yet I am still distracted by doubts, remembering the pleasantry of her female companions respecting her wish for a husband.

Priyamvadā (*looking with a smile at* Shakuntalā, *and then turning towards the* King). You seem desirous, Sir, of asking something further.

(Shakuntalā *makes a chiding gesture with her finger.*)

King. You conjecture truly. I am so eager to hear the particulars of your friend's history, that I have still another question to ask.

Priyamvadā. Scruple not to do so. Persons who lead the life of hermits may be questioned unreservedly.

King. I wish to ascertain one point respecting your friend—

Will she be bound by solitary vows
Opposed to love, till her espousals only?
Or ever dwell with these her cherished fawns,
Whose eyes, in luster vieing with her own,
Return her gaze of sisterly affection?

Priyamvadā. Hitherto, Sir, she has been engaged in the practice of religious duties, and has lived in subjection to her foster-father; but it is now his fixed intention to give her away in marriage to a husband worthy of her.

King (*aside*). His intention may be easily carried into effect,

Be hopeful, O my heart, thy harrowing doubts
Are past and gone; that which thou didst believe
To be as unapproachable as fire,
Is found a glittering gem that may be touched.

Shakuntalā (*pretending anger*). Anasūyā, I shall leave you.

Anasūyā. Why so?

Shakuntalā. That I may go and report this impertinent Priyamvadā to the venerable matron, Gautamī.

[1] Vishvāmitra was tempted because excessive devotions were considered by the inferior gods to be a menace to their powers. The King finds out here that he can marry Shakuntalā since one of her parents was a nymph.

Anasūyā. Surely, dear friend, it would not be right to leave a distinguished guest before he has received the rights of hospitality, and quit his presence in this wilful manner.

(Shakuntalā, *without answering a word, moves away.*)

King (*making a movement to arrest her departure, but checking himself. Aside*). Ah! a lover's feelings betray themselves by his gestures.
When I would fain have stayed the maid, a sense
Of due decorum checked my bold design:
Though I have stirred not, yet my mien betrays
My eagerness to follow on her steps.

Priyamvadā (*holding* Shakuntalā *back*). Dear, it does not become you to go away in this manner.

Shakuntalā (*frowning*). Why not, pray?

Priyamvadā. You are under a promise to water two more shrubs for me. When you have paid your debt, you shall go, and not before.

(*Forces her to turn back.*)

King. Spare her this trouble, gentle maiden. The exertion of watering the shrubs has already fatigued her.
The water-jar has overtasked the strength
Of her slim arms; her shoulders droop, her hands
Are ruddy with the glow of quickened pulses;
E'en now her agitated breath imparts
Unwonted tremor to her heaving breast;
The pearly drops that mar the recent bloom
Of the Shirīsha pendant in her ear,
Gather in clustering circles on her cheek;
Loosed is the fillet of her hair: her hand
Restrains the locks that struggle to be free.
Suffer me, then, thus to discharge the debt for you.[1]

(*Offers a ring to* Priyamvadā. *Both the maidens, reading the name* Dushyanta *on the seal, look at each other with surprise.*)

King. Nay, think not that I am King Dushyanta. I am only the king's officer, and this is the ring which I have received from him as my credentials.

[1] Service in a hermitage for several years was considered a religious duty.

Priyamvadā. The greater the reason you ought not t
part with the ring from your finger. I am content to re
lease her from her obligation at your simple request. (*Wit*
a smile.) Now, Shakuntalā my love, you are at liberty t
retire, thanks to the intercession of this noble stranger
or rather of this mighty prince.

Shakuntalā (*aside*). My movements are no longer under m
own control. (*Aloud.*) Pray, what authority have you ove
me, either to send me away or keep me back?

King (*gazing at* Shakuntalā. *Aside*). Would I could ascertai
whether she is affected towards me as I am towards her
At any rate, my hopes are free to indulge themselves. Be
cause,

Although she mingles not her words with mine,
Yet doth her listening ear drink in my speech;
Although her eye shrinks from my ardent gaze,
No form but mine attracts its timid glances.

A Voice (*behind the scenes*). O hermits, be ready to protec
the animals belonging to our hermitage. King Dushyanta
amusing himself with hunting, is near at hand.

Lo! by the feet of prancing horses raised,
Thick clouds of moving dust, like glittering swarms
Of locusts in the glow of eventide,
Fall on the branches of our sacred trees;
Where hang the dripping vests of woven bark,
Bleached by the waters of the cleansing fountain.
And see!
Scared by the royal chariot in its course,
With headlong haste an elephant invades
The hallowed precincts of our sacred grove;
Himself the terror of the startled deer,
And an embodied hindrance to our rites.
The hedge of creepers clinging to his feet,
Feeble obstruction to his mad career,
Is dragged behind him in a tangled chain;
And with terrific shock one tusk he drives
Into the riven body of a tree,
Sweeping before him all impediments.

King (*aside*). Out upon it! my retinue are looking for me
and are disturbing this holy retreat. Well! there is no hel
for it; I must go and meet them.

Priyamvadā and *Anasūyā.* Noble Sir, we are terrified b
the accidental disturbance caused by the wild elephant
Permit us to return into the cottage.

King (*hastily*). Go, gentle maidens. It shall be our care tha
no injury happen to the hermitage.

(*All rise up.*)

Priyamvadā and *Anasūyā.* After such poor hospitality we are ashamed to request the honor of a second visit from you.

King. Say not so. The mere sight of you, sweet maidens, has been to me the best entertainment.

Shakuntalā. Anasūyā, a pointed blade of Kusha-grass [k] has pricked my foot; and my bark-mantle is caught in the branch of a Kuruvaka bush. Be so good as to wait for me until I have disentangled it.

(*Exit with her two companions, after making pretexts for delay, that she may steal glances at the* King.)

King. I have no longer any desire to return to the city. I will therefore rejoin my attendants, and make them encamp somewhere in the vicinity of this sacred grove. In good truth, Shakuntalā has taken such possession of my thoughts, that I cannot turn myself in any other direction.
My limbs drawn onward leave my heart behind,
Like silken pennon borne against the wind.

[k] A sacred grass used at religious ceremonies.

ACT II

Scene—A plain on the skirts of the forest

Enter the jester, Mādhavya, *in a melancholy mood.*

Mādhavya (*sighing*). Heigh-ho! what an unlucky fellow I am! worn to a shadow by my royal friend's sporting propensities. "Here's a deer!" "There goes a boar!" "Yonder's a tiger!" This is the only burden of our talk, while in the heat of the meridian sun we toil on from jungle to jungle, wandering about in the paths of the woods, where the trees afford us no shelter. Are we thirsty? We have nothing to drink but the foul water of some mountain stream, filled with dry leaves which give it a most pungent flavor. Are we hungry? We have nothing to eat but roast game, which we must swallow down at odd times, as best we can. Even at night there is no peace to be had. Sleeping is out of the question, with joints all strained by dancing attendance upon my sporting friend; or if I do happen to doze, I am awakened at the very earliest dawn by the horrible din of a lot of rascally beaters and huntsmen, who must needs surround the wood before sunrise, and deafen me with their clatter. Nor are these my only troubles. Here's a fresh grievance, like a new boil rising upon an old one! Yesterday, while we were lagging behind, my royal friend entered yonder hermitage after a deer; and there, as ill-luck would have it, caught sight of a beautiful girl, called Shakuntalā, the hermit's daughter. From that moment, not another thought about returning to the city! and all last night, not a wink of sleep did he get for thinking of the damsel. What is to be done? At any rate, I will be on the watch for him as soon as he has finished his toilet. (*Walking and looking about.*) Oh! here he comes, attended by the Yavana women with bows in their hands, and wearing garlands of wild flowers. What shall I do? I have it. I will pretend to stand in the easiest attitude for resting my bruised and crippled limbs.

(*Stands leaning on a staff.*)

Enter King Dushyanta, *followed by a retinue in the manner described.*

King. True, by no easy conquest may I win her,
Yet are my hopes encouraged by her mien.
Love is not yet triumphant; but, methinks,
The hearts of both are ripe for his delights.
(*Smiling.*) Ah! thus does the lover delude himself; judging of the state of his loved one's feelings by his own desires. But yet,
The stolen glance with half-averted eye,
The hesitating gait, the quick rebuke
Addressed to her companion, who would fain
Have stayed her counterfeit departure; these
Are signs not unpropitious to my suit.
So eagerly the lover feeds his hopes,
Claiming each trivial gesture for his own.

Mādhavya (*still in the same attitude*). Ah, friend, my hands cannot move to greet you with the usual salutation. I can only just command my lips to wish your majesty victory.

King. Why, what has paralyzed your limbs?

Mādhavya. You might as well ask me how my eye comes to water after you have poked your finger into it.

King. I don't understand you; speak more intelligibly.

Mādhavya. Ah, my dear friend, is yonder upright reed transformed into a crooked plant by its own act, or by the force of the current?

King. The current of the river causes it, I suppose.

Mādhavya. Aye; just as you are the cause of my crippled limbs.

King. How so?

Mādhavya. Here are you living the life of a wild man of the woods in a savage, unfrequented region, while your state affairs are left to shift for themselves; and as for poor me, I am no longer master of my own limbs, but have to follow you about day after day in your chases after wild animals, till my bones are all crippled and out of joint. Do, my dear friend, let me have one day's rest.

King (*aside*). This fellow little knows, while he talks in this manner, that my mind is wholly engrossed by recollections of the hermit's daughter, and quite as disinclined to the chase as his own.

No longer can I bend my well-braced bow
Against the timid deer; nor e'er again
With well-aimed arrows can I think to harm
These her beloved associates, who enjoy
The privilege of her companionship;
Teaching her tender glances in return.

Mādhavya (*looking in the* King's *face*). I may as well speak to the winds, for any attention you pay to my requests. I suppose you have something on your mind, and are talking it over to yourself.

King (*smiling*). I was only thinking that I ought not to disregard a friend's request.

Mādhavya. Then may the King live forever!

(*Moves off.*)

King. Stay a moment, my dear friend. I have something else to say to you.

Mādhavya. Say on, then.

King. When you have rested, you must assist me in another business, which will give you no fatigue.

Mādhavya. In eating something nice, I hope.

King. You shall know at some future time.

Mādhavya. No time better than the present.

King. What ho! there.

Warder (*entering*). What are your Majesty's commands?

King. O Raivataka! bid the General of the forces attend.

Warder. I will, Sire. (*Exits and reenters with the* General.) Come forward, General; his Majesty is looking towards you, and has some order to give you.

General (*looking at the* King). Though hunting is known to produce ill effects, my royal master has derived only benefit from it. For

Like the majestic elephant that roams
O'er mountain wilds, so does the King display
A stalwart frame, instinct with vigorous life.
His brawny arms and manly chest are scored
By frequent passage of the sounding string;
Unharmed he bears the mid-day sun; no toil
His mighty spirit daunts; his sturdy limbs,

Stripped of redundant flesh, relinquish nought
Of their robust proportions, but appear
In muscle, nerve, and sinewy fiber cased.
(*Approaching the* King.) Victory to the King! We have tracked the wild beasts to their lairs in the forest. Why delay, when everything is ready?

King. My friend Mādhavya here has been disparaging the chase, till he has taken away all my relish for it.

General (*aside to* Mādhavya). Persevere in your opposition, my good fellow; I will sound the King's real feelings, and humor him accordingly. (*Aloud.*) The blockhead talks nonsense, and your Majesty, in your own person, furnishes the best proof of it. Observe, Sire, the advantage and pleasure the hunter derives from the chase.
Freed from all grosser influences, his frame
Loses its sluggish humors, and becomes
Buoyant, compact, and fit for bold encounter.
'Tis his to mark with joy the varied passions,
Fierce heats of anger, terror, blank dismay,
Of forest animals that cross his path.
Then what a thrill transports the hunter's soul,
Pierces the moving mark! Oh! 'tis conceit
In moralists to call the chase a vice;
What recreation can compare with this?

Mādhavya (*angrily*). Away! tempter, away! The King has recovered his senses, and is himself again. As for you, you may, if you choose, wander about from forest to forest, till some old bear seizes you by the nose, and makes a mouthful of you.

King. My good General, as we are just now in the neighborhood of a consecrated grove, your panegyric upon hunting is somewhat ill-timed, and I cannot assent to all you have said. For the present,
All undisturbed the buffaloes shall sport
In yonder pool, and with their ponderous horns
Scatter its tranquil waters, while the deer,
Couched here and there in groups beneath the shade
Of spreading branches, ruminate in peace.
And all securely shall the herd of boars
Freed on the marshy sedge; and thou, my bow,
With slackened string enjoy a long repose.

General. So please your Majesty, it shall be as you desire.

King. Recall, then, the beaters who were sent in advance to surround the forest. My troops must not be allowed to disturb this sacred retreat, and irritate its pious inhabitants.

Know that within the calm and cold recluse
Lurks unperceived a germ of smothered flame,
All-potent to destroy; a latent fire
That rashly kindled bursts with fury forth:—
As in the disc of crystal that remains
Cool to the touch, until the solar ray
Falls on its polished surface, and excites
The burning heat that lies within concealed.

General. Your Majesty's commands shall be obeyed.

Mādhavya. Off with you, you son of a slave! Your nonsense won't go down here, my fine fellow. (*Exit* General.)

King (*looking at his attendants*). Here, women, take my hunting-dress; and you, Raivataka, keep guard carefully outside.

Attendants. We will, sire. (*Exeunt.*)

Mādhavya. Now that you have got rid of these plagues, who have been buzzing about us like so many flies, sit down, do, on that stone slab, with the shade of the tree as your canopy, and I will seat myself by you quite comfortably.

King. Go you, and sit down first.

Mādhavya. Come along, then.

(*Both walk on a little way, and seat themselves.*)

King. Mādhavya, it may be said of you that you have never beheld anything worth seeing: for your eyes have not yet looked upon the loveliest object in creation.

Mādhavya. How can you say so, when I see your Majesty before me at this moment?

King. It is very natural that everyone should consider his own friend perfect; but I was alluding to Shakuntalā, the brightest ornament of these hallowed groves.

Mādhavya (*aside*). I understand well enough, but I am not going to humor him. (*Aloud.*) If, as you intimate, she is a hermit's daughter, you cannot lawfully ask her in marriage. You may as well, then, dismiss her from your mind, for any good the mere sight of her can do.

King. Think you that a descendant of the mighty Puru could fix his affections on an unlawful object?
Though, as men say, the offspring of the sage,
The maiden to a nymph celestial owes
Her being, and by her mother left on earth,
Was found and nurtured by the holy man
As his own daughter, in this hermitage;—
So, when dissevered from its parent stalk,

Some falling blossom of the jasmine, wafted
Upon the sturdy sunflower, is preserved
By its support from premature decay.

Mādhavya (smiling). This passion of yours for a rustic maiden, when you have so many gems of women at home in your palace, seems to me very like the fancy of a man who is tired of sweet dates, and longs for sour tamarinds as a variety.

King. You have not seen her, or you would not talk in this fashion.

Mādhavya. I can quite understand it must require something surpassingly attractive to excite the admiration of such a great man as you.

King. I will describe her, my dear friend, in a few words—

Man's all-wise Maker, wishing to create
A faultless form, whose matchless symmetry
Should far transcend Creation's choicest works,
Did call together by his mighty will,
And garner up in his eternal mind,
A bright assemblage of all lovely things:—
And then, as in a picture, fashion them
Into one perfect and ideal form.
Such the divine, the wondrous prototype,
Whence her fair shape was molded into being.

Mādhavya. If that's the case, she must indeed throw all other beauties into the shade.

King. To my mind she really does.

This peerless maid is like a fragrant flower,
Whose perfumed breath has never been diffused;
A tender bud, that no profaning hand
Has dared to sever from its parent stalk;
A gem of priceless water, just released
Pure and unblemished from its glittering bed.
Or may the maiden haply be compared
To sweetest honey, that no mortal lip
Has sipped; or, rather to the mellowed fruit
Of virtuous actions in some former birth,
Now brought to full perfection? Lives the man
Whom bounteous heaven has destined to espouse her?

Mādhavya. Make haste, then, to her aid; you have no time to lose, if you don't wish this fruit of all the virtues to drop into the mouth of some greasy-headed rustic of devout habits.

King. The lady is not her own mistress, and her foster-father is not at home.

Mādhavya. Well, but tell me, did she look at all kindl
upon you?

King. Maidens brought up in a hermitage are naturally sh
and reserved; but for all that,

She did look towards me, though she quick withdrew
Her stealthy glances when she met my gaze;
She smiled upon me sweetly, but disguised
With maiden grace the secret of her smiles.
Coy love was half unveiled; then, sudden checked
By modesty, left half to be divined.

Mādhavya. Why, of course, my dear friend, you neve
could seriously expect that at the very first sight she woul
fall over head and ears in love with you, and withou
more ado come and sit in your lap.

King. When we parted from each other, she betrayed he
liking for me by clearer indications, but still with th
utmost modesty.

Scarce had the fair one from my presence passed,
When, suddenly, without apparent cause,
She stopped, and counterfeiting pain, exclaimed,
"My foot is wounded by this prickly grass."
Then glancing at me tenderly, she feigned
Another charming pretext for delay,
Pretending that a bush had caught her robe,
And turned as if to disentangle it.

Mādhavya. I trust you have laid in a good stock of provi
sions, for I see you intend making this consecrated grov
your game-preserve, and will be roaming here in ques
of sport for some time to come.

King. You must know, my good fellow, that I have bee
recognized by some of the inmates of the hermitage. Nov
I want the assistance of your fertile invention, in devisin
some excuse for going there again.

Mādhavya. There is but one expedient that I can suggest
You are the King, are you not?

King. What then?

Mādhavya. Say you have come for the sixth part of thei
grain, which they owe you for tribute.

King. No, no, foolish man; these hermits pay me a ver
different kind of tribute, which I value more than heap
of gold or jewels; observe,

The tribute which my other subjects bring
Must molder into dust, but holy men
Present me with a portion of the fruits
Of penitential services and prayers—
A precious and imperishable gift.

A Voice (*behind the scenes*). We are fortunate; here is the object of our search.

King (*listening*). Surely those must be the voices of hermits, to judge by their deep tones.

Warder (*entering*). Victory to the King! two young hermits are in waiting outside, and solicit an audience of your Majesty.

King. Introduce them immediately.

Warder. I will, my liege. (*Goes out, and reenters with two young* hermits.) This way, Sirs, this way.

(*Both the* Hermits *look at the* King.)

First Hermit. How majestic in his mien, and yet what confidence it inspires! But this might be expected in a king whose character and habits have earned for him a title only one degree removed from that of a Saint.

In this secluded grove, whose sacred joys
All may participate, he deigns to dwell
Like one of us; and daily treasures up
A store of purest merit for himself,
By the protection of our holy rites.
In his own person wondrously are joined
Both majesty and saintlike holiness:—
And often chanted by inspirèd bards,
His hallowed title of "Imperial Sage"
Ascends in joyous accents to the skies.

Second Hermit. Bear in mind, Gautamī, that this is the great Dushyanta, the friend of Indra.[1]

First Hermit. What of that?

Second Hermit. Where is the wonder if his nervous arm,
Puissant and massive as the iron bar
That binds a castle-gateway, singly sways
The scepter of the universal earth,
E'en to its dark-green boundary of waters?
Or if the gods, beholden to his aid
In their fierce warfare with the powers of hell,
Should blend his name with Indra's in their songs
Of victory, and gratefully accord
No lower meed of praise to his braced bow,
Than to the thunders of the god of heaven?

Both the Hermits (*approaching*). Victory to the King!

King (*rising from his seat*). Hail to you both!

[1] Indra and other inferior gods used and needed the assistance of mortal heroes in some of their battles against demons.

Both the Hermits. Heaven bless your Majesty!

(*They offer fruits.*)

King (*respectfully receiving the offering*). Tell me, I pra you, the object of your visit.

Both the Hermits. The inhabitants of the hermitage, havin heard of your Majesty's sojourn in our neighborhoo make this humble petition.

King. What are their commands?

Both the Hermits. In the absence of our Superior, the grea Sage Kanva, evil demons are disturbing our sacrifici rites.[m] Deign, therefore, accompanied by your charioteer to take up your abode in our hermitage for a few days.

King. I am honored by your invitation.

Mādhavya (*aside*). Most opportune and convenient, ce tainly!

King (*smiling*). Ho! there, Raivataka! Tell the chariotee from me to bring round the chariot with my bow.

Warder. I will, Sire. (*Exit.*

Both the Hermits (*joyfully*). Well it becomes the King b acts of grace
To emulate the virtues of his race.
Such acts thy lofty destiny attest;
Thy mission is to succor the distressed.

King (*bowing to the* hermits). Go first, reverend Sirs, I wi follow you immediately.

Both the Hermits. May victory attend you! (*Exeunt.*

King. My dear Mādhavya, are you not full of longing t see Shakuntalā?

Mādhavya. To tell you the truth, though I was just no brimful of desire to see her, I have not a drop left sinc this piece of news about the demons.

King. Never fear; you shall keep close to me for protectio

Mādhavya. Well, you must be my guardian-angel, and ac the part of a very Vishnu[n] to me.

Warder (*entering*). Sire, the chariot is ready, and only wait to conduct you to victory. But here is a messenger name Karabhaka, just arrived from your capital, with a messag from the Queen, your mother.

King (*respectfully*). How say you? a messenger from th venerable Queen?

[m] The purpose of the warrior caste is to protect the priestl caste. Certain demons called *rākshasas* harassed the pious hermit

[n] i.e., a preserver.

Warder. Even so.

King. Introduce him at once.

Warder. I will, Sire. (*Goes out and reenters with* Karabhaka.) Behold the King! Approach.

Karabhaka. Victory to the King! The Queen-mother bids me say that in four days from the present time she intends celebrating a solemn ceremony for the advancement and preservation of her son. She expects that your Majesty will honor her with your presence on that occasion.

King. This places me in a dilemma. Here, on the one hand, is the commission of these holy men to be executed; and, on the other, the command of my revered parent to be obeyed. Both duties are too sacred to be neglected. What is to be done?

Mādhavya. You will have to take up an intermediate position between the two, like King Trishanku,° who was suspended between heaven and earth, because the sage Vishvāmitra commanded him to mount up to heaven, and the gods ordered him down again.

King. I am certainly very much perplexed. For here,

Two different duties are required of me
In widely distant places; how can I
In my own person satisfy them both?
Thus is my mind distracted and impelled
In opposite directions, like a stream
That, driven back by rocks, still rushes on
Forming two currents in its eddying course.

(*Reflecting.*) Friend Mādhavya, as you were my playfellow in childhood, the Queen has always received you like a second son; go you, then, back to her and tell her of my solemn engagement to assist these holy men. You can supply my place in the ceremony, and act the part of a son to the Queen.

Mādhavya. With the greatest pleasure in the world; but don't suppose that I am really coward enough to have the slightest fear of those trumpery demons.

King (*smiling*). Oh! of course not; a great Brahman like you could not possibly give way to such weakness.

Mādhavya. You must let me travel in a manner suitable to the King's younger brother.

King. Yes, I shall send my retinue with you, that there may be no further disturbance in this sacred forest.

Mādhavya (*with a strut*). Already I feel quite like a young prince.

° A character in the Hindu epic, the *Rāmāyana.*

King (*aside*). This is a giddy fellow, and in all probability he will let out the truth about my present pursuit to the women of the palace. What is to be done? I must say something to deceive him. (*Aloud to* Mādhavya, *taking him by the hand.*) Dear friend, I am going to the hermitage wholly and solely out of respect for its pious inhabitants, and not because I have really any liking for Shakuntalā, the hermit's daughter. Observe,

What suitable communion could there be
Between a monarch and a rustic girl?
I did but feign an idle passion, friend,
Take not in earnest what was said in jest.

Mādhavya. Don't distress yourself; I quite understand.

(*Exeunt.*)

Prelude to Act III

Scene—The hermitage

Enter a young Brahman, *carrying bundles of Kusha-grass for the use of the sacrificing priests.*

Young Brahman. How wonderful is the power of King Dushyanta! No sooner did he enter our hermitage, than we were able to proceed with our sacrificial rites, unmolested by the evil demons.

No need to fix the arrow to the bow;
The mighty monarch sounds the quivering string,
Our demon foes are scattered to the wind.

I must now, therefore, make haste and deliver to the sacrificing priests these bundles of Kusha-grass, to be strewn round the altar. (*Walking and looking about; then addressing someone off the stage.*) Why, Priyamvadā, for whose use are you carrying that ointment of Usīra-root and those lotus leaves with fibers attached to them? (*Listening for her answer.*) What say you?—that Shakuntalā is suffering from fever produced by exposure to the sun, and that this ointment is to cool her burning frame? Nurse her with care, then, Priyamvadā, for she is cherished by our reverend Superior as the very breath of his nostrils. I, for my part, will contrive that soothing waters, hallowed in the sacrifice, be administered to her by the hands of Gautamī. (*Exit.*)

ACT III

Scene—The Sacred Grove

Enter King Dushyanta, *with the air of one in love.*

King (*sighing thoughtfully*). The holy sage possesses magi
power
In virtue of his penance; she, his ward,
Under the shadow of his tutelage
Rests in security. I know it well;
Yet sooner shall the rushing cataract
In foaming eddies re-ascend the steep,
Than my fond heart turn back from its pursuit.
God of Love! God of the flowery shafts! we are all o
us cruelly deceived by thee, and by the Moon, howeve
deserving of confidence you may both appear.
For not to us do these thine arrows seem
Pointed with tender flowerets; not to us
Doth the pale moon irradiate the earth
With beams of silver fraught with cooling dews:—
But on our fevered frames the moon-beams fall
Like darts of fire, and every flower-tipped shaft
Of Kāma,[p] as it probes our throbbing hearts,
Seems to be barbed with hardest adamant.
Adorable god of love! hast thou no pity for me? (*In a
tone of anguish.*) How can thy arrows be so sharp wher
they are pointed with flowers? Ah! I know the reason:
E'en now in thine unbodied essence lurks
The fire of Shiva's anger,[q] like the flame

[p] The god of love, envisioned as a figure like Cupid.

[q] Always an enemy of austerities, the god Kāma was blasted to a cinder by Shiva, whom he angered by reminding of his wife's love.

That ever hidden in the secret depths
Of ocean, smolders there unseen. How else
Couldst thou, all immaterial as thou art,
Inflame our hearts thus fiercely?—thou, whose form
Was scorched to ashes by a sudden flash
From the offended god's terrific eye.
Yet, methinks,
Welcome this anguish, welcome to my heart
These rankling wounds inflicted by the god,
Who on his scutcheon bears the monster-fish
Slain by his prowess: welcome death itself,
So that, commissioned by the lord of love,
This fair one be my executioner.
Adorable divinity! Can I by no reproaches excite your commiseration?
Have I not daily offered at thy shrine
Innumerable vows, the only food
Of thine ethereal essence? Are my prayers
Thus to be slighted? Is it meet that thou
Shouldst aim thy shafts at thy true votary's heart,
Drawing thy bow-string even to thy ear?
(*Pacing up and down in a melancholy manner.*) Now that the holy men have completed their rites, and have no more need of my services, how shall I dispel my melancholy? (*Sighing.*) I have but one resource. Oh for another sight of the idol of my soul! I will seek her. (*Glancing at the sun.*) In all probability, as the sun's heat is now at its height, Shakuntalā is passing her time under the shade of the bowers on the banks of the Mālinī, attended by her maidens. I will go and look for her there. (*Walking and looking about.*) I suspect the fair one has but just passed by this avenue of young trees.
Here, as she tripped along, her fingers plucked
The opening buds: these lacerated plants,
Shorn of their fairest blossoms by her hand,
Seem like dismembered trunks, whose recent wounds
Are still unclosed; while from the bleeding socket
Of many a severed stalk, the milky juice
Still slowly trickles, and betrays her path.
(*Feeling a breeze.*) What a delicious breeze meets me in this spot!
Here may the zephyr, fragrant with the scent
Of lotuses, and laden with the spray
Caught from the waters of the rippling stream,
Fold in its close embrace my fevered limbs.
(*Walking and looking about.*) She must be somewhere in

the neighborhood of this arbor of overhanging creepers, enclosed by plantations of cane. (*Looking down.*)

For at the entrance here I plainly see
A line of footsteps printed in the sand.
Here are the fresh impressions of her feet;
Their well-known outline faintly marked in front,
More deeply towards the heel; betokening
The graceful undulation of her gait.

I will peep through those branches. (*Walking and looking. With transport.*) Ah! now my eyes are gratified by an entrancing sight. Yonder is the beloved of my heart reclining on a rock strewn with flowers, and attended by her two friends. How fortunate! Concealed behind the leaves, I will listen to their conversation, without raising their suspicions.

(*Stands concealed, and gazes at them.*)

Shakuntalā *and her two attendants, holding fans in their hands, are discovered as described.*

Priyamvadā and *Anasūyā* (*fanning her. In a tone of affection*). Dearest Shakuntalā, is the breeze raised by these broad lotus leaves refreshing to you?

Shakuntalā. Dear friends, why should you trouble yourselves to fan me?

(Priyamvadā *and* Anasūyā *look sorrowfully at one another.*)

King. Shakuntalā seems indeed to be seriously ill. (*Thoughtfully.*) Can it be the intensity of the heat that has affected her? or does my heart suggest the true cause of her malady? (*Gazing at her passionately.*) Why should I doubt it?

The maiden's spotless bosom is o'erspread
With cooling balsam; on her slender arm
Her only bracelet, twined with lotus stalks,
Hangs loose and withered; her recumbent form
Expresses languor. Ne'er could noon-day sun
Inflict such fair disorder on a maid—
No, love, and love alone, is here to blame.

Priyamvadā (*aside to* Anasūyā). I have observed, Anasūyā, that Shakuntalā has been indisposed ever since her first interview with King Dushyanta. Depend upon it, her ailment is to be traced to this source.

Anasūyā. The same suspicion, dear Priyamvadā, has crossed

my mind. But I will at once ask her and ascertain the truth. (*Aloud.*) Dear Shakuntalā, I am about to put a question to you. Your indisposition is really very serious.

Shakuntalā (*half-rising from her couch*). What were you going to ask?

Anasūyā. We know very little about love-matters, dear Shakuntalā; but for all that, I cannot help suspecting your present state to be something similar to that of the lovers we have read about in romances. Tell us frankly what is the cause of your disorder. It is useless to apply a remedy, until the disease be understood.

King. Anasūyā bears me out in my suspicion.

Shakuntalā (*aside*). I am, indeed, deeply in love; but cannot rashly disclose my passion to these young girls.

Priyamvadā. What Anasūyā says, dear Shakuntalā, is very just. Why give so little heed to your ailment? Every day you are becoming thinner; though I must confess your complexion is still as beautiful as ever.

King. Priyamvadā speaks most truly.

Sunk is her velvet cheek; her wasted bosom
Loses its fulness; e'en her slender waist
Grows more attenuate; her face is wan,
Her shoulders droop;—as when the vernal blasts
Sear the young blossoms of the Mādhavī,
Blighting their bloom; so mournful is the change,
Yet in its sadness, fascinating still,
Inflicted by the mighty lord of love
On the fair figure of the hermit's daughter.

Shakuntalā. Dear friends, to no one would I rather reveal the nature of my malady than to you; but I should only be troubling you.

Priyamvadā and *Anasūyā.* Nay, this is the very point about which we are so solicitous. Sorrow shared with affectionate friends is relieved of half its poignancy.

King. Pressed by the partners of her joys and griefs,
Her much beloved companions, to reveal
The cherished secret locked within her breast,
She needs must utter it; although her looks
Encourage me to hope, my bosom throbs
As anxiously I listen for her answer.

Shakuntalā. Know then, dear friends, that from the first moment the illustrious Prince, who is the guardian of our grove, presented himself to my sight—

(*Stops short, and appears confused.*)

Priyamvadā and *Anasūyā*. Say on, dear Shakuntalā, say on

Shakuntalā. Ever since that happy moment, my heart's affections have been fixed upon him, and my energies of mind and body have all deserted me, as you see.

King (*with rapture*). Her own lips have uttered the words I most longed to hear.

Love lit the flame, and Love himself allays
My burning fever, as when gathering clouds
Rise o'er the earth in summer's dazzling noon,
And grateful showers dispel the morning heat.

Shakuntalā. You must consent, then, dear friends, to contrive some means by which I may find favor with the King, or you will have ere long to assist at my funeral.

King (*with rapture*). Enough! These words remove all my doubts.

Priyamvadā (*aside to* Anasūyā). She is far gone in love, dear Anasūyā, and no time ought to be lost. Since she has fixed her affections on a monarch who is the ornament of Puru's line, we need not hesitate for a moment to express our approval.

Anasūyā. I quite agree with you.

Priyamvadā (*aloud*). We wish you joy, dear Shakuntalā. Your affections are fixed on an object in every respect worthy of you. The noblest river will unite itself to the ocean, and the lovely Mādhavī-creeper clings naturally to the mango, the only tree capable of supporting it.

King. Why need we wonder if the beautiful constellation Vishākhā pines to be united with the Moon.

Anasūyā. By what stratagem can we best secure to our friend the accomplishment of her heart's desire, both speedily and secretly?

Priyamvadā. The latter point is all we have to think about. As to "speedily," I look upon the whole affair as already settled.

Anasūyā. How so?

Priyamvadā. Did you not observe how the King betrayed his liking by the tender manner in which he gazed upon her, and how thin he has become the last few days, as if he had been lying awake thinking of her?

King (*looking at himself*). Quite true! I certainly am becoming thin from want of sleep:—

As night by night in anxious thought I raise
This wasted arm to rest my sleepless head,
My jeweled bracelet, sullied by the tears
That trickle from my eyes in scalding streams,
Slips towards my elbow from my shriveled wrist.

Oft I replace the bauble, but in vain;
So easily it spans the fleshless limb
That e'en the rough and corrugated skin,
Scarred by the bow-string, will not check its fall.

Priyamvadā (*thoughtfully*). An idea strikes me. Anasūyā. Let Shakuntalā write a love-letter; I will conceal it in a flower, and contrive to drop it in the King's path. He will surely mistake it for the remains of some sacred offering, and will, in all probability, pick it up.

Anasūyā. A very ingenious device! It has my entire approval; but what says Shakuntalā?

Shakuntalā. I must consider before I can consent to it.

Priyamvadā. Could you not, dear Shakuntalā, think of some pretty composition in verse, containing a delicate declaration of your love?

Shakuntalā. Well, I will do my best; but my heart trembles when I think of the chances of a refusal.

King (*with rapture*). Too timid maid, here stands the man from whom
Thou fearest a repulse; supremely blessed
To call thee all his own. Well might he doubt
His title to thy love; but how couldst thou
Believe thy beauty powerless to subdue him?

Priyamvadā and *Anasūyā*. You undervalue your own merits, dear Shakuntalā. What man in his senses would intercept with the skirt of his robe the bright rays of the autumnal moon, which alone can allay the fever of his body?

Shakuntalā (*smiling*). Then it seems I must do as I am bid.

(*Sits down and appears to be thinking.*)

King. How charming she looks! My very eyes forget to wink, jealous of losing even for an instant a sight so enchanting.
How beautiful the movement of her brow,
As through her mind love's tender fancies flow!
And, as she weighs her thoughts, how sweet to trace
The ardent passion mantling in her face!

Shakuntalā. Dear girls, I have thought of a verse, but I have no writing-materials at hand.

Priyamvadā. Write the letters with your nail on this lotus leaf, which is smooth as a parrot's breast.

Shakuntalā (*after writing the verse*). Listen, dear friends, and tell me whether the ideas are appropriately expressed.

Priyamvadā and *Anasūyā*. We are all attention.

Shakuntalā (*reads*).
I know not the secret thy bosom conceals,
Thy form is not near me to gladden my sight;
But sad is the tale that my fever reveals,
Of the love that consumes me by day and by night.

King (*advancing hastily towards her*).
Nay, Love does but warm thee, fair maiden—thy frame
Only droops like the bud in the glare of the noon;
But me he consumes with a pitiless flame,
As the beams of the day-star destroy the pale moon.

Priyamvadā and *Anasūyā* (*looking at him joyfully, and rising to salute him*). Welcome, the desire of our hearts, that so speedily presents itself!

(Shakuntalā *makes an effort to rise.*)

King. Nay, trouble not thyself, dear maiden,
Move not to do me homage; let thy limbs
Still softly rest upon their flowery couch,
And gather fragrance from the lotus stalks
Bruised by the fevered contact of thy frame.

Anasūyā. Deign, gentle Sir, to seat yourself on the rock on which our friend is reposing.

(*The* King *sits down.* Shakuntalā *is confused.*)

Priyamvadā. Anyone may see at a glance that you are deeply attached to each other. But the affection I have for my friend prompts me to say something of which you hardly require to be informed.

King. Do not hesitate to speak out, my good girl. If you omit to say what is in your mind, you may be sorry for it afterwards.

Priyamvadā. Is it not your special office as a King to remove the suffering of your subjects who are in trouble?

King. Such is my duty, most assuredly.

Priyamvadā. Know, then, that our dear friend has been brought to her present state of suffering entirely through love for you. Her life is in your hands; take pity on her and restore her to health.

King. Excellent maiden, our attachment is mutual. It is I who am the most honored by it.

Shakuntalā (*looking at* Priyamvadā). What do you mean by detaining the King, who must be anxious to return to his royal consorts after so long a separation?

King. Sweet maiden, banish from thy mind the thought
That I could love another. Thou dost reign
Supreme, without a rival, in my heart,
And I am thine alone: disown me not,
Else must I die a second deadlier death—
Killed by thy words, as erst by Kāma's shafts.

Anasūyā. Kind Sir, we have heard it said that kings have many favorite consorts. You must not, then, by your behavior towards our dear friend, give her relations cause to sorrow for her.

King. Listen, gentle maiden, while in a few words I quiet your anxiety.
Though many beauteous forms my palace grace,
Henceforth two things alone will I esteem
The glory of my royal dynasty;—
My sea-girt realm, and this most lovely maid.

Priyamvadā and *Anasūyā.* We are satisfied by your assurances.

Priyamvadā (*glancing on one side*). See, Anasūyā, there is our favorite little fawn running about in great distress, and turning its eyes in every direction as if looking for its mother; come, let us help the little thing to find her.

(*Both move away.*)

Shakuntalā. Dear friends, dear friends, leave me not alone and unprotected. Why need you both go?

Priyamvadā and *Anasūyā.* Unprotected! when the Protector of the world is at your side. (*Exeunt.*)

Shakuntalā. What! have they both really left me?

King. Distress not thyself, sweet maiden. Thy adorer is at hand to wait upon thee.
Oh, let me tend thee, fair one, in the place
Of thy dear friends; and, with broad lotus fans,
Raise cooling breezes to refresh thy frame;
Or shall I rather, with caressing touch,
Allay the fever of thy limbs, and soothe
Thy aching feet, beauteous as blushing lilies?

Shakuntalā. Nay, touch me not. I will not incur the censure of those whom I am bound to respect.

(*Rises and attempts to go.*)

King. Fair one, the heat of noon has not yet subsided, and thy body is still feeble.
How canst thou quit thy fragrant couch of flowers,

And from thy throbbing bosom cast aside
Its covering of lotus leaves, to brave
With weak and fainting limbs the noon-day heat?

(*Forces her to turn back.*)

Shakuntalā. Infringe not the rules of decorum, mighty de scendant of Puru. Remember, though I love you, I hav no power to dispose of myself.

King. Why this fear of offending your relations, timid maid When your venerable foster-father hears of it, he will nc find fault with you. He knows that the law permits us t be united without consulting him.

In Indra's heaven, so at least 'tis said,
No nuptial rites prevail,[1] nor is the bride
Led to the altar by her future spouse;
But all in secret does the bridegroom plight
His troth, and each unto the other vow
Mutual allegiance. Such espousals, too,
Are authorized on earth, and many daughters
Of royal saints thus wedded to their lords,
Have still received their father's benison.

Shakuntalā. Leave me, leave me; I must take counsel wit my female friends.

King. I will leave thee when—

Shakuntalā. When?

King. When I have gently stolen from thy lips
Their yet untasted nectar, to allay
The raging of my thirst, e'en as the bee
Sips the fresh honey from the opening bud.

(*Attempts to raise her face.* Shakuntalā *tries to prevent him.*)

A Voice (*behind the scenes*). The loving birds, doomed by fate to nightly separation, must bid farewell to each other for evening is at hand.

Shakuntalā (*in confusion*). Great Prince, I hear the voice of the matron Gautamī. She is coming this way, to inquire after my health. Hasten and conceal yourself behind the branches.

King. I will.

(*Conceals himself.*)

[1] The so-called *gāndharva* form of marriage was a simple pledge without the usual ceremonies. It was supposed to be used by nymphs in Indra's paradise.

Enter Gautamī *with a vase in her hand, preceded by two attendants.*

Attendants. This way, most venerable Gautamī.

Gautamī (*approaching* Shakuntalā). My child, is the fever of thy limbs allayed?

Shakuntalā. Venerable mother, there is certainly a change for the better.

Gautamī. Let me sprinkle you with this holy water, and all your ailments will depart. (*Sprinkling* Shakuntalā *on the head.*) The day is closing, my child; come, let us go to the cottage.

(*They all move away.*)

Shakuntalā (*aside*). Oh my heart! thou didst fear to taste of happiness when it was within thy reach. Now that the object of thy desires is torn from thee, how bitter will be thy remorse, how distracting thine anguish! (*Moving on a few steps and stopping. Aloud.*) Farewell! bower of creepers, sweet soother of my sufferings, farewell! may I soon again be happy under thy shade.

(*Exit reluctantly with the others.*)

King (*returning to his former seat in the arbor. Sighing.*) Alas! how many are the obstacles to the accomplishment of our wishes!

Albeit she did coyly turn away
Her glowing cheek, and with her fingers guard
Her pouting lips, that murmured a denial
In faltering accents, she did yield herself
A sweet reluctant captive to my will,
As eagerly I raised her lovely face:
But ere with gentle force I stole the kiss,
Too envious Fate did mar my daring purpose.

Whither now shall I betake myself? I will tarry for a brief space in this bower of creepers, so endeared to me by the presence of my beloved Shakuntalā.

(*Looking round.*)

Here printed on the flowery couch I see
The fair impression of her slender limbs;
Here is the sweet confession of her love,
Traced with her nail upon the lotus leaf—
And yonder are the withered lily stalks
That graced her wrist. While all around I view

Things that recall her image, can I quit
This bower, e'en though its living charm be fled?

A Voice (*in the air*). Great King,
Scarce is our evening sacrifice begun,
When evil demons, lurid as the clouds
That gather round the dying orb of day,
Cluster in hideous troops, obscene and dread,
About our altars, casting far and near
Terrific shadows, while the sacred fire
Sheds a pale luster o'er their ghostly shapes.

King. I come to the rescue, I come. (*Exit.*

Prelude to Act IV

Scene—The garden of the hermitage

Enter Priyamvadā *and* Anasūyā *in the act of gathering flowers.*

Anasūyā. Although, dear Priyamvadā, it rejoices my heart to think that Shakuntalā has been happily united to a husband in every respect worthy of her, by the form of marriage prevalent among Indra's celestial musicians, nevertheless, I cannot help feeling somewhat uneasy in my mind.

Priyamvadā. How so?

Anasūyā. You know that the pious King was gratefully dismissed by the hermits on the successful termination of their sacrificial rites. He has now returned to his capital, leaving Shakuntalā under our care; and it may be doubted whether, in the society of his royal consorts, he will not forget all that has taken place in this hermitage of ours.

Priyamvadā. On that score be at ease. Persons of his noble nature are not so destitute of all honorable feeling. I confess, however, that there is one point about which I am rather anxious. What, think you, will Father Kanva say when he hears what has occurred?

Anasūyā. In my opinion, he will approve the marriage.

Priyamvadā. What makes you think so?

Anasūyā. From the first, it was always his fixed purpose to bestow the maiden on a husband worthy of her; and since heaven has given her such a husband, his wishes have been realized without any trouble to himself.

Priyamvadā (*looking at the flower-basket*). We have gathered flowers enough for the sacred offering, dear Anasūyā.

Anasūyā. Well, then, let us now gather more, that we ma have wherewith to propitiate the guardian-deity of ou dear Shakuntalā.

Priyamvadā. By all means.

(*They continue gathering.*)

A Voice (*behind the scenes*). Ho there! See you not that am here?

Anasūyā (*listening*). That must be the voice of a guest an nouncing his arrival.

Priyamvadā. Surely, Shakuntalā is not absent from the co tage. (*Aside.*) Her heart at least is absent, I fear.

Anasūyā. Come along, come along; we have gathere flowers enough.

(*They move away.*)

The same voice (*behind the scenes*). Woe to thee, maiden for daring to slight a guest like me!

Shall I stand here unwelcomed; even I,
A very mine of penitential merit,
Worthy of all respect? Shalt thou, rash maid,
Thus set at nought the ever sacred ties
Of hospitality? and fix thy thoughts
Upon the cherished object of thy love,
While I am present? Thus I curse thee, then—
He, even he of whom thou thinkest, he
Shall think no more of thee; nor in his heart
Retain thy image. Vainly shalt thou strive
To waken his remembrance of the past;
He shall disown thee, even as the sot,
Roused from his midnight drunkenness, denies
The words he uttered in his revelings.

Priyamvadā. Alas! alas! I fear a terrible misfortune ha occurred. Shakuntalā, from absence of mind, must hav offended some guest whom she was bound to treat wit respect. (*Looking behind the scenes.*) Ah! yes; I see, an no less a person than the great sage Durvāsas,[s] who i known to be most irascible. He it is that has just curse her, and is now retiring with hasty strides, trembling wit passion, and looking as if nothing could turn him. Hi wrath is like a consuming fire.

[s] This is the sage Durvāsas, who had a reputation for quick an ger—and severe penalties for those who did not honor him as h wished to be honored. His punishment of Shakuntalā's girlish neg ligence is excessive.

Anasūyā. Go quickly, dear Priyamvadā, throw yourself at his feet, and persuade him to come back, while I prepare a propitiatory offering for him, with water and refreshments.

Priyamvadā. I will. (*Exit.*)

Anasūyā (*advancing hastily a few steps and stumbling*). Alas! alas! this comes of being in a hurry. My foot has slipped and my basket of flowers has fallen from my hand.

(*Stays to gather them up.*)

Priyamvadā (*reentering*). Well, dear Anasūyā, I have done my best; but what living being could succeed in pacifying such a cross-grained, ill-tempered old fellow? However, I managed to mollify him a little.

Anasūyā (*smiling*). Even a little was much for him. Say on.

Priyamvadā. When he refused to turn back, I implored his forgiveness in these words: "Most venerable sage, pardon, I beseech you, this first offense of a young and inexperienced girl, who was ignorant of the respect due to your saintly character and exalted rank."

Anasūyā. And what did he reply?

Priyamvadā. "My word must not be falsified; but at the sight of the ring of recognition the spell shall cease." So saying, he disappeared.

Anasūyā. Oh! then we may breathe again; for now I think of it, the King himself, at his departure, fastened on Shakuntalā's finger, as a token of remembrance, a ring on which his own name was engraved. She has, therefore, a remedy for her misfortune at her own command.

Priyamvadā. Come, dear Anasūyā, let us proceed with our religious duties.

(*They walk away.*)

Priyamvadā (*looking off the stage*). See, Anasūyā, there sits our dear friend, motionless as a statue, resting her face on her left hand, her whole mind absorbed in thinking of her absent husband. She can pay no attention to herself, much less to a stranger.

Anasūyā. Priyamvadā, let this affair never pass our lips. We must spare our dear friend's feelings. Her constitution is too delicate to bear much emotion.

Priyamvadā. I agree with you. Who would think of watering a tender jasmine with hot water?

ACT IV

Scene—The neighborhood of the hermitage

Enter one of Kanva's *pupils, just arisen from his couch at the dawn of day.*

Pupil. My master, the venerable Kanva, who is but lately returned from his pilgrimage, has ordered me to ascertain how the time goes. I have therefore come into the open air to see if it be still dark. (*Walking and looking about.*) Oh! the dawn has already broken.

Lo! in one quarter of the sky, the Moon,
Lord of the herbs and night-expanding flowers,
Sinks towards his bed behind the western hills;
While in the east, preceded by the Dawn,
His blushing charioteer, the glorious Sun
Begins his course, and far into the gloom
Casts the first radiance of his orient beams.
Hail! co-eternal orbs, that rise to set,
And set to rise again; symbols divine
Of man's reverses, life's vicissitudes.
And now,
While the round Moon withdraws his looming disc
Beneath the western sky, the full-blown flower
Of the night-loving lotus sheds her leaves
In sorrow for his loss, bequeathing nought
But the sweet memory of her loveliness
To my bereavèd sight: e'en as the bride
Disconsolately mourns her absent lord,
And yields her heart a prey to anxious grief.

Anasūyā (*entering abruptly*). Little as I know of the

ways of the world, I cannot help thinking that King Dushyanta is treating Shakuntalā very improperly.

Pupil. Well, I must let my revered preceptor know that it is time to offer the burnt oblation. (*Exit.*)

Anasūyā. I am broad awake, but what shall I do? I have no energy to go about my usual occupations. My hands and feet seem to have lost their power. Well, Love has gained his object; and Love only is to blame for having induced our dear friend, in the innocence of her heart, to confide in such a perfidious man. Possibly, however, the imprecation of Durvāsas may be already taking effect. Indeed, I cannot otherwise account for the King's strange conduct, in allowing so long a time to elapse without even a letter; and that, too, after so many promises and protestations. I cannot think what to do, unless we send him the ring which was to be the token of recognition. But which of these austere hermits could we ask to be the bearer of it? Then, again, Father Kanva has just returned from his pilgrimage: and how am I to inform him of Shakuntalā's marriage to King Dushyanta, and her expectation of being soon a mother? I never could bring myself to tell him, even if I felt that Shakuntalā had been in fault, which she certainly has not. What is to be done?

Priyamvadā (*entering; joyfully*). Quick! quick! Anasūyā! come and assist in the joyful preparations for Shakuntalā's departure to her husband's palace.

Anasūyā. My dear girl, what can you mean?

Priyamvadā. Listen, now, and I will tell you all about it. I went just now to Shakuntalā, to inquire whether she had slept comfortably—

Anasūyā. Well, well; go on.

Priyamvadā. She was sitting with her face bowed down to the very ground with shame, when Father Kanva entered and, embracing her, of his own accord offered her his congratulations. "I give thee joy, my child," he said, "we have had an auspicious omen. The priest who offered the oblation dropped it into the very center of the sacred fire, though thick smoke obstructed his vision. Henceforth thou wilt cease to be an object of compassion. This very day I purpose sending thee, under the charge of certain trusty hermits, to the King's palace; and shall deliver thee into the hands of thy husband, as I would commit knowledge to the keeping of a wise and faithful student."

Anasūyā. Who, then, informed the holy Father of what passed in his absence?

Priyamvadā. As he was entering the sanctuary of the consecrated fire, an invisible being chanted a verse in celestial strains.

Anasūyā (with astonishment). Indeed! pray repeat it.

Priyamvadā (repeats the verse).

Glows in thy daughter King Dushyanta's glory,
 As in the sacred tree the mystic fire.
Let worlds rejoice to hear the welcome story;
 And may the son immortalize the sire.

Anasūyā (embracing Priyamvadā*).* Oh, my dear Priyamvadā, what delightful news! I am pleased beyond measure; yet when I think that we are to lose our dear Shakuntalā this very day, a feeling of melancholy mingles with my joy.

Priyamvadā. We shall find means of consoling ourselves after her departure. Let the dear creature only be made happy, at any cost.

Anasūyā. Yes, yes, Priyamvadā, it shall be so; and now to prepare our bridal array. I have always looked forward to this occasion, and some time since, I deposited a beautiful garland of Keshara flowers in a cocoa-nut box, and suspended it on a bough of yonder mango-tree. Be good enough to stretch out your hand and take it down, while I compound unguents and perfumes with this consecrated paste and these blades of sacred grass.

Priyamvadā. Very well.

(*Exit* Anasūyā. Priyamvadā *takes down the flowers.*)

A Voice (behind the scenes). Gautamī, bid Shārngarava and the others hold themselves in readiness to escort Shakuntalā.

Priyamvadā (listening). Quick, quick, Anasūyā! They are calling the hermits who are to go with Shakuntalā to Hastināpur.[t]

Anasūyā (reentering, with the perfumed unguents in her hand). Come along then, Priyamvadā; I am ready to go with you.

(*They walk away.*)

Priyamvadā (looking). See! there sits Shakuntalā, her locks arranged even at this early hour of the morning. The

[t] Dushyanta's city, on the Ganges near Delhi in north central India.

holy women of the hermitage are congratulating her, and invoking blessings on her head, while they present her with wedding-gifts and offerings of consecrated wild-rice. Let us join them.

'hey approach.)

akuntalā *is seen seated, with women surrounding her, occupied in the manner described.*

rst Woman (*to* Shakuntalā). My child, may'st thou receive the title of "Chief-queen," and may thy husband delight to honor thee above all others!

cond Woman. My child, may'st thou be the mother of a hero!

iird Woman. My child, may'st thou be highly honored by thy lord!

:xeunt all the women, excepting Gautamī, *after blessing* Shakuntalā.)

'iyamvadā and *Anasūyā* (*approaching*). Dear Shakuntalā, we are come to assist you at your toilet, and may a blessing attend it!

ıakuntalā. Welcome, dear friends, welcome. Sit down here.

'iyamvadā and *Anasūyā* (*taking the baskets containing the bridal decorations, and sitting down*). Now, then, dearest, prepare to let us dress you. We must first rub your limbs with these perfumed unguents.

ıakuntalā. I ought indeed to be grateful for your kind offices, now that I am so soon to be deprived of them. Dear, dear friends, perhaps I shall never be dressed by you again.

Bursts into tears.)

riyamvadā and *Anasūyā.* Weep not, dearest, tears are out of season on such a happy occasion.

They wipe away her tears and begin to dress her.)

riyamvadā. Alas! these simple flowers and rude ornaments which our hermitage offers in abundance, do not set off your beauty as it deserves.

Enter two young hermits, *bearing costly presents.*

Both Hermits. Here are ornaments suitable for a queen.

(*The women look at them in astonishment.*)

Gautamī. Why, Nārada, my son, whence came these?
First Hermit. You owe them to the devotion of Fat
Kanva.
Gautamī. Did he create them by the power of his o
mind?
Second Hermit. Certainly not; but you shall hear. T
venerable sage ordered us to collect flowers for Shakunt
from the forest-trees; and we went to the wood for t
purpose, when

Straightway depending from a neighboring tree
Appeared a robe of linen tissue, pure
And spotless as a moon-beam—mystic pledge
Of bridal happiness; another tree
Distilled a roseate dye wherewith to stain
The lady's feet; and other branches near
Glistened with rare and costly ornaments.
While, 'midst the leaves, the hands of forest-nymphs,
Vying in beauty with the opening buds,
Presented us with sylvan offerings.

Priyamvadā (*looking at* Shakuntalā). The wood-nym
have done you honor, indeed. This favor doubtless signi
that you are soon to be received as a happy wife i
your husband's house, and are from this forward to
come the partner of his royal fortunes.

(Shakuntalā *appears confused.*)

First Hermit. Come, Gautamī; Father Kanva has finis
his ablutions. Let us go and inform him of the fa
we have received from the deities who preside over
trees.
Second Hermit. By all means. (*Exeun*
Priyamvadā and *Anasūyā.* Alas! what are we to
We are unused to such splendid decorations, and are a
loss how to arrange them. Our knowledge of paint
must be our guide. We will dispose the ornaments as
have seen them in pictures.
Shakuntalā. Whatever pleases you, dear girls, will ple
me. I have perfect confidence in your taste.

hey commence dressing her.)

ter Kanva, *having just finished his ablutions.*

anva. This day my loved one leaves me, and my heart
Is heavy with its grief: the streams of sorrow
Choked at the source, repress my faltering voice.
I have no words to speak; mine eyes are dimmed
By the dark shadows of the thoughts that rise
Within my soul. If such the force of grief
In an old hermit parted from his nursling,
What anguish must the stricken parent feel—
Bereft forever of an only daughter?

dvances toward Shakuntalā.)

iyamvadā and *Anasūyā.* Now, dearest Shakuntalā, we have finished decorating you. You have only to put on the two linen mantles.

hakuntalā *rises and puts them on.*)

autamī. Daughter, see, here comes thy foster-father; he is eager to fold thee in his arms; his eyes swim with tears of joy. Hasten to do him reverence.

akuntalā (*reverently*). My father, I salute you.

anva. My daughter,
May'st thou be highly honored by thy lord,
E'en as Yayāti Sharmishthā adored! [u]
And, as she bore him Puru, so may'st thou
Bring forth a son to whom the world shall bow!

autamī. Most venerable father, she accepts your benediction as if she already possessed the boon it confers.

anva. Now come this way, my child, and walk reverently round these sacrificial fires.

They all walk round.)

anva (*repeats a prayer in the metre of the Rig-veda*).
Holy flames, that gleam around
Every altar's hallowed ground;
Holy flames, whose frequent food
Is the consecrated wood,

[u] Dushyanta is of the dynasty of Puru, and Sharmishthā was the other of Puru, the king's great ancestor. Her ancestors were partly pernatural: Yayāti was a lunar god.

And for whose encircling bed,
Sacred Kusha-grass is spread;
Holy flames, that waft to heaven
Sweet oblations daily given,
Mortal guilt to purge away;—
Hear, oh hear me, when I pray—
Purify my child this day!

Now then, my daughter, set out on thy journey. (*Loo[k]ing on one side.*) Where are thy attendants, Shārngara[va], and the others?

Young Hermit (*entering*). Here we are, most venerab[le] father.

Kanva. Lead the way for thy sister.

Shārngarava. Come, Shakuntalā, let us proceed.

(*All move away.*)

Kanva. Hear me, ye trees that surround our hermitage!

Shakuntalā ne'er moistened in the stream
Her own parched lips, till she had fondly poured
Its purest water on your thirsty roots;
And oft, when she would fain have decked her hair
With your thick-clustering blossoms, in her love
She robbed you not e'en of a single flower.
Her highest joy was ever to behold
The early glory of your opening buds:
Oh, then, dismiss her with a kind farewell!
This very day she quits her father's home,
To seek the palace of her wedded lord.

(*The note of a Köil is heard.*)

Hark! heard'st thou not the answer of the trees,
Our sylvan sisters, warbled in the note
Of the melodious Köil? [v] they dismiss
Their dear Shakuntalā with loving wishes.

Voices (*in the air*).

Fare thee well, journey pleasantly on amid streams
Where the lotuses bloom, and the sun's glowing beams
Never pierce the deep shade of the wide-spreading tree[s],
While gently around thee shall sport the cool breeze;
Then light be thy footsteps and easy thy tread,
Beneath thee shall carpets of lilies be spread.

[v] A bird like the cuckoo, and a favorite in Indian poetry as t[he] nightingale is in the West.

Journey on to thy lord, let thy spirit be gay,
For the smiles of all Nature shall gladden thy way.

ll listen with astonishment.)

autamī. Daughter! thy nymphs of the wood, who love thee with the affection of a sister, dismiss thee with kind wishes for thy happiness. Take thou leave of them reverentially.

akuntalā (bowing respectfully and walking on. Aside to her friend). Eager as I am, dear Priyamvadā, to see my husband once more, yet my feet refuse to move, now that I am quitting forever the home of my girlhood.

iyamvadā. You are not the only one, dearest, to feel the bitterness of parting. As the time of separation approaches, the whole grove seems to share your anguish.

In sorrow for thy loss, the herd of deer
Forget to browse; the peacock on the lawn
Ceases its dance; the very trees around us
Shed their pale leaves, like tears, upon the ground.

akuntalā (recollecting herself). My father, let me, before I go, bid adieu to my pet jasmine, the Moonlight of the Grove. I love the plant almost as a sister.

anva. Yes, yes, my child, I remember thy sisterly affection for the creeper. Here it is on the right.

akuntalā (approaching the jasmine). My beloved jasmine, most brilliant of climbing plants, how sweet it is to see thee cling thus fondly to thy husband, the mango-tree; yet, prithee, turn thy twining arms for a moment in this direction to embrace thy sister; she is going far away, and may never see thee again.

anva. Daughter, the cherished purpose of my heart
Has ever been to wed thee to a spouse
That should be worthy of thee; such a spouse
Hast thou thyself, by thine own merits, won.
To him thou goest, and about his neck
Soon shalt thou cling confidingly, as now
Thy favorite jasmine twines its loving arms
Around the sturdy mango. Leave thou it
To its protector—e'en as I consign
Thee to thy lord, and henceforth from my mind
Banish all anxious thought on thy behalf.
Proceed on thy journey, my child.

akuntalā (to Priyamvadā *and* Anasūyā*).* To you, my sweet companions, I leave it as a keepsake. Take charge of it when I am gone.

Priyamvadā and *Anasūyā* (*bursting into tears*). And whose charge do you leave us, dearest? Who will care f us when you are gone?

Kanva. For shame, Anasūyā! dry your tears. Is this t way to cheer your friend at a time when she needs yo support and consolation?

(*All move on.*)

Shakuntalā. My father, see you there my pet deer, grazi close to the hermitage? She expects soon to fawn, a even now the weight of the little one she carries hinde her movements. Do not forget to send me word when s becomes a mother.

Kanva. I will not forget it.

Shakuntalā (*feeling herself drawn back*). What can this b fastened to my dress?

(*Turns round.*)

Kanva. My daughter,

It is the little fawn, thy foster-child.
Poor helpless orphan! it remembers well
How with a mother's tenderness and love
Thou didst protect it, and with grains of rice
From thine own hand didst daily nourish it;
And, ever and anon, when some sharp thorn
Had pierced its mouth, how gently thou didst tend
The bleeding wound, and pour in healing balm.
The grateful nursling clings to its protectress,
Mutely imploring leave to follow her.

Shakuntalā. My poor little fawn, dost thou ask to follo an unhappy woman who hesitates not to desert her cor panions? When thy mother died, soon after thy birth, supplied her place, and reared thee with my own han and now that thy second mother is about to leave the who will care for thee? My father, be thou a mother her. My child, go back, and be a daughter to my fathe

(*Moves on, weeping.*)

Kanva. Weep not, my daughter, check the gathering te

That lurks beneath thine eyelid, ere it flow
And weaken thy resolve; be firm and true—
True to thyself and me; the path of life
Will lead o'er hill and plain, o'er rough and smooth,

And all must feel the steepness of the way;
Though rugged be thy course, press boldly on.

ārngarava. Venerable sire! the sacred precept is—"Accompany thy friend as far as the margin of the first stream." Here then, we are arrived at the border of a lake. It is time for you to give us your final instructions and return.

nva. Be it so; let us tarry for a moment under the shade of this fig-tree.

hey do so.)

nva (aside). I must think of some appropriate message to send to his majesty King Dushyanta.

eflects.)

ıkuntalā (aside to Anasūyā). See, see, dear Anasūyā, the poor female Chakravāka-bird,[w] whom cruel fate dooms to nightly separation from her mate, calls to him in mournful notes from the other side of the stream, though he is only hidden from her view by the spreading leaves of the water-lily. Her cry is so piteous that I could almost fancy she was lamenting her hard lot in intelligible words.

asūyā. Say not so, dearest.

Fond bird! though sorrow lengthen out her night
Of widowhood, yet with a cry of joy
She hails the morning light that brings her mate
Back to her side. The agony of parting
Would wound us like a sword, but that its edge
Is blunted by the hope of future meeting.

nva. Shārngarava, when you have introduced Shakuntalā into the presence of the King, you must give him this message from me.

ārngarava. Let me hear it, venerable Father.

nva. This is it—

Most puissant prince! we here present before thee
One thou art bound to cherish and receive
As thine own wife; yea, even to enthrone
As thine own queen—worthy of equal love
With thine imperial consorts. So much, Sire,
We claim of thee as justice due to us,
In virtue of our holy character—
In virtue of thine honorable rank—

[w] A kind of water-fowl separated every night from its mate by te.

In virtue of the pure spontaneous love
That secretly grew up 'twixt thee and her,
Without consent or privity of us.
We ask no more—the rest we freely leave
To thy just feeling and to destiny.

Shārngarava. A most suitable message. I will take care deliver it correctly.

Kanva. And now, my child, a few words of advice thee. We hermits, though we live secluded from the wor are not ignorant of worldly matters.

Shārngarava. No, indeed. Wise men are conversant with subjects.

Kanva. Listen, then, my daughter. When thou reachest husband's palace, and art admitted into his family,
Honor thy betters; ever be respectful.
To those above thee; and, should others share
Thy husband's love, ne'er yield thyself a prey
To jealousy; but ever be a friend,
A loving friend, to those who rival thee
In his affections. Should thy wedded lord
Treat thee with harshness, thou must never be
Harsh in return, but patient and submissive.
Be to thy menials courteous, and to all
Placed under thee, considerate and kind.
Be never self-indulgent, but avoid
Excess in pleasure; and, when fortune smiles,
Be not puffed up. Thus to thy husband's house
Wilt thou a blessing prove, and not a curse.
What thinks Gautamī of this advice?

Gautamī. An excellent compendium, truly, of every wif duties! Lay it well to heart, my daughter.

Kanva. Come, my beloved child, one parting embrace f me and for thy companions, and then we leave thee.

Shakuntalā. My father, must Priyamvadā and Anasū really return with you? They are very dear to me.

Kanva. Yes, my child; they, too, in good time, will given in marriage to suitable husbands. It would not proper for them to accompany thee to such a public plac But Gautamī shall be thy companion.

Shakuntalā (embracing him). Removed from thy boso my beloved father, like a young tendril of the sand tree torn from its home in the western mountains, ho shall I be able to support life in a foreign soil?

Kanva. Daughter, thy fears are groundless:—
Soon shall thy lord prefer thee to the rank
Of his own consort; and unnumbered cares

Befitting his imperial dignity
Shall constantly engross thee. Then the bliss
Of bearing him a son—a noble boy,
Bright as the day-star—shall transport thy soul
With new delights, and little shalt thou reck
Of the light sorrow that afflicts thee now
At parting from thy father and thy friends.

(Shakuntalā *throws herself at her foster-father's feet.*)

Kanva. Blessings on thee, my child! May all my hopes of thee be realized!

Shakuntalā (*approaching her friends*). Come, my two loved companions, embrace me—both of you together.

Priyamvadā and *Anasūyā* (*embracing her*). Dear Shakuntalā, remember, if the King should by any chance be slow in recognizing you, you have only to show him this ring, on which his own name is engraved.

Shakuntalā. The bare thought of it puts me in a tremor.

Priyamvadā and *Anasūyā.* There is no real cause for fear, dearest. Excessive affection is too apt to suspect evil where none exists.

Shārngarava. Come, lady, we must hasten on. The sun is rising in the heavens.

Shakuntalā (*looking towards the hermitage*). Dear father, when shall I ever see this hallowed grove again?

Kanva. I will tell thee; listen—
When thou hast passed a long and blissful life
As King Dushyanta's queen, and jointly shared
With all the earth his ever-watchful care;
And hast beheld thine own heroic son,
Matchless in arms, united to a spouse
In happy wedlock; when his aged sire,
Thy faithful husband, hath to him resigned
The helm of state; then, weary of the world,
Together with Dushyanta thou shalt seek
The calm seclusion of thy former home:—
There amid holy scenes to be at peace,
Till thy pure spirit gain its last release.[x]

Gautamī. Come, my child, the favorable time for our journey is fast passing. Let thy father return. Venerable Sire, be thou the first to move homewards, or these last words will never end.

[x] Kings frequently felt it a pious duty to abdicate and retire to a religious life in old age, sometimes with their wives.

Kanva. Daughter, detain me no longer. My religious duties must not be interrupted.

Shakuntalā (*again embracing her foster-father*). Beloved father, thy frame is much enfeebled by penitential exercises. Do not, oh! do not, allow thyself to sorrow too much on my account.

Kanva (*sighing*). How, O my child, shall my bereavèd heart
Forget its bitterness, when, day by day,
Full in my sight shall grow the tender plants
Reared by thy care, or sprung from hallowed grain
Which thy loved hands have strewn around the door—
A frequent offering to our household gods?
Go, my daughter, and may thy journey be prosperous.
(*Exit* Shakuntalā *with her escort.*)

Priyamvadā and *Anasūyā* (*gazing after* Shakuntalā). Alas! alas! she is gone, and now the trees hide our darling from our view.

Kanva (*sighing*). Well, Anasūyā, your sister has departed. Moderate your grief, both of you, and follow me. I go back to the hermitage.

Priyamvadā and *Anasūyā.* Holy father, the sacred grove will be a desert without Shakuntalā. How can we ever return to it?

Kanva. It is natural enough that your affection should make you view it in this light. (*Walking pensively on.*) As for me, I am quite surprised at myself. Now that I have fairly dismissed her to her husband's house, my mind is easy: for indeed,
A daughter is a loan—a precious jewel
Lent to a parent till her husband claim her.
And now that to her rightful lord and master
I have delivered her, my burdened soul
Is lightened, and I seem to breathe more freely. (*Exeunt.*)

ACT V

Scene—A room in the palace

The King Dushyanta *and the jester* Mādhavya *are discovered seated.*

Mādhavya (*listening*). Hark! my dear friend, listen a minute, and you will hear sweet sounds proceeding from the music-room. Someone is singing a charming air. Who can it be? Oh! I know. The queen Hansapadikā is practicing her notes, that she may greet you with a new song.

King. Hush! Let me listen.

A Voice (*sings behind the scenes*).

How often hither didst thou rove,
Sweet bee, to kiss the mango's cheek;
Oh! leave not, then, thy early love,
The lily's honeyed lip to seek.

King. A most impassioned strain, truly!

Mādhavya. Do you understand the meaning of the words?

King (*smiling*). She means to reprove me, because I once paid her great attention, and have lately deserted her for the queen Vasumatī. Go, my dear fellow, and tell Hansapadikā from me that I take her delicate reproof as it is intended.

Mādhavya. Very well. (*Rising from his seat*.) But stay—I don't much relish being sent to bear the brunt of her jealousy. The chances are that she will have me seized by the hair of the head and beaten to a jelly. I would as soon expose myself, after a vow of celibacy, to the seductions of a lovely nymph, as encounter the fury of a jealous woman.

King. Go, go; you can disarm her wrath by a civil speech; but give her my message.

Mādhavya. What must be must be, I suppose. (*Exit.*)

King (*aside*). Strange! that song has filled me with a most peculiar sensation. A melancholy feeling has come over me, and I seem to yearn after some long-forgotten object of affection. Singular, indeed! but,

Not seldom in our happy hours of ease,
When thought is still, the sight of some fair form,
Or mournful fall of music breathing low,
Will stir strange fancies, thrilling all the soul
With a mysterious sadness, and a sense
Of vague yet earnest longing. Can it be
That the dim memory of events long past,
Or friendships formed in other states of being,
Flits like a passing shadow o'er the spirit?

(*Remains pensive and sad.*)

Enter the chamberlain.

Chamberlain. Alas! to what an advanced period of life have I attained!

Even this wand betrays the lapse of years;
In youthful days 'twas but a useless badge
And symbol of my office; now it serves
As a support to prop my tottering steps.

Ah me! I feel very unwilling to announce to the King that a deputation of young hermits from the sage Kanva has arrived, and craves an immediate audience. Certainly, his Majesty ought not to neglect a matter of sacred duty, yet I hardly like to trouble him when he has just risen from the judgment-seat. Well, well; a monarch's business is to sustain the world, and he must not expect much repose; because—

Onward, forever onward, in his car
The unwearied Sun pursues his daily course,
Nor tarries to unyoke his glittering steeds.
And ever moving speeds the rushing Wind
Through boundless space, filling the universe
With his life-giving breezes. Day and night,
The King of Serpents on his thousand heads
Upholds the incumbent earth; and even so,
Unceasing toil is aye the lot of kings,
Who, in return, draw nurture from their subjects.

I will therefore deliver my message. (*Walking on and looking about.*) Ah! here comes the King:—
His subjects are his children; through the day,
Like a fond father, to supply their wants,
Incessantly he labors; wearied now,
The monarch seeks seclusion and repose—
E'en as the prince of elephants defies
The sun's fierce heat, and leads the fainting herd
To verdant pastures, ere his wayworn limbs
He yields to rest beneath the cooling shade.
(*Approaching.*) Victory to the King! So please your majesty, some hermits who live in a forest near the Snowy Mountains have arrived here, bringing certain women with them. They have a message to deliver from the sage Kanva, and desire an audience. I await your Majesty's commands.

King (*respectfully*). A message from the sage Kanva, did you say?

Chamberlain. Even so, my liege.

King. Tell my domestic priest, Somarāta, to receive the hermits with due honor, according to the prescribed form. He may then himself introduce them into my presence. I will await them in a place suitable for the reception of such holy guests.

Chamberlain. Your Majesty's commands shall be obeyed. (*Exit.*)

King (*rising and addressing the* warder). Vetravatī, lead the way to the chamber of the consecrated fire.

Warder. This way, Sire.

King (*walking on, with the air of one oppressed by the cares of government*). People are generally contented and happy when they have gained their desires; but kings have no sooner attained the object of their aspirations than all their troubles begin.
'Tis a fond thought that to attain the end
And object of ambition is to rest;
Success doth only mitigate the fever
Of anxious expectation; soon the fear
Of losing what we have, the constant care
Of guarding it doth weary. Ceaseless toil
Must be the lot of him who with his hands
Supports the canopy that shields his subjects.

Two Heralds (*behind the scenes*). May the King be victorious!

First Herald. Honor to him who labors day by day
For the world's weal, forgetful of his own.
Like some tall tree that with its stately head

Endures the solar beam, while underneath
It yields refreshing shelter to the weary.

Second Herald. Let but the monarch wield his threatening rod
And e'en the guilty tremble; at his voice
The rebel spirit cowers; his grateful subjects
Acknowledge him their guardian; rich and poor
Hail him a faithful friend, a loving kinsman.

King. Weary as I was before, this complimentary address has refreshed me.

(*Walks on.*)

Warder. Here is the terrace of the hallowed fire-chamber, and yonder stands the cow that yields the milk for the oblations. The sacred enclosure has been recently purified, and looks clean and beautiful. Ascend, Sire.

King (*leans on the shoulders of his attendants, and ascends*). Vetravatī, what can possibly be the message that the venerable Kanva has sent me by these hermits?—
Perchance their sacred rites have been disturbed
By demons, or some evil has befallen
The innocent herds, their favorites, that graze
Within the precincts of the hermitage;
Or haply, through my sins, some withering blight
Has nipped the creeping plants that spread their arms
Around the hallowed grove. Such troubled thoughts
Crowd through my mind, and fill me with misgiving.

Warder. If you ask my opinion, Sire, I think the hermits merely wish to take an opportunity of testifying their loyalty, and are therefore come to offer homage to your Majesty.

Enter the hermits, *leading* Shakuntalā, *attended by* Gautamī; *and, in advance of them, the* chamberlain *and the domestic* priest.

Chamberlain. This way, reverend sirs, this way.

Shārngarava. O Shāradvata,
'Tis true the monarch lacks no royal grace,
Nor ever swerves from justice; true, his people,
Yea such as in life's humblest walks are found,
Refrain from evil courses; still to me,
A lonely hermit reared in solitude,
This throng appears bewildering, and methinks
I look upon a burning house, whose inmates

Are running to and fro in wild dismay.

Shāradvata. It is natural that the first sight of the King's capital should affect you in this manner; my own sensations are very similar.

As one just bathed beholds the man polluted;
As one late purified, the yet impure:—
As one awake looks on the yet unwakened;
Or as the freeman gazes on the thrall,
So I regard this crowd of pleasure-seekers.

Shakuntalā (feeling a quivering sensation in her right eye-lid, and suspecting a bad omen). Alas! what means this throbbing of my right eye-lid? [y]

Gautamī. Heaven avert the evil omen, my child! May the guardian deities of thy husband's family convert it into a sign of good fortune!

(*Walks on.*)

Priest (pointing to the King*).* Most reverend sirs, there stands the protector of the four classes of the people; the guardian of the four orders of the priesthood. He has just left the judgment-seat, and is waiting for you. Behold him!

Shārngarava. Great Brahman, we are happy in thinking that the King's power is exerted for the protection of all classes of his subjects. We have not come as petitioners —we have the fullest confidence in the generosity of his nature.

The loftiest trees bend humbly to the ground
Beneath the teeming burden of their fruit;
High in the vernal sky the pregnant clouds
Suspend their stately course, and hanging low,
Scatter their sparkling treasures o'er the earth:—
And such is true benevolence; the good
Are never rendered arrogant by riches.

Warder. So please your Majesty, I judge from the placid countenance of the hermits that they have no alarming message to deliver.

King (looking at Shakuntalā*).* But the lady there—
Who can she be, whose form of matchless grace
Is half concealed beneath her flowing veil?
Among the somber hermits she appears
Like a fresh bud 'mid sere and yellow leaves.

Warder. So please your Majesty, my curiosity is also roused,

[y] The left side is a sign of good omens for women, the reverse is true for men.

but no conjecture occurs to my mind. This at least is certain, that she deserves to be looked at more closely.

King. True; but it is not right to gaze at another man's wife.

Shakuntalā (*placing her hand on her bosom. Aside*). O my heart, why this throbbing? Remember thy lord's affection, and take courage.

Priest (*advancing*). These holy men have been received with all due honor. One of them has now a message to deliver from his spiritual superior. Will your Majesty deign to hear it?

King. I am all attention.

Hermits (*extending their hands*). Victory to the King!

King. Accept my respectful greeting.

Hermits. May the desires of your soul be accomplished!

King. I trust no one is molesting you in the prosecution of your religious rites.

Hermits. Who dares disturb our penitential rites
When thou art our protector? Can the night
Prevail to cast her shadows o'er the earth
While the sun's beams irradiate the sky?

King. Such, indeed, is the very meaning of my title—"Defender of the Just." I trust the venerable Kanva is in good health. The world is interested in his well-being.

Hermits. Holy men have health and prosperity in their own power. He bade us greet your Majesty, and, after kind inquiries, deliver this message.

King. Let me hear his commands.

Shārngarava. He bade us say that he feels happy in giving his sanction to the marriage which your Majesty contracted with this lady, his daughter, privately and by mutual agreement. Because
By us thou art esteemed the most illustrious
Of noble husbands; and Shakuntalā
Virtue herself in human form revealed.
Great Brahma hath in equal yoke united
A bride unto a husband worthy of her:—
Henceforth let none make blasphemous complaint
That he is pleased with ill-assorted unions.
Since, therefore, she expects soon to be the mother of thy child, receive her into thy palace, that she may perform, in conjunction with thee, the ceremonies prescribed by religion on such an occasion.

Gautamī. So please your Majesty, I would add a few words: but why should I intrude my sentiments when an opportunity of speaking my mind has never been allowed me? She took no counsel with her kindred; thou

Didst not confer with thine, but all alone
Didst solemnize thy nuptials with thy wife.
Together, then, hold converse; let us leave you.

hakuntalā (*aside*). Ah! how I tremble for my lord's reply.

ing. What strange proposal is this?

hakuntalā (*aside*). His words are fire to me.

hārngarava. What do I hear? Dost thou, then, hesitate? Monarch, thou art well acquainted with the ways of the world, and knowest that

A wife, however virtuous and discreet,
If she live separate from her wedded lord,
Though under shelter of her parent's roof,
Is mark for vile suspicion. Let her dwell
Beside her husband, though he hold her not
In his affection. So her kinsmen will it.

ing. Do you really mean to assert that I married this lady?

hakuntalā (*despondingly. Aside*). O my heart, thy worst misgivings are confirmed.

hārngarava. Is it becoming in a monarch to depart from the rules of justice, because he repents of his engagements?

ing. I cannot answer a question which is based on a mere fabrication.

hārngarava. Such inconstancy is fortunately not common, excepting in men intoxicated by power.

ing. Is that remark aimed at me?

autamī. Be not ashamed, my daughter. Let me remove thy veil for a little space. Thy husband will then recognize thee.

Removes her veil.)

ing (*gazing at* Shakuntalā. *Aside*). What charms are here revealed before mine eyes!

Truly no blemish mars the symmetry
Of that fair form; yet can I ne'er believe
She is my wedded wife; and like a bee
That circles round the flower whose nectared cup
Teems with the dew of morning, I must pause
Ere eagerly I taste the proffered sweetness.

Remains wrapped in thought.)

Varder. How admirably does our royal master's behavior prove his regard for justice! Who else would hesitate for a moment when good fortune offered for his acceptance a form of such rare beauty?

Shārngarava. Great King, why art thou silent?

King. Holy men, I have revolved the matter in my mind; bu the more I think of it, the less able am I to recollect that ever contracted an alliance with this lady. What answe then, can I possibly give you when I do not believe myse to be her husband, and I plainly see that she is soon to be come a mother?

Shakuntalā (*aside*). Woe! woe! Is our very marriage to b called in question by my own husband? Ah me! is this t be the end of all my bright visions of wedded happiness?

Shārngarava. Beware!

Beware how thou insult the holy Sage!
Remember how he generously allowed
Thy secret union with his foster-child;
And how, when thou didst rob him of his treasure,
He sought to furnish thee excuse, when rather
He should have cursed thee for a ravisher.

Shāradvata. Shārngarava, speak to him no more. Shakun talā, our part is performed: we have said all we had to say and the King has replied in the manner thou hast heard. is now thy turn to give him convincing evidence of th marriage.

Shakuntalā (*aside*). Since his feeling towards me has unde gone a complete revolution, what will it avail to revive ol recollections? One thing is clear—I shall soon have t mourn my own widowhood. (*Aloud.*) My revered husban ——(*Stops short.*) But no—I dare not address thee by th title, since thou hast refused to acknowledge our union Noble descendant of Puru! It is not worthy of thee to be tray an innocent-minded girl, and disown her in such term after having so lately and so solemnly plighted thy vows t her in the hermitage.

King (*stopping his ears*). I will hear no more. Be such crime far from my thoughts!

What evil spirit can possess thee, lady,
That thou dost seek to sully my good name
By base aspersions? like a swollen torrent,
That, leaping from its narrow bed, o'erthrows
The tree upon its bank, and strives to blend
Its turbid waters with the crystal stream?

Shakuntalā. If, then, thou really believest me to be the wi of another, and thy present conduct proceeds from som cloud that obscures thy recollection, I will easily convin thee by this token.

King. An excellent idea!

hakuntalā (feeling for the ring). Alas! alas! woe is me! There is no ring on my finger!

Looks with anguish at Gautamī.)

autamī. The ring must have slipped off when thou wast in the act of offering homage to the holy water of Shachī's sacred pool, near Shakrāvatāra.

ing (smiling). People may well talk of the readiness of woman's invention! Here is an instance of it.

hakuntalā. Say, rather, of the omnipotence of fate. I will mention another circumstance, which may yet convince thee.

ing. By all means let me hear it at once.

hakuntalā. One day, while we were seated in a jasmine bower, thou didst pour into the hollow of thine hand some water, sprinkled by a recent shower in the cup of a lotus blossom——

ing. I am listening; proceed.

hakuntalā. At that instant, my adopted child, the little fawn, with soft, long eyes, came running towards us. Upon which, before tasting the water thyself, thou didst kindly offer some to the little creature, saying fondly—"Drink first, gentle fawn." But she could not be induced to drink from the hand of a stranger; though immediately afterwards, when I took the water in my own hand, she drank with perfect confidence. Then, with a smile, thou didst say —"Every creature confides naturally in its own kind. You are both inhabitants of the same forest, and have learnt to trust each other."

ing. Voluptuaries may allow themselves to be seduced from the path of duty by falsehoods such as these, expressed in honeyed words.

autamī. Speak not thus, illustrious Prince. This lady was brought up in a hermitage, and has never learnt deceit.

ing. Holy matron,

E'en in untutored brutes, the female sex
Is marked by inborn subtlety—much more
In beings gifted with intelligence.
The wily Köil, ere towards the sky
She wings her sportive flight, commits her eggs
To other nests, and artfully consigns
The rearing of her little ones to strangers.

hakuntalā (angrily). Dishonorable man, thou judgest of others by thine own evil heart. Thou, at least, art unrivaled in perfidy, and standest alone—a base deceiver in the garb of virtue and religion—like a deep pit whos yawning mouth is concealed by smiling flowers.

King (*aside*). Her anger, at any rate, appears genuine, an makes me almost doubt whether I am in the right. Fo indeed,

When I had vainly searched my memory,
And so with stern severity denied
The fabled story of our secret loves,
Her brows, that met before in graceful curves,
Like the arched weapon of the god of love,
Seemed by her frown dissevered; while the fire
Of sudden anger kindled in her eyes.

(*Aloud.*) My good lady, Dushyanta's character is wel known to all. I comprehend not your meaning.

Shakuntalā. Well do I deserve to be thought a harlot fc having, in the innocence of my heart, and out of the co fidence I reposed in a Prince of Puru's race, intrusted m honor to a man whose mouth distils honey, while his hea is full of poison.

(*Covers her face with her mantle, and bursts into tears.*)

Shārngarava. Thus is it that burning remorse must ev follow rash actions which might have been avoided, an for which one has only one's self to blame.

Not hastily should marriage be contracted,
And specially in secret. Many a time,
In hearts that know not each the other's fancies,
Fond love is changed into most bitter hate.

King. How now! Do you give credence to this woman rath than to me, that you heap such accusations on me?

Shārngarava (*sarcastically*). That would be too absurd, ce tainly. You have heard the proverb—

Hold in contempt the innocent words of those
Who from their infancy have known no guile.—
But trust the treacherous counsels of the man
Who makes a very science of deceit.

King. Most veracious Brahman, grant that you are in th right, what end would be gained by betraying this lady?

Shārngarava. Ruin.

King. No one will believe that a Prince of Puru's race woul seek to ruin others or himself.

Shāradvata. This altercation is idle, Shārngarava. We hav executed the commission of our preceptor; come, let us r turn. (*To the* King.)

Shakuntalā is certainly thy bride;

Receive her or reject her, she is thine.
Do with her, King, according to thy pleasure—
The husband o'er the wife is absolute.
Go on before us, Gautamī.

(*They move away.*)

Shakuntalā. What! is it not enough to have been betrayed by this perfidious man? Must you also forsake me, regardless of my tears and lamentations?

(*Attempts to follow them.*)

Gautamī (*stopping*). My son Shārngarava, see, Shakuntalā is following us, and with tears implores us not to leave her. Alas! poor child, what will she do here with a cruel husband who casts her from him?

Shārngarava (*turning angrily towards her*). Wilful woman, dost thou seek to be independent of thy lord?

(Shakuntalā *trembles with fear.*)

Shārngarava. Shakuntalā!
If thou art really what the King proclaims thee,
How can thy father e'er receive thee back
Into his house and home? but, if thy conscience
Be witness to thy purity of soul,
E'en should thy husband to a handmaid's lot
Condemn thee, thou may'st cheerfully endure it,
When ranked among the number of his household.
Thy duty, therefore, is to stay. As for us, we must return immediately.

King. Deceive not the lady, my good hermit, by any such expectations.
The moon expands the lotus of the night,
The rising sun awakes the lily; each
Is with his own contented. Even so
The virtuous man is master of his passions,
And from another's wife averts his gaze.

Shārngarava. Since thy union with another woman has rendered thee oblivious of thy marriage with Shakuntalā, whence this fear of losing thy character for constancy and virtue?

King (*to the* priest). You must counsel me, revered sir, as to my course of action. Which of the two evils involves the greater or less sin?

Whether by some dark veil my mind be clouded,
Or this designing woman speak untruly,
I know not. Tell me, must I rather be
The base disowner of my wedded wife,
Or the defiling and defiled adulterer?

Priest (*after deliberation*). You must take an intermediat course.

King. What course, revered sir? Tell me at once.

Priest. I will provide an asylum for the lady in my own house until the birth of her child; and my reason, i you ask me, is this. Soothsayers have predicted that you first-born will have universal dominion. Now, if the her mit's daughter bring forth a son with the discus or mark of empire in the lines of his hand, you must admit he immediately into your royal apartments with great re joicings; if not, then determine to send her back as soon a possible to her father.

King. I bow to the decision of my spiritual adviser.

Priest. Daughter, follow me.

Shakuntalā. O divine earth, open and receive me into th bosom!

(*Exit* Shakuntalā *weeping, with the* priest *and the* hermits *The* King *remains absorbed in thinking of her, though th curse still clouds his recollection*).

A Voice (*behind the scenes*). A miracle! a miracle!

King (*listening*). What has happened now?

Priest (*entering with an air of astonishment*). Great Prince a stupendous prodigy has just occurred!

King. What is it?

Priest. May it please your Majesty, so soon as Kanva's pupils had departed,
Shakuntalā, her eyes all bathed in tears,
With outstretched arms bewailed her cruel fate——

King. Well, well, what happened then?

Priest. When suddenly a shining apparition,
In female shape, descended from the skies,
Near the nymphs' pool, and bore her up to heaven.

(*All remain motionless with astonishment*.)

King. My good priest, from the very first I declined having anything to do with this matter. It is now all over, and we can never, by our conjectures, unravel the mystery; let i rest; go, seek repose.

Priest (*looking at the* King). Be it so. Victory to the King!

(*Exit*.)

King. Vetravatī, I am tired out; lead the way to the bed-chamber.

Warder. This way, Sire.

(*They move away*.)

King. Do what I will, I cannot call to mind
That I did e'er espouse the sage's daughter—
Therefore I have disowned her; yet 'tis strange
How painfully my agitated heart
Bears witness to the truth of her assertion,
And makes me credit her against my judgment. (*Exeunt*.)

Prelude to Act VI

Scene—A street

Enter the King's *brother-in-law as Superintendent of the cit police; and with him two* constables, *dragging a poo* fisherman,[z] *who has his hands tied behind his back.*

Both the Constables (*striking the prisoner*). Take that for rascally thief that you are; and now tell us, sirrah, wher you found this ring—aye, the King's own signet-ring. See here is the royal name engraved on the setting of the jewe

Fisherman (*with a gesture of alarm*). Mercy! kind sir mercy! I did not steal it; indeed I did not.

First Constable. Oh! then I suppose the King took you fc some fine Brahman, and made you a present of it?

Fisherman. Only hear me. I am but a poor fisherman, liv ing at Shakrāvatāra——

Second Constable. Scoundrel, who ever asked you, pray for a history of your birth and parentage?

Superintendent (*to one of the* constables). Sūchaka, let th fellow tell his own story from the beginning. Don't inte rupt him.

Both Constables. As you please, master. Go on, then, sirrah and say what you've got to say.

Fisherman. You see in me a poor man, who supports hi family by catching fish with nets, hooks, and the like.

Superintendent (*laughing*). A most refined occupation, cer tainly!

Fisherman. Blame me not for it, master.

[z] The Hindu religious aversion to eating flesh made the occup tions of butcher and fisherman very lowly.

The father's occupation, though despised
By others, casts no shame upon the son,
And he should not forsake it. Is the priest
Who kills the animal for sacrifice
Therefore deemed cruel? Sure a lowborn man
May, though a fisherman, be tender-hearted.

Superintendent. Well, well; go on with your story.

Fisherman. One day I was cutting open a large carp I had just hooked, when the sparkle of a jewel caught my eye, and what should I find in the fish's maw but that ring! Soon afterwards, when I was offering it for sale, I was seized by your honors. Now you know everything. Whether you kill me, or whether you let me go, this is the true account of how the ring came into my possession.

Superintendent (*to one of the* constables). Well, Jānuka, the rascal emits such a fishy odor that I had no doubt of his being a fisherman; but we must inquire a little more closely into this queer story about the finding of the ring. Come, we'll take him before the King's household.

Both Constables. Very good, master. Get on with you, you cut-purse.

(*All move on.*)

Superintendent. Now attend, Sūchaka; keep you guard here at the gate; and hark ye, sirrahs, take good care your prisoner does not escape, while I go in and lay the whole story of the discovery of this ring before the King in person. I will soon return and let you know his commands.

Constable. Go in, master, by all means; and may you find favor in the King's sight! (*Exit* Superintendent.)

First Constable (*after an interval*). I say, Jānuka, the Superintendent is a long time away.

Second Constable. Aye, aye; kings are not to be got at so easily. Folks must bide the proper opportunity.

First Constable. Jānuka, my fingers itch to strike the first blow at this royal victim here. We must kill him with all the honors, you know. I long to begin binding the flowers round his head.

(*Pretends to strike a blow at the* fisherman.)

Fisherman. Your honor surely will not put an innocent man to a cruel death.

Second Constable (*looking*). There's our Superintendent at last, I declare. See, he is coming towards us with a paper in his hand. We shall soon know the King's command; so prepare, my fine fellow, either to become food for the vultures, or to make acquaintance with some hungry cur.

Superintendent (*entering*). Ho, there, Sūchaka! set the fisherman at liberty, I tell you. His story about the ring is all correct.

Sūchaka. Oh! very good, sir; as you please.

Second Constable. The fellow had one foot in hell, and now here he is in the land of the living.

(*Releases him.*)

Fisherman (*bowing to the* Superintendent). Now, master, what think you of my way of getting a livelihood?

Superintendent. Here, my good man, the King desired me to present you with this purse. It contains a sum of money equal to the full value of the ring.

(*Gives him the money.*)

Fisherman (*taking it and bowing*). His Majesty does me too great honor.

Sūchaka. You may well say so. He might as well have taken you from the gallows to seat you on his state elephant.

Jānuka. Master, the King must value the ring very highly, or he would never have sent such a sum of money to this ragamuffin.

Superintendent. I don't think he prizes it as a costly jewel so much as a memorial of some person he tenderly loves. The moment it was shown to him he became much agitated, though in general he conceals his feelings.

Sūchaka. Then you must have done a great service——

Jānuka. Yes, to this husband of a fish-wife.

(*Looks enviously at the* fisherman.)

Fisherman. Here's half the money for you, my masters. It will serve to purchase the flowers you spoke of, if not to buy me your good-will.

Jānuka. Well, now, that's just as it should be.

Superintendent. My good fisherman, you are an excellent fellow, and I begin to feel quite a regard for you. Let us seal our fast friendship over a glass of good liquor. Come along to the next wine-shop and we'll drink your health.

All. By all means. (*Exeunt.*)

ACT VI

Scene—The garden of the palace

The nymph Sānumatī *is seen descending in a celestial car.*

Sānumatī. Behold me just arrived from attending in my proper turn at the nymphs' pool, where I have left the other nymphs to perform their ablutions, whilst I seek to ascertain, with my own eyes, how it fares with King Dushyanta. My connection with the nymph Menakā has made her daughter Shakuntalā dearer to me than my own flesh and blood; and Menakā it was who charged me with this errand on her daughter's behalf. (*Looking round in all directions.*) How is it that I see no preparations in the King's household for celebrating the great vernal festival?[a] I could easily discover the reason by my divine faculty of meditation; but respect must be shown to the wishes of my friend. How then shall I arrive at the truth? I know what I will do. I will become invisible, and place myself near those two maidens who are tending the plants in the garden.

(*Descends and takes her station.*)

Enter a maiden, *who stops in front of a mango-tree and gazes at the blossom. Another* maiden *is seen behind her.*

First Maiden. Hail to thee, lovely harbinger of spring!
The varied radiance of thy opening flowers

[a] The spring festival celebrates Krishna and his son Kāma, the god of love.

Is welcome to my sight. I bid thee hail,
Sweet mango, soul of this enchanting season.

Second Maiden. Parabhartikā, what are you saying there to yourself?

First Maiden. Dear Madhukarikā, am I not named after the Köil? and does not the Köil sing for joy at the first appearance of the mango-blossom?

Second Maiden (*approaching hastily, with transport*). What! is spring really come?

First Maiden. Yes, indeed, Madhukarikā, and with it the season of joy, love, and song.

Second Maiden. Let me lean upon you, dear, while I stand on tip-toe and pluck a blossom of the mango, that I may present it as an offering to the god of love.

First Maiden. Provided you let me have half the reward which the god will bestow in return.

Second Maiden. To be sure you shall, and that without asking. Are we not one in heart and soul, though divided in body? (*Leans on her friend and plucks a mango-blossom.*) Ah! here is a bud just bursting into flower. It diffuses a delicious perfume, though not yet quite expanded. (*Joining her hands reverentially.*)

God of the bow, who with spring's choicest flowers
Dost point thy five unerring shafts; to thee
I dedicate this blossom; let it serve
To barb thy truest arrow; be its mark
Some youthful heart that pines to be beloved.

(*Throws down a mango-blossom.*)

Chamberlain (*entering in a hurried manner, angrily*). Hold there, thoughtless woman. What are you about, breaking off those mango-blossoms, when the King has forbidden the celebration of the spring festival?

Both Maidens (*alarmed*). Pardon us, kind sir, we have heard nothing of it.

Chamberlain. You have heard nothing of it? Why, all the vernal plants and shrubs, and the very birds that lodge in their branches, show more respect to the King's order than you do.

Yon mango-blossoms, though long since expanded,
Gather no down upon their tender crests;
The flower still lingers in the amaranth,
Imprisoned in its bud; the tuneful Köil,
Though winter's chilly dews be overpast,
Suspends the liquid volume of his song

Scarce uttered in his throat; e'en Love, dismayed,
Restores the half-drawn arrow to his quiver.

Both Maidens. The mighty power of King Dushyanta is not to be disputed.

First Maiden. It is but a few days since Mitrāvasu, the King's brother-in-law, sent us to wait upon his Majesty; and, during the whole of our sojourn here, we have been intrusted with the charge of the royal pleasure-grounds. We are therefore strangers in this place, and heard nothing of the order until you informed us of it.

Chamberlain. Well then, now you know it, take care you don't continue your preparations.

Both Maidens. But tell us, kind sir, why has the King prohibited the usual festivities? We are curious to hear, if we may.

Sānumatī (*aside*). Men are naturally fond of festive entertainments. There must be some good reason for the prohibition.

Chamberlain. The whole affair is now public; why should I not speak of it! Has not the gossip about the King's rejection of Shakuntalā reached your ears yet?

Both Maidens. Oh yes, we heard the story from the King's brother-in-law, as far, at least, as the discovery of the ring.

Chamberlain. Then there is little more to tell you. As soon as the King's memory was restored by the sight of his own ring, he exclaimed, "Yes, it is all true. I remember now my secret marriage with Shakuntalā. When I repudiated her, I had lost my recollection." Ever since that moment, he has yielded himself a prey to the bitterest remorse.

He loathes his former pleasures; he rejects
The daily homage of his ministers.
On his lone couch he tosses to and fro,
Courting repose in vain. Whene'er he meets
The ladies of his palace, and would fain
Address them with politeness, he confounds
Their names; or, calling them "Shakuntalā,"
Is straightway silent and abashed with shame.

Sānumatī (*aside*). To me this account is delightful.

Chamberlain. In short, the King is so completely out of his mind that the festival has been prohibited.

Both Maidens. Perfectly right.

A Voice (*behind the scenes*). The King! the King! This way, Sire, this way.

Chamberlain (*listening*). Oh! here comes his Majesty in this direction. Pass on, maidens; attend to your duties.

Both Maidens. We will, sir. (*Exeunt.*)

Enter King Dushyanta, *dressed in deep mourning, attended by his jester,* Mādhavya, *and preceded by* Vetravatī.

Chamberlain (*gazing at the* King). Well, noble forms are certainly pleasing, under all varieties of outward circumstances. The King's person is as charming as ever, notwithstanding his sorrow of mind.

Though but a single golden bracelet spans
His wasted arm; though costly ornaments
Have given place to penitential weeds;
Though oft-repeated sighs have blanched his lips,
And robbed them of their bloom; though sleepless care
And carking thought have dimmed his beaming eye;
Yet does his form, by its inherent luster
Dazzle the gaze; and, like a priceless gem
Committed to some cunning polisher,
Grow more effulgent by the loss of substance.

Sānumatī (*aside. Looking at the* King). Now that I have seen him, I can well understand why Shakuntalā should pine after such a man, in spite of his disdainful rejection of her.

King (*walking slowly up and down, in deep thought*).

When fatal lethargy o'erwhelmed my soul,
My loved one strove to rouse me, but in vain:—
And now when I would fain in slumber deep
Forget myself, full soon remorse doth wake me.

Sānumatī (*aside*). My poor Shakuntalā's sufferings are very similar.

Mādhavya (*aside*). He is taken with another attack of this odious Shakuntalā fever. How shall we ever cure him?

Chamberlain (*approaching*). Victory to the King! Great Prince, the royal pleasure-grounds have been put in order. Your Majesty can resort to them for exercise and amusement whenever you think proper.

King. Vetravatī, tell the worthy Pishuna, my prime minister, from me, that I am so exhausted by want of sleep that I cannot sit on the judgment-seat to-day. If any case of importance be brought before the tribunal he must give it his best attention, and inform me of the circumstances by letter.

Vetravatī. Your Majesty's commands shall be obeyed. (*Exit.*)

King (*to the* chamberlain). And you, Vātāyana, may go about your own affairs.

Chamberlain. I will, Sire. (*Exit*)

Mādhavya. Now that you have rid yourself of these troublesome fellows, you can enjoy the delightful coolness of your pleasure-grounds without interruption.

King. Ah! my dear friend, there is an old adage—"When affliction has a mind to enter, she will find a crevice somewhere"—and it is verified in me.

Scarce is my soul delivered from the cloud
That darkened its remembrance of the past,
When lo! the heart-born deity of love
With yonder blossom of the mango barbs
His keenest shaft, and aims it at my breast.

Mādhavya. Well, then, wait a moment; I will soon demolish Master Kāma's arrow with a cut of my cane.

(*Raises his stick and strikes off the mango-blossom.*)

King (*smiling*). That will do. I see very well the god of Love is not a match for a Brahman. And now, my dear friend, where shall I sit down, that I may enchant my sight by gazing on the twining plants, which seem to remind me of the graceful shape of my beloved?

Mādhavya. Do you not remember? you told Chaturikā you should pass the heat of the day in the jasmine bower; and commanded her to bring the likeness of your queen Shakuntalā, sketched with your own hand.

King. True. The sight of her picture will refresh my soul. Lead the way to the arbor.

Mādhavya. This way, Sire.

(*Both move on, followed by* Sānumatī.)

Mādhavya. Here we are at the jasmine bower. Look, it has a marble seat, and seems to bid us welcome with its offerings of delicious flowers. You have only to enter and sit down. (*Both enter and seat themselves.*)

Sānumatī (*aside*). I will lean against these young jasmines. I can easily, from behind them, glance at my friend's picture, and will then hasten to inform her of her husband's ardent affection.

(*Stands leaning against the creepers.*)

King. Oh! my dear friend, how vividly all the circumstances of my union with Shakuntalā present themselves to my recollection at this moment! But tell me now how it was that, between the time of my leaving her in the hermitage and my subsequent rejection of her, you never breathed her name to me! True, you were not by my side when I disowned her; but I had confided to you the story of my love and you were acquainted with every particular. Did it pass out of your mind as it did out of mine?

Mādhavya. No, no; trust me for that. But, if you remember, when you had finished telling me about it, you added that I was not to take the story in earnest, for that you were not really in love with a country girl, but were only jesting; and I was dull and thick-headed enough to believe you. But so fate decreed, and there is no help for it.

Sānumatī (*aside*). Exactly.

King (*after deep thought*). My dear friend, suggest some relief for my misery.

Mādhavya. Come, come, cheer up; why do you give way? Such weakness is unworthy of you. Great men never surrender themselves to uncontrolled grief. Do not mountains remain unshaken even in a gale of wind?

King. How can I be otherwise than inconsolable, when I call to mind the agonized demeanor of the dear one on the occasion of my disowning her?

When cruelly I spurned her from my presence,
She fain had left me; but the young recluse,
Stern as the Sage, and with authority
As from his saintly master, in a voice
That brooked not contradiction, bade her stay.
Then through her pleading eyes, bedimmed with tears,
She cast on me one long reproachful look,
Which like a poisoned shaft torments me still.

Sānumatī (*aside*). Alas! such is the force of self-reproach following a rash action. But his anguish only rejoices me.

Mādhavya. An idea has just struck me. I should not wonder if some celestial being had carried her off to heaven.

King. Very likely. Who else would have dared to lay a finger on a wife, the idol of her husband? It is said that Menakā, the nymph of heaven, gave her birth. The suspicion has certainly crossed my mind that some of her celestial companions may have taken her to their own abode.

Sānumatī (*aside*). His present recollection of every circumstance of her history does not surprise me so much as his former forgetfulness.

Mādhavya. If that's the case, you will be certain to meet her before long.

King. Why?

Mādhavya. No father and mother can endure to see a daughter suffering the pain of separation from her husband.

King. Oh! my dear Mādhavya,

Was it a dream? or did some magic dire,
Dulling my senses with a strange delusion,
O'ercome my spirit? or did destiny,
Jealous of my good actions, mar their fruit,
And rob me of their guerdon? It is past,
Whate'er the spell that bound me. Once again
Am I awake, but only to behold
The precipice o'er which my hopes have fallen.

Mādhavya. Do not despair in this manner. Is not this very ring a proof that what has been lost may be unexpectedly found?

King (*gazing at the ring*). Ah! this ring, too, has fallen from a station which it will not easily regain, and deserves all my sympathy.

O gem, deserved the punishment we suffer,
And equal is the merit of our works,
When such our common doom. Thou didst enjoy
The thrilling contact of those slender fingers,
Bright as the dawn; and now how changed thy lot!

Sānumatī (*aside*). Had it found its way to the hand of any other person, then indeed its fate would have been deplorable.

Mādhavya. Pray, how did the ring ever come upon her hand at all?

Sānumatī. I myself am curious to know.

King. You shall hear. When I was leaving my beloved Shakuntalā that I might return to my own capital, she said to me, with tears in her eyes, "How long will it be ere my lord send for me to his palace and make me his queen?"

Mādhavya. Well, what was your reply?

King. Then I placed the ring on her finger, and thus addressed her—

Repeat each day one letter of the name
Engraven on this gem; ere thou hast reckoned
The tale of syllables, my minister
Shall come to lead thee to thy husband's palace.

But, hard-hearted man that I was, I forgot to fulfil n promise, owing to the infatuation that took possession me.

Sānumatī (*aside*). A pleasant arrangement! Fate, howeve ordained that the appointment should not be kept.

Mādhavya. But how did the ring contrive to pass into th stomach of that carp which the fisherman caught and w cutting up?

King. It must have slipped from my Shakuntalā's hand, an fallen into the stream of the Ganges, while she was o fering homage to the water of Shachī's holy pool.

Mādhavya. Very likely.

Sānumatī (*aside*). Hence it happened, I suppose, that th King, always fearful of committing the least injustice, can to doubt his marriage with my poor Shakuntalā. But wh should affection so strong as his stand in need of any toke of recognition?

King. Let me now address a few words of reproof to th ring.

Mādhavya (*aside*). He is going stark mad, I verily believ

King. Hear me, thou dull and undiscerning bauble!

For so it argues thee, that thou couldst leave
The slender fingers of her hand, to sink
Beneath the waters. Yet what marvel is it
That thou shouldst lack discernment? let me rather
Heap curses on myself, who, though endowed
With reason, yet rejected her I loved.

Mādhavya (*aside*). And so, I suppose, I must stand here be devoured by hunger, whilst he goes on in this sent mental strain.

King. O forsaken one, unjustly banished from my presenc take pity on thy slave, whose heart is consumed by th fire of remorse, and return to my sight.

Enter Chaturikā *hurriedly, with a picture in her hand.*

Chaturikā. Here is the Queen's portrait.

(*Shows the picture.*)

Mādhavya. Excellent, my dear friend, excellent! The imit tion of nature is perfect, and the attitude of the figur is really charming. They stand out in such bold reli that the eye is quite deceived.

Sānumatī (*aside*). A most artistic performance! I admi the King's skill, and could almost believe that Shakunta herself was before me.

ing. I own 'tis not amiss, though it portrays
But feebly her angelic loveliness.
Aught less than perfect is depicted falsely,
And fancy must supply the imperfection.

ānumatī (*aside*). A very just remark from a modest man, whose affection is exaggerated by the keenness of his remorse.

Iādhavya. Tell me—I see three female figures drawn on the canvas, and all of them beautiful; which of the three is her Majesty, Shakuntalā?

ānumatī (*aside*). If he cannot distinguish her from the others, the simpleton might as well have no eyes in his head.

ing. Which should you imagine to be intended for her?

Iādhavya. She who is leaning, apparently a little tired, against the stem of that mango-tree, the tender leaves of which glitter with the water she has poured upon them. Her arms are gracefully extended; her face is somewhat flushed with the heat; and a few flowers have escaped from her hair, which has become unfastened, and hangs in loose tresses about her neck. That must be the queen Shakuntalā, and the others, I presume, are her two attendants.

ing. I congratulate you on your discernment. Behold the proof of my passion;
My finger, burning with the glow of love,
Has left its impress on the painted tablet;
While here and there, alas! a scalding tear
Has fallen on the cheek and dimmed its brightness.
Chaturikā, the garden in the background of the picture is only half-painted. Go, fetch the brush that I may finish it.

haturikā. Worthy Mādhavya, have the kindness to hold the picture until I return.

ing. Nay, I will hold it myself.

(*Takes the picture. Exit* Chaturikā.)

ing. My loved one came but lately to my presence
And offered me herself, but in my folly
I spurned the gift, and now I fondly cling
To her mere image; even as a madman
Would pass the waters of the gushing stream,
And thirst for airy vapors of the desert.

Iādhavya (*aside*). He has been fool enough to forego the reality for the semblance, the substance for the shadow. (*Aloud.*) Tell us, pray, what else remains to be painted.

ānumatī (*aside*). He longs, no doubt, to delineate some

favorite spot where my dear Shakuntalā delighted t
ramble.

King. You shall hear——

I wish to see the Mālinī portrayed,
Its tranquil course by banks of sand impeded—
Upon the brink a pair of swans: beyond,
The hills adjacent to Himālaya,
Studded with deer; and, near the spreading shade
Of some large tree, where 'mid the branches hang
The hermits' vests of bark, a tender doe,
Rubbing its downy forehead on the horn
Of a black antelope, should be depicted.

Mādhavya (*aside*). Pooh! if I were he, I would fill up th
vacant spaces with a lot of grizzly-bearded old hermits.

King. My dear Mādhavya, there is still a part of Shakun
talā's dress which I purposed to draw, but find I hav
omitted.

Mādhavya. What is that?

Sānumatī (*aside*). Something suitable, I suppose, to the sin
ple attire of a young and beautiful girl dwelling in a fores

King. A sweet Shirīsha blossom should be twined
Behind her ear, its perfumed crest depending
Towards her cheek; and, resting on her bosom,
A lotus-fiber necklace, soft and bright
As an autumnal moon-beam, should be traced.

Mādhavya. Pray, why does the Queen cover her lips wit
the tips of her fingers, bright as the blossom of a lily, a
if she were afraid of something? (*Looking more closely*
Oh! I see; a vagabond bee, intent on thieving the honey o
flowers, has mistaken her mouth for a rose-bud, and
trying to settle upon it.

King. A bee! drive off the impudent insect, will you?

Mādhavya. That's your business. Your royal prerogati
gives you power over all offenders.

King. Very true. Listen to me, thou favorite guest of flowe
ing plants; why give thyself the trouble of hovering here
See where thy partner sits on yonder flower,
And waits for thee ere she will sip its dew.

Sānumatī (*aside*). A most polite way of warning him o

Mādhavya. You'll find the obstinate creature is not to b
sent about his business so easily as you think.

King. Dost thou presume to disobey? Now hear me—
An thou but touch the lips of my beloved,
Sweet as the opening blossom, whence I quaffed
In happier days love's nectar, I will place thee
Within the hollow of yon lotus cup,

And there imprison thee for thy presumption.

Mādhavya. He must be bold indeed not to show any fear when you threaten him with such an awful punishment. (*Smiling, aside.*) He is stark mad, that's clear; and I believe, by keeping him company, I am beginning to talk almost as wildly. (*Aloud.*) Look, it is only a painted bee.

King. Painted? impossible!

Sānumatī (*aside*). Even I did not perceive it; how much less should he?

King. Oh! my dear friend, why were you so ill-natured as to tell me the truth?

While, all entranced, I gazed upon her picture,
My loved one seemed to live before my eyes,
Till every fiber of my being thrilled
With rapturous emotion. Oh! 'twas cruel
To dissipate the day-dream, and transform
The blissful vision to a lifeless image.

(*Sheds tears.*)

Sānumatī (*aside*). Separated lovers are very difficult to please; but he seems more difficult than usual.

King. Alas! my dear Mādhavya, why am I doomed to be the victim of perpetual disappointment?

Vain is the hope of meeting her in dreams,
For slumber night by night forsakes my couch:
And now that I would fain assuage my grief
By gazing on her portrait here before me,
Tears of despairing love obscure my sight.

Sānumatī (*aside*). You have made ample amends for the wrong you did Shakuntalā in disowning her.

Chaturikā (*entering*). Victory to the King! I was coming along with the box of colors in my hand——

King. What now?

Chaturikā. When I met the Queen Vasumatī, attended by Taralikā. She insisted on taking it from me, and declared she would herself deliver it into your Majesty's hands.

Mādhavya. By what luck did you contrive to escape her?

Chaturikā. While her maid was disengaging her mantle, which had caught in the branch of a shrub, I ran away.

King. Here, my good friend, take the picture and conceal it. My attentions to the Queen have made her presumptuous. She will be here in a minute.

Mādhavya. Conceal the picture! conceal myself, you mean. (*Getting up and taking the picture.*) The Queen has a bitter draught in store for you, which you will have to swallow as Shiva did the poison at the Deluge.[b] When you are well quit of her, you may send and call me from the Palace of Clouds,[c] where I shall take refuge.

(*Exit, running.*)

Sānumatī (*aside*). Although the King's affections are transferred to another object, yet he respects his previous attachments. I fear his love must be somewhat fickle.

Vetravatī (*entering with a dispatch in her hand*). Victory to the King!

King. Vetravatī, did you observe the Queen Vasumatī coming in this direction?

Vetravatī. I did; but when she saw that I had a dispatch in my hand for your Majesty, she turned back.

King. The Queen has too much regard for propriety to interrupt me when I am engaged with state-affairs.

Vetravatī. So please your Majesty, your Prime Minister begs respectfully to inform you that he has devoted much time to the settlement of financial calculations, and only one case of importance has been submitted by the citizens for his consideration. He has made a written report of the facts, and requests your Majesty to cast your eyes over it.

King. Hand me the paper.

(Vetravatī *delivers it.*)

King (*reading*). What have we here? "A merchant named Dhanamitra, trading by sea, was lost in a late shipwreck. Though a wealthy trader, he was childless; and the whole of his immense property becomes by law forfeited to the King." So writes the minister. Alas! alas! for his childlessness. But surely, if he was wealthy, he must have had many wives. Let an inquiry be made whether any of them is expecting to give birth to a child.

Vetravatī. They say that his wife, the daughter of the foreman of a guild belonging to Ayodhyā, has just completed the ceremonies usual upon such expectations.

King. The unborn child has a title to his father's property. Such is my decree. Go, bid my minister proclaim it so.

Vetravatī. I will, my liege. (*Going.*)

King. Stay a moment.

[b] The powerful god Shiva, destroyer of all things through death and time, during the creation period drank a deadly poison churned from the cosmic ocean. This turned his neck blue, but he saved the other gods.

[c] A poetic description of Dushyanta's lofty palace.

etravatī. I am at your Majesty's service.

ing. Let there be no question whether he may or may not have left offspring;

Rather be it proclaimed that whosoe'er
Of King Dushyanta's subjects be bereaved
Of any loved relation, an it be not
That his estates are forfeited for crimes,
Dushyanta will himself to them supply
That kinsman's place in tenderest affection.

etravatī. It shall be so proclaimed.

(*Exit* Vetravatī, *and reenter after an interval.*)

etravatī. Your Majesty's proclamation was received with acclamations of joy, like grateful rain at the right season.

ing (*drawing a deep sigh*). So then, the property of rich men, who have no lineal descendants, passes over to a stranger at their decease. And such, alas! must be the fate of the fortunes of the race of Puru at my death; even as when fertile soil is sown with seed at the wrong season.

etravatī. Heaven forbid!

ing. Fool that I was to reject such happiness when it offered itself for my acceptance!

ānumatī (*aside*). He may well blame his own folly when he calls to mind his treatment of my beloved Shakuntalā.

ing. Ah! woe is me! when I forsook my wife—

My lawful wife—concealed within her breast
There lay my second self, a child unborn,
Hope of my race, e'en as the choicest fruit
Lies hidden in the bosom of the earth.

ānumatī (*aside*). There is no fear of your race being cut off for want of a son.

haturikā (*aside to* Vetravatī). The affair of the merchant's death has quite upset our royal master, and caused him sad distress. Had you not better fetch the worthy Mādhavya from the Palace of Clouds to comfort him?

etravatī. A very good idea. (*Exit.*)

ing. Alas! the shades of my forefathers are even now beginning to be alarmed, lest at my death they may be deprived of their funeral libations.

No son remains in King Dushyanta's place
To offer sacred homage to the dead
Of Puru's noble line: my ancestors
Must drink these glistening tears, the last libation
A childless man can ever hope to make them.

Falls down in an agony of grief.)

Chaturikā (*looking at him in consternation*). Great King compose yourself.

Sānumatī (*aside*). Alas! alas! though a bright light is shin ing near him, he is involved in the blackest darkness, b reason of the veil that obscures his sight. I will now re veal all, and put an end to his misery. But no; I heard th mother of the great Indra, when she was consoling Shakun talā, say, that the gods will soon bring about a joyfu union between husband and wife, being eager for the sacri fice which will be celebrated in their honor on the oc casion. I must not anticipate the happy moment, but wil return at once to my dear friend and cheer her with a account of what I have seen and heard.

(*Rises aloft and disappears.*)

A Voice (*behind the scenes*). Help! help! to the rescue!

King (*recovering himself. Listening*). Ha! I heard a cry o distress, and in Mādhavya's voice. What ho there!

Vetravatī (*entering*). Your friend is in danger; save him great King.

King. Who dares insult the worthy Mādhavya?

Vetravatī. Some evil demon, invisible to human eyes, ha seized him, and carried him to one of the turrets of th Palace of Clouds.

King (*rising*). Impossible! Have evil spirits power over m subjects, even in my private apartments? Well, well—

Daily I seem less able to avert
Misfortune from myself, and o'er my actions
Less competent to exercise control;
How can I then direct my subjects' ways,
Or shelter them from tyranny and wrong?

A Voice (*behind the scenes*). Halloo there! my dear friend Help! help!

King (*advancing with rapid strides*). Fear nothing——

The same voice (*behind the scenes*). Fear nothing, indeed How can I help fearing when some monster is twistin back my neck, and is about to snap it as he would sugar-cane?

King (*looking around*). What ho there! my bow.

Slave (*entering with a bow*). Behold your bow, Sire, an your armguard.

(*The* King *snatches up the bow and arrows.*)

Another Voice (behind the scenes). Here, thirsting for thy life-blood, will I slay thee,
As a fierce tiger rends his struggling prey.
Call now thy friend Dushyanta to thy aid;
His bow is mighty to defend the weak;
Yet all its vaunted power shall be as nought.

King (with fury). What! dares he defy me to my face? Hold there, monster! Prepare to die, for your time is come. (*Stringing his bow.*) Vetravatī, lead the way to the terrace.

Vetravatī. This way, Sire.

(*They advance in haste.*)

King (looking on every side). How's this? there is nothing to be seen.

A Voice (behind the scenes). Help! Save me! I can see you, though you cannot see me. I am like a mouse in the claws of a cat; my life is not worth a moment's purchase.

King. Avaunt, monster! You may pride yourself on the magic that renders you invisible, but my arrow shall find you out. Thus do I fix a shaft
That shall discern between an impious demon
And a good Brahman; bearing death to thee,
To him deliverance—even as the swan
Distinguishes the milk from worthless water.

(*Takes aim.*)

Enter Mātali, *holding* Mādhavya, *whom he releases.*

Mātali. Turn thou thy deadly arrows on the demons;
Such is the will of Indra; let thy bow
Be drawn against the enemies of the gods;
But on thy friends cast only looks of favor.

King (putting back his arrow). What, Mātali! Welcome, most noble charioteer of the mighty Indra.

Mādhavya. So, here is a monster who thought as little about slaughtering me as if I had been a bullock for sacrifice, and you must e'en greet him with a welcome.

Mātali (smiling). Great Prince, hear on what errand Indra sent me into your presence.

King. I am all attention.

Mātali. There is a race of giants, the descendants of Kālanemi,[d] whom the gods find difficult to subdue.

[d] A demon with a hundred arms and heads.

King. So I have already heard from Nārada.[e]

Mātali. Heaven's mighty lord, who deigns to call thee "friend,"
Appoints thee to the post of highest honor,
As leader of his armies; and commits
The subjugation of this giant brood
To thy resistless arms, e'en as the sun
Leaves the pale moon to dissipate the darkness.
Let your Majesty, therefore, ascend at once the celestial car of Indra; and, grasping your arms, advance to victory.

King. The mighty Indra honors me too highly by such a mark of distinction. But tell me, what made you act thus towards my poor friend Mādhavya?

Mātali. I will tell you. Perceiving that your Majesty's spirit was completely broken by some distress of mind under which you were laboring, I determined to rouse your energies by moving you to anger. Because
To light a flame, we need but stir the embers;
The cobra, when incensed, extends his head
And springs upon his foe; the bravest men
Display their courage only when provoked.

King (*aside to* Mādhavya). My dear Mādhavya, the commands of the great Indra must not be left unfulfilled. Go you and acquaint my minister, Pishuna, with what has happened, and say to him from me,
Dushyanta to thy care confides his realm—
Protect with all the vigor of thy mind
The interests of my people; while my bow
Is braced against the enemies of heaven.

Mādhavya. I obey. (*Exit.*)

Mātali. Ascend, illustrious Prince.

(*The* King *ascends the car. Exeunt.*)

[e] A celebrated wise man.

ACT VII

Scene—The sky

Enter King Dushyanta *and* Mātali *in the car of Indra, moving in the air.*

King. My good Mātali, it appears to me incredible that I can merit such a mark of distinction for having simply fulfilled the behests of the great Indra.

Mātali (*smiling*). Great Prince, it seems to me that neither of you is satisfied with himself—

You underrate the service you have rendered,
And think too highly of the god's reward:
He deems it scarce sufficient recompense
For your heroic deeds on his behalf.

King. Nay, Mātali, say not so. My most ambitious expectations were more than realized by the honor conferred on me at the moment when I took my leave. For,

Tinged with celestial sandal,[f] from the breast
Of the great Indra, where before it hung,
A garland of the ever-blooming tree
Of Nandana was cast about my neck
By his own hand: while, in the very presence
Of the assembled gods, I was enthroned
Beside their mighty lord, who smiled to see
His son Jayanta envious of the honor.

Mātali. There is no mark of distinction which your Majesty does not deserve at the hands of the immortals. See,

Heaven's hosts acknowledge thee their second saviour;
For now thy bow's unerring shafts (as erst

[f] Dyed yellow with sandalwood, an aromatic cosmetic.

The lion-man's terrific claws)[g] have purged
The empyreal sphere from taint of demons foul.

King. The praise of my victory must be ascribed to the majesty of Indra.

When mighty gods make men their delegates
In martial enterprise, to them belongs
The palm of victory; and not to mortals.
Could the pale Dawn dispel the shades of night,
Did not the god of day, whose diadem
Is jeweled with a thousand beams of light,
Place him in front of his effulgent car?

Mātali. A very just comparison. (*Driving on.*) Great King, behold! the glory of thy fame has reached even to the vault of heaven.

Hark! yonder inmates of the starry sphere
Sing anthems worthy of thy martial deeds,
While with celestial colors they depict
The story of thy victories on scrolls
Formed of the leaves of heaven's immortal trees.

King. My good Mātali, yesterday, when I ascended the sky, I was so eager to do battle with the demons, that the road by which we were traveling towards Indra's heaven escaped my observation. Tell me, in which path of the seven winds are we now moving?

Mātali. We journey in the path of Parivaha;
The wind that bears along the triple Ganges,
And causes Ursa's seven stars to roll
In their appointed orbits, scattering
Their several rays with equal distribution.
'Tis the same path that once was sanctified
By the divine impression of the foot
Of Vishnu, when, to conquer haughty Bali,[h]
He spanned the heavens in his second stride.

King. This is the reason, I suppose, that a sensation of calm repose pervades all my senses. (*Looking down at the wheels.*) Ah! Mātali, we are descending towards the earth's atmosphere.

Mātali. What makes you think so?

King. The car itself instructs me; we are moving
O'er pregnant clouds, subcharged with rain; below us
I see the moisture-loving Chātakas
In sportive flight dart through the spokes; the steeds

[g] To save the three worlds (heaven, earth, the lower regions), the god Vishnu turned into a half-man, half-lion to fight demons.

[h] A demon who had gained control of the world by austerities, but was vanquished by Vishnu.

Of Indra glisten with the lightning's flash;
And a thick mist bedews the circling wheels.

Mātali. You are right; in a little while the chariot will touch the ground, and you will be in your own dominions.

King (looking down). How wonderful is the appearance of the earth as we rapidly descend!

Stupendous prospect! yonder lofty hills
Do suddenly uprear their towering heads
Amid the plain, while from beneath their crests
The ground receding sinks; the trees, whose stems
Seemed lately hid within their leafy tresses,
Rise into elevation, and display
Their branching shoulders; yonder streams, whose waters,
Like silver threads, but now were scarcely seen,
Grow into mighty rivers; lo! the earth
Seems upward hurled by some gigantic power.

Mātali. Well described! (*Looking with awe.*) Grand, indeed, and lovely is the spectacle presented by the earth.

King. Tell me, Mātali, what is that range of mountains which, like a bank of clouds illumined by the setting sun, pours down a stream of gold? On one side its base dips into the eastern ocean, and on the other side into the western.

Mātali. Great Prince, it is called "Golden-peak,"[1] and is the abode of the attendants of the god of Wealth. In this spot the highest forms of penance are wrought out.

There Kashyapa, the great progenitor
Of demons and of gods, himself the offspring
Of the divine Marīchi, Brahma's son,
With Aditi, his wife, in calm seclusion,
Does holy penance for the good of mortals.

King. Then I must not neglect so good an opportunity of obtaining his blessing. I should much like to visit this venerable personage and offer him my homage.

Mātali. By all means! An excellent idea.

(*Guides the car to the earth.*)

King (in a tone of wonder). How's this?

Our chariot wheels move noiselessly. Around
No clouds of dust arise; no shock betokened
Our contact with the earth; we seem to glide
Above the ground, so lightly do we touch it.

Mātali. Such is the difference between the car of Indra and

[1] A sacred range of mountains in the Himalāya chain, the abode of Kuvera, god of wealth.

that of your Majesty.

King. In which direction, Mātali, is Kashyapa's sacred retreat?

Mātali (pointing). Where stands yon anchorite, towards the orb
Of the meridian sun, immovable
As a tree's stem, his body half-concealed
By a huge ant-hill. Round about his breast
No sacred cord is twined, but in its stead
A hideous serpent's skin. In place of necklace,
The tendrils of a withered creeper chafe
His wasted neck. His matted hair depends
In thick entanglement about his shoulders,
And birds construct their nests within its folds.[j]

King. I salute thee, thou man of austere devotion.

Mātali (holding in the reins of the car). Great Prince, we are now in the sacred grove of the holy Kashyapa—the grove that boasts as its ornament one of the five trees of Indra's heaven, reared by Aditi.

King. This sacred retreat is more delightful than heaven itself. I could almost fancy myself bathing in a pool of nectar.

Mātali (stopping the chariot). Descend, mighty Prince.

King (descending). And what will you do, Mātali?

Mātali. The chariot will remain where I have stopped it. We may both descend. (*Doing so.*) This way, great King. (*Walking on.*) You see around you the celebrated region where the holiest sages devote themselves to penitential rites.

King. I am filled with awe and wonder as I gaze.
In such a place as this do saints of earth
Long to complete their acts of penance; here,
Beneath the shade of everlasting trees,
Transplanted from the groves of Paradise,
May they inhale the balmy air, and need
No other nourishment; here may they bathe
In fountains sparkling with the golden dust
Of lilies, here, on jeweled slabs of marble,
In meditation rapt, may they recline;
Here, in the presence of celestial nymphs,
E'en passion's voice is powerless to move them.

Mātali. So true is it that the aspirations of the good and great are ever soaring upwards. (*Turning round and speak-*

[j] An idealized picture of the ascetic doing penance: he lives on air.

ing off the stage.) Tell me, Vriddha-shākalya, how is the divine son of Marīchi now engaged? What sayest thou? that he is conversing with Aditi and some of the wives of the great sages, and that they are questioning him respecting the duties of a faithful wife?

King (*listening*). Then we must await the holy father's leisure.

Mātali (*looking at the* King). If your Majesty will rest under the shade, at the foot of this Ashoka-tree, I will seek an opportunity of announcing your arrival to Indra's reputed father.

King. As you think proper.

(*Remains under the tree.*)

Mātali. Great King, I go. (*Exit.*)

King (*feeling his arm throb*). Wherefore this causeless throbbing, O mine arm?

All hope has fled forever; mock me not
With presages of good, when happiness
Is lost, and nought but misery remains.

A Voice (*behind the scenes*). Be not so naughty. Do you begin already to show a refractory spirit?

King (*listening*). This is no place for petulance. Who can it be whose behavior calls for such a rebuke? (*Looking in the direction of the sound and smiling.*) A child, is it? closely attended by two holy women. His disposition seems anything but childlike. See,

He braves the fury of yon lioness
Suckling its savage offspring, and compels
The angry whelp to leave the half-sucked dug,
Tearing its tender mane in boisterous sport.

Enter a child, *attended by two women of the hermitage, in the manner described.*

Child. Open your mouth, my young lion, I want to count your teeth.

First Attendant. You naughty child, why do you tease the animals? Know you not that we cherish them in this hermitage as if they were our own children? In good sooth, you have a high spirit of your own, and are beginning already to do justice to the name Sarvadamana,[k] given you by the hermits.

[k] Sarvadamana means "all-taming."

King. Strange! My heart inclines towards the boy with almost as much affection as if he were my own child. What can be the reason? I suppose my own childlessness makes me yearn towards the sons of others.

Second Attendant. This lioness will certainly attack you if you do not release her whelp.

Child (*laughing*). Oh! indeed! let her come. Much I fear her, to be sure.

(*Pouts his under-lip in defiance.*)

King. The germ of mighty courage lies concealed
Within this noble infant, like a spark
Beneath the fuel, waiting but a breath
To fan the flame and raise a conflagration.

First Attendant. Let the young lion go, like a dear child, and I will give you something else to play with.

Child. Where is it? Give it me first.

(*Stretches out his hand.*)

King (*looking at his hand*). How's this? His hand exhibits one of those mystic marks[1] which are the sure prognostic of universal empire. See!
His fingers stretched in eager expectation
To grasp the wished-for toy, and knit together
By a close-woven web, in shape resemble
A lotus-blossom, whose expanding petals
The early dawn has only half unfolded.

Second Attendant. We shall never pacify him by mere words, dear Suvratā. Be kind enough to go to my cottage, and you will find there a plaything belonging to Mārkāndeya, one of the hermit's children. It is a peacock made of China-ware, painted in many colors. Bring it here for the child.

First Attendant. Very well. (*Exit.*)

Child. No, no; I shall go on playing with the young lion.

(*Looks at the female attendant and laughs.*)

King. I feel an unaccountable affection for this wayward child.
How blessed the virtuous parents whose attire

[1] The mark of a discus (mentioned earlier), which means he will be a king or hero.

Is soiled with dust, by raising from the ground
The child that asks a refuge in their arms!
And happy are they while with lisping prattle,
In accents sweetly inarticulate,
He charms their ears; and with his artless smiles
Gladdens their hearts, revealing to their gaze
His tiny teeth, just budding into view.

Attendant. I see how it is. He pays me no manner of attention. (*Looking off the stage.*) I wonder whether any of the hermits are about here. (*Seeing the* King.) Kind Sir, could you come hither a moment and help me to release the young lion from the clutch of this child, who is teasing him in boyish play?

King (*approaching and smiling*). Listen to me, thou child of a mighty saint.

Dost thou dare show a wayward spirit here?
Here, in this hallowed region? Take thou heed
Lest, as the serpent's young defiles the sandal,[m]
Thou bring dishonor on the holy sage,
Thy tender-hearted parent, who delights
To shield from harm the tenants of the wood.

Attendant. Gentle Sir, I thank you; but he is not the saint's son.

King. His behavior and whole bearing would have led me to doubt it, had not the place of his abode encouraged the idea.

(*Follows the* child, *and takes him by the hand, according to the request of the attendant. Speaking aside.*)

I marvel that the touch of this strange child
Should thrill me with delight; if so it be,
How must the fond caresses of a son
Transport the father's soul who gave him being!

Attendant (*looking at them both*). Wonderful! Prodigious!

King. What excites your surprise, my good woman?

Attendant. I am astonished at the striking resemblance between the child and yourself; and, what is still more extraordinary, he seems to have taken to you kindly and submissively, though you are a stranger to him.

King (*fondling the* child). If he be not the son of the great sage, of what family does he come, may I ask?

Attendant. Of the race of Puru.

King (*aside*). What! are we, then, descended from the same

[m] Serpents were supposed to like the perfumed sandalwood tree.

ancestry? This, no doubt, accounts for the resemblanc she traces between the child and me. Certainly it ha always been an established usage among the princes o Puru's race,

To dedicate the morning of their days
To the world's weal, in palaces and halls,
'Mid luxury and regal pomp abiding;
Then, in the wane of life, to seek release
From kingly cares, and make the hallowed shade
Of sacred trees their last asylum, where
As hermits they may practice self-abasement,
And bind themselves by rigid vows of penance.

(*Aloud.*) But how could mortals by their own power gai admission to this sacred region?

Attendant. Your remark is just; but your wonder will ceas when I tell you that his mother is the offspring of celestial nymph, and gave him birth in the hallowed grov of Kashyapa.

King (*aside*). Strange that my hopes should be again ex cited! (*Aloud.*) But what, let me ask, was the name of th prince whom she deigned to honor with her hand?

Attendant. How could I think of polluting my lips by th mention of a wretch who had the cruelty to desert hi lawful wife?

King (*aside*). Ha! the description suits me exactly. Would could bring myself to inquire the name of the child' mother! (*Reflecting.*) But it is against propriety to mak too minute inquiries about the wife of another man.

First Attendant (*entering with the china peacock in her hand*) Sarvadamana, Sarvadamana, see, see, what a beautifu Shakunta (bird).

Child (*looking round*). My mother! Where? Let me go t her.

Both Attendants. He mistook the word Shakunta for Sha kuntalā. The boy dotes upon his mother, and she i ever uppermost in his thoughts.

Second Attendant. Nay, my dear child, I said, Look at th beauty of this Shakunta.

King (*aside*). What! is his mother's name Shakuntalā? Bu the name is not uncommon among women. Alas! I fear th mere similarity of a name, like the deceitful vapor of th desert, has once more raised my hopes only to dash them t the ground.

Child (*takes the toy*). Dear nurse, what a beautiful pea cock!

First Attendant (*looking at the child. In great distress*). Alas! alas! I do not see the amulet on his wrist.

King. Don't distress yourself. Here it is. It fell off while he was struggling with the young lion.

(*Stoops to pick it up.*)

Both Attendants. Hold! hold! touch it not, for your life. How marvelous! He has actually taken it up without the slightest hesitation.

(*Both raise their hands to their breasts and look at each other in astonishment.*)

King. Why did you try to prevent my touching it?

First Attendant. Listen, great Monarch. This amulet, known as "The Invincible," was given to the boy by the divine son of Marīchi, soon after his birth, when the natal ceremony was performed. Its peculiar virtue is, that when it falls on the ground, no one excepting the father or mother of the child can touch it unhurt.

King. And suppose another person touches it?

First Attendant. Then it instantly becomes a serpent, and bites him.

King. Have you ever witnessed the transformation with your own eyes?

Both Attendants. Over and over again.

King (*with rapture. Aside*). Joy! joy! Are then my dearest hopes to be fulfilled?

(*Embraces the* child.)

Second Attendant. Come, my dear Suvratā, we must inform Shakuntalā immediately of this wonderful event, though we have to interrupt her in the performance of her religious vows. (*Exeunt.*)

Child (*to the* King). Do not hold me. I want to go to my mother.

King. We will go to her together, and give her joy, my son.

Child. Dushyanta is my father, not you.

King (*smiling*). His contradiction convinces me only the more.

Enter Shakuntalā, *in widow's apparel, with her long hair twisted into a single braid.*

Shakuntalā (*aside*). I have just heard that Sarvadamana amulet has retained its form, though a stranger raised from the ground. I can hardly believe in my good for- tune. Yet why should not Sānumatī's prediction be veri- fied?

King (*gazing at* Shakuntalā). Alas! can this indeed be my Shakuntalā?

Clad in the weeds of widowhood, her face
Emaciate with fasting, her long hair
Twined in a single braid, her whole demeanor
Expressive of her purity of soul:
With patient constancy she thus prolongs
The vow to which my cruelty condemned her.

Shakuntalā (*gazing at the* King, *who is pale with remorse*). Surely this is not like my husband; yet who can it be that dares pollute by the pressure of his hand my child whose amulet should protect him from a stranger's touch?

Child (*going to his mother*). Mother, who is this man that has been kissing me and calling me his son?

King. My best beloved, I have indeed treated thee most cruelly, but am now once more thy fond and affectionate lover. Refuse not to acknowledge me as thy husband.

Shakuntalā (*aside*). Be of good cheer, my heart. The anger of Destiny is at last appeased. Heaven regards thee with compassion. But is he in very truth my husband?

King. Behold me, best and loveliest of women,
Delivered from the cloud of fatal darkness
That erst oppressed my memory. Again
Behold us brought together by the grace
Of the great lord of Heaven. So the moon
Shines forth from dim eclipse, to blend his rays
With the soft luster of his Rohinī.

Shakuntalā. May my husband be victorious——

(*She stops short, her voice choked with tears.*)

King. O fair one, though the utterance of thy prayer
Be lost amid the torrent of thy tears,
Yet does the sight of thy fair countenance,
And of thy pallid lips, all unadorned
And colorless in sorrow for my absence,
Make me already more than conqueror.

Child. Mother, who is this man?

Shakuntalā. My child, ask the deity that presides over thy destiny.

King (falling at Shakuntalā's *feet).* Fairest of women, banish from thy mind
The memory of my cruelty; reproach
The fell delusion that o'erpowered my soul,
And blame not me, thy husband; 'tis the curse
Of him in whom the power of darkness reigns,
That he mistakes the gifts of those he loves
For deadly evils. Even though a friend
Should wreathe a garland on a blind man's brow,
Will he not cast it from him as a serpent?

Shakuntalā. Rise, my own husband, rise. Thou wast not to blame. My own evil deeds, committed in a former state of being, brought down this judgment upon me. How else could my husband, who was ever of a compassionate disposition, have acted so unfeelingly? (*The* King *rises.*) But tell me, my husband, how did the remembrance of thine unfortunate wife return to thy mind?

King. As soon as my heart's anguish is removed, and its wounds are healed, I will tell thee all.
Oh! let me, fair one, chase away the drop
That still bedews the fringes of thine eye;
And let me thus efface the memory
Of every tear that stained thy velvet cheek,
Unnoticed and unheeded by thy lord,
When in his madness he rejected thee.

(*Wipes away the tear.*)

Shakuntalā (seeing the signet-ring on his finger). Ah! my dear husband, is that the Lost Ring?

King. Yes; the moment I recovered it, my memory was restored.

Shakuntalā. The ring was to blame in allowing itself to be lost at the very time when I was anxious to convince my noble husband of the reality of my marriage.

King. Receive it back, as the beautiful twining plant receives again its blossom in token of its reunion with the spring.

Shakuntalā. Nay; I can never more place confidence in it. Let my husband retain it.

Enter Mātali.

Mātali. I congratulate your Majesty. Happy are you in your reunion with your wife: happy are you in beholding the face of your son.

King. Yes, indeed. My heart's dearest wish has born sweet fruit. But tell me, Mātali, is this joyful ever known to the great Indra?

Mātali (*smiling*). What is unknown to the gods? But com with me, noble Prince, the divine Kashyapa graciousl permits thee to be presented to him.

King. Shakuntalā, take our child and lead the way. W will together go into the presence of the holy Sage.

Shakuntalā. I shrink from entering the august presence c the great Saint, even with my husband at my side.

King. Nay; on such a joyous occasion it is highly prope Come, come; I entreat thee.

(*All advance.*)

Kashyapa *is discovered seated on a throne with his wif* Aditi.

Kashyapa (*gazing at* Dushyanta. *To his wife*). O Adit
This is the mighty hero, King Dushyanta,
Protector of the earth; who, at the head
Of the celestial armies of thy son,
Does battle with the enemies of heaven.
Thanks to his bow, the thunderbolt of Indra
Rests from its work, no more the minister
Of death and desolation to the world,
But a mere symbol of divinity.

Aditi. He bears in his noble form all the marks of dignity

Mātali (*to* Dushyanta). Sire, the venerable progenitors c the celestials are gazing at your Majesty with as much af fection as if you were their son. You may advance toward them.

King. Are these, O Mātali, the holy pair,
Offspring of Daksha and divine Marīchi,
Children of Brahma's sons, by sages deemed
Sole fountain of celestial light, diffused
Through twelve effulgent orbs?[n] Are these the pair
From whom the ruler of the triple world,
Sovereign of gods and lord of sacrifice,
Sprang into being? That immortal pair
Whom Vishnu, greater than the self-existent,
Chose for his parents, when, to save mankind,
He took upon himself the shape of mortals?

Mātali. Even so.

[n] The twelve months, born to Aditi and Kashyapa.

King (prostrating himself). Most august of beings, Dushyanta, content to have fulfilled the commands of your son Indra, offers you his adoration.

Kashyapa. My son, long may'st thou live, and happily may'st thou reign over the earth!

Aditi. My son, may'st thou ever be invincible in the field of battle!

Shakuntalā. I also prostrate myself before you, most adorable beings, and my child with me.

Kashyapa. My daughter,

Thy lord resembles Indra, and thy child
Is noble as Jayanta, Indra's son;
I have no worthier blessing left for thee,
May'st thou be faithful as the god's own wife!

Aditi. My daughter, may'st thou be always the object of thy husband's fondest love; and may thy son live long to be the joy of both his parents! Be seated.

(*All sit down in the presence of* Kashyapa.)

Kashyapa (regarding each of them by turns). Hail to the beautiful Shakuntalā!

Hail to her noble son! and hail to thee,
Illustrious Prince! Rare triple combination
Of virtue, wealth, and energy united!

King. Most venerable Kashyapa, by your favor all my desires were accomplished even before I was admitted to your presence. Never was mortal so honored that his boon should be granted ere it was solicited. Because,

Bloom before fruit, the clouds before the rain—
Cause first and then effect, in endless sequence,
Is the unchanging law of constant nature:
But, ere the blessing issued from thy lips,
The wishes of my heart were all fulfilled.

Mātali. It is thus that the great progenitors of the world confer favors.

King. Most reverend Sage, this thy handmaid was married to me by the Gāndharva ceremony, and after a time was conducted to my palace by her relations. Meanwhile a fatal delusion seized me; I lost my memory and rejected her, thus committing a grievous offense against the venerable Kanva, who is of thy divine race. Afterwards the sight of this ring restored my faculties, and brought back to my mind all the circumstances of my union with his daughter. But my conduct still seems to me incomprehensible;

As foolish as the fancies of a man

Who, when he sees an elephant, denies
That 'tis an elephant, yet afterwards,
When its huge bulk moves onward, hesitates,
Yet will not be convinced till it has passed
Forever from his sight, and left behind
No vestige of its presence save its footsteps.

Kashyapa. My son, cease to think thyself in fault. Even th delusion that possessed thy mind was not brought abo by any act of thine. Listen to me.

King. I am attentive.

Kashyapa. Know that when the nymph Menakā, the mot er of Shakuntalā, became aware of her daughter's anguis in consequence of the loss of the ring at the nymph pool, and of thy subsequent rejection of her, she broug her and confided her to the care of Aditi. And I no soon saw her than I ascertained by my divine power of medit tion, that thy repudiation of thy poor faithful wife ha been caused entirely by the curse of Durvāsas—not thine own fault—and that the spell would terminate c the discovery of the ring.

King (*drawing a deep breath*). Oh! what a weight is take off my mind, now that my character is cleared of reproac

Shakuntalā (*aside*). Joy! joy! My revered husband did nc then, reject me without good reason, though I have r recollection of the curse pronounced upon me. But, in a probability, I unconsciously brought it upon myself, whe I was so distracted on being separated from my husbar soon after our marriage. For I now remember that n two friends advised me not to fail to show the ring in ca he should have forgotten me.

Kashyapa. At last, my daughter, thou art happy, and ha gained thy heart's desire. Indulge, then, no feeling of r sentment against thy partner. See, now,

Though he repulsed thee, 'twas the Sage's curse
That clouded his remembrance; 'twas the curse
That made thy tender husband harsh towards thee.
Soon as the spell was broken, and his soul
Delivered from its darkness, in a moment
Thou didst gain thine empire o'er his heart.
So on the tarnished surface of a mirror
No image is reflected, till the dust
That dimmed its wonted luster is removed.

King. Holy father, see here the hope of my royal race.

(*Takes his child by the hand.*)

Kashyapa. Know that he, too, will become the monarch of the whole earth. Observe,

Soon, a resistless hero, shall he cross
The trackless ocean, borne above the waves
In an aerial car; and shall subdue
The earth's seven sea-girt isles.[o] Now has he gained,
As the brave tamer of the forest-beasts,
The title Sarvadamana; but then
Mankind shall hail him as King Bharata,[p]
And call him the supporter of the world.

King. We cannot but entertain the highest hopes of a child for whom your highness performed the natal rites.

Aditi. My revered husband, should not the intelligence be conveyed to Kanva, that his daughter's wishes are fulfilled, and her happiness complete? He is Shakuntalā's foster-father. Menakā, who is one of my attendants, is her mother, and dearly does she love her daughter.

Shakuntalā (*aside*). The venerable matron has given utterance to the very wish that was in my mind.

Kashyapa. His penances have gained for him the faculty of omniscience, and the whole scene is already present to his mind's eye.

King. Then most assuredly he cannot be very angry with me.

Kashyapa. Nevertheless it becomes us to send him intelligence of this happy event, and hear his reply. What, ho there!

Pupil (*entering*). Holy father, what are your commands?

Kashyapa. My good Gālava, delay not an instant, but hasten through the air and convey to the venerable Kanva, from me, the happy news that the fatal spell has ceased, that Dushyanta's memory is restored, that his daughter Shakuntalā has a son, and that she is once more tenderly acknowledged by her husband.

Pupil. Your highness's commands shall be obeyed. (*Exit.*)

Kashyapa. And now, my dear son, take thy consort and thy child, re-ascend the car of Indra, and return to thy imperial capital.

King. Most holy father, I obey.

Kashyapa. And accept this blessing—

For countless ages may the god of gods,
Lord of the atmosphere, by copious showers

[o] The universe was regarded as seven islands surrounded by seven seas, the earth being the central island.

[p] Shakuntalā's child becomes a greater king than his father, so great that India is often called Bharata.

Secure abundant harvest to thy subjects;
And thou by frequent offerings preserve
The Thunderer's friendship! Thus, by interchange
Of kindly actions, may you both confer
Unnumbered benefits on earth and heaven!

King. Holy father, I will strive, as far as I am able, to attain this happiness.

Kashyapa. What other favor can I bestow on thee, my son?

King. What other can I desire? If, however, you permit me to form another wish, I would humbly beg that the saying of the sage Bharata be fulfilled:—

May kings reign only for their subjects' weal!
May the divine Saraswati, the source
Of speech, and goddess of dramatic art,
Be ever honored by the great and wise!
And may the purple self-existent god,
Whose vital Energy pervades all space,
From future transmigrations save my soul! [q]

(*Exeunt omnes.*)

[q] By pious conduct one escapes from temporal desires and the world of flesh and no longer suffers endless reincarnation.

The Little Clay Cart

(*MṚCCHAKAṬIKĀ*)
Anonymous
(*traditionally attributed to King Sūdraka*)

From The Little Clay Cart, *translated by Arthur William Ryder. Cambridge, Mass.: Harvard University Press. Harvard Oriental Series, Vol. IX, 1905. Reprinted by permission of Harvard University Press.*

The Little Clay Cart

The manuscripts of the play always attribute it to a sage or to King Sūdraka. There is unfortunately no information on such a person and it has been held to be doubtful if he lived at all. Sūdraka does indeed appear in collections of stories like the *Ocean of Story* of Somadeva, an Indian anthology somewhat like the *Arabian Nights*. However, modern scholars conjecture that the illustrious name of a legendary sage was attached to the play to conceal the fact that it is a revision of a play by the well-known Sanskrit dramatist Bhāsa,[1] who flourished perhaps in the third century A.D. *The Little Clay Cart* cannot be later than 800 A.D. and may well have been written in the time of Kālidāsa, about 400 A.D. The conservatism of the Indian dramatic tradition, in any case, would make the date of the play less important than it might otherwise be.

The Little Clay Cart is quite different from the surviving plays of the other major Sanskrit dramatists. Its characters are not kings and ministers of state, it avoids the supernatural, and it emphasizes plot more heavily than poetry. In these respects it is unconventional, and perhaps for these reasons it has appealed to Western students of Indian literature. There is a double plot, like many a Renaissance drama in the West—one plot concerned with political intrigue and the other with the love of the hero Chārudatta and the beautiful courtesan Vasantasenā. The author is highly skilled at the realistic depiction of characters drawn from city life and it may be due to this that the play is easily appreciated by Westerners.

There are many striking scenes, but two may be singled

[1] On the problem of the authorship of the play see the translation by Revilo P. Oliver, pp. 12–28 (see Bibliography).

out. The trial scene at the end is exciting and skillfully con
trived, though the hero's being snatched from death at th
last moment will not seem to us very original. And, al
though the author's verbal gifts run more to wit than to po
etic descriptions, the elaborateness of the description of th
dwelling place of Vasantasenā is a minor masterpiece. In
finite varieties of sensual opulence suggest themselves in Ac
IV as Maitreya wanders through the eight courts of the pal
ace. ("Triple heaven in a nut-shell," he irreverently re
marks.)

CHARACTERS

Chārudatta, *a Brahman merchant who was once wealthy and is now impoverished*
Rohasena, *his son*
Maitreya, *his friend, also an indigent Brahman*
Vardhamānaka, *a servant in his house*
Sansthānaka, *brother-in-law of King Palāka*
Sthāvaraka, *his servant*
Another servant of Sansthānaka
A Courtier
Aryaka, *an exiled prince, now a herdsman*
Sharvilaka, *a Brahman by birth and a professional thief; friend of Aryaka and in love with Madanikā*
A Shampooer, *who becomes a Buddhist monk*
Māthura, *a gambling-master*
Darduraka, *an impoverished gentleman-gambler, friend of Sharvilaka*
Another gambler
Karnapūraka, Kumbhīlaka } *servants of Vasantasenā*
Vīraka, Chandanaka } *policemen*
Goha, Ahīnta } *headsmen*
Bastard pages, in Vasantasenā's house
A Judge, the chief of the merchant's guild, a Clerk, and a Bailiff or Beadle
Vasantasenā, *a beautiful courtesan*
Her Mother
Madanikā, *maid to Vasantasenā*
Another maid to Vasantasena
The wife of Chārudatta
Radanikā, *a maid in Chārudatta's house*
Stage Director and Actress (*in the Prologue*)

Scene: The city of Ujjayinī (also called Avanti), not far from the modern town of Ujjain in Gwalior, north central India

The Little Clay Cart

PROLOGUE

Benediction upon the audience [a]

His bended knees the knotted girdle holds,[b]
Fashioned by doubling of a serpent's folds;
His sensive organs, so he checks his breath,
Are numbed, till consciousness seems sunk in death;
Within himself, with eye of truth, he sees
The All-soul, free from all activities.
May His, may Shiva's meditation be
Your strong defense; on the Great Self thinks he,
Knowing full well the world's vacuity. 1

And again:

May Shiva's neck shield you from every harm,
That seems a threatening thunder-cloud, whereon,
Bright as the lightning-flash, lies Gaurī's [c] arm. 2

Stage Director. Enough of this tedious work, which fritters away the interest of the audience! Let me then most reverently salute the honorable gentlemen, and announce our intention to produce a drama called "The Little Clay Cart." Its author was a man

Who vied with elephants in lordly grace;
Whose eyes were those of the chakora bird
That feeds on moonbeams; glorious his face
As the full moon; his person, all have heard,
Was altogether lovely. First in worth
Among the twice-born was this poet, known
As Sūdraka [d] far over all the earth,—

[a] This is recited to the audience by a performer.

[b] The god Shiva holds a serpent, which symbolizes the Cycles of Existence. In his yoga-like trance he sees ultimate Reality.

[c] Wife of Shiva.

[d] Proper names ending in *-a* are masculine; those ending in *-ā* are feminine.

His virtue's depth unfathomed and alone. 3

And again:

The Sama-veda, the Rig-veda[e] too,
The science mathematical, he knew;
The arts wherein fair courtezans excel[f]

And all the lore of elephants as well.
Through Shiva's grace, his eye was never dim;
He saw his son a king in place of him.
The difficult horse-sacrifice he tried
Successfully; entered the fiery tide,[g]
One hundred years and ten days old, and died 4

And yet again:

Eager for battle; sloth's determined foe;
Of scholars chief, who to the Veda cling;
Rich in the riches that ascetics know;
Glad, gainst the foeman's elephant to show
His valor;—such was Sūdraka, the king. 5

And in this work of his,

Within the town, Avanti named,
Dwells one called Chārudatta, famed
No less for youth than poverty;
A merchant's son and Brahman, he.

His virtues have the power to move
Vasantasenā's inmost love;
Fair as the springtime's radiancy,
And yet a courtezan is she. 6

So here king Sūdraka the tale imparts
Of love's pure festival in these two hearts,
Of prudent acts, a lawsuit's wrong and hate,
A rascal's nature, and the course of fate. 7

(*He walks about and looks around him.*) Why, this music-room of ours is empty. I wonder where the actors have gone. (*Reflecting.*) Ah, I understand.

Empty his house, to whom no child was born;
Thrice empty his, who lacks true friends and sure;
To fools, the world is empty and forlorn;
But all that is, is empty to the poor. 8

I have finished the concert. And I've been practicing so

[e] Two of the most sacred scriptures of the Hindus.

[f] Erotics is considered a science and has a sacred book, the *Kāmasūtra.*

[g] At a great age, he ended his life by casting himself into the flames.

long that the pupils of my eyes are dancing, and I'm so hungry that my eyes are crackling like a lotus-seed, dried up by the fiercest rays of the summer sun. I'll just call my wife and ask whether there is anything for breakfast or not.

Hello! here I am—but no! Both the particular occasion and the general custom demand that I speak Prākrit. (*Speaking in Prākrit.*) Confound it! I've been practicing so long and I'm so hungry that my limbs are as weak as dried-up lotus-stalks. Suppose I go home and see whether my good wife has got anything ready or not. (*He walks about and looks around him.*) Here I am at home. I'll just go in. (*He enters and looks about.*) Merciful heavens! Why in the world is everything in our house turned upside down! A long stream of rice-water is flowing down the street. The ground, spotted black where the iron kettle has been rubbed clean, is as lovely as a girl with the beauty-marks of black cosmetic on her face.[h] It smells so good that my hunger seems to blaze up and hurts me more than ever. Has some hidden treasure come to light? or am I hungry enough to think the whole world is made of rice? There surely isn't any breakfast in our house, and I'm starved to death. But everything seems topsyturvy here. One girl is preparing cosmetics, another is weaving garlands of flowers. (*Reflecting.*) What does it all mean? Well, I'll call my good wife and learn the truth. (*He looks toward the dressing-room.*) Mistress, will you come here a moment?

Enter an actress.

Actress. Here I am, sir.

Director. You are very welcome, mistress.

Actress. Command me, sir. What am I to do?

Director. Mistress, I've been practicing so long and I'm so hungry that my limbs are as weak as dried-up lotus-stalks. Is there anything to eat in the house or not?

Actress. There's everything, sir.

Director. Well, what?

Actress. For instance: there's rice with sugar, melted butter, curdled milk, rice; and, all together, it makes you a

[h] Pastes made of perfumed chalks or powdered sandalwood were used as cosmetics and were considered cooling. Certain cosmetic marks (like the red spot on the forehead of married women) indicated social status.

dish fit for heaven. May the gods always be thus gracious to you!

Director. All that in our house? or are you joking?

Actress (*aside*). Yes, I will have my joke. (*Aloud.*) It's in the market-place, sir.

Director (*angrily*). You wretched woman, thus shall your own hope be cut off! And death shall find you out! For my expectations, like a scaffolding, have been raised so high, only to fall again.

Actress. Forgive me, sir, forgive me! It was only a joke.

Director. But what do these unusual preparations mean? One girl is preparing cosmetics, another is weaving garlands, and the very ground is adorned with sacrificial flowers of five different colors.

Actress. This is a fast day, sir.

Director. What fast?

Actress. The fast for a handsome husband.

Director. In this world, mistress, or the next?

Actress. In the next world, sir.

Director (*wrathfully*). Gentlemen! look at this. She is sacrificing my food to get herself a husband in the next world.

Actress. Don't be angry, sir. I am fasting in the hope that you may be my husband in my next birth, too.

Director. But who suggested this fast to you?

Actress. Your own dear friend Jūrnavriddha.

Director (*angrily*). Ah, Jūrnavriddha, son of a slave-wench! When, oh, when shall I see King Pālaka angry with you? Then you will be parted, as surely as the scented hair of some young bride.

Actress. Don't be angry, sir. It is only that I may have you in the next world that I celebrate this fast.

(*She falls at his feet.*)

Director. Stand up, mistress, and tell me who is to officiate at this fast.

Actress. Some Brahman of our own sort whom we must invite.

Director. You may go then. And I will invite some Brahman of our own sort.

Actress. Very well, sir. (*Exit.*)

Director (*walking about*). Good heavens! In this rich city of Ujjayinī how am I to find a Brahman of our own sort? (*He looks about him.*) Ah, here comes Chārudatta's friend Maitreya. Good! I'll ask him. Maitreya, you must be the first to break bread in our house to-day.

A voice behind the scenes. You must invite some other Brahman. I am busy.

Director. But, man, the feast is set and you have it all to yourself. Besides, you shall have a present.

The voice. I said no once. Why should you keep on urging me?

Director. He says no. Well, I must invite some other Brahman.

(*Exit.*)

ACT I

The Gems are Left Behind

Enter, with a cloak in his hand, Maitreya.

Maitreya. "You must invite some other Brahman. I am busy." And yet I really ought to be seeking invitations from a stranger. Oh, what a wretched state of affairs! When good Chārudatta was still wealthy, I used to eat my fill of the most deliciously fragrant sweetmeats, prepared day and night with the greatest of care. I would sit at the door of the courtyard, where I was surrounded by hundreds of dishes, and there, like a painter with his paint-boxes, I would simply touch them with my fingers and thrust them aside. I would stand chewing my cud like a bull in the city market. And now he is so poor that I have to run here, there, and everywhere, and come home, like the pigeons, only to roost. Now here is this jasmine-scented cloak, which Chārudatta's good friend Jūrnavriddha has sent him. He bade me give it to Chārudatta, as soon as he had finished his devotions. So now I will look for Chārudatta. (*He walks about and looks around him.*) Chārudatta has finished his devotions, and here he comes with an offering for the divinities of the house.[1]

Enter Chārudatta *as described, and* Radanikā.

Chārudatta (*looking up and sighing wearily*).

Upon my threshold, where the offering
 Was straightway seized by swans and flocking cranes,
The grass grows now, and these poor seeds I fling

[1] Daily devotions, which include an offering of food to all living creatures, done by all pious Brahmans.

Fall where the mouth of worms their sweetness stains. 9

(*He walks about very slowly and seats himself.*)

Maitreya. Chārudatta is here. I must go and speak to him. (*Approaching.*) My greetings to you. May happiness be yours.

Chārudatta. Ah, it is my constant friend Maitreya. You are very welcome, my friend. Pray be seated.

Maitreya. Thank you. (*He seats himself.*) Well, comrade, here is a jasmine-scented cloak which your good friend Jūrnavriddha has sent. He bade me give it you as soon as you had finished your devotions. (*He presents the cloak.* Chārudatta *takes it and remains sunk in thought.*) Well, what are you thinking about?

Chārudatta. My good friend,

A candle shining through the deepest dark
Is happiness that follows sorrow's strife;
But after bliss when man bears sorrow's mark,
His body lives a very death-in-life. 10

Maitreya. Well, which would you rather, be dead or be poor?

Chārudatta. Ah, my friend.

Far better death than sorrows sure and slow;
Some passing suffering from death may flow,
But poverty brings never-ending woe. 11

Maitreya. My dear friend, be not thus cast down. Your wealth has been conveyed to them you love, and like the moon, after she has yielded her nectar to the gods, your waning fortunes win an added charm.

Chārudatta. Comrade, I do not grieve for my ruined fortunes. But

This is my sorrow. They whom I
Would greet as guests, now pass me by.
"This is a poor man's house," they cry.

As flitting bees, the season o'er,
Desert the elephant, whose store
Of ichor[j] spent, attracts no more. 12

Maitreya. Oh, confound the money! It is a trifle not worth thinking about. It is like a cattle-boy in the woods afraid of wasps; it doesn't stay anywhere where it is used for food.

[j] During the mating season, the elephant secretes from his forehead a pungent substance that attracts bees.

Chārud. Believe me, friend.

My sorrow does not spring
From simple loss of gold;
For fortune is a fickle, changing thing,
Whose favors do not hold;
But he whose sometime wealth has taken wing,
Finds bosom-friends grow cold. 13

Then too:

A poor man is a man ashamed; from shame
Springs want of dignity and worthy fame;
Such want gives rise to insults hard to bear;
Thence comes despondency; and thence, despair;
Despair breeds folly; death is folly's fruit.—
Ah! the lack of money is all evil's root! 14

Maitreya. But just remember what a trifle money is, after all, and be more cheerful.

Chārudatta. My friend, the poverty of a man is to him

A home of cares, a shame that haunts the mind,
Another form of warfare with mankind;
The abhorrence of his friends, a source of hate
From strangers, and from each once-loving mate;
But if his wife despise him, then 't were meet
In some lone wood to seek a safe retreat.
The flame of sorrow, torturing his soul,
Burns fiercely, yet contrives to leave him whole. 15

Comrade, I have made my offering to the divinities of the house. Do you too go and offer sacrifice to the Divine Mothers [k] at a place where four roads meet.

Maitreya. No!

Chārudatta. Why not?

Maitreya. Because the gods are not gracious to you even when thus honored. So what is the use of worshiping?

Chārudatta. Not so, my friend, not so! This is the constant duty of a householder.

The gods feel ever glad content
In the gifts, and the self-chastisement,
The meditations, and the prayers,
Of those who banish worldly cares. 16

Why then do you hesitate? Go and offer sacrifice to the Mothers.

Maitreya. No, I'm not going. You must send somebody else. Anyway, everything seems to go wrong with me, poor Brahman that I am! It's like a reflection in a mirror; the right side becomes the left, and the left becomes

[k] Representations of the female principle in nature.

the right.[l] Besides, at this hour of the evening, people are abroad upon the king's highway—courtezans, courtiers, servants, and royal favorites. They will take me now for fair prey, just as the black-snake out frog-hunting snaps up the mouse in his path. But what will you do sitting here?

Chārudatta. Good then, remain; and I will finish my devotions.

Voices behind the scenes. Stop, Vasantasenā, stop!

Enter Vasantasenā, *pursued by the* courtier, *by* Sansthānaka, *and the* servant.

Courtier. Vasantasenā! Stop, stop!

Ah, why should fear transform your tenderness?
Why should the dainty feet feel such distress,
That twinkle in the dance so prettily?
Why should your eyes, thus startled into fear,
Dart sidelong looks? Why, like the timid deer
Before pursuing hunters, should you flee? 17

Sansthānaka. Shtop,[m] Vasantasenā, shtop!

Why flee? and run? and shtumble in your turning?
Be kind! You shall not die. Oh, shtop your feet!
With love, shweet girl, my tortured heart is burning
As on a heap of coals a piece of meat. 18

Servant. Stop, courtezan, stop!

In fear you flee
Away from me,
As a summer peahen should;
But my lord and master
Struts fast and faster,
Like a woodcock in the wood. 19

Courtier. Vasantasenā! Stop, stop!

Why should you tremble, should you flee,
A-quiver like the plantain tree?
Your garment's border, red and fair,
Is all a-shiver in the air;
Now and again, a lotus-bud
Falls to the ground, as red as blood.

[l] The same contrast as in the West between the right side (*dexter*) which is favorable and the left (*sinister*) which is evil or unfavorable.

[m] A bragging and vulgar character who speaks in a way that is not socially acceptable.

A red realgar [n] vein you seem,
Whence, smitten, drops of crimson stream. 20

Sansthānaka. Shtop, Vasantasenā, shtop!
You wake my passion, my desire, my love;
You drive away my shleep in bed at night;
Both fear and terror sheem your heart to move;
You trip and shtumble in your headlong flight.
But Rāvana forced Kuntī [o] to his will;
Jusht sho shall I enjoy you to the fill. 21

Courtier. Ah, Vasantasenā,
Why should your fleeter flight
Outstrip my flying feet?
Why, like a snake in fright
Before the bird-king's might,
Thus seek to flee, my sweet?
Could I not catch the storm-wind in his flight?
Yet would not seize upon you, though I might. 22

Sansthānaka. Lishten to me, shir!
Thish whip of robber Love,[p] thish dancing-girl,
Eater of fish, deshtroyer of her kin,
Thish shnubnose, shtubborn, love-box, courtezan,
Thish clothes-line, [q] wanton creature, maid of sin—
I gave her ten shweet names, and shtill
She will not bend her to my will. 23

Courtier. As courtier's fingers strike the lute's tense string,
The dancing ear-ring smites your wounded cheek.
Why should you flee, with dreadful terror weak,
As flees the crane when heaven's thunders ring? 24

Sansth. Your jingling gems, girl, clink like anything;
Like Draupadī you flee, when Rāma kisshed her.
I'll sheize you quick, as once the monkey-king
Sheized Subhadrā, Vishvāvasu's shweet shister.[r] 25

Servant. He's the royal protégé;
Do whatever he may say,
And you shall have good fish and flesh to eat.
For when dogs have all the fish
And the flesh that they can wish,
Even carrion seems to them no longer sweet. 26

Courtier. Mistress Vasantasenā,

[n] A vein of red arsenic, used as a cosmetic.

[o] Attempting to sound educated, Sansthānaka badly mixes up mythology from two Indian epics, the *Rāmāyana* and the *Mahābhārata.*

[p] Kāma, the god of love, who carries a whip.

[q] On which beautiful ornaments are hung.

[r] More badly scrambled mythology.

The girdle drooping low upon your hips
Flashes as brilliant as the shining stars;
The wondrous terror of your fleeing mars
Your charms; for red realgar, loosened, slips
As on an imaged god, from cheek and lips. 2

Sansth. We're chasing you with all our main and might,
As dogs a jackal when they hunt and find it;
But you are quick and nimble in your flight,
And shteal my heart with all the roots that bind it. 2

Vasantasenā. Pallavaka! Parabhritikā!

Sansthānaka. Mashter! a man! a man!

Courtier. Don't be a coward.

Vasantasenā. Mādhavikā! Mādhavikā!

Courtier (*laughing*). Fool! She is calling her servants.

Sansthānaka. Mashter! Is she calling a woman?

Courtier. Why, of course.

Sansthānaka. Women! I kill hundreds of 'em. I'm a brav man.

Vasantasenā (*seeing that no one answers*). Alas, how come it that my very servants have fallen away from me? shall have to defend myself by mother-wit.

Courtier. Don't stop the search.

Sansthānaka. Shqueal, Vasantasenā, shqueal for you cuckoo Parabhritikā, or for your blosshom Pallavaka or fo all the month of May! Who's going to save you when I'n chasing you?

Why shpeak of Bhīmasena? Or the shon
Of Jamadagni, that thrice-mighty one?
The ten-necked ogre? Shon of Kuntī fair?
Jusht look at me! My fingers in your hair,
Jusht like Duhshāsana, I'll tear, and tear.[8] 29

Look, look!

My shword is sharp; good-by, poor head!
Let's chop it off, or kill you dead.
Then do not try my wrath to shun;
When you musht die, your life is done. 30

Vasantasenā. Sir, I am a weak woman.

Courtier. That is why you are still alive.

Sansthānaka. That is why you're not murdered.

Vasantasenā (*aside*). Oh! his very courtesy frightens me. Come, I will try this. (*Aloud.*) Sir, what do you expect from this pursuit? my jewels?

Courtier. Heaven forbid! A garden creeper, Mistress Vasan-

[8] All of these characters are celebrated warriors from the epics.

tasenā, should not be robbed of its blossoms. Say no more about the jewels.

Vasantasenā. What is then your desire?

Sansthānaka. I'm a man, a big man, a regular Vāsudeva.[t] You musht love me.

Vasantasenā (indignantly). Heavens! You weary me. Come, leave me! Your words are an insult.

Sansthānaka (laughing and clapping his hands). Look, mashter, look! The courtezan's daughter is mighty affectionate with me, isn't she? Here she says "Come on! Heavens, you're weary. You're tired!" No, I haven't been walking to another village or another city. No, little mishtress, I shwear by the gentleman's head, I shwear by my own feet! It's only by chasing about at your heels that I've grown tired and weary.

Courtier (aside). What! is it possible that the idiot does not understand when she says "You weary me"? (*Aloud.*) Vasantasenā, your words have no place in the dwelling of a courtezan,

> Which, as you know, is friend to every youth;
>   Remember, you are common as the flower
> That grows beside the road; in bitter truth,
>   Your body has its price; your beauty's dower
> Is his, who pays the market's current rate:
> Then serve the man you love, and him you hate. 31

And again:

> The wisest Brahman and the meanest fool
> Bathe in the selfsame pool;
> Beneath the peacock, flowering plants bend low,
> No less beneath the crow;
> The Brahman, warrior, merchant, sail along
> With all the vulgar throng.
> You are the pool, the flowering plant, the boat;
> And on your beauty every man may dote. 32

Vasantasenā. Yet true love would be won by virtue, not violence.

Sansthānaka. But, mashter, ever since the shlave-wench went into the park where Kāma's[u] temple shtands, she has been in love with a poor man, with Chārudatta, and she doesn't love me any more. His house is to the left. Look out and don't let her shlip out of our hands.

Courtier (aside). Poor fool, he has said the very thing he

[t] A name for Krishna, an amorous god who was supposed to have had 16,000 wives.

[u] The god of love.

should have concealed. So Vasantasenā is in love with Chārudatta? The proverb is right. Pearl suits with pearl. Well, I have had enough of this fool. (*Aloud.*) Did you say the good merchant's house was to the left, you jackass?

Sansthānaka. Yes. His house is to the left.

Vasantasenā (*aside*). Oh, wonderful! If his house is really at my left hand, then the scoundrel has helped me in the very act of hurting me, for he has guided me to my love.

Sansthānaka. But mashter, it's pitch dark and it's like hunting for a grain of soot in a pile of shpotted beans. Now you shee Vasantasenā and now you don't.

Courtier. Pitch dark it is indeed.

The sudden darkness seems to steal
The keenness of my sight;
My open eyes, as with a seal,
Are closed by blackest night. 33

And again:

Darkness anoints my body, and the sky
Drops ointment of thick darkness, till mine eye
Is all unprofitable grown to me,
Like service done to them who cheat and lie. 34

Sansthānaka. Mashter, I'm looking for Vasantasenā.

Courtier. Is there anything you can trace her by, jackass?

Sansthānaka. Like what, for inshtance?

Courtier. Like the tinkling of her jewels, for instance, or the fragrance of her garlands.

Sansthānaka. I hear the shmell of her garlands, but my nose is shtuffed so full of darkness that I don't shee the shound of her jewels very clearly.

Courtier (*to* Vasantasenā. *Aside*). Vasantasenā,

'Tis true, the night is dark, O timid maid,
And like the lightning hidden in the cloud,
You are not seen; yet you will be betrayed
By fragrant garlands and by anklets loud. 35

Have you heard me, Vasantasenā?

Vasantasenā (*to herself*). Heard and understood. (*She removes the ankle-rings, lays aside the garlands, and takes a few steps, feeling her way.*) I can feel the wall of the house, and here is a side-entrance. But alas! my fingers tell me that the door is shut.

Chārudatta (*who is within the house*). Comrade, my prayer is done. Go now and offer sacrifice to the Mothers.

Maitreya. No, I'm not going.

Chārudatta. Alas!

The poor man's kinsmen do not heed his will;

The friends who loved him once, now stand afar;
His sorrows multiply; his strength is nil;
Behold! his character's bright-shining star
Fades like the waning moon; and deeds of ill
That others do, are counted to him still. 36

And again:

No man holds converse with him; none will greet
With due respect the poor man when they meet.
Where rich men hold a feast, if he draw near,
He meets with scornful looks for looks of cheer.
Where vulgar throngs are gathered, 'tis the same;
His scanty raiment wakes his heartfelt shame.
Five are the deadly sins [v] we knew before;
Alas! I find the sixth is—to be poor. 37

And yet again:

Ah, Poverty, I pity thee, that so
To me thou clingest, as thy dearest friend;
When my poor life has met its woeful end,
I sadly wonder, whither thou wilt go. 38

Maitreya (*betraying his embarrassment*). Well, comrade, if I must go, at least let Radanikā go with me, to keep me company.

Chārudatta. Radanikā, you are to accompany Maitreya.

Radanikā. Yes, sir.

Maitreya. Mistress Radanikā, do you take the offering and the candle while I open the side-door.

(*He does so.*)

Vasantasenā. It seems as if the door took pity on me and opened of itself. I will lose no time, but enter. (*She looks in.*) What? a candle? Oh dear, oh dear!

(*She puts it out with her skirt and enters.*)

Chārudatta. What was that, Maitreya?

Maitreya. I opened the side-door and the wind came through all in a lump and blew out the candle. Suppose you go out by the side-door, Radanikā, and I will follow as soon as I have gone into the courtyard and lighted the candle again. (*Exit.*)

[v] The five deadly sins are the murder of a Brahman, drunkenness, theft, adultery with the wife of one's teacher, and association with anyone guilty of any of these sins.

Sansthānaka. Mashter! mashter! I'm looking for Vasantasenā.

Courtier. Keep on looking, keep on looking!

Sansthānaka (does so). Mashter! mashter! I've caught her! I've caught her!

Courtier. Idiot, you've caught me.

Sansthānaka. You shtand right here, mashter, and shtay where you're put. (*He renews the search and seizes the servant.*) Mashter! mashter! I've caught her! I've caught her!

Servant. Master, you've caught me, your servant.

Sansthānaka. Mashter here, shervant here! Mashter, shervant; shervant, mashter. Now shtay where you're put, both of you. (*He renews the search and seizes* Radanikā *by the hair.*) Mashter! mashter! Thish time I've caught her! I've caught Vasantasenā!

Through the black night she fled, fled she;
Her garland's shmell betrayed her;
Like Chānakya caught Draupadī,[w]
I caught her hair and shtayed her. 39

Courtier. Ah, proud to be so young, so fair!
Too high thy love must not aspire;
For now thy blossom-fragrant hair,
That merits richest gems and rare,
Serves but to drag thee through the mire. 40

Sansth. I've got your head, girl, got it tight,
By the hair, the locks, and the curls, too.
Now shcream, shqueak, shqueal with all your might
"Shiva! Ishvara! Shankara! Shambhu!" [x] 41

Radanikā (in terror). Oh, sirs, what does this mean?

Courtier. You jackass! It's another voice.

Sansthānaka. Mashter, the wench has changed her voice, the way a cat changes her voice, when she wants shome cream of curdled milk.

Courtier. Changed her voice? Strange! Yet why so strange?
She trod the stage; she learned the arts;
She studied to deceive our hearts;
And now she practices her parts. 42

Enter Maitreya.

[w] Another preposterous allusion. Chānakya was an historical character; Draupadī is the heroine of the *Mahābhārata.*

[x] All of these are names for the god Shiva.

Maitreya. Look! In the gentle evening breeze the flame of the candle is fluttering like the heart of a goat that goes to the altar. (*He approaches and discovers* Radanikā.) Mistress Radanikā!

Sansthānaka. Mashter, mashter! A man! a man!

Maitreya. This is right, this is perfectly right, that strangers should force their way into the house, just because Chārudatta is poor.

Radanikā. Oh, Maitreya, see how they insult me.

Maitreya. What! insult you? No, they are insulting us.

Radanikā. Very well. They are insulting you, then.

Maitreya. But they aren't using violence?

Radanikā. Yes, yes!

Maitreya. Really?

Radanikā. Really.

Maitreya (*raising his staff angrily*). No, sir! Man, a dog will show his teeth in his own kennel, and I am a Brahman! My staff is crooked as my fortunes, but it can still split a dry bamboo or a rascal's pate.

Courtier. Have mercy, O great Brahman, have mercy.

Maitreya (*discovers the* courtier). He is not the sinner. (*Discovers* Sansthānaka.) Ah, here is the sinner. Well, you brother-in-law to the king, Sansthānaka, you scoundrel, you coward, this is perfectly proper, isn't it? Chārudatta the good is a poor man now—true, but are not his virtues an ornament to Ujjayinī? And so men break into his house and insult his servants!

Insult not him, laid low by poverty;
For none are counted poor by mighty fate:
Yet he who falls from virtue's high estate,
Though he be rich, no man is poor as he. 43

Courtier (*betraying his embarrassment*). Have mercy, O great Brahman, have mercy. We intended no insolence; we merely mistook this lady for another. For

We sought an amorous maiden,

Maitreya. What! this one?

Courtier. Heaven forbid!

one whose youth
Is in the guidance of her own sweet will;
She disappeared; unconscious of the truth,
We did what seems a purposed deed of ill. 44

I pray you, accept this all-in-all of humblest supplication.

(*He drops his sword, folds his hands, and falls at* Maitreya's *feet.*)

Maitreya. Good man, rise, rise. When I reviled you, I did not know you. Now I know you and I ask your pardon.

Courtier. It is I who should ask pardon. I will rise on one condition.

Maitreya. And that is—

Courtier. That you will not tell Chārudatta what has happened here.

Maitreya. I will be silent.

Courtier. Brahman, this gracious act of thine
I bow my neck to bear;
For never could this sword of mine
With virtue's steel compare. 45

Sansthānaka (*indignantly*). But mashter, what makes you fold your hands sho helplesshly and fall at the feet of thish manikin?

Courtier. I was afraid.

Sansthānaka. What were *you* afraid of?

Courtier. Of Chārudatta's virtues.

Sansthānaka. Virtues? He? You can go into his houshe and not find a thing to eat.

Courtier. No, no.
His loving-kindness unto such as we
Has brought him low at last;
From him could no man learn what insults be,
Or e'er his wealth was past.
This well-filled pool, that in its summer day
Gave others drink, itself is dried away. 46

Sansthānaka (*impatiently*). Who is the shon of a shlave-wench anyway?
Brave Shvetaketu is he, Pāndu's child?
Or Rādhā's shon, the ten-necked ogre wild?
Or Indradatta? or again, is he
Shon of brave Rāma and of fair Kuntī?
Or Dharmaputra? Ashvatthāman bold?
Perhaps Jatāyu's shelf, that vulture old? [y] 47

Courtier. Fool! I will tell you who Chārudatta is.
A tree of life to them whose sorrows grow,
Beneath its fruit of virtue bending low;
Father to good men; virtue's touchstone he;
The mirror of the learned; and the sea
Where all the tides of character unite;
A righteous man, whom pride could never blight;
A treasure-house, with human virtues stored;

[y] More mythological characters foolishly connected.

Courtesy's essence, honor's precious hoard.
He doth to life its fullest meaning give,
So good is he; we others breathe, not live. 48

Let us be gone.

Sansthānaka. Without Vasantasenā?

Courtier. Vasantasenā has disappeared.

Sansthānaka. How?

Courtier. Like sick men's strength, or like the blind man's sight,
Like the fool's judgment, like the sluggard's might,
Like thoughtless scoundrels' store of wisdom's light,
Like love, when foemen fan our slumbering wrath,
So did *she* vanish, when you crossed her path. 49

Sansthānaka. I'm not going without Vasantasenā.

Courtier. And did you never hear this?

To hold a horse, you need a rein;
To hold an elephant, a chain;
To hold a woman, use a heart;
And if you haven't one, depart. 50

Sansthānaka. If you're going, go along. I'm not going.

Courtier. Very well. I will go. (*Exit.*)

Sansthānaka. Mashter's gone, sure enough. (*To* Maitreya.) Well, you man with the head that looks like a caret,[z] you manikin, take a sheat, take a sheat.

Maitreya. We have already been invited to take a seat.

Sansthānaka. By whom?

Maitreya. By destiny.

Sansthānaka. Shtand up, then, shtand up!

Maitreya. We shall.

Sansthānaka. When?

Maitreya. When fate is kind again.

Sansthānaka. Weep, then, weep!

Maitreya. We have wept.

Sansthānaka. Who made you?

Maitreya. Poverty.

Sansthānaka. Laugh, then, laugh!

Maitreya. Laugh we shall.

Sansthānaka. When?

Maitreya. When Chārudatta is happy once more.

Sansthānaka. You manikin, give poor little Chārudatta thish messhage from me. "Thish wench with golden ornaments and golden jewels, thish female shtage-manager looking after the rehearsal of a new play, thish Vasanta-

[z] The typographical symbol used to indicate an insertion. In India it is lopsided (elongated on the left side).

senā—she has been in love with you ever shince she went into the park where Kāma's temple shtands. And when we tried to conciliate her by force, she went into your houshe. Now if you shend her away yourshelf and hand her over to me, if you reshtore her at once, without any lawshuit[a] in court, than I'll be friends with you forever. But if you don't reshtore her, there will be a fight to the death." Remember:

> Shmear a pumpkin-shtalk with cow-dung;
> Keep your vegetables dried;
> Cook your rice in winter evenings;
> And be sure your meat is fried.
> Then let 'em shtand, and they will not
> Bothershomely shmell and rot. 51

Tell it to him prettily, tell it to him craftily. Tell it to him sho that I can hear it as I roosht in the dove-cote on the top of my own palace. If you shay it different, I'll chew your head like an apple caught in the crack of a door.

Maitreya. Very well. I shall tell him.

Sansthānaka (*aside*). Tell me, shervant. Is mashter really gone?

Servant. Yes, sir.

Sansthānaka. Then we will go as quickly as we can.

Servant. Then take your sword, master.

Sansthānaka. You can keep it.

Servant. Here it is, master. Take your sword, master.

Sansthānaka (*taking it by the wrong end*).

> My shword, red as a radish shkin,
> Ne'er finds the time to molder;
> Shee how it shleeps its sheath within!
> I put it on my shoulder.
> While curs and bitches yelp at me, I roam,
> Like a hunted jackal, home. 52

(Sansthānaka *and the* servant *walk about, then exeunt.*)

Maitreya. Mistress Radanikā, you must not tell good Chārudatta of this outrage. I am sure you would only add to the poor man's sorrows.

Radanikā. Good Maitreya, you know Radanikā. Her lips are sealed.

Maitreya. So be it.

[a] Possibly at this time courtesans could be compelled by law to accept all patrons who could produce the fee.

Chārudatta (*to* Vasantasenā). Radanikā, Rohasena likes the fresh air, but he will be cold in the evening chill. Pray bring him into the house, and cover him with this mantle.

(*He gives her the mantle.*)

Vasantasenā (*to herself*). See! He thinks I am his servant. (*She takes the mantle and perceives its perfume. Ardently to herself.*) Oh, beautiful! The mantle is fragrant with jasmine. His youthful days are not wholly indifferent to the pleasures of the world.

(*She wraps it about her, without letting* Chārudatta *see.*)

Chārudatta. Come, Radanikā, take Rohasena and enter the heart of the house.

Vasantasenā (*to herself*). Ah me unhappy, that have little part or lot in your heart!

Chārudatta. Come, Radanikā, will you not even answer? Alas!

When man once sees that miserable day,
When fate almighty sweeps his wealth away,
Then ancient friendships will no longer hold,
Then all his former bosom-friends grow cold. 53

Maitreya (*drawing near to* Radanikā). Sir, here is Radanikā.

Chārudatta. Here is Radanikā? Who then is this—
This unknown lady, by my robe
Thus clinging, desecrated,

Vasantasenā (*to herself*). Say rather "consecrated."

Chārudatta. Until she seems the crescent moon,
With clouds of autumn mated? 54

But no! I may not gaze upon another's wife.

Maitreya. Oh, you need not fear that you are looking at another man's wife. This is Vasantasenā, who has been in love with you ever since she saw you in the garden where Kāma's temple stands.

Chārudatta. What! this is Vasantasenā? (*Aside.*)
My love for whom—my fortune spent—
My wretched self in twain has rent,
Like coward's anger, inward bent. 55

Maitreya. My friend, that brother-in-law of the king says—

Chārudatta. Well?

Maitreya. "This wench with golden ornaments and golden jewels, this female stage-manager looking after the rehearsal of a new play, this Vasantasenā—she has been in love with you ever since she went into the park where Kāma's temple stands. And when we tried to conciliate her by force, she went into your house."

Vasantasenā (*to herself*). "Tried to conciliate me by force"—truly, I am honored by these words.

Maitreya. "Now if you send her away yourself and hand her over to me, if you restore her at once, without any lawsuit in court, then I'll be friends with you forever. Otherwise, there will be a fight to the death."

Chārudatta (*contemptuously*). He is a fool. (*To himself.*) How is this maiden worthy of the worship that we pay a goddess! For now

Although I bade her enter, yet she seeks
To spare my poverty, nor enters here;
Though men are known to her, yet all she speaks
Contains no word to wound a modest ear. 56

(*Aloud.*) Mistress Vasantasenā, I have unwittingly made myself guilty of an offense; for I greeted as a servant one whom I did not recognize. I bend my neck to ask your pardon.

Vasantasenā. It is I who have offended by this unseemly intrusion. I bow my head to seek your forgiveness.

Maitreya. Yes, with your pretty bows you two have knocked your heads together, till they look like a couple of rice fields. I also bow my head like a camel colt's knee and beseech you both to stand up.

(*He does so, then rises.*)

Chārudatta. Very well, let us no longer trouble ourselves with conventions.

Vasantasenā (*to herself*). What a delightfully clever hint. But it would hardly be proper to spend the night, considering how I came hither. Well, I will at least say this much. (*Aloud.*) If I am to receive thus much of your favor, sir, I should be glad to leave these jewels in your house. It was for the sake of the jewels that those scoundrels pursued me.

Chārudatta. This house is not worthy of the trust.

Vasantasenā. You mistake, sir! It is to men that treasures are entrusted, not to houses.

Chārudatta. Maitreya, will you receive the jewels?
Vasantasenā. I am much indebted to you.

(*She hands him the jewels.*)

Maitreya (*receiving them*). Heaven bless you, madam.
Chārudatta. Fool! They are only entrusted to us.
Maitreya (*aside*). Then the thieves may take them, for all I care.
Chārudatta. In a very short time—
Maitreya. What she has entrusted to us, belongs to us.
Chārudatta. I shall restore them.
Vasantasenā. I should be grateful, sir, if this gentleman would accompany me home.
Chārudatta. Maitreya, pray accompany our guest.
Maitreya. She walks as gracefully as a female swan, and you are the gay flamingo to accompany her. But I am only a poor Brahman, and wherever I go, the people will fall upon me just as dogs will snap at a victim dragged to the cross-roads.
Chārudatta. Very well. I will accompany her myself. Let the torches be lighted, to ensure our safety on the highway.[b]
Maitreya. Vardhamānaka, light the torches.
Vardhamānaka (*aside to* Maitreya). What! light torches without oil?
Maitreya (*aside to* Chārudatta). These torches of ours are like courtezans who despise their poor lovers. They won't light up unless you feed them.
Chārudatta. Enough, Maitreya! We need no torches. See, we have a lamp upon the king's highway.

Attended by her starry servants all,
And pale to see as a loving maiden's cheeks,
Rises before our eyes the moon's bright ball,
Whose pure beams on the high-piled darkness fall
Like streaming milk that dried-up marshes seeks. 57

(*His voice betraying his passion.*) Mistress Vasantasenā, we have reached your home. Pray enter. (Vasantasenā *gazes ardently at him, then exit.*) Comrade, Vasantasenā is gone. Come, let us go home.

All creatures from the highway take their flight;
The watchmen pace their rounds before our sight;

[b] In an effort to curb crime, the law required that wayfarers at night carry torches so that they would be visible and identifiable.

To forestall treachery, is just and right,
For many sins find shelter in the night. 58
(*He walks about.*) And you shall guard this golden casket by night, and Vardhamānaka by day.

Maitreya. Very well. (*Exeunt ambo.*)

ACT II

The Shampooer[c] Who Gambled

Enter a maid.

Maid. I am sent with a message to my mistress by her mother. I must go in and find my mistress. (*She walks about and looks around her.*) There is my mistress. She is painting a picture, and putting her whole heart into it. I must go and speak to her.

Then appear the love-lorn Vasantasenā, *seated, and* Madanikā.

Vasantasenā. Well, girl, and then—
Madanikā. But mistress, you were not speaking of anything. What do you mean?
Vasantasenā. Why, what did I say?
Madanikā. You said, "and then"—
Vasantasenā (*puckering her brows*). Oh, yes. So I did.
Maid (*approaching*). Mistress, your mother sends word that you should bathe and then offer worship to the gods.
Vasantasenā. You may tell my mother that I shall not take the ceremonial bath to-day. A Brahman must offer worship in my place.
Maid. Yes, mistress. (*Exit.*)
Madanikā. My dear mistress, it is love, not naughtiness, that asks the question—but what does this mean?
Vasantasenā. Tell me, Madanikā. How do I seem to you?
Madanikā. My mistress is so absent-minded that I know her heart is filled with longing for somebody.
Vasantasenā. Well guessed. My Madanikā is quick to fathom another's heart.

[c] *Masseur* would be an equally accurate translation.

Madanikā. I am very, very glad. Yes, Kāma is indeed mighty, and his great festival is welcome when one is young. But tell me, mistress, is it a king, or a king's favorite, whom you worship?

Vasantasenā. Girl, I wish to love, not to worship.

Madanikā. Is it a Brahman that excites your passion, some youth distinguished for very particular learning?

Vasantasenā. A Brahman I should have to reverence.

Madanikā. Or is it some young merchant, grown enormously wealthy from visiting many cities?

Vasantasenā. A merchant, girl, must go to other countries and leave you behind, no matter how much you love him. And the separation makes you very sad.

Madanikā. It isn't a king, nor a favorite, nor a Brahman, nor a merchant. Who is it then that the princess loves?

Vasantasenā. Girl! Girl! You went with me to the park where Kāma's temple stands?

Madanikā. Yes, mistress.

Vasantasenā. And yet you ask, as if you were a perfect stranger.

Madanikā. Now I know. Is it the man who comforted you when you asked to be protected?

Vasantasenā. Well, what was his name?

Madanikā. Why, he lives in the merchants' quarter.

Vasantasenā. But I asked you for his name.

Madanikā. His name, mistress, is a good omen in itself. His name is Chārudatta.[d]

Vasantasenā (*joyfully*). Good, Madanikā, good. You have guessed it.

Madanikā (*aside*). So much for that. (*Aloud.*) Mistress, they say he is poor.

Vasantasenā. That is the very reason why I love him. For a courtezan who sets her heart on a poor man is blameless in the eyes of the world.

Madanikā. But mistress, do the butterflies visit the mango tree when its blossoms have fallen?

Vasantasenā. That is just why we call *that* sort of a girl a butterfly.

Madanikā. Well, mistress, if you love him, why don't you go and visit him at once?

Vasantasenā. Girl, if I should visit him at once, then, because he can't make any return—no, I don't mean that, but it would be hard to see him.

[d] Chārudatta means "beautifully endowed."

Madanikā. Is that the reason why you left your jewels with him?

Vasantasenā. You have guessed it.

A voice[e] *behind the scenes.* Oh, sir, a shampooer owes me ten gold-pieces, and he got away from us. Hold him, hold him! (*To the fleeing* shampooer.) Stop, stop! I see you from here.

Enter hurriedly a frightened shampooer.

Shampooer. Oh, confound this gambling business!

Freed from its tether, the ace—
I might better say "ass"—how it kicks me!
And the cast of the dice called the "spear"
Proves true to its name; for it sticks me. 1

The keeper's whole attention
Was busy with the score;
So it took no great invention
To vanish through the door.
But I cannot stand forever
In the unprotected street.
Is there no one to deliver?
I would fall before his feet. 2

While the keeper and the gambler are looking somewhere else for me, I'll just walk backwards into this empty temple and turn goddess.

(*He makes all sorts of gestures, takes his place, and waits.*)

Enter Māthura *and the* gambler.

Māthura. Oh, sir, a shampooer owes me ten gold-pieces, and he got away from us. Hold him, hold him! Stop, stop! I see you from here.

Gambler. You may run to hell, if they'll take you in;
With Indra,[f] the god, you may stay:
For there's never a god can save your skin,
While Māthura wants his pay. 3

Māthura. Oh, whither flee you, nimble rambler,
You that cheat an honest gambler?
You that shake with fear and shiver,
All a-tremble, all a-quiver;

[e] That of Māthura, keeper of the gambling house.

[f] Indra is the god of heaven.

You that cannot trip enough,
On the level ground and rough;
You that stain your social station,
Family, and reputation!

Gambler (*examining the footprints*). Here he goes. And here the tracks are lost.

Māthura (*gazes at the footprints. Reflectively*). Look! The feet are turned around. And the temple hasn't any image. (*After a moment's thought.*) That rogue of a shampooer has gone into the temple with his feet turned around.

Gambler. Let's follow him.

Māthura. All right.

(*They enter the temple and take a good look, then make signs to each other.*)

Gambler. What! a wooden image?

Māthura. Of course not. It's stone. (*He shakes it with all his might, then makes signs.*) What do we care? Come, let's have a game.

(*He starts to gamble as hard as he can.*)

Shampooer (*trying with all his might to repress the gambling fever. Aside*). Oh, oh!

Oh, the rattle of dice is a charming thing,
When you haven't a copper left;
It works like a drum on the heart of a king,
Of all his realm bereft.
For gamblers leap down a mountain steep—
I know I shall not play.
Yet the rattle of dice is as sweet as the peep
Of nightingales in May.

Gambler. My turn, my turn!

Māthura. Not much! it's my turn.

Shampooer (*coming up quickly from behind*). Isn't it my turn?

Gambler. We've got our man.

Māthura (*seizing him*). You jail-bird, you're caught. Pay me my ten gold-pieces.

Shampooer. I'll pay you this very day.

Māthura. Pay me this very minute!

Shampooer. I'll pay you. Only have mercy!

Māthura. Come, will you pay me now?

Shampooer. My head is getting dizzy.

(*He falls to the ground. The others beat him with all their might.*)

Māthura. There (*drawing the gamblers' ring*)[g] you're bound by the gamblers' ring.

Shampooer (*rises. Despairingly*). What! bound by the gamblers' ring? Confound it! That is a limit which we gamblers can't pass. Where can I get the money to pay him?

Māthura. Well then, you must give surety.

Shampooer. I have an idea. (*He nudges the* gambler.) I'll give you half, if you'll forgive me the other half.

Gambler. All right.

Shampooer (*to* Māthura). I'll give you surety for a half. You might forgive me the other half.

Māthura. All right. Where's the harm?

Shampooer (*aloud*). You forgave me a half, sir?

Māthura. Yes.

Shampooer (*to the* gambler). And you forgave me a half?

Gambler. Yes.

Shampooer. Then I think I'll be going.

Māthura. Pay me my ten gold-pieces! Where are you going?

Shampooer. Look at this, gentlemen, look at this! Here I just gave surety to one of them for a half, and the other forgave me a half. And even after that he is dunning me, poor helpless me!

Māthura (*seizing him*). My name is Māthura, the clever swindler, and you're not going to swindle me this time. Pay up, jail-bird, every bit of my money, and this minute, too.

Shampooer. How can I pay?

Māthura. Sell your father and pay.

Shampooer. Where can I get a father?

Māthura. Sell your mother and pay.

Shampooer. Where can I get a mother?

Māthura. Sell yourself and pay.

Shampooer. Have mercy! Lead me to the king's highway.

Māthura. Go ahead.

Shampooer. If it must be. (*He walks about.*) Gentlemen, will you buy me for ten gold-pieces from this gambling-master? (*He sees a passer-by and calls out.*) What is that? You wish to know what I can do? I will be your house-

[g] Magic circles drawn around people and objects abound in mythology and folktales, but the meaning of the "gamblers' ring" here is not clear.

servant. What! he has gone without even answering. Well, here's another. I'll speak to him. (*He repeats his offer.*) What! this one too takes no notice of me. He is gone. Confound it! I've had hard luck ever since Chārudatta lost his fortune.

Māthura. Will you pay?

Shampooer. How can I pay? (*He falls down.* Māthura *drags him about.*) Good gentlemen, save me, save me!

Enter Darduraka.

Darduraka. Yes, gambling is a kingdom without a throne.

You do not mind defeat at all;
Great are the sums you spend and win;
While kingly revenues roll in,
Rich men, like slaves, before you fall. 7

And again:

You earn your coin by gambling,
Your friends and wife by gambling,
Your gifts and food by gambling;
Your last cent goes by gambling. 8

And again:

My cash was taken by the trey;
The deuce then took my health away;
The ace then set me on the street;
The four completed my defeat. 9

(*He looks before him.*) Here comes Māthura, our sometime gambling-master. Well, as I can't escape, I think I'll put on my veil. (*He makes any number of gestures with his cloak, then examines it.*)

This cloth is sadly indigent in thread;
This lovely cloth lets in a lot of light;
This cloth's protective power is nearly fled;
This cloth is pretty when it's rolled up tight. 10

Yet after all, what more could a poor saint do? For you see,

One foot I've planted in the sky,
The other on the ground must lie.[h]
The elevation's rather high,
But the sun stands it. Why can't I? 11

Māthura. Pay, pay!

Shampooer. How can I pay?

[h] He compares himself in poverty to an Indian ascetic and makes a humorous reference to the exaggerated postures of the yogi.

(Māthura *drags him about.*)

Darduraka. Well, well, what is this I see? (*He addresses a bystander.*) What did you say, sir? "This shampooer is being maltreated by the gambling-master, and no one will save him"? I'll save him myself. (*He presses forward.*) Stand back, stand back! (*He takes a look.*) Well, if this isn't that swindler Māthura. And here is the poor saintly shampooer; a saint to be sure,

> Who does not hang with bended head
> Rigid till set of sun,
> Who does not rub his back with sand
> Till boils begin to run,
> Whose shins dogs may not browse upon,
> As they pass him in their rambling.[1]
> Why should this tall and dainty man
> Be so in love with gambling? 12

Well, I must pacify Māthura. (*He approaches.*) How do you do, Māthura?

(Māthura *returns the greeting.*)

Darduraka. What does this mean?
Māthura. He owes me ten gold-pieces.
Darduraka. A mere bagatelle!
Māthura (*pulling the rolled-up cloak from under* Darduraka's *arm*). Look, gentlemen, look! The man in the ragged cloak calls ten gold-pieces a mere bagatelle.
Darduraka. My good fool, don't I risk ten gold-pieces on a cast of the dice? Suppose a man has money—is that any reason why he should put it in his bosom and show it? But you,

> You'll lose your caste, you'll lose your soul,
> For ten gold-pieces that he stole,
> To kill a man that's sound and whole,
> With five good senses in him. 13

Māthura. Ten gold-pieces may be a mere bagatelle to you, sir. To me they are a fortune.
Darduraka. Well then, listen to me. Just give him ten more, and let him go to gambling again.
Māthura. And what then?
Darduraka. If he wins, he will pay you.
Māthura. And if he doesn't win?
Darduraka. Then he won't pay you.

[1] Actual practices of Indian ascetics.

Māthura. This is no time for nonsense. If you say that, you can give him the money yourself. My name is Māthura. I'm a swindler and I play a crooked game, and I'm not afraid of anybody. You are an immoral scoundrel.

Darduraka. Who did you say was immoral?

Māthura. You're immoral.

Darduraka. Your father is immoral.

(*He gives the* shampooer *a sign to escape.*)

Māthura. You cur! That is just the way that you gamble.

Darduraka. That is the way I gamble?

Māthura. Come, shampooer, pay me my ten gold-pieces.

Shampooer. I'll pay you this very day. I'll pay at once.

(Māthura *drags him about.*)

Darduraka. Fool! You may maltreat him when I am away, but not before my eyes.

(Māthura *seizes the* shampooer *and hits him on the nose. The* shampooer *bleeds, faints, and falls flat.* Darduraka *approaches and interferes.* Māthura *strikes* Darduraka, *and* Darduraka *strikes back.*)

Māthura. Oh, oh, you accursèd hound! But I'll pay you for this.

Darduraka. My good fool, I was walking peaceably along the street, and you struck me. If you strike me to-morrow in court, then you will open your eyes.

Māthura. Yes, I'll open my eyes.

Darduraka. How will you open your eyes?

Māthura (*opening his eyes wide*). This is the way I'll open my eyes.

(Darduraka *throws dust in* Māthura's *eyes, and gives the shampooer a sign to escape.* Māthura *shuts his eyes and falls down. The* shampooer *escapes.*)

Darduraka (*aside*). I have made an enemy of the influential gambling-master Māthura. I had better not stay here. Besides, my good friend Sharvilaka told me that a young herdsman named Aryaka has been designated by a soothsayer as our future king. Now everybody in my condition is running after him. I think I will join myself to him.

(*Exit.*)

Shampooer (*trembles as he walks away and looks about him*). Here is a house where somebody has left the side-door open. I will go in. (*He enters and perceives* Vasantasenā.) Madam, I throw myself upon your protection.

Vasantasenā. He who throws himself upon my protection shall be safe. Close the door, girl. (*The maid does so.*)

Vasantasenā. What do you fear?

Shampooer. A creditor, madam.

Vasantasenā. You may open the door now, girl.

Shampooer (*to himself*). Ah! Her reasons for not fearing a creditor are in proportion to her innocence. The proverb is right:

The man who knows his strength and bears a load
Proportioned to that strength, not more nor less,
Is safe from stumbling and from sore distress,
Although he wander on a dreary road. 14

That means me.

Māthura (*wiping his eyes. To the* gambler). Pay, pay!

Gambler. While we are quarreling with Darduraka, sir, the man escaped.

Māthura. I broke that shampooer's nose for him with my fist. Come on! Let's trace him by the blood.

(*They do so.*)

Gambler. He went into Vasantasenā's house, sir.

Māthura. Then that is the end of the gold-pieces.

Gambler. Let's go to court and lodge a complaint.

Māthura. The swindler would leave the house and escape. No, we must besiege him and so capture him.

(Vasantasenā *gives* Madanikā *a sign*.)

Madanikā. Whence are you, sir? or who are you, sir? or whose son are you, sir? or what is your business, sir? or what are you afraid of?

Shampooer. Listen, madam. My birthplace is Pātaliputra,[j] madam. I am the son of a householder. I practice the trade of a shampooer.

Vasantasenā. It is a very dainty art, sir, which you have mastered.

Shampooer. Madam, as an art I mastered it. It has now become a mere trade.

[j] On the Ganges some 600 miles east of Ujjayinī.

Madanikā. Your answers are most disconsolate, sir. Pray continue.

Shampooer. Yes, madam. When I was at home, I used to hear travelers tell tales, and I wanted to see new countries, and so I came here. And when I had come here to Ujjayinī, I became the servant of a noble gentleman. Such a handsome, courteous gentleman! When he gave money away, he did not boast; when he was injured, he forgot it. To cut a long story short: he was so courteous that he regarded his own person as the possession of others, and had compassion on all who sought his protection.

Madanikā. Who may it be that adorns Ujjayinī with the virtues which he has stolen from the object of my mistress' desires?

Vasantasenā. Good, girl, good! I had the same thought in mind.

Madanikā. But to continue, sir—

Shampooer. Madam, he was so compassionate and so generous that now—

Vasantasenā. His riches have vanished?

Shampooer. I didn't say it. How did you guess it, madam?

Vasantasenā. What was there to guess? Virtue and money seldom keep company. In the pools from which men cannot drink there is so much the more water.

Madanikā. But sir, what is his name?

Shampooer. Madam, who does not know the name of this moon of the whole world? He lives in the merchants' quarter. He whose name is worthy of all honor is named Chārudatta.

Vasantasenā (*joyfully rising from her seat*). Sir, this house is your own. Give him a seat, girl, and take this fan. The gentleman is weary.

(Madanikā *does as she is bid.*)

Shampooer (*aside*). What! so much honor because I mentioned Chārudatta's name? Heaven bless you, Chārudatta! You are the only man in the world who really lives. All others merely breathe. (*He falls at* Vasantasenā's *feet.*) Enough, madam, enough. Pray be seated, madam.

Vasantasenā (*seating herself*). Where is he who is so richly your creditor, sir?

Shamp. The good man's wealth consists in kindly deeds;
All other wealth is vain and quickly flies.
The man who honors not his neighbor's needs,
Does that man know what honor signifies? 15

Vasantasenā. But to continue—

Shampooer. So I became a servant in his employ. And when his wealth was reduced to his virtue, I began to live by gambling. But fate was cruel, and I lost ten gold-pieces.

Māthura. I am ruined! I am robbed!

Shampooer. There are the gambling-master and the gambler, looking for me. You have heard my story, madam. The rest is your affair.

Vasantasenā. Madanikā, the birds fly everywhither when the tree is shaken in which they have their nests. Go, girl, and give the gambling-master and the gambler this bracelet. And tell them that this gentleman sends it.

(*She removes a bracelet from her arm, and gives it to* Madanikā.)

Madanikā (*receiving the bracelet*). Yes, mistress. (*She goes out.*)

Māthura. I am ruined! I am robbed!

Madanikā. Inasmuch as these two are looking up to heaven, and sighing, and chattering, and fastening their eyes on the door, I conclude that they must be the gambling-master and the gambler. (*Approaching.*) I salute you, sir.

Māthura. May happiness be yours.

Madanikā. Sir, which of you is the gambling-master?

Māth. O maiden, fair but something less than shy,
With red lip wounded in love's ardent play,
On whom is bent that sweet, coquettish eye?
For whom that lisp that steals the heart away? 16

I haven't got any money. You'll have to look somewhere else.

Madanikā. You are certainly no gambler, if you talk that way. Is there any one who *owes* you money?

Māthura. There is. He owes ten gold-pieces. What of him?

Madanikā. In his behalf my mistress sends you this bracelet. No, no! He sends it himself.

Māthura (*seizing it joyfully*). Well, well, you may tell the noble youth that his account is squared. Let him come and seek delight again in gambling.

(*Exeunt* Māthura *and the* gambler.)

Madanikā (*returning to* Vasantasenā). Mistress, the gambling-master and the gambler have gone away well-pleased.

Vasantasenā. Go, sir, and comfort your kinsfolk.

Shampooer. Ah, madam, if it may be, these hands would gladly practice their art in your service.

Vasantasenā. But sir, he for whose sake you mastered the art, who first received your service, he should have your service still.

Shampooer (*aside*). A very pretty way to decline my services. How shall I repay her kindness? (*Aloud.*) Madam, thus dishonored as a gambler, I shall become a Buddhist monk. And so, madam, treasure these words in your memory: "He was a shampooer, a gambler, a Buddhist monk."

Vasantasenā. Sir, you must not act too precipitately.

Shampooer. Madam, my mind is made up. (*He walks about.*)

I gambled, and in gambling I did fall,
  Till every one beheld me with dismay.
Now I shall show my honest face to all,
  And walk abroad upon the king's highway. 17

(*Tumultuous cries behind the scenes.*)

Shampooer (*listening*). What is this? What is this? (*Addressing some one behind the scenes.*) What did you say? "Post-breaker, Vasantasenā's rogue elephant, is at liberty!" Hurrah! I must go and see the lady's best elephant. No, no! What have I to do with these things? I must hold to my resolution. (*Exit.*)

Then enter hastily Karnapūraka, *highly delighted, wearing a gorgeous mantle.*

Karnapūraka. Where is she? Where is my mistress?

Madanikā. Insolent! What can it be that so excites you? You do not see your mistress before your very eyes.

Karnapūraka (*perceiving* Vasantasenā). Mistress, my service to you.

Vasantasenā. Karnapūraka, your face is beaming. What is it?

Karnapūraka (*proudly*). Oh, mistress! You missed it! You didn't see Karnapūraka's heroism to-day!

Vasantasenā. What, Karnapūraka, What?

Karnapūraka. Listen. Post-breaker, my mistress' rogue elephant, broke the stake he was tied to, killed his keeper, and ran into the street, making a terrible commotion. You should have heard the people shriek,

Take care of the babies, as quick as you can,
  And climb up a roof or a tree!
The elephant rogue wants the blood of a man.
  Escape! Run away! Can't you see? 18

And:

How they lose their ankle-rings!
Girdles, set with gems and things,

Break away from fastenings!
As they stumble, trip, and blunder,
See the bracelets snap asunder,
Each a tangled, pearly wonder! 19

And that rogue of an elephant dives with his trunk and his feet and his tusks into the city of Ujjayinī, as if it were a lotus-pond in full flower. At last he comes upon a Buddhist monk.[k] And while the man's staff and his water-jar and his begging-bowl fly every which way, he drizzles water over him and gets him between his tusks. The people see him and begin to shriek again, crying "Oh, oh, the monk is killed!"

Vasantasenā (*anxiously*). Oh, what carelessness, what carelessness!

Karnapūraka. Don't be frightened. Just listen, mistress. Then, with a big piece of the broken chain dangling about him, he picked him up, picked up the monk between his tusks, and just then Karnapūraka saw him, *I* saw him, no, no! the slave who grows fat on my mistress' rice-cakes saw him, stumbled with his left foot over a gambler's score, grabbed up an iron pole out of a shop, and challenged the mad elephant—

Vasantasenā. Go on! Go on!

Karnap. I hit him—in a fit of passion, too—

He really looked like some great mountain peak.
And from between those tusks of his I drew
The sacred hermit meek. 20

Vasantasenā. Splendid, splendid! But go on!

Karnapūraka. Then, mistress, all Ujjayinī tipped over to one side, like a ship loaded unevenly, and you could hear nothing but "Hurrah, hurrah for Karnapūraka!" Then, mistress, a man touched the places where he ought to have ornaments, and, finding that he hadn't any, looking up, heaved a long sigh, and threw this mantle over me.

Vasantasenā. Find out, Karnapūraka, whether the mantle is perfumed with jasmine or not.

Karnapūraka. Mistress, the elephant perfume is so strong that I can't tell for sure.

Vasantasenā. Then look at the name.

Karnapūraka. Here is the name. You may read it, mistress.

(*He hands her the mantle.*)

Vasantasenā (*reads*). Chārudatta.

[k] The former shampooer. The Sanskrit drama is not as concerned about realistic time intervals as is the Western drama.

(*She seizes the mantle eagerly and wraps it about her.*)

Madanikā. The mantle is very becoming to her Karnapūraka.
Karnapūraka. Oh, yes, the mantle is becoming enough.
Vasantasenā. Here is your reward, Karnapūraka.

(*She gives him a gem.*)

Karnapūraka (*taking it and bowing low*). Now the mantle is most wonderfully becoming.
Vasantasenā. Karnapūraka, where is Chārudatta now?
Karnapūraka. He started to go home along this very street
Vasantasenā. Come, girl! Let us go to the upper balcony and see Chārudatta. (*Exeunt omnes.*)

ACT III

The Hole in the Wall

Enter Chārudatta's *servant,* Vardhamānaka.

Vardh. A master, kindly and benevolent,
His servants love, however poor he be.
The purse-proud, with a will on harshness bent,
Pays service in the coin of cruelty. 1

And again:
A bullock greedy for a feast of corn
You never can prevent;
A wife who wants her lord to wear a horn
You never can prevent;
A man who loves to gamble night and morn
You never can prevent;
And blemishes that with a man are born
You never can prevent. 2

It is some time since Chārudatta went to the concert. It is past midnight, and still he does not come. I think I will go into the outer hall and take a nap. (*He does so.*)

Enter Chārudatta *and* Maitreya.

Chārudatta. How beautifully Rebhila sang! The lute is indeed a pearl, a pearl not of the ocean.
Gently the anxious lover's heart befriending,
Consoling when true lovers may not meet,
To love-lorn souls the dearest comforts sending,
It adds to sweetest love its more of sweet. 3

Maitreya. Well then, let's go into the house.
Chārudatta. But how wonderfully Master Rebhila sang!
Maitreya. There are just two things that always make me

laugh. One is a woman talking Sanskrit,[1] and the other is a man who tries to sing soft and low. Now when a woman talks Sanskrit, she is like a heifer with a new rope through her nose; all you hear is "soo, soo, soo." And when a man tries to sing soft and low, he reminds me of an old priest muttering texts, while the flowers in his chaplet dry up. No, I don't like it!

Chārudatta. My friend, Master Rebhila sang most wonderfully this evening. And still you are not satisfied.

The notes of love, peace, sweetness, could I trace,
The note that thrills, the note of passion too,
The note of woman's loveliness and grace—
Ah, my poor words add nothing, nothing new!
But as the notes in sweetest cadence rang,
I thought it was my hidden love who sang. 4
The melody of song, the stricken strings
In undertone that half-unconscious clings,
More clearly sounding when the passions rise,
But ever sweeter as the music dies.
Words that strong passion fain would say again,
Yet checks their second utterance—in vain;
For music sweet as this lives on, until
I walk as hearing sweetest music still. 5

Maitreya. But see, my friend! The very dogs are sound asleep in the shops that look out on the market. Let us go home. (*He looks before him.*) Look, look! The blessèd moon seems to give place to darkness, as she descends from her palace in heaven.

Chārudatta. True.

The moon gives place to darkness as she dips
Behind the western mountain; and the tips
Of her uplifted horns alone appear,
Like two sharp-pointed tusks uplifted clear,
Where bathes an elephant in waters cool,
Who shows naught else above the jungle pool. 6

Maitreya. Well, here is our house. Vardhamānaka, Vardhamānaka, open the door!

Vardhamānaka. I hear Maitreya's voice. Chārudatta has returned. I must open the door for him. (*He does so.*) Master, I salute you. Maitreya, I salute you too. The couch is ready. Pray be seated.

(Chārudatta *and* Maitreya *enter and seat themselves.*)

[1] Even highly educated women do not speak Sanskrit on the stage except in unusual cases.

Maitreya. Vardhamānaka, call Radanikā to wash our feet.

Chārudatta (compassionately). She sleeps. Do not wake her.

Vardhamānaka. I will bring the water, Maitreya, and you may wash Chārudatta's feet.

Maitreya (angrily). Look, man. He acts like the son of a slave that he is, for he is bringing water. But he makes me wash your feet, and I am a Brahman.

Chārudatta. Good Maitreya, do you bring the water, and Vardhamānaka shall wash my feet.

Vardhamānaka. Yes, Maitreya. Do you bring the water.

(Maitreya *does so.* Vardhamānaka *washes* Chārudatta's *feet, then moves away.*)

Chārudatta. Let water be brought for the Brahman's feet.

Maitreya. What good does water do my feet? I shall have to roll in the dirt again, like a beaten ass.

Vardhamānaka. Maitreya, you are a Brahman.

Maitreya. Yes, like a slow-worm[m] among all the other snakes, so am I a Brahman among all the other Brahmans.

Vardhamānaka. Maitreya, I will wash your feet after all. (*He does so.*) Maitreya, this golden casket I was to keep by day, you by night. Take it.

(*He gives it to* Maitreya, *then exit.*)

Maitreya (receiving the casket). The thing is here still. Isn't there a single thief in Ujjayinī to steal the wretch that robs me of my sleep? Listen. I am going to take it into the inner court.

Chārud. Such lax attention we can ill afford.

> If we are trusted by a courtezan,
> Then, Brahman, prove yourself an honest man,
> And guard it safely, till it be restored.

(*He nods, repeating the stanza* "The melody of a song, the stricken strings:" *page 166.*)

Maitreya. Are you going to sleep?

Chārudatta. Yes, so it seems.

> For conquering sleep, descending on mine eyes,
> First smites the brow with unresisted blow;
> Unseen, elusive, like old age, she tries
> To gather strength by weakening her foe. 8

Maitreya. Then let's go to sleep. (*He does so.*)

[m] A very minor snake, a garter snake.

Enter Sharvilaka.[n]

Sharv. I made an entrance for my body's round
By force of art and arms, a path to deeds!
I skinned my sides by crawling on the ground,
Like a snake that sloughs the skin no longer sound;
And now I go where my profession leads.
(*He gazes at the sky. Joyfully.*) See! The blessèd moon is setting. For well I know,
My trade would fain from watchmen's eyes be shrouded;
Valiant, I force the dwelling of another.
But see, the stars in deepest dark are clouded,
And the night shields me like a careful mother. 10
I made a breach in the orchard wall and entered. And now I must force my way into the inner court as well.
Yes, let men call it vulgar, if they will,
The trade that thrives while sleeps the sleepyhead;
Yes, knavery, not bravery, call it still,
To overreach confiding folk a-bed.
Far better blame and hissing, fairly won,
Than the pay of genuflecting underlings;
This antique path was trod by Drona's son,
Who slew the sleeping, unsuspecting kings. 11
But where shall I make the breach?
Where is the spot which falling drops decayed?
For each betraying sound is deadened there.
No yawning breach should in the walls be made,
So treatises on robbery declare.
Where does the palace crumble? Where the place
That niter-eaten bricks false soundness wear?
Where shall I 'scape the sight of woman's face?[o]
Fulfilment of my wishes waits me there. 12
(*He feels the wall.*) Here is a spot weakened by constant sun and sprinkling and eaten by saltpeter rot. And here is a pile of dirt thrown up by a mouse. Now heaven be praised! My venture prospers. This is the first sign of success for Skanda's[p] sons. Now first of all, how shall I make the breach? The blessèd Bearer of the Golden

[n] The Hindu love of science resulted in elaborate classification systems and treatises on methodology for everything: the treatise on housebreaking lists seven prescribed breaches to be made in the walls of houses. All aspects of love are classified in the *Kāmasūtra* (various translations). For the classification of emotions in the drama see the *Dasharupa* (see Bibliography).

[o] The rules for burglary made it mandatory that it not be carried out in the presence of a woman.

[p] The patron saint of thieves.

Lance[q] has prescribed four varieties of breach, thus: if the bricks are baked, pull them out; if they are unbaked, cut them; if they are made of earth, wet them; if they are made of wood, split them. Here we have baked bricks; ergo, pull out the bricks.

Now what shall be the shape I give the breach?
A "lotus," "cistern," "crescent moon," or "sun"?
"Oblong," or "cross," or "bulging pot"? for each
The treatises permit. Which one? which one?
And where shall I display my sovereign skill,
That in the morning men may wonder still? 13

In this wall of baked bricks, the "bulging pot" would be effective. I will make that.

At other walls that I have pierced by night,
And at my less successful ventures too,
The crowd of neighbors gazed by morning light,
Assigning praise or blame, as was my due. 14

Praise to the boon-conferring god, to Skanda of immortal youth! Praise to him, the Bearer of the Golden Lance, the Brahman's god, the pious! Praise to him, the Child of the Sun! Praise to him, the teacher of magic, whose first pupil I am! For he found pleasure in me and gave me magic ointment,[r]

With which so I anointed be,
No watchman's eye my form shall see;
And edgèd sword that falls on me
From cruel wounds shall leave me free. 15

(*He anoints himself.*) Alas, I have forgotten my measuring line. (*Reflecting.*) Aha! This sacred cord[s] shall be my measuring line. Yes, the sacred cord is a great blessing to a Brahman, especially to one like me. For, you see,

With this he measures, ere he pierce a wall,
And picks the lock, when jewels are at stake.
It serves as key to bolted door and hall,
As tourniquet for bite of worm and snake. 16

The measuring is done. I begin my task. (*He does so, then takes a look.*) My breach lacks but a single brick. Alas, I am bitten by a snake. (*He binds his finger with the sacred cord, and manifests the workings of poison.*) I have applied the remedy, and now I am restored. (*He continues*

[q] An epithet for Skanda.

[r] The ointment is supposed to make him invisible.

[s] A sacred thread worn over the left shoulder and under the right arm by members of the three upper castes.

his work, then gazes.) Ah, there burns a candle. See!

Though jealous darkness hems it round,
  The golden-yellow candle from its place
Shines through the breach upon the ground,
  Like a streak of gold upon the touchstone's face. 17

(*He returns to his work.*) The breach is finished. Good! I enter. But no, I will not enter yet. I will shove a dummy in. (*He does so.*) Ah, no one is there. Praise be to Skanda! (*He enters and looks about.*) See! Two men asleep. Come, for my own protection I will open the door. But the house is old and the door squeaks. I must look for water. Now where might water be? (*He looks about, finds water, and sprinkles the door. Anxiously.*) I hope it will not fall upon the floor and make a noise. Come, this is the way. (*He puts his back against the door and opens it cautiously.*) Good! So much for that. Now I must discover whether these two are feigning sleep, or whether they are asleep in the fullest meaning of the term. (*He tries to terrify them, and notes the effect.*) Yes, they must be asleep in the fullest meaning of the term. For see!

Their breath first calmly rises, ere it sink;
  Its regularity all fear defies.
  Unmoving in their socket-holes, the eyes
Are tightly closed, and never seem to wink.
The limbs relaxed, at ease the bodies lie,
  I see their feet beyond the bedstead peep,
The lighted candle vexes not the eye;
  It would, if they were only feigning sleep. 18

(*He looks about him.*) What! a drum? And here is a flute. And here, a snare-drum. And here, a lute. And reed-pipes. And yonder, manuscripts. Is this the house of a dancing-master? But no! When I entered, I was convinced that this was a palatial residence. Now then, is this man poor in the fullest meaning of the term, or, from fear of the king[t] or of thieves, does he keep his property buried? Well, my own property is buried, too. But I will scatter the seeds that betray subterranean gold. (*He does so.*) The scattered seeds nowhere swell up. Ah, he is poor in the fullest meaning of the term. Good! I go.

Maitreya (*talking in his sleep*). Look, man. I see something like a hole in the wall. I see something like a thief. You had better take this golden casket.

Sharvilaka. I wonder if the man has discovered that I have entered, and is showing off his poverty in order to make fun

[t] That is, tax collectors.

of me. Shall I kill him, or is the poor devil talking in his sleep? (*He takes a look.*) But see! This thing wrapped in a ragged bath-clout, now that I inspect it by the light of my candle, is in truth a jewel-casket. Suppose I take it. But no! It is hardly proper to rob a man of good birth, who is as poor as I am. I go.

Maitreya. My friend, by the wishes of cows [u] and Brahmans I conjure you to take this golden casket.

Sharvilaka. One may not disregard the sacred wish of a cow and the wish of a Brahman. I will take it. But look! There burns the candle. I keep about me a moth for the express purpose of extinguishing candles. I will let him enter the flame. This is his place and hour. May this moth [v] which I here release, depart to flutter above the flame in varying circles. The breeze from the insect's wings has translated the flame into accursèd darkness. Or shall I not rather curse the darkness brought by me upon my Brahmanic family? For my father was a man who knew the four Vedas, who would not accept a gift; and I, Sharvilaka, his son, and a Brahman, I am committing a crime for the sake of that courtezan girl Madanikā. Now I will grant the Brahman's wish.

(*He reaches out for the casket.*)

Maitreya. How cold your fingers are, man!

Sharvilaka. What carelessness! My fingers are cold from touching water. Well, I will put my hand in my armpit.

(*He warms his left hand and takes the casket.*)

Maitreya. Have you got it?

Sharvilaka. I could not refuse a Brahman's request. I have it.

Maitreya. Now I shall sleep as peacefully as a merchant who has sold his wares.

Sharvilaka. O great Brahman, sleep a hundred years! Alas that a Brahman family should thus be plunged in darkness for the sake of Madanikā, a courtezan! Or better, I myself am thus plunged in darkness.

> A curse on poverty, I say!
> 'Tis stranger to the manly will;
> This act that shuns the light of day
> I curse indeed, but do it still. 19

[u] The cow is regarded as sacred in India.

[v] These moths were part of the scientific thief's equipment.

Well then, I must go to Vasantasenā's house to buy Madanikā's freedom. (*He walks about and looks around him.*) Ah, I think I hear footsteps. I hope they are not those of policemen. Never mind. I will pretend to be a pillar, and wait. But after all, no policemen exist for me, for Sharvilaka? Why, I am

A cat for crawling, and a deer for flight,
A hawk for rending, and a dog for sight
To judge the strength of men that wake or sleep,
A snake, when 'tis advisable to creep,
Illusion's self, to seem a saint or rogue,
Goddess of Speech in understanding brogue;
A light in blackest night, in holes a lizard I can be,
A horse on terra firma, and a ship upon the sea. 20

And again:

Quick as a snake, and steady as a hill;
In flight the prince of birds can show no greater skill;
In searching on the ground I am as keen as any hare,
In strength I am a lion, and a wolf to rend and tear. 21

Radanikā (*entering*). Dear me! Vardhamānaka went to sleep in the outer court, and now he is not there. Well, I will call Maitreya.

(*She walks about.*)

Sharvilaka (*prepares to strike down* Radanikā, *but first takes a look*). What! a woman? Good! I go. (*Exit.*)

Radanikā (*recoiling in terror*). Oh, oh, a thief has cut a hole in the wall of our house and is escaping. I must go and wake Maitreya. (*She approaches* Maitreya.) Oh, Maitreya, get up, get up! A thief has cut a hole in the wall of our house and has escaped.

Maitreya (*rising*). What do you mean, wench? "A hole in the wall has cut a thief and has escaped"?

Radanikā. Poor fool! Stop your joking. Don't you see it?

Maitreya. What do you mean, wench? "It looks as if a second door had been thrown open"? Get up, friend Chārudatta, get up! A thief has made a hole in the wall of our house and has escaped.

Chārudatta. Yes, yes! a truce to your jests!

Maitreya. But it isn't a jest. Look!

Chārudatta. Where?

Maitreya. Why, here.

Chārudatta (*gazing*). What a very remarkable hole!

The bricks are drawn away below, above;
The top is narrow, but the center wide;

As if the great house-heart had burst with pride,
Fearing lest the unworthy share its love. 22

To think that science should be expended on a task like this!

Maitreya. My friend, this hole must have been made by one of two men; either by a stranger, or else for practice by a student of the science of robbery. For what man here in Ujjayinī does not know how much wealth there is in our house?

Chārud. Stranger he must have been who made the breach,
His customed harvest in my house to reap;
He has not learned that vanished riches teach
A calm, untroubled sleep.
He saw the sometime greatness of my home
And forced an entrance; for his heart did leap
With short-lived hope; now he must elsewhere roam,
And over broken hopes must sorely weep. 23

Just think of the poor fellow telling his friends: "I entered the house of a merchant's son, and found—nothing."

Maitreya. Do you mean to say that you pity the rascally robber? Thinks he—"Here's a great house. Here's a great house. Here's the place to carry off a jewel-casket or a gold-casket." (*He remembers the casket. Despondently. Aside.*) Where *is* that golden casket? (*He remembers the events of the night. Aloud.*) Look, man! You are always saying "Maitreya is a fool, Maitreya is no scholar." But I certainly acted wisely in handing over that golden casket to you. If I hadn't, the son of a slave would have carried it off.

Chārudatta. A truce to your jests!

Maitreya. Just because I'm a fool, do you suppose I don't even know the place and time for a jest?

Chārudatta. But when did this happen?

Maitreya. Why, when I told you that your fingers were cold.

Chārudatta. It might have been. (*He searches about. Joyfully.*) My friend, I have something pleasant to tell you.

Maitreya. What? Wasn't it stolen?

Chārudatta. Yes.

Maitreya. What is the pleasant news, then?

Chārudatta. The fact that he did not go away disappointed.

Maitreya. But it was only entrusted to our care.

Chārudatta. What! entrusted to our care?

(*He swoons.*)

Maitreya. Come to yourself, man. Is the fact that a thief stole what was entrusted to you, any reason why you should swoon?

Chārudatta (*coming to himself*). Ah, my friend,

Who will believe the truth?
Suspicion now is sure.
This world will show no ruth
To the inglorious poor. 24

Alas!

If envious fate before
Has wooed my wealth alone,
Why should she seek my store
Of virtue as her own? 25

Maitreya. I intend to deny the whole thing. Who gave anybody anything? who received anything from anybody? who was a witness?

Chārudatta. And shall I tell a falsehood now?
No! I will beg until I earn
The wherewithal my debt to pay.
Ignoble falsehood I will spurn,
That steals the character away. 26

Radanikā. I will go and tell his good wife.

(*She goes out, returning with* Chārudatta's *wife.*)

Wife (*anxiously*). Oh! Is it true that my lord is uninjured, and Maitreya too?

Radanikā. It is true, mistress. But the gems which belong to the courtezan have been stolen. (Chārudatta's *wife swoons.*) O my good mistress! Come to yourself!

Wife (*recovering*). Girl, how can you say that my lord is uninjured? Better that he were injured in body than in character. For now the people of Ujjayinī will say that my lord committed this crime because of his poverty. (*She looks up and sighs.*) Ah, mighty Fate! The destinies of the poor, uncertain as the water-drops which fall upon a lotus-leaf, seem to thee but playthings. There remains to me this one necklace, which I brought with me from my mother's house. But my lord would be too proud to accept it. Girl, call Maitreya hither.

Radanikā. Yes, mistress. (*She approaches* Maitreya.) Maitreya, my lady summons you.

Maitreya. Where is she?

Radanikā. Here. Come!

Maitreya (*approaching*). Heaven bless you!

Wife. I salute you, sir. Sir, will you look straight in front of you?

Maitreya. Madam, here stands a man who looks straight in front of him.

Wife. Sir, you must accept this.

Maitreya. Why?

Wife. I have observed the Ceremony of the Gems. And on this occasion one must make as great a present as one may to a Brahman. This I have not done, therefore pray accept this necklace.

Maitreya (*receiving the necklace*). Heaven bless you! I will go and tell my friend.

Wife. You must not do it in such a way as to make me blush, Maitreya. (*Exit.*)

Maitreya (*in astonishment*). What generosity!

Chārudatta. How Maitreya lingers! I trust his grief is not leading him to do what he ought not. Maitreya, Maitreya!

Maitreya (*approaching*). Here I am. Take that.

(*He displays the necklace.*)

Chārudatta. What is this?

Maitreya. Why, that is the reward you get for marrying such a wife.

Chārudatta. What! my wife takes pity on me? Alas, now am I poor indeed!

When fate so robs him of his all,
That on her pity he must call,
The man to woman's state doth fall,
The woman is the man. 27

But no, I am not poor. For I have a wife

Whose love outlasts my wealthy days;
In thee a friend through good and ill;
And truth that naught could take away;
Ah, this the poor man lacketh still. 28

Maitreya, take the necklace and go to Vasantasenā. Tell her in my name that we have gambled away the golden casket, forgetting that it was not our own; that we trust she will accept this necklace in its place.

Maitreya. But you must not give away this necklace, the pride of the four seas,[w] for that cheap thing that was stolen before we had a bite or a drink out of it.

Chārudatta. Not so, my friend.

[w] When the gods churned the ocean, fourteen jewels were produced, of which one was the pearl.

She showed her trust in leaving us her treasure;
The price of confidence has no less measure. 29

Friend, I conjure you by this gesture, not to return until you have delivered it into her hands. Vardhamānaka do you speedily

Fill up the opening with the selfsame bricks;
Thus will I thwart the process of the law,
For the blemish of so great a scandal sticks. 30

And, friend Maitreya, you must show your pride by not speaking too despondently.

Maitreya. How can a poor man help speaking despondently?

Chārudatta. Poor I am not, my friend. For I have a wife

Whose love outlasts my wealthy day;
In thee a friend through good and ill;
And truth that naught could take away:
Ah, this the poor man lacketh still. (28)

Go then, and after performing rites of purification, I will offer my morning prayer. (*Exeunt omnes.*)

ACT IV

Madanikā and Sharvilaka

Enter a maid.

Maid. I am entrusted with a message for my mistress by her mother. Here is my mistress. She is gazing at a picture and is talking with Madanikā. I will go to her.

(*She walks about. Then enter* Vasantasenā, *as described, and* Madanikā.)

Vasantasenā. Madanikā girl, is this portrait really like Chārudatta?
Madanikā. Very like.
Vasantasenā. How do you know?
Madanikā. Because my mistress' eyes are fastened so lovingly upon it.
Vasantasenā. Madanikā girl, do you say this because courtezan courtesy demands it?
Madanikā. But mistress, is the courtesy of a girl who lives in a courtezan's house, necessarily false?
Vasantasenā. Girl, courtezans meet so many kinds of men that they do learn a false courtesy.
Madanikā. But when the eyes of my mistress find such delight in a thing, and her heart too, what need is there to ask the reason?
Vasantasenā. But I should not like to have my friends laugh at me.
Madanikā. You need not be afraid. Women understand women.
Maid (*approaching*). Mistress, your mother sends word that a covered cart is waiting at the side-door, and that you are to take a drive.

Vasantasenā. Tell me, is it Chārudatta who invites me?
Maid. Mistress, the man who sent ornaments worth ten thousand gold-pieces with the cart—
Vasantasenā. Is who?
Maid. Is the king's brother-in-law, Sansthānaka.
Vasantasenā (*indignantly*). Go! and never come again on such an errand.
Maid. Do not be angry, mistress. I was only sent with the message.
Vasantasenā. But it is the message which makes me angry.
Maid. But what shall I tell your mother?
Vasantasenā. Tell my mother never to send me another such message, unless she wishes to kill me.
Maid. As you will. (*Exit.*)

Enter Sharvilaka.

Sharv. Blame for my sin I laid upon the night;
I conquered sleep and watchmen of the king;
But darkness wanes, and in the sun's clear light
My light is like the moon's—a faded thing. 1
And again:
Whoever cast at me a passing look,
Or neared me, anxious, as they quickly ran,
All such my laden soul for foes mistook;
For sin it was wherein man's fear began. 2
Well, it was for Madanikā's sake that I did the deed of sin.
I paid no heed to any one who talked with serving-men;
The houses ruled by women-folk—these I avoided most;
And when policemen seemed to have me almost in their ken,
I stood stock-still and acted just exactly like a post.
A hundred such maneuvers did I constantly essay,
And by such means succeeded in turning night to day. 3

(*He walks about.*)

Vasantasenā. Girl, lay this picture on my sofa and come back at once with a fan.
Madanikā. Yes, mistress. (*Exit with the picture.*)
Sharvilaka. This is Vasantasenā's house. I will enter. (*He does so.*) I wonder where I can find Madanikā. (*Enter* Madanikā *with the fan.* Sharvilaka *discovers her.*) Ah, it is Madanikā.

Surpassing Madana[x] himself in charm,
She seems the bride of Love, in human guise;
Even while my heart the flames of passion harm,
She brings a sandal[y] coolness to my eyes. 4

Madanikā!

Madanikā (*discovers* Sharvilaka). Oh, oh, oh, Sharvilaka! I am so glad, Sharvilaka. Where have you been?

Sharvilaka. I will tell you.

(*They gaze at each other passionately.*)

Vasantasenā. How Madanikā lingers! I wonder where she is. (*She looks through a bull's-eye window.*) Why, there she stands, talking with a man. Her loving glance does not waver, and she gazes as if she would drink him in. I imagine he must be the man who wishes to make her free. Well, let her stay, let her stay. Never interrupt anybody's happiness. I will not call her.

Madanikā. Tell me, Sharvilaka. (Sharvilaka *looks about him uneasily.*) What is it, Sharvilaka? You seem uneasy.

Sharvilaka. I will tell you a secret. Are we alone?

Madanikā. Of course we are.

Vasantasenā. What! a deep secret? I will not listen.

Sharvilaka. Tell me, Madanikā. Will Vasantasenā take a price for your freedom?

Vasantasenā. The conversation has to do with me? Then I will hide behind this window and listen.

Madanikā. I asked my mistress about it, Sharvilaka, and she said that if she could have *her* way, she would free all her servants for nothing. But Sharvilaka, where did you find such a fortune that you can think of buying my freedom from my mistress?

Sharvilaka. A victim to my pauper plight,
And your sweet love to win,
For you, my timid maid, last night
I did the deed of sin. 5

Vasantasenā. His face is tranquil. It would be troubled, if he had sinned.

Madanikā. Oh, Sharvilaka! For a mere nothing—for a woman—you have risked both things!

Sharvilaka. What things?

Madanikā. Your life and your character.

Sharvilaka. My foolish girl, fortune favors the brave.

[x] Another name for Kāma, the god of love.

[y] Sandalwood has a "cool" fragrance.

Madanikā. Oh, Sharvilaka! Your character was without a stain. You didn't do anything *very* bad, did you, when for my sake you did the deed of sin?

Sharv. The gems that magnify a woman's charm,
As flowers the creeping plant, I do not harm.
I do not rob the Brahman of his pelf,
Nor seize the sacrificial gold myself.
I do not steal the baby from the nurse,
Simply because I need to fill my purse.
Even as a thief, I strive with main and might
For just distinction 'twixt the wrong and right. 6

And so you may tell Vasantasenā this:
These ornaments were made for you to don,
Or so it seems to me;
But as you love me, never put them on
Where other folks may see. 7

Madanikā. But Sharvilaka, ornaments that nobody may see, and a courtezan—the two things do not hang together. Give me the jewels. I want to see them.

Sharvilaka. Here they are.

(*He gives them to her with some uneasiness.*)

Madanikā (*examining the jewels*). It seems to me I have seen these before. Tell me. Where did you get them?

Sharvilaka. What does that matter to you, Madanikā? Take them.

Madanikā (*angrily*). If you can't trust me, why do you wish to buy my freedom?

Sharvilaka. Well, this morning I heard in the merchant's quarter that the merchant Chārudatta—

(Vasantasenā *and* Madanikā *swoon.*)

Sharvilaka. Madanikā! Come to yourself! Why is it that now
Your figure seems to melt in limp despair,
Your eyes are wildly rolling here and there?
That when I come, sweet girl, to make you free,
You fall to trembling, not to pitying me? 8

Madanikā (*coming to herself*). O you reckless man! When you did what you ought not to have done for my sake, you didn't kill anybody or hurt anybody in that house?

Sharvilaka. Madanikā, Sharvilaka does not strike a terrified man or a man asleep. I did not kill anybody or hurt anybody.

Madanikā. Really?

Sharvilaka. Really.

Vasantasenā (*recovering consciousness*). Ah, I breathe again.

Madanikā. Thank heaven!

Sharvilaka (*jealously*). What does this "Thank heaven" mean, Madanikā?

I sinned for you, when love had made me pine,
  Although my house was good since time began;
Love took my virtue, but my pride is mine.
  You call me friend and love another man? 9

(*Meaningly.*) A noble youth is like a goodly tree;
    His wealth, the fruit so fair;
  The courtezan is like a bird; for she
    Pecks him and leaves him bare. 10

  Love is a fire, whose flame is lust,
    Whose fuel is gallantry,
  Wherein our youth and riches must
    Thus sacrificèd be. 11

Vasantasenā (*with a smile*). His excitement is a little out of place.

Sharvilaka. Yes!

Those man are fools, it seems to me,
  Who trust to women or to gold;
For gold and girls, 'tis plain to see,
  Are false as virgin snakes and cold. 12

Love not a woman; if you ever do,
  She mocks at you, and plays the gay deceiver:
Yet if she loves you, you may love her too;
  But if she doesn't, leave her. 13

Too true it is that
A courtezan will laugh and cry for gold;
  She trusts you not, but waits your trustful hour.
If virtue and a name are yours, then hold!
  Avoid her as you would a graveyard flower. 14

And again:

As fickle as the billows of the sea,
  Glowing no longer than the evening sky,
A woman takes your gold, then leaves you free;
  You're worthless, like cosmetics, when you're dry. 15

Yes, women are indeed fickle.

One man perhaps may hold her heart in trust,
  She lures another with coquettish eyes,
Sports with another in unseemly lust,
  Another yet her body satisfies. 16

As some one has well said:

On mountain-tops no lotuses are grown;
The horse's yoke no ass will ever bear;
Rice never springs from seeds of barely sown;
A courtezan is not an honest fair. 17
Accursèd Chārudatta, you shall not live!

(*He takes a few steps.*)

Madanikā (*seizing the hem of his garment*). O you foolish man! Your anger is so ridiculous.
Sharvilaka. Ridiculous? how so?
Madanikā. Because these jewels belong to my mistress
Sharvilaka. And what then?
Madanikā. And she left them with that gentleman.
Sharvilaka. What for?
Madanikā (*whispers*). That's why.
Sharvilaka (*sheepishly*). Confound it!
The sun was hot one summer day;
I sought the shadow, there to stay:
Poor fool! the kindly branch to pay,
I stole its sheltering leaves away. 18
Vasantasenā. How sorry he seems. Surely, he did this thing in ignorance.
Sharvilaka. What is to be done now, Madanikā?
Madanikā. Your own wit should tell you that.
Sharvilaka. No. For you must remember,
Nature herself gives woman wit;
Men learn from books a little bit. 19
Madanikā. Sharvilaka, if you will take my advice, restore the jewels to that righteous man.
Sharvilaka. But Madanikā, what if he should prosecute me
Madanikā. No cruel heat comes from the moon.
Vasantasenā. Good, Madanikā, good!
Sharvilaka. Madanikā,
For what I did, I feel no grief nor fear;
Why tell me of this good man's virtues high?
Shame for my baseness touches me more near;
What can this king do to such rogues as I? 20
Nevertheless, your suggestion is inconsistent with prudence. You must discover some other plan.
Madanikā. Yes, there is another plan.
Vasantasenā. I wonder what it will be.
Madanikā. Pretend to be a servant of that gentleman, and give the jewels to my mistress.
Sharvilaka. And what then?
Madanikā. Then you are no thief, Chārudatta has dis

charged his obligation, and my mistress has her jewels.

Sharvilaka. But isn't this course too reckless?

Madanikā. I tell you, give them to her. Any other course is too reckless.

Vasantasenā. Good, Madanikā, good! Spoken like a free woman.

Sharvilaka. Risen at last is wisdom's light,
Because I followed after you;
When clouds obscure the moon by night,
'Tis hard to find a guide so true. 21

Madanikā. Then you must wait here a moment in Kāma's shrine, while I tell my mistress that you have come.

Sharvilaka. I will.

Madanikā (*approaches* Vasantasenā). Mistress, a Brahman has come from Chārudatta to see you.

Vasantasenā. But girl, how do you know that he comes from Chārudatta?

Madanikā. Should I not know my own, mistress?

Vasantasenā (*shaking her head and smiling. Aside*). Splendid! (*Aloud.*) Bid him enter.

Madanikā. Yes, mistress. (*Approaching* Sharvilaka.) Enter, Sharvilaka.

Sharvilaka (*approaches. With some embarrassment*). My greetings to you.

Vasantasenā. I salute you, sir. Pray be seated.

Sharvilaka. The merchant sends this message: "My house is so old that it is hard to keep this casket safe. Pray take it back."

(*He gives it to* Madanikā, *and starts to leave.*)

Vasantasenā. Sir, will you undertake a return commission of mine?

Sharvilaka (*aside*). Who will carry it? (*Aloud.*) And this commission is—

Vasantasenā. You will be good enough to accept Madanikā.

Sharvilaka. Madam, I do not quite understand.

Vasantasenā. But I do.

Sharvilaka. How so?

Vasantasenā. Chārudatta told me that I was to give Madanikā to the man who should return these jewels. You are therefore to understand that he makes you a present of her.

Sharvilaka (*aside*). Ah, she sees through me. (*Aloud.*) Good, Chārudatta, good!

On virtue only set your heart's desire;
The righteous poor attain to heights whereto
The wicked wealthy never may aspire. 22

And again:

On virtue let the human heart be set;
To virtue nothing serves as check or let.
The moon, attaining unattainable, is led
By virtue to her seat on Shiva's head.[z] 23

Vasantasenā. Is my driver there?

Enter a servant *with a bullock-cart.*[a]

Servant. Mistress, the cart is ready.

Vasantasenā. Madanikā girl, you must show me a happy face. You are free. Enter the bullock-cart. But do not forget me.

Madanikā (*weeping*). My mistress drives me away.

(*She falls at her feet.*)

Vasantasenā. You are now the one to whom honor should be paid.[b] Go then, enter the cart. But do not forget me.

Sharvilaka. Heaven bless you! and you, Madanikā,

Turn upon her a happy face,
And hail with bended head the grace
That gives you now the name of wife,
As a veil to keep you safe through life. 24

(*He enters the bullock-cart with* Madanikā, *and starts away.*)

A voice behind the scenes. Men! Men! We have the following orders from the chief of police: "A soothsayer has declared that a young herdsman named Aryaka is to become king. Trusting to this prophecy, and alarmed thereat, King Pālaka has taken him from his hamlet, and thrown him into strict confinement. Therefore be watchful, and every man at his post."

Sharvilaka (*listening*). What! King Pālaka has imprisoned my good friend Aryaka? And here I am, a married man. Confound it! But no,

[z] Shiva is frequently represented as wearing the crescent moon on his brow.

[a] A two-wheeled cart, completely enclosed by cloth or netting, drawn by two oxen.

[b] That is to say, you are now a legal wife, while I am still a courtesan.

Two things alone—his friend, his wife—
Deserve man's love below;
A hundred brides may forfeit life
Ere he should suffer so. 25

Good! I will get out.

(*He does so.*)

Madanikā (*folding her hands. Tearfully*). My lord, if you must, at least bring me first to your parents.

Sharvilaka. Yes, my love, I will. I had the same thought in mind. (*To the* servant.) My good fellow, do you know the house of the merchant Rebhila?

Servant. Certainly.

Sharvilaka. Bring my wife thither.

Servant. Yes, sir.

Madanikā. If you desire it, dear. But dear, you must be very careful. (*Exit.*)

Sharvilaka. Now as for me,

I'll rouse my kin, the kitchen cabinet,
Those high in fame by strength of good right arm,
And those who with the king's contempt have met,
And royal slaves, to save my friend from harm:
Like old Yaugandharāyana [c]
For the good king Udayana. 26

And again:

My friend has causeless been confined
By wicked foes of timid kind;
I fly, I fly to free him soon,
Like the eclipse-oppressèd moon. (*Exit.*) 27

Maid (*entering*). Mistress, I congratulate you. A Brahman has come with a message from Chārudatta.

Vasantasenā. Ah, this is a joyful day. Show him every mark of respect, girl, and have him conducted hither by one of the pages.

Maid. Yes, mistress. (*Exit.*)

Enter Maitreya *with a* page.

Maitreya. Well! Rāvana, the king of the demons, travels with his chariot that they call the "Blossom." He earned it

[c] Yaugandharāyana, the minister of King Udayana, came to Ujjayinī in disguise during the reign of King Pālaka's father, and by intrigue released Udayana from captivity. This is the subject of Bhāsa's drama, *The Minister's Vows.*

by his penances. Now I am a Brahman, and though I never performed any penances, I travel with another sort of blossom—a woman of the town.[d]

Maid. Sir, will you inspect our gateway.

Maitreya (*gazes admiringly*). It has just been sprinkled and cleaned and received a coat of green. The threshold of it is pretty as a picture with the offerings of all sorts of fragrant flowers. It stretches up its head as if it wanted to peep into the sky. It is adorned with strings of jasmine garlands that hang down and toss about like the trunk of the heavenly elephant. It shines with its high ivory portal. It is lovely with any number of holiday banners that gleam red as great rubies and wave their coquettish fingers as they flutter in the breeze and seem to invite me to enter. Both sides are decorated with holiday water-jars of crystal, which are charming with their bright-green mango twigs, and are set at the foot of the pillars that sustain the portal. The doors are of gold, thickly set with diamonds as hard to pierce as a giant's breast. It actually wearies a poor devil's envy. Yes, Vasantasenā's house-door is a beautiful thing. Really, it forcibly challenges the attention of a man who doesn't care about such things.

Maid. Come, sir, and enter the first court.

Maitreya (*enters and looks about*). Well! Here in the first court are rows of balconies brilliant as the moon, or as sea-shells, or as lotus-stalks; whitened by handfuls of powder strewn over them; gleaming with golden stairways inlaid with all sorts of gems: they seem to gaze down on Ujjayinī with their round faces, the crystal windows, from which strings of pearls are dangling. The porter sits there and snoozes as comfortably as a professor. The crows which they tempt with rice-gruel and curdled milk will not eat the offering, because they can't distinguish it from the mortar. Show me the way, madam.

Maid. Come, sir, and enter the second court.

Maitreya (*enters and looks about*). Well! Here in the second court the cart-bullocks are tied. They grow fat on mouthfuls of grass and pulse-stalks which are brought them, right and left, by everybody. Their horns are smeared with oil. And here is another, a buffalo, snorting like a gentleman insulted. And here is a ram[e] having his neck rubbed, like a prize-fighter after the fight. And

[d] A pun. "Flower-bearer," the name of the chariot of Rāvana, a god of evil, also means "prostitute."

[e] Rams were trained to fight.

here are others, horses having their manes put in shape. And here in a stall is another, a monkey, tied fast like a thief. (*He looks in another direction.*) And here is an elephant, taking from his drivers a cake of rice and drippings and oil. Show me the way, madam.

Maid. Come, sir, and enter the third court.

Maitreya (*enters and looks about*). Well! Here in the third court are these seats, prepared for young gentlemen to sit on. A half-read book is lying on the gaming-table. And the table itself has its own dice, made out of gems. And here, again, are courtezans and old hangers-on at court, past masters in the war and peace of love, wandering about and holding in their fingers pictures painted in many colors. Show me the way, madam.

Maid. Come, sir, and enter the fourth court.

Maitreya (*enters and looks about*). Well! Here in the fourth court the drums that maiden fingers beat are booming like the thunder; the cymbals are falling, as the stars fall from heaven when their merit is exhausted;[f] the pipe is discoursing music as sweet as the humming of bees. And here, again, is a lute that somebody is holding on his lap like a girl who is excited by jealousy and love, and he is stroking it with his fingers. And here, again, are courtezan girls that sing as charmingly as honey-drunken bees, and they are made to dance and recite a drama with love in it. And water-coolers are hanging in the windows so as to catch the breeze. Show me the way, madam.

Maid. Come, sir, and enter the fifth court.

Maitreya (*enters and looks about*). Well! Here in the fifth court the overpowering smell of asafetida and oil is attractive enough to make a poor devil's mouth water. The kitchen is kept hot all the time, and the gusts of steam, laden with all sorts of good smells, seem like sighs issuing from its mouth-like doors. The smell of the preparation of all kinds of foods and sauces makes me smack my lips. And here, again, is a butcher's boy washing a mess of chitterlings as if it were an old loin-cloth.[g] The cook is preparing every kind of food. Sweetmeats are being constructed, cakes are being baked. (*To himself.*) I wonder if I am to get a chance to wash my feet and an invitation to eat what I can hold. (*He looks in another direction.*) There

[f] Virtuous souls after death may attain happiness as stars, but when their acquired merit is used up, they fall to earth again.

[g] Meat was more a favorite food with Hindus in early days than it is today, when abstinence from meat is considered praiseworthy.

are courtezans and bastard pages, adorned with any number of jewels, just like Gāndharvas[h] and Apsarases.[i] Really, this house is heaven. Tell me, who are you bastards anyway?

Pages. Why, we are bastard pages—

Petted in a stranger's court,
  Fed on stranger's food,
Stranger's money makes us sport—
  Not so very good.
Stranger women gave us birth,
  Stranger men begot;
Baby elephants in mirth,
  We're a bastard lot. 28

Maitreya. Show me the way, madam.

Maid. Come, sir, and enter the sixth court.

Maitreya (*enters and looks about*). Well! Here in the sixth court they are working in gold and jewels. The arches set with sapphires look as if they were the home of the rainbow. The jewelers are testing the lapis lazuli, the pearls, the corals, the topazes, the sapphires, the cat's-eyes, the rubies, the emeralds, and all the other kinds of gems. Rubies are being set in gold. Golden ornaments are being fashioned. Pearls are being strung on a red cord. Pieces of lapis lazuli are being cleverly polished. Shells are being pierced. Corals are being ground. Wet bundles of saffron are being dried. Musk is being moistened. Sandalwood is being ground to make sandal-water. Perfumes are being compounded. Betel-leaves and camphor are being given to courtezans and their lovers. Coquettish glances are being exchanged. Laughter is going on. Wine is being drunk incessantly with sounds of glee. Here are men-servants, here are maid-servants, and here are men who forget child and wife and money. When the courtezans, who have drunk the wine from the liquor-jars, give them the mitten, they—drink. Show me the way, madam.

Maid. Come, sir, and enter the seventh court.

Maitreya (*enters and looks about*). Well! Here in the seventh court the mated doves are sitting comfortably in their snug dove-cotes, billing and cooing and nothing else, and perfectly happy. And there is a parrot in a cage chanting like a Brahman with a bellyful of curdled milk and rice. And here, again, is a talking thrush, chattering like a housemaid who spreads herself because some-

[h] The musicians of Indra's heaven.

[i] The nymphs of heaven.

body noticed her. A cuckoo, her throat still happy from tasting all sorts of fruit-syrups, is cooing like a procuress. Rows of cages are hanging from pegs. Quails are being egged on to fight. Partridges are being made to talk. Caged pigeons are being provoked. A tame peacock that looks as if he was adorned with all sorts of gems is dancing happily about, and as he flaps his wings, he seems to be fanning the roof which is distressed by the rays of the sun. (*He looks in another direction.*) Here are pairs of flamingos like moonbeams rolled into a ball, that wander about after pretty girls, as if they wanted to learn how to walk gracefully. And here, again, are tame cranes, walking around like ancient eunuchs. Well, well! This courtezan keeps a regular menagerie of birds. Really, the courtezan's house seems to me like Indra's heaven. Show me the way, madam.

Maid. Come, sir, and enter the eighth court.

Maitreya (*enters and looks about*). Madam, who is this in the silk cloak, adorned with such astonishingly tautologous ornaments, who wanders about, stumbling and stretching his limbs?

Maid. Sir, this is my mistress' brother.

Maitreya. What sort of ascetic exercises does a man have to perform, in order to be born as Vasantasenā's brother? But no,

> He may be shiny, may be greasy,
> And perfumed may he be.
> And yet I warn you to go easy;
> He's a graveyard champak-tree 29

(*He looks in another direction.*) But madam, who is that in the expansive garment, sitting on the throne? She has shoes on her greasy feet.

Maid. Sir, that is my mistress' mother.

Maitreya. Lord! What an extensive belly the dirty old witch has got! I suppose they couldn't put that superb portal on the house till after they had brought the idol in?

Maid. Rascal! You must not make fun of our mother so. She is pining away under a quartan ague.[j]

Maitreya (*bursts out laughing*). O thou blessèd quartan ague! Look thou upon a Brahman, even upon me, with this thy favor!

Maid. Rascal! May death strike you.

Maitreya (*bursts out laughing*). Why, wench, a pot-belly like that is better dead.

[j] Dropsy.

Drinking brandy, rum, and wine,
Mother fell extremely ill.
If mother now should peak and pine,
A jackal-pack would have its fill. 30

Well, I have seen Vasantasenā's palace with its many incidents and its eight courts, and really, it seems as if I had seen the triple heaven in a nut-shell. I haven't the eloquence to praise it. Is this the house of a courtezan, or a piece of Kubera's [k] palace? Where's your mistress?

Maid. She is here in the orchard. Enter, sir.

Maitreya (*enters and looks about*). Well! What a beautiful orchard! There are any number of trees planted here, and they are covered with the most wonderful flowers. Silken swings are hung under the thick-set trees, just big enough for a girl to sit in. The golden jasmine, the shephālikā, the white jasmine, the jessamine, the navamallikā, the amaranth, the spring creeper, and all the other flowers have fallen of themselves, and really, it makes Indra's heaven look dingy. (*He looks in another direction.*) And the pond here looks like the morning twilight, for the lilies and red lotuses are as splendid as the rising sun. And again:

The ashoka-tree, whose twigs so merry
And crimson flowers have just appeared,
Seems like a battling mercenary,
With clotting crimson gore besmeared. 31

Good! Now where's your mistress?

Maid. If you would stop star-gazing, sir, you would see her.

Maitreya (*perceives* Vasantasenā *and approaches*). Heaven bless you!

Vasantasenā (*speaking in Sanskrit* [1]). Ah, Maitreya! (*Rising.*) You are very welcome. Here is a seat. Pray be seated.

Maitreya. When you are seated, madam.

(*They both seat themselves.*)

Vasantasenā. Is the merchant's son well?

Maitreya. Well, madam.

Vasantasenā. Tell me, good Maitreya,

Do friends, like birds, yet seek a shelter free
Beneath the modest boughs of this fair tree,

[k] The god of wealth.

[1] Vasantasenā speaks Sanskrit for a number of lines. This is unusual, as women almost always speak Prākrit, and it shows her excellent education.

Whose leaves are virtues, confidence its root,
Its blossoms honor, good its precious fruit? 32

Maitreya (*aside*). A good description by a naughty woman. (*Aloud.*) They do, indeed.

Vasantasenā. Tell me, what is the purpose of your coming?

Maitreya. Listen, madam. The excellent Chārudatta folds his hands[m] and requests—

Vasantasenā (*folding her hands*). And commands—

Maitreya. He says he imagined that that golden casket was his own and gambled it away. And nobody knows where the gambling-master has gone, for he is employed in the king's business.

Maid. Mistress, I congratulate you. The gentleman has turned gambler.

Vasantasenā (*aside*). It was stolen by a thief, and he is so proud that he says he gambled it away. I love him for that.

Maitreya. He requests that you will therefore be good enough to accept in its place this necklace of pearls.

Vasantasenā (*aside*). Shall I show him the jewels? (*Reflecting.*) No, not yet.

Maitreya. Why don't you take this necklace?

Vasantasenā (*laughs and looks at her friend*). Why should I not take the necklace, Maitreya? (*She takes it and lays it away. Aside.*) How is it possible that drops of honey fall from the mango-tree, even after its blossoms are gone? (*Aloud.*) Sir, pray tell the worthy gambler Chārudatta in my name that I shall pay him a visit this evening.

Maitreya (*aside*). What else does she expect to get out of a visit to our house? (*Aloud.*) Madam, I will tell him—(*aside*) to have nothing more to do with this courtezan.

(*Exit.*)

Vasantasenā. Take these jewels, girl. Let us go and bring cheer to Chārudatta.

Maid. But mistress, see! An untimely storm is gathering.

Vasant. The clouds may come, the rain may fall forever,
The night may blacken in the sky above;
For this I care not, nor I will not waver;
My heart is journeying to him I love. 33

Take the necklace, girl, and come quickly.

(*Exeunt omnes.*)

[m] A gesture of respectful entreaty.

ACT V

The Storm

The love-lorn Chārudatta *appears, seated.*

Chārudatta (*looks up*). An untimely storm[n] is gathering. For see!

The peacocks gaze and lift their fans on high;
  The swans forget their purpose to depart;
The untimely storm afflicts the blackened sky,
  And the wistful lover's heart. 1

And again:

The wet bull's belly wears no deeper dye;
  In flashing lightning's golden mantle clad,
  While cranes, his buglers, make the heaven glad,
The cloud, a second Vishnu,[o] mounts the sky. 2

And yet again:

As dark as Vishnu's form, with circling cranes
To trumpet him, instead of bugle strains,
  And garmented in lightning's silken robe,
Approaches now the harbinger of rains. 3

When lightning's lamp is lit, the silver river
  Impetuous falls from out the cloudy womb;
  Like severed lace from heaven-cloaking gloom,
It gleams an instant, then is gone forever. 4

Like shoaling fishes, or like dolphins shy,
Or like to swans, toward heaven's vault that fly,
  Like paired flamingos, male and mate together,
Like mighty pinnacles that tower on high,

[n] It is in the rainy season that lovers most want to be togethe[r] and the pain of separation grows intense. The rainy season comes a[t] the end of summer.

[o] One of the names of the god Vishnu means "black."

In thousand forms the tumbling clouds embrace,
Though torn by winds, they gather, interlace,
And paint the ample canvas of the sky. 5
The sky is black as Dhritarāshtra's face;[p]
Proud as the champion of Kuru's race,
The haughty peacock shrills his joy abroad;
The cuckoo, in Yudhishthira's sad case,
Is forced to wander if he would not die;
The swans must leave their forest-homes and fly,[q]
Like Pāndu's sons, to seek an unknown place. 6

(*Reflecting.*) It is long since Maitreya went to visit Vasantasenā. And even yet he does not come.

Enter Maitreya.

Maitreya. Confound the courtezan's avarice and her incivility! To think of her making so short a story of it! Over and over she repeats something about the affection she feels, and then without more ado she pockets the necklace. She is rich enough so that she might at least have said: "Good Maitreya, rest a little. You must not go until you have had a cup to drink." Confound the courtezan! I hope I'll never set eyes on her again. (*Wearily.*) The proverb is right. "It is hard to find a lotus-plant without a root, a merchant who never cheats, a goldsmith who never steals, a village-gathering without a fight, and a courtezan without avarice." Well, I'll find my friend and persuade him to have nothing more to do with this courtezan. (*He walks about until he discovers* Chārudatta.) Ah, my good friend is sitting in the orchard. I'll go to him. (*Approaching.*) Heaven bless you! May happiness be yours.

Chārudatta (*looking up*). Ah, my friend Maitreya has returned. You are very welcome, my friend. Pray be seated.

Maitreya. Thank you.

Chārudatta. Tell me of your errand, my friend.

Maitreya. My errand went all wrong.

Chārudatta. What! did she not accept the necklace?

Maitreya. How could we expect such a piece of luck? She put her lotus-tender hands to her brow, and took it.

Chārudatta. Then why do you say "went wrong"?

[p] Dhritarāshtra and Yudhishthira are characters in the wars fought when the sons of Pāndu attempted to gain control of the empire of the Kurus. This is narrated in the epic *Mahābhārata.*

[q] The swans migrated during the rainy season to an unknown place.

Maitreya. Why not, when we lost a necklace that was the pride of the four seas for a cheap golden casket, that was stolen before we had a bite or a drink out of it?

Chārudatta. Not so, my friend.

She showed her trust in leaving us her treasure;
The price of confidence has no less measure. 7

Maitreya. Now look here! I have a second grievance. She tipped her friend the wink, covered her face with the hem of her dress, and laughed at me. And so, Brahman though I am, I hereby fall on my face before you and beg you not to have anything more to do with this courtezan. That sort of society does any amount of damage. A courtezan is like a pebble in your shoe. It hurts before you get rid of it. And one thing more, my friend. A courtezan, an elephant, a scribe, a mendicant friar, a swindler, and an ass—where these dwell, not even rogues are born.

Chārudatta. Oh, my friend, a truce to all your detraction! My poverty of itself prevents me. For consider:

The horse would gladly hasten here and there,
  But his legs fail him, for his breath departs.
So men's vain wishes wander everywhere,
  Then, weary grown, return into their hearts. 8

Then too, my friend:

If wealth is thine, the maid is thine,
  For maids are won by gold;
(*Aside.*) And not by virtue cold. (*Aloud.*)
But wealth is now no longer mine,
  And her I may not hold. 9

Maitreya (*looks down. Aside*). From the way he looks up and sighs, I conclude that my effort to distract him has simply increased his longing. The proverb is right. "You can't reason with a lover." (*Aloud.*) Well, she told me to tell you that she would have to come here this evening. I suppose she isn't satisfied with the necklace and is coming to look for something else.

Chārudatta. Let her come, my friend. She shall not depart unsatisfied.

Enter Kumbhīlaka.

Kumbhīlaka. Listen, good people.

The more it rains in sheets,
  The more my skin gets wet;
The more the cold wind beats,
  The more I shake and fret. 10

(*He bursts out laughing.*)

I make the sweet flute speak from seven holes,
I make the loud lute speak on seven strings;
In singing, I essay the donkey's rôles:
No god can match my music when he sings. 11

My mistress Vasantasenā said to me, "Kumbhīlaka, go and tell Chārudatta that I am coming." So here I am, on my way to Chārudatta's house. (*He walks about, and, as he enters, discovers* Chārudatta.) Here is Chārudatta in the orchard. And here is that wretched jackanapes, too. Well, I'll go up to them. What! the orchard-gate is shut? Good! I'll give this jackanapes a hint.

(*He throws lumps of mud.*)

Maitreya. Well! Who is this pelting me with mud, as if I were an apple-tree inside a fence?

Chārudatta. Doubtless the pigeons that play on the roof of the garden-house.

Maitreya. Wait a minute, you confounded pigeon! With this stick I'll bring you down from the roof to the ground, like an over-ripe mango.

(*He raises his stick and starts to run.*)

Chārudatta (*holding him back by the sacred cord*). Sit down, my friend. What do you mean? Leave the poor pigeon alone with his mate.

Kumbhīlaka. What! he sees the pigeon and doesn't see me? Good? I'll hit him again with another lump of mud.

(*He does so.*)

Maitreya (*looks about him*). What! Kumbhīlaka? I'll be with you in a minute. (*He approaches and opens the gate.*) Well, Kumbhīlaka, come in. I'm glad to see you.

Kumbhīlaka (*enters*). I salute you, sir.

Maitreya. Where do you come from, man, in this rain and darkness?

Kumbhīlaka. You see, she's here.

Maitreya. Who's she? Who's here?

Kumbhīlaka. She. See? She.

Maitreya. Look here, you son of a slave! What makes you sigh like a half-starved old beggar in a famine, with your "shesheshe"?

Kumbhīlaka. And what makes you hoot like an owl with your "whowhowho"?
Maitreya. All right. Tell me.
Kumbhīlaka (aside). Suppose I say it this way. (*Aloud.*) I'll give you a riddle, man.
Maitreya. And I'll give you the answer with my foot on your bald spot.
Kumbhīlaka. Not till you've guessed it. In what season do the mango-trees blossom?
Maitreya. In summer, you jackass.
Kumbhīlaka (laughing). Wrong!
Maitreya (aside). What shall I say now? (*Reflecting.*) Good! I'll go and ask Chārudatta. (*Aloud.*) Just wait a moment. (*Approaching* Chārudatta.) My friend, I just wanted to ask you in what season the mango-trees blossom.
Chārudatta. You fool, in spring, in *vasanta.*
Maitreya (returns to Kumbhīlaka*).* You fool, in spring, in *vasanta.*
Kumbhīlaka. Now I'll give you another. Who guards thriving villages?
Maitreya. Why, the guard.
Kumbhīlaka (laughing). Wrong!
Maitreya. Well, I'm stuck. (*Reflecting.*) Good! I'll ask Chārudatta again.

(*He returns and puts the question to* Chārudatta.)

Chārudatta. The army, my friend, the *senā.*
Maitreya (comes back to Kumbhīlaka*).* The army, you jackass, the *senā.*
Kumbhīlaka. Now put the two together and say 'em fast.
Maitreya. Senā-vasanta.
Kumbhīlaka. Say it turned around.
Maitreya (turns around). Senā-vasanta.
Kumbhīlaka. You fool! you jackanapes! Turn the parts of the thing around!
Maitreya (turns his feet around). Senā-vasanta.
Kumbhīlaka. You fool! Turn the parts of the word around!
Maitreya (after reflection). Vasanta-senā.
Kumbhīlaka. She's here.
Maitreya. Then I must tell Chārudatta. (*Approaching.*) Well, Chārudatta, your creditor is here.
Chārudatta. How should a creditor come into my family?
Maitreya. Not in the family perhaps, but at the door. Vasantasenā is here.
Chārudatta. Why do you deceive me, my friend?

Maitreya. If you can't trust me, then ask Kumbhīlaka here. Kumbhīlaka, you jackass, come here.
Kumbhīlaka (*approaching*). I salute you, sir.
Chārudatta. You are welcome, my good fellow. Tell me, is Vasantasenā really here?
Kumbhīlaka. Yes, she's here. Vasantasenā is here.
Chārudatta (*joyfully*). My good fellow, I have never let the bearer of welcome news go unrewarded. Take this as your recompense.

(*He gives him his mantle.*)

Kumbhīlaka (*takes it and bows. Gleefully*). I'll tell my mistress. (*Exit.*)
Maitreya. Do you see why she comes in a storm like this?
Chārudatta. I do not quite understand, my friend.
Maitreya. I know. She has an idea that the pearl necklace is cheap, and the golden casket expensive. She isn't satisfied, and she has come to look for something more.
Chārudatta (*aside*). She shall not depart unsatisfied.

Then enter the love-lorn Vasantasenā, *in a splendid garment, fit for a woman who goes to meet her lover, a* maid *with an umbrella, and the* courtier.

Courtier (*referring to* Vasantasenā).
Lakshmī[r] without the lotus-flower is she,
Loveliest arrow of god Kāma's bow,[s]
The sweetest blossom on love's magic tree.
See how she moves, so gracefully and slow!
In passion's hour she still loves modesty;
In her, good wives their dearest sorrow know.
When passion's drama shall enacted be,
When on love's stage appears the passing show,
A host of wanderers shall bend them low,
Glad to be slaves in such captivity. 12
See, Vasantasenā, see!
The clouds hang drooping to the mountain peaks,[t]
Like a maiden's heart, that distant lover seeks:
The peacocks startle, when the thunder booms,

[r] Goddess of fortune and wife of Vishnu. She is also a goddess of beauty called *Shri,* the "radiant one." She was born of the ocean, like Aphrodite, and is represented by a lotus blossom.
[s] The arrows of Kāma (here a figure like Cupid) are flowers.
[t] The heart of a woman yearning for her beloved is supposed to be surrounded by a fog-like exhalation.

And fan the heaven with all their jeweled plumes. 13

And again:

Mud-stained, and pelted by the streaming rain,
To drink the falling drops the frogs are fain;
Full-throated peacocks love's shrill passion show,
And nīpa flowers like brilliant candles glow;
Unfaithful clouds obscure the hostage moon,
Like knaves, unworthy of so dear a boon;
Like some poor maid of better breeding bare,
The impatient lightning rests not anywhere. 14

Vasantasenā. Sir, what you say is most true. For

The night, an angry rival, bars my way;
Her thunders fain would check and hinder me:
"Fond fool! with him I love thou shalt not stay,
'Tis I, 'tis I, he loves," she seems to say,
"Nor from my swelling bosom shall he flee." [u] 15

Courtier. Yes, yes. That is right. Scold the night.

Vasantasenā. And yet, sir, why scold one who is so ignorant of woman's nature? For you must remember:

The clouds may rain, may thunder ne'er so bold,
May flash the lightning from the sky above;
That woman little recks of heat or cold,
Who journeys to her love. 16

Courtier. But see, Vasantasenā! Another cloud,

Sped by the fickle fury of the air—
A flood of arrows in his rushing streams,
His drum, the roaring thunder's mighty blare,
His banner, living lightning's awful gleams—
Rages within the sky, and shows him bold
'Mid beams that to the moon allegiance owe,
Like a hero-king within the hostile hold
Of his unwarlike foe. 17

Vasantasenā. True, true. And more than this:

As dark as elephants, these clouds alone
Fall like a cruel dart—
With streaks of lightning and with white birds strewn—
To wound my wretched heart.
But, oh, why should the heron, bird of doom,
With that perfidious sound [v]
Of "Rain! Rain! Rain!"—grim summons to the tomb

[u] Her verses are in Sanskrit. Only princesses of the royal blood and the highest class of courtesans are likely to use Sanskrit in the drama.

[v] The cry of the heron resembles the Sanskrit word for "rain." The sorrows of the loved one, who may pine away and die, are a favorite theme in Sanskrit poetry.

For her who spends her lonely hours in gloom—
Strew salt upon the wound? 18

Courtier. Very true, Vasantasenā. And yet again:
It seems as if the sky would take the guise
Of some fierce elephant to service bred;
The lightning like a waving streamer flies,
And white cranes serve to deck his mighty head. 19

Vasantasenā. But look, sir, look!
Clouds, black as wet tamāla-leaves, the ball
Of heaven hide from our sight;
Rain-smitten homes of ants decay and fall
Like beasts that arrows smite;
Like golden lamps within a lordly hall
Wander the lightnings bright;
As when men steal the wife of some base thrall,
Clouds rob the moon of light. 20

Courtier. See, Vasantasenā, see!
Clouds, harnessed in the lightning's gleams,
Like charging elephants dash by;
At Indra's bidding, pour their streams,
Until with silver cords it seems
That earth is linked with sky. 21

And look yonder!
As herds of buffaloes the clouds are black;
The winds deny them ease;
They fly on lightning wings and little lack
Of seeming troubled seas.
Smitten with falling drops, the fragrant sod,
Upon whose bosom greenest grasses nod,
Seems pierced with pearls, each pearl an arrowy rod. 22

Vasantasenā. And here is yet another cloud.
The peacock's shrill-voiced cry
Implores it to draw nigh;
And ardent cranes on high
Embrace it lovingly.
The wistful swans espy
The lotus-sweeter sky;
The darkest colors lie
On heaven clingingly. 23

Courtier. True. For see!
A thousand lotuses that bloom by night,
A thousand blooming when the day is bright,
Nor close nor ope their eyes to heaven's sight;
There is no night nor day.
The face of heaven, thus shrouded in the night,
Is only for a single instant bright,

When momentary lightning gives us sight;
Else is it dark alway.
Now sleeps the world as still as in the night
Within the house of rain where naught is bright,
Where hosts of swollen clouds seem to our sight
One covering veil of gray. 24

Vasantasenā. True. And see!
The stars are lost like mercies given
To men of evil heart;
Like lonely-parted wives, the heaven
Sees all her charms depart.
And, molten in the cruel heat
Of Indra's bolt, it seems
As if the sky fell at our feet
In liquid, flowing streams. 25

And yet again:
The clouds first darkly rise, then darkly fall,
Send forth their floods of rain, and thunder all;
Assuming postures strange and manifold,
Like men but newly blest with wealth untold. 26

Courtier. True.
The heaven is radiant with the lightning's glare;
Its laughter is the cry of myriad cranes;
Its voice, the bolts that whistle through the air;
Its dance, that bow whose arrows are the rains.
It staggers at the winds, and seems to smoke
With clouds, which form its black and snaky cloak. 27

Vasantasenā. O shameless, shameless sky!
To thunder thus, while I
To him I love draw nigh.
Why do thy thunders frighten me and pain?
Why am I seized upon by hands of rain? 28

O Indra, mighty Indra!
Did I then give thee of my love before,
That now thy clouds like mighty lions roar?
Ah no! Thou shouldst not send thy streaming rain,
To fill my journey to my love with pain. 29

Remember:
For Ahalyā's sweet sake thou once didst lie; [w]
Thou knowest lover's pain.
As thou didst suffer then, now suffer I;
O cruel, cease thy rain. 30

And yet:
Thunder and rain and lighten hundredfold

[w] The love of Indra for Ahalyā in Hindu mythology is almost identical with the Greek story of Zeus and Alcmene.

Forth from thy sky above;
The woman canst thou not delay nor hold
Who journeys to her love. 31
Let thunders roar, for men were cruel ever;
But oh, thou maiden lightning! didst thou never
Know pains that maidens know? 32

Courtier. But mistress, do not scold the lightning. She is your friend,

This golden cord that trembles on the breast
Of great Airāvata;[x] upon the crest
Of rocky hills this banner all ablaze;
This lamp in Indra's palace; but most blest
As telling where your most belovèd stays. 33

Vasantasenā. And here, sir, is his house.

Courtier. You know all the arts, and need no instruction now. Yet love bids me prattle. When you enter here, you must not show yourself too angry.

Where anger is, there love is not;
Or no! except for anger hot,
There is no love.
Be angry! make him angry then!
Be kind! and make him kind again—
The man you love. 34

So much for that. Who is there? Let Chārudatta know, that

While clouds look beautiful, and in the hour
Fragrant with nīpa and kadamba flower,
She comes to see her lover, very wet,
With dripping locks, but pleased and loving yet.
Though lightning and though thunder terrifies,
She comes to see you; 'tis for you she sighs.
The mud still soils the anklets on her feet,
But in a moment she will have them sweet. 35

Chārudatta (*listening*). My friend, pray discover what this means.

Maitreya. Yes, sir. (*He approaches* Vasantasenā. *Respectfully.*) Heaven bless you!

Vasantasenā. I salute you, sir. I am very glad to see you. (*To the* courtier.) Sir, the maid with the umbrella is at your service.

Courtier (*aside*). A very clever way to get rid of me. (*Aloud.*) Thank you. And mistress Vasantasenā,

Pride and tricks and lies and fraud
Are in your face;

[x] The elephant of Indra, god of the thunderstorm.

False playground of the lustful god,
Such is your face;
The wench's stock in trade, in fine,
Epitome of joys divine,
I mean, your face—
For sale! the price is courtesy.
I trust you'll find a man to buy
Your face. (*Exit.*) 36

Vasantasenā. Good Maitreya, where is your gambler?

Maitreya (*aside*). "Gambler"? Ah, she's paying a compliment to my friend. (*Aloud.*) Madam, here he is in the dry orchard.

Vasantasenā. But sir, what do you call a dry orchard?

Maitreya. Madam, it's a place where there's nothing to eat or drink. (Vasantasenā *smiles.*) Pray enter, madam.

Vasantasenā (*aside to her* maid). What shall I say when I enter?

Maid. "Gambler, what luck this evening?"

Vasantasenā. Shall I dare to say it?

Maid. When the time comes, it will say itself.

Maitreya. Enter, madam.

Vasantasenā (*enters, approaches* Chārudatta, *and strikes him with the flowers which she holds*). Well, gambler, what luck this evening?

Chārudatta (*discovers her*). Ah, Vasantasenā is here. (*He rises joyfully.*) Oh, my belovèd,

My evenings pass in watching ever,
My nights from sighs are never free;
This evening cannot else than sever—
In bringing you—my grief and me. 37

You are very, very welcome. Here is a seat. Pray be seated.

Maitreya. Here is a seat. Be seated, madam.

(Vasantasenā *sits, then the others.*)

Chārudatta. But see, my friend,

The dripping flower that decks her ear, droops down,
And one sweet breast
Anointed is, like a prince who wears the crown,
With ointment blest. 38

My friend, Vasantasenā's garments are wet. Let other, and most beautiful, garments be brought.

Maitreya. Yes, sir.

Maid. Good Maitreya, do you stay here. I will wait upon my mistress.

(*She does so.*)

Maitreya (*aside to* Chārudatta). My friend, I'd just like to ask the lady a question.

Chārudatta. Then do so.

Maitreya (*aloud*). Madam, what made you come here, when it is so stormy and dark that you can't see the moon?

Maid. Mistress, the Brahman is very plain-spoken.

Vasantasenā. You might better call him clever.

Maid. My mistress came to ask how much that pearl necklace is worth.

Maitreya (*aside to* Chārudatta). There! I told you so. She thinks the pearl necklace is cheap, and the golden casket is expensive. She isn't satisfied. She has come to look for something more.

Maid. For my mistress imagined that it was her own, and gambled it away. And nobody knows where the gambling-master has gone, for he is employed in the king's business.

Maitreya. Madam, you are simply repeating what somebody said before.

Maid. While we are looking for him, pray take this golden casket. (*She displays the casket.* Maitreya *hesitates.*) Sir, you examine it very closely. Did you ever see it before?

Maitreya. No, madam, but the skillful workmanship captivates the eye.

Maid. Your eyes deceive you, sir. This *is* the golden casket.

Maitreya (*joyfully*). Well, my friend, here is the golden casket, the very one that thieves stole from our house.

Chārudatta. My friend,

> The artifice we tried before,
> Her stolen treasure to restore,
> Is practiced now on us. But no,
> I cannot think 'tis really so. 39

Maitreya. But it is so. I swear it on my Brahmanhood.

Chārudatta. This is welcome news.

Maitreya (*aside to* Chārudatta). I'm going to ask where they found it.

Chārudatta. I see no harm in that.

Maitreya (*whispers in the* maid's *ear*). There!

Maid (*whispers in* Maitreya's ear). So there!

Chārudatta. What is it? and why are we left out?

Maitreya (*whispers in* Chārudatta's *ear*). So there!

Chārudatta. My good girl, is this really the same golden casket?

Maid. Yes, sir, the very same.

Chārudatta. My good girl, I have never let the bearer of welcome news go unrewarded. Take this ring as your recompense.

(*He looks at his finger, notices that the ring is gone, and betrays his embarrassment.*)

Vasantasenā (*to herself*). I love you for that.
Chārudatta (*aside to* Maitreya). Alas,

When in this world a man has lost his all,
Why should he set his heart on longer life?
His angers and his favors fruitless fall,
His purposes and powers are all at strife. 40
Like wingless birds, dry pools, or withered trees,
Like fangless snakes—the poor are like to these. 41
Like man-deserted houses, blasted trees,
Like empty wells—the poor are like to these.
For them no pleasant hours serve happy ends;
They are forgotten of their sometime friends. 42

Maitreya. But you must not grieve thus beyond reason. (*He bursts out laughing. Aloud.*) Madam, please give me back my bath-clout.
Vasantasenā. Chārudatta, it was not right that you should show your distrust of me by sending me this pearl necklace.
Chārudatta (*with an embarrassed smile*). But remember, Vasantasenā,

Who will believe the truth?
Suspicion now is sure.
This world will show no ruth
To the inglorious poor. 43

Maitreya. Tell me, girl, are you going to sleep here to-night?
Maid (*laughing*). But good Maitreya, you show yourself most remarkably plain-spoken now.
Maitreya. See, my friend, the rain enters again in great streams, as if it wanted to drive people away when they are sitting comfortably together.
Chārudatta. You are quite right.

The falling waters pierce the cloud,
As lotus-shoots the soil;
And tears the face of heaven's shroud,
Who weeps the moon's vain toil. 44

And again:

In streams as pure as thoughts to good men given,
But merciless as darts that Arjun[y] hurls,
And black as Baladeva's cloak, the heaven
Seems to pour out all Indra's hoarded pearls. 45

See, my belovèd, see!

The heaven is painted with the blackest dye,

[y] Arjuna, the greater archer and hero of the *Mahābhārata.*

And fanned by cool and fragrant evening airs;
Red lightning, glad in union, clasps the sky
With voluntary arms, and shows on high
The love that maiden heart to lover bears. 46

(Vasantasenā *betrays her passion, and throws her arms about* Chārudatta. Chārudatta *feels her touch, and embraces her.*)

Chārudatta. More grimly yet, O thunder, boom;
For by thy grace and power
My love-distracted limbs now bloom
Like the kadamba flower.[z]
Her dear touch all my being thrills,
And love my inmost spirit fills. 47

Maitreya. Confound you, storm! You are no gentleman, to frighten the lady with the lightning.

Chārudatta. Do not rebuke the storm, my friend.
Let ceaseless rain a hundred years endure,[a]
The lightning quiver, and the thunder peal;
For what I deemed impossible is sure:
Her dear-loved arms about my neck I feel. 48

And oh, my friend,
He only knows what riches are,
Whose love comes to him from afar,
Whose arms that dearest form enfold,
While yet with rain 'tis wet and cold. 49

Vasantasenā, my belovèd,
The masonry is shaken; and so old
The awning, that 'twill not much longer hold.
Heavy with water is the painted wall,
From which dissolving bits of mortar fall. 50

(*He looks up.*) The rainbow! See, my belovèd, see!
See how they yawn, the cloudy jaws of heaven,
As by a tongue, by forkèd lightning riven;
And to the sky great Indra's fiery bow
In lieu of high-uplifted arms is given. 51

Come, let us seek a shelter. (*He rises and walks about.*)
On palm-trees shrill,
On thickets still,
On boulders dashing,

[z] The kadamba tree is said to bloom at the touch of a beautiful girl.

[a] He wants the rainy season to last forever because it is the season of love.

On waters splashing,
Like a lute that, smitten, sings,
The rainy music rings. 52

(*Exeunt omnes.*)

ACT VI

The Swapping of the Bullock-Carts

Enter a maid.

Maid. Isn't my mistress awake yet? Well, I must go in and wake her. (*She walks about.* Vasantasenā *appears, dressed, but still asleep. The* maid *discovers her.*) It is time to get up, mistress. The morning is here.

Vasantasenā (*awakening*). What! is the night over? is it morning?

Maid. For us it is morning. But for my mistress it appears to be night still.

Vasantasenā. But girl, where is your gambler?

Maid. Mistress, after giving Vardhamānaka his orders, Chārudatta went to the old garden Pushpakaranda.

Vasantasenā. What orders?

Maid. To have the bullock-cart ready before daylight; for, he said, Vasantasenā was to come—

Vasantasenā. Where, girl?

Maid. Where Chārudatta is.

Vasantasenā (*embraces the* maid). I did not have a good look at him in the evening. But to-day I shall see him face to face. Tell me, girl. Have I found my way into the inner court?

Maid. You have found your way not only into the inner court, but into the heart of every one who lives here.

Vasantasenā. Tell me, are Chārudatta's servants vexed?

Maid. They will be.

Vasantasenā. When?

Maid. When my mistress goes away.

Vasantasenā. But not so much as I shall be. (*Persuasively.*) Here, girl, take this pearl necklace. You must go and give it to my lady sister, his good wife. And give her this message: "Worthy Chārudatta's virtues have won me made me his slave, and therefore your slave also. And so I hope that these pearls may adorn your neck."

Maid. But mistress, Chārudatta will be angry with you.

Vasantasenā. Go. He will not be angry.

Maid (*takes the necklace*). Yes, mistress. (*She goes out, then returns.*) Mistress, his lady wife says that her lord made you a present of it, and it would not be right for her to accept it. And further, that you are to know that her lord and her husband is her most excellent adornment.

Enter Radanikā, *with* Chārudatta's *little son.*

Radanikā. Come, dear, let's play with your little cart.

Rohasena (*peevishly*). I don't like this little clay cart Radanikā. Give me my gold cart.

Radanikā (*sighing wearily*). How should we have anything to do with gold now, my child? When your papa is rich again, then you shall have a gold cart to play with. But I'll amuse him by taking him to see Vasantasenā. (*She approaches* Vasantasenā.) Mistress, my service to you.

Vasantasenā. I am glad to see you, Radanikā. But whose little boy is this? He wears no ornaments, yet his dear little face makes my heart happy.

Radanikā. This is Chārudatta's son, Rohasena.

Vasantasenā (*stretches out her arms*). Come, my boy and put your little arms around me. (*She takes him on her lap.*) He looks just like his father.

Radanikā. More than looks like him, he *is* like him. At least I think so. His father is perfectly devoted to him.

Vasantasenā. But what is he crying about?

Radanikā. He used to play with a gold cart that belongs to the son of a neighbor. But that was taken away, and when he asked for it, I made him this little clay cart. But when gave it to him, he said, "I don't like this little clay cart Radanikā. Give me my gold cart."

Vasantasenā. Oh, dear! To think that this little fellow has to suffer because others are wealthy. Ah, mighty Fate! the destinies of men, uncertain as the water-drops which fall upon a lotus-leaf, seem to thee but playthings! (*Tearfully.*) Don't cry, my child. You shall have a gold cart to play with

Rohasena. Who is she, Radanikā?

Vasantasenā. A slave of your father's, won by his virtues

Radanikā. My child, the lady is your mother.

Rohasena. That's a lie, Radanikā. If the lady is my mother, why does she wear those pretty ornaments?

Vasantasenā. My child, your innocent lips can say terrible things. (*She removes her ornaments. Weeping.*) Now I am your mother. You shall take these ornaments and have a gold cart made for you.

Rohasena. Go away! I won't take them. You're crying.

Vasantasenā (*wiping away her tears*). I'll not cry, dear. There! go and play. (*She fills the clay cart with her jewels.*) There, dear, you must have a little gold cart made for you.

(*Exit* Radanikā, *with* Rohasena.)

Enter Vardhamānaka, *driving a bullock-cart.*

Vardhamānaka. Radanikā, Radanikā! Tell Mistress Vasantasenā that the covered cart is standing ready at the side-door.

Radanikā (*entering*). Mistress, Vardhamānaka is here, and he says that the cart is waiting at the side-door.

Vasantasenā. He must wait a minute, girl, while I get ready.

Rad. Wait a minute, Vardhamānaka, while she gets ready.

(*Exit.*)

Vardhamānaka. Hello, I've forgotten the cushion. I must go and get it. But the nose-rope makes the bullocks skittish. I suppose I had better take the cart along with me. (*Exit.*)

Vasantasenā. Bring me my things, girl. I must make myself ready. (*She does so.*)

Enter, driving a bullock-cart, Sthāvaraka, *servant to* Sansthānaka.

Sthāvaraka. Sansthānaka, the king's brother-in-law, said to me, "Take a bullock-cart, Sthāvaraka, and come as quick as you can to the old garden Pushpakaranda." Well, I'm on my way there. Get up, bullocks, get up! (*He drives about and looks around.*) Why, the road is blocked with villagers' carts. What am I to do now? (*Haughtily.*) Get out of my way, you! Get out of my way! (*He listens.*) What's that? you want to know whose cart this is? This cart belongs to Sansthānaka, the king's brother-in-law. So get out of my way—and this minute, too! (*He looks about.*) Why, here's a man going in the other direction as fast as he can. He is trying to hide like a runaway gambler, and he looks at me as if I were the gambling-master. I wonder who he is.[b] But then, what business is it of mine? I must get there as soon as I can. Get out of my way, you villagers, get out of my way! What's that? you want me to wait a minute and put a shoulder to your wheel? Confound you! A brave man like me, that serves Sansthānaka, the king's brother-in-law, put a shoulder to your wheel? After all, the poor fellow is quite alone. I'll do it. I'll stop my cart at the side-door to Chārudatta's orchard. (*He does so.*) I'm coming! (*Exit.*)

Maid. Mistress, I think I hear the sound of wheels. The cart must be here.

Vasantasenā. Come, girl. My heart grows impatient. Go with me to the side-door.

Maid. Follow me, mistress.

Vasantasenā (*walks about*). You have earned a rest, girl.

Maid. Thank you, mistress. (*Exit.*)

Vasantasenā (*feels her right eye twitch*[c] *as she enters the cart*). Why should my right eye twitch now? But the sight of Chārudatta will smooth away the bad omen.

Enter Sthāvaraka.

Sthāvaraka. I've cleared the carts out of the way, and now I'll go ahead. (*He mounts and drives away. To himself.*) The cart has grown heavy. But I suppose it only seems so, because I got tired helping them with that wheel. Well, I'll go along. Get up, bullocks, get up!

A voice behind the scenes. Police! Police! Every man at his post! The young herdsman has just broken jail, killed the jailer, broken his fetters, escaped, and run away. Catch him! Catch him!

Enter, in excited haste, Aryaka, *an iron chain on one foot. Covering his face, he walks about.*

Sthāvaraka (*to himself*). There is great excitement in the city. I must get out of the way as fast as I possibly can. (*Exit.*)

Aryaka.[d] I leave behind me that accursed sea.
Of human woe and human misery,

[b] This person is Aryaka, who has been freed from prison by Sharvilaka.

[c] A bad omen, in the case of a woman. The left eye would be a good omen. The reverse is true for a man.

[d] He speaks Sanskrit as he is of royal blood.

The prison of the king.
Like elephants that break their chains and flee,
I drag a fettered foot most painfully
In flight and wandering. 1

King Pālaka was frightened by a prophecy, took me from the hamlet where I lived, fettered me, and thrust me into a solitary cell, there to await my death.[e] But with the help of my good friend Sharvilaka I escaped. (*He sheds tears.*)

If such my fate, no sin is mine at least,
That he should cage me like a savage beast.
A man may fight with kings, though not with fate—
And yet, can helpless men contend with great? 2

Whither shall I go with my wretchedness? (*He looks about.*) Here is the house of some good man who hasn't locked the side-door.

The house is old, the door without a lock,
The hinges all awry.
Some man, no doubt, who feels misfortune's shock
As cruelly as I. 3

I will enter here and wait.

A voice behind the scenes. Get up, bullocks, get up!

Aryaka (listening). Ah, a bullock-cart is coming this way.

If this should prove to be a picnic rig,
Its occupants not peevishly inclined;
Some noble lady's waiting carriage trig;
Or rich man's coach, that leaves the town behind—
And if it empty be, fate proving kind,
'Twould seem a godsend to my anxious mind. 4

Enter Vardhamānaka *with the bullock-cart.*

Vardhamānaka. There, I've got the cushion. Radanikā, tell mistress Vasantasenā that the cart is ready and waiting for her to get in and drive to the old garden Pushpakaranda.

Aryaka (listening). This is a courtezan's cart, going out of the city. Good, I'll climb in.

(*He approaches cautiously.*)

Vardhamānaka (hears him coming). Ah, the tinkling of ankle-rings! The lady is here. Mistress, the nose-rope makes the bullocks skittish. You had better climb in

[e] Starvation in prison was a frequent way of eliminating troublesome persons.

behind. (*Aryaka does so.*) The ankle-rings tinkle only whe the feet are moving, and the sound has ceased. Beside the cart has grown heavy. I am sure the lady must hav climbed in by this time. I'll go ahead. Get up, bullocks, ge up!

(*He drives about. Enter* Vīraka.)

Vīraka. Come, come! Jaya, Jayamāna, Chandanaka, Man gala, Phullabhadra, and the rest of you!

So calm, when the herdsman, slipping his tether,
Breaks jail and the heart of the king together?

Here! You stand at the east gate of the main street, yo at the west, you at the south, you at the north. I'll climb up the broken wall here with Chandanaka and take a look Come on, Chandanaka, come on! This way!

Enter Chandanaka, *in excitement.*

Chandanaka. Come, come! Vīraka, Vishalya, Bhīmāngada Dandakāla, Dandashūra, and the rest of you!

Come quick, my reliables! Work! Now begin!
Lest the old king go out, and a new king come in.
Search gardens, and dives, and the town, and the stree
The market, the hamlet, wherever you meet
With what looks suspicious. Now, Vīraka, say,
Who saved the young herdsman that just broke away?
Who was born when the sun in his eighth mansion stooc
Or the moon in her fourth, or when Jupiter could
Be seen in his sixth, or when Saturn was resting
In his ninth, in her sixth house when Venus was nesting
Or Mars in his fifth?[f] Who will dare to be giving
The herdsman protection, while I am still living? 9, 1

Vīraka. Chandanaka, you mercenary!

I swear on your heart, he's been long out of prison,
For the herdsman escaped ere the sun was half risen. 1

Vardhamānaka. Get up, bullocks, get up!

Chandanaka (*discovers him*). Look, man, look!

A covered cart is moving in the middle of the road;
Investigate it, whose it is, and where it takes its load! 1

Vīraka (*discovers him*). Here, driver, stop your cart! Whose cart is this? who is in it? where is it going?

Vardhamānaka. This is Chārudatta's cart. Mistress Vasanta

[f] These horoscopes indicate, respectively, distress, colic, stupid ity, poverty, sorrow, and destruction.

senā is in it. I am taking her to the old garden Pushpakaranda to meet Chārudatta.

Vīraka (*approaches* Chandanaka). The driver says it is Chārudatta's cart; that Vasantasenā is in it; that he is taking her to the old garden Pushpakaranda.

Chandanaka. Then let it pass.

Vīraka. Without inspection?

Chandanaka. Certainly.

Vīraka. On whose authority?

Chandanaka. On Chārudatta's.

Vīraka. Who is Chārudatta, or who is Vasantasenā, that the cart should pass without inspection?

Chandanaka. Don't you know Chārudatta, man? nor Vasantasenā? If you don't know Chārudatta, nor Vasantasenā, then you don't know the moon in heaven, nor the moonlight.

Who doesn't know this moon of goodness, virtue's lotus-flower,
This gem of four broad seas, this savior in man's luckless hour? 13
These two are wholly worshipful, our city's ornaments,
Vasantasenā, Chārudatta, sea of excellence. 14

Vīraka. Well, well, Chandanaka! Chārudatta? Vasantasenā?
I know them perfectly, as well as I know anything;
But I do not know my father when I'm serving of my king. 15

Aryaka (*to himself*). In a former existence the one must have been my enemy, the other my kinsman. For see!

Their business is the same; their ways
Unlike, and their desire:
Like flames that gladden wedding days,
And flames upon the pyre. 16

Chandanaka. You are a most careful captain whom the king trusts. I am holding the bullocks. Make your inspection.

Vīraka. You too are a corporal whom the king trusts. Make the inspection yourself.

Chandanaka. If I make the inspection, that's just the same as if you had made it?

Vīraka. If you make the inspection, that's just the same as if King Pālaka had made it.

Chandanaka. Lift the pole, man!

(Vardhamānaka *does so.*) [g]

[g] To lower the back of the vehicle so that the occupant can dismount easily.

Aryaka (*to himself*). Are the policemen about to inspec
me? And I have no sword, worse luck! But at least,

Bold Bhīma's spirit I will show;
My arm shall be my sword.
Better a warrior's death than woe
That cells and chains afford. 17

But the time to use force has not yet come. (*Chandanaka enters the cart and looks about.*) I seek your protection.

Chandanaka (*speaking in Sanskrit*).[h] He who seeks protection shall be safe.

Aryaka. Whene'er he fight, that man will suffer hurts,
Will be abandoned of his friends and kin,
Becomes a mock forever, who deserts
One seeking aid; 'tis an unpardoned sin. 18

Chandanaka. What! the herdsman Aryaka? Like a bird that flees from a hawk, he has fallen into the hands of the fowler. (*Reflecting.*) He is no sinner, this man who seeks my protection and sits in Chārudatta's cart. Besides, he is the friend of good Sharvilaka, who saved my life. On the other hand, there are the king's orders. What is a man to do in a case like this? Well, what must be, must be. I promised him my protection just now.

He who gives aid to frightened men,
And joys his neighbor's ills to cure,
If he must die, he dies; but then,
His reputation is secure. 19

(*He gets down uneasily.*) I saw the gentleman—(*correcting himself*) I mean, the lady Vasantasenā, and she says, "Is it proper, is it gentlemanly, when I am going to visit Chārudatta, to insult me on the highway?"

Vīraka. Chandanaka, I have my suspicions.

Chandanaka. Suspicions? How so?

Vīraka. You gurgled in your craven throat; it seems a trifle shady.
You said, "I saw the gentleman," and then, "I saw the lady." 20

That's why I'm not satisfied.

Chandanaka. What's the matter with you, man? We southerners don't speak plain. We know a thousand dialects of the barbarians—the Khashas, the Khattis, the Kadas, the Kadatthobilas, the Karnātas, the Karnas, the Prāvaranas, the Drāvidas, the Cholas, the Chīnas, the Barbaras, the

[h] He employs Sanskrit here and in the speech beginning after line 20. Here he may be indicating that he is a person of some culture. In the second speech he sounds affected, but he is trying to confuse Vīraka.

Kheras, the Khānas, the Mukhas, the Madhughātas, and all the rest of 'em, and it all depends on the way we feel whether we say "he" or "she," "gentleman" or "lady."

Vīraka. Can't I have a look, too? It's the king's orders. And the king trusts me.

Chandanaka. I suppose the king doesn't trust *me!*

Vīraka. Isn't it his Majesty's command?

Chandanaka (aside). If people knew that the good herdsman escaped in Chārudatta's cart, then the king would make Chārudatta suffer for it. What's to be done? (*Reflecting.*) I'll stir up a quarrel the way they do down in the Carnatic.[i] (*Aloud.*) Well, Vīraka, I made one inspection myself—my name is Chandanaka—and you want to do it over again. Who are you?

Vīraka. Confound it! Who are you, anyway?

Chandanaka. An honorable and highly respectable person, and you don't remember your own family.

Vīraka (angrily). Confound you! What is my family?

Chandanaka. Who speaks of such things?

Vīraka. Speak!

Chandanaka. I think I'd better not.

I know your family, but I won't say;
'Twould not be modest, such things to betray;
What good's a rotten apple anyway? 21

Vīraka. Speak, speak! (*Chandanaka makes a significant gesture.*) [j] Confound you! What does that mean?

Chand. A broken whetstone in one hand—a thing
That looks like scissors in the other wing—
To trim the scrubby beards that curl and cling,
And you—why, you're a captain of the king! 22

Vīraka. Well, Chandanaka, you highly respectable person, you don't remember your own family either.

Chandanaka. Tell me. What is the family I belong to, I, Chandanaka, pure as the moon? [k]

Vīraka. Who speaks of such things?

Chandanaka. Speak, speak! (Vīraka *makes a significant gesture.*) Confound you! What does that mean?

Vīraka. Listen.

Your house is pure; your father is a drum,

[i] Apparently a tribe with a reputation for either quick tempers or a tradition of elaborate or formal argumentativeness.

[j] All of the gestures on the Indian stage are significant, but the meaning of this one is not clear.

[k] The Sanskrit word for moon is *Chandra.* This is a pun.

Your mother is a kettledrum, you scum!
Your brother is a tambourine—tum, tum!
And you—why, you're a captain of the king![1] 23

Chandanaka (*wrathfully*). I, Chandanaka, a tanner! You can look at the cart.

Vīraka. You! driver! turn the cart around. I want to look in.

Vardhamānaka *does so.* Vīraka *starts to climb in.* Chandanaka *seizes him violently by the hair, throws him down, and kicks him.*)

Vīraka (*rising. Wrathfully*). Confound you! I was peaceably going about the king's business, when you seized me violently by the hair and kicked me. So listen! If I don't have you drawn and quartered in the middle of the courtroom, my name's not Vīraka.

Chandanaka. All right. Go to court or to a hall of justice. What do I care for a puppy like you?

Vīraka. I will. (*Exit.*)

Chandanaka (*looks about him*). Go on, driver, go on! If anybody asks you, just say, "The cart has been inspected by Chandanaka and Vīraka." Mistress Vasantasenā, let me give you a passport.

(*He hands* Aryaka *a sword.*)

Aryaka (*takes it. Joyfully to himself.*)
A sword, a sword! My right eye twitches fast.
Now all is well, and I am safe at last. 24

Chandanaka. Madam,
As I have given you a passage free,
So may I live within your memory.
To utter this, no selfish thoughts could move;
Ah no, I speak in plenitude of love. 25

Aryaka. Chandanaka is rich in virtues pure;
My friend is he—Fate willed it—true and tried.
I'll not forget Chandanaka, be sure,
What time the oracle is justified. 26

Chand. May Shiva, Vishnu, Brahma, Three in One,
Protect thee, and the Moon, and blessèd Sun;
Slay all thy foes, as mighty Pārvatī
Slew Shumbha and Nishumbha—fearfully. 27

[1] Hindu respect for the cow as a giver of milk—and fuel in the form of dung—makes the killing of cattle abominable and the work of the butcher and tanner very offensive. Vīraka is being very insulting.

(*Exit* Vardhamānaka, *with the bullock-cart.* Chandanaka *looks toward the back of the stage.*) Aha! As he goes away, my good friend Sharvilaka is following him. Well, I've made an enemy of Vīraka, the chief constable and the king's favorite; so I think I too had better be following him, with all my sons and brothers. (*Exit.*)

ACT VII

Aryaka's Escape

Enter Chārudatta *and* Maitreya.

Maitreya. How beautiful the old garden Pushpakaranda is!
Chārudatta. You are quite right, my friend. For see!

> The trees, like merchants, show their wares;
> Each several tree his blossoms bears,
> While bees, like officers, are flitting,
> To take from each what toll is fitting. 1

Maitreya. This simple stone is very attractive. Pray be seated.
Chārudatta (*seats himself*). How Vardhamānaka lingers, my friend!
Maitreya. I told Vardhamānaka to bring Vasantasenā and come as quickly as he could.
Chārudatta. Why then does he linger?

> Is he delayed by some slow-moving load?
> Has he returned with broken wheel or traces?
> Obstructions bid him seek another road?
> His bullocks, or himself, choose these slow paces? 2

Enter Vardhamānaka *with the bullock-cart, in which* Aryaka *lies hidden.*

Vardhamānaka. Get up, bullocks, get up!
Aryaka (*aside*).

> And still I fear the spies that serve the king;
> Escape is even yet a doubtful thing,
> While to my foot these cursèd fetters cling.
> Some good man 'tis, within whose cart I lie,
> Like cuckoo chicks, whose heartless mothers fly,
> And crows must rear the fledglings, or they die. 3

I have come a long distance from the city. Shall I get out of the cart and seek a hiding-place in the grove? or shall I wait to see the owner of the cart? On second thoughts, I will not hide myself in the grove; for men say that the noble Chārudatta is ever helpful to them that seek his protection. I will not go until I have seen him face to face.

'Twill bring contentment to this good man's heart
To see me rescued from misfortune's sea.[m]
This body, in its suffering, pain, and smart,
Is saved through his sweet magnanimity. 4

Vardhamānaka. Here is the garden. I'll drive in. (*He does so.*) Maitreya!

Maitreya. Good news, my friend. It is Vardhamānaka's voice. Vasantasenā must have come.

Chārudatta. Good news, indeed.

Maitreya. You son of a slave, what makes you so late?

Vardhamānaka. Don't get angry, good Maitreya. I remembered that I had forgotten the cushion, and I had to go back for it, and that is why I am late.

Chārudatta. Turn the cart around, Vardhamānaka. Maitreya, my friend, help Vasantasenā to get out.

Maitreya. Has she got fetters on her feet, so that she can't get out by herself? (*He rises and lifts the curtain of the cart.*) Why, this isn't Mistress Vasantasenā—this is Mister Vasantasena.

Chārudatta. A truce to your jests, my friend. Love cannot wait. I will help her to get out myself.

(*He rises.*)

Aryaka (*discovers him*). Ah, the owner of the bullock-cart! He is attractive not only to the ears of men, but also to their eyes. Thank heaven! I am safe.

Chārudatta (*enters the bullock-cart and discovers* Aryaka). Who then is this?

As trunk of elephant his arms are long,
His chest is full, his shoulders broad and strong,
His great eyes restless-red;[n]
Why should this man be thus enforced to fight—
So noble he—with such ignoble plight,
His foot to fetters wed? 5

Who are you, sir?

[m] A metaphor for the prison of the king.

[n] These physiognomical characteristics fit a king or man of destiny.

Aryaka. I am one who seeks your protection, Aryaka, by birth a herdsman.
Chārudatta. Are you he whom King Pālaka took from the hamlet where he lived and thrust into prison?
Aryaka. The same.
Chārudatta. 'Tis fate that brings you to my sight;
May I be reft of heaven's light,
Ere I desert you in your hapless plight. 6

(Aryaka *manifests his joy.*)

Chārudatta. Vardhamānaka, remove the fetters from his foot.
Vardhamānaka. Yes, sir. (*He does so.*) Master, the fetters are removed.
Aryaka. But you have bound me with yet stronger fetters of love.
Maitreya. Now you may put on the fetters yourself. He is free anyway. And it's time for us to be going.
Chārudatta. Peace! For shame!
Aryaka. Chārudatta, my friend, I entered your cart somewhat unceremoniously. I beg your pardon.
Chārudatta. I feel honored that you should use no ceremony with me.
Aryaka. If you permit it, I now desire to go.
Chārudatta. Go in peace.
Aryaka. Thank you. I will alight from the cart.
Chārudatta. No, my friend. The fetters have but this moment been removed, and you will find walking difficult. In this spot where men seek pleasure, a bullock-cart will excite no suspicion. Continue your journey then in the cart.
Aryaka. I thank you, sir.
Chārud. Seek now thy kinsmen. Happiness be thine!
Aryaka. Ah, I have found thee, blessèd kinsman mine!
Chārud. Remember me, when thou hast cause to speak.
Aryaka. Thy name, and not mine own, my words shall seek.
Chārud. May the immortal gods protect thy ways!
Aryaka. Thou didst protect me, in most perilous days.
Chārud. Nay, it was fate that sweet protection lent.
Aryaka. But thou wast chosen as fate's instrument. 7
Chārudatta. King Pālaka is aroused, and protection will prove difficult. You must depart at once.
Aryaka. Until we meet again, farewell. (*Exit.*)
Chārud. From royal wrath I now have much to fear;
It were unwise for me to linger here.

Then throw the fetters in the well; for spies °
Serve to their king as keen, far-seeing eyes. 8

(*His left eye twitches.*) Maitreya, my friend, I long to see Vasantasenā. For now, because

I have not seen whom I love best,
My left eye twitches; and my breast
Is causeless-anxious and distressed. 9

Come, let us go. (*He walks about.*) See! a Buddhist monk approaches, and the sight bodes ill. (*Reflecting.*) Let him enter by that path, while we depart by this. (*Exit.*)

° Elaborate spy networks were considered essential to the government and are discussed in works on the theory of statecraft.

ACT VIII

The Strangling of Vasantasenā

Enter a monk, *with a wet garment in his hand.*

Monk. Ye ignorant, lay by a store of virtue!
Restrain the belly; watch eternally,
Heeding the beat of contemplation's drum.
For else the senses—fearful thieves they be—
Will steal away all virtue's hoarded sum. 1

And further: I have seen that all things are transitory, so that now I am become the abode of virtues alone.

Who slays the Five Men,[p] and the Female Bane,
By whom protection to the Town is given,
By whom the Outcaste impotent is slain,
He cannot fail to enter into heaven. 2

Though head be shorn and face be shorn,
The heart unshorn, why should man shave him?
But he whose inmost heart is shorn
Needs not the shaven head to save him. 3

I have dyed this robe of mine yellow. And now I will go into the garden of the king's brother-in-law, wash it in the pond, and go away as soon as I can.

(*He walks about and washes the robe.*)

A voice behind the scenes. Shtop, you confounded monk, shtop!

Monk (*discovers the speaker. Fearfully*). Heaven help me! Here is the king's brother-in-law, Sansthānaka. Just be-

[p] The five men are the five senses. Ignorance is the female bane. The town is the human body. The outcaste is the illusion of individuality, which prevents people from attaining liberation or nirvana.

cause one monk committed an offense, now, wherever he sees a monk, whether it is the same one or not, he bores a hole in his nose and drives him around like a bullock. Where shall a defenseless man find a defender? But after all, the blessèd Lord Buddha is my defender.

Enter the courtier, *carrying a sword, and* Sansthānaka.

Sansthānaka. Shtop, you confounded monk, shtop! I'll pound your head like a red radish[a] at a drinking party.

(*He strikes him.*)

Courtier. You jackass, you should not strike a monk who wears the yellow robes of renunciation. Why heed him? Look rather upon this garden, which offers itself to pleasure.

To creatures else forlorn, the forest trees
Do works of mercy, granting joy and ease;
Like a sinner's heart, the park unguarded lies,
Like some new-founded realm, an easy prize. 4

Monk. Heaven bless you! Be merciful, servant of the Blessèd One!

Sansthānaka. Did you hear that, shir? He's inshulting me.

Courtier. What does he say?

Sansthānaka. Shays I'm a shervant. What do you take me for? a barber?

Courtier. A servant of the Blessèd One he calls you, and this is praise.

Sansthānaka. Praise me shome more, monk!

Monk. You are virtuous! You are a brick!

Sansthānaka. Shee? He shays I'm virtuous. He shays I'm a brick. What do you think I am? a materialistic philosopher? or a watering-trough? or a pot-maker?

Courtier. You jackass, he praises you when he says that you are virtuous, that you are a brick.

Sansthānaka. Well, shir, what did he come here for?

Monk. To wash this robe.

Sansthānaka. Confound the monk! My shishter's husband gave me the finesht garden there is, the garden Pushpakaranda. Dogs and jackals drink the water in thish pond. Now I'm an arishtocrat, I'm a man, and I don't even take a bath. And here you bring your shtinking clothes, all shtained with shtale bean-porridge, and wash 'em! I think one good shtroke will finish you.

[a] Used as an appetizer.

Courtier. You jackass, I am sure he has not long been a monk.

Sansthānaka. How can you tell, shir?

Courtier. It doesn't take much to tell that. See!

His hair is newly shorn; the brow still white;
The rough cloak has not yet the shoulder scarred;
He wears it awkwardly; it clings not tight;
And here above, the fit is sadly marred.

Monk. True, servant of the Blessèd One. I have been a monk but a short time.

Sansthānaka. Then why haven't you been one all your life?

(*He beats him.*)

Monk. Buddha be praised!

Courtier. Stop beating the poor fellow. Leave him alone. Let him go.

Sansthānaka. Jusht wait a minute, while I take counshel.

Courtier. With whom?

Sansthānaka. With my own heart.

Courtier. Poor fellow! Why didn't he escape?

Sansthānaka. Blesshèd little heart, my little shon and mashter, shall the monk go, or shall the monk shtay? (*To himself.*) Neither go, nor shtay. (*Aloud.*) Well, shir, I took counshel with my heart, and my heart shays—

Courtier. Says what?

Sansthānaka. He shall neither go, nor shtay. He shall neither breathe up, nor breathe down. He shall fall down right here and die, before you can shay "boo."

Monk. Buddha be praised! I throw myself upon your protection.

Courtier. Let him go.

Sansthānaka. Well, on one condition.

Courtier. And what is that?

Sansthānaka. He musht shling mud in, without making the water dirty. Or better yet, he musht make the water into a ball, and shling it into the mud.

Courtier. What incredible folly!

The patient earth is burdened by
So many a fool, so many a drone,
Whose thoughts and deeds are all awry—
These trees of flesh, these forms of stone.

(*The* monk *makes faces at* Sansthānaka.)

Sansthānaka. What does he mean?

Courtier. He praises you.
Sansthānaka. Praise me shome more! Praise me again!

(*The* monk *does so, then exit.*)

Courtier. See how beautiful the garden is, you jackass.
See yonder trees, adorned with fruit and flowers,
O'er which the clinging creepers interlace;
The watchmen guard them with the royal powers;
They seem like men whom loving wives embrace. 7
Sansthānaka. A good deshcription, shir.
The ground is mottled with a lot of flowers;
The blosshom freight bends down the lofty trees;
And, hanging from the leafy tree-top bowers,
The monkeys bob, like breadfruit in the breeze. 8
Courtier. Will you be seated on this stone bench, you jackass?
Sansthānaka. I am sheated. (*They seat themselves.*) Do you know, shir, I remember that Vasantasenā even yet. She is like an inshult. I can't get her out of my mind.
Courtier (*aside*). He remembers her even after such a repulse. For indeed,
The mean man, whom a woman spurns,
But loves the more;
The wise man's passion gentler burns,
Or passes o'er. 9
Sansthānaka. Shome time has passhed, shir, shince I told my shervant Sthāvaraka to take the bullock-cart and come as quick as he could. And even yet he is not here. I've been hungry a long time, and at noon a man can't go a-foot. For shee!
The shun is in the middle of the shky,
And hard to look at as an angry ape;
Like Gāndhārī,[r] whose hundred shons did die,
The earth is hard dishtresshed and can't eshcape. 10
Courtier. True.
The cattle all—their cuds let fall—
Lie drowsing in the shade;
In heated pool their lips to cool,
Deer throng the woodland glade;
A prey to heat, the city street
Makes wanderers afraid;

[r] Gāndhāri was the wife of Dhritarāshtra, the king whose side lost the Bhāratī war described in the *Mahābhārata.* She bore one hundred sons, the Kauravas, all of whom died in the war.

The cart must shun the midday sun,
And thus has been delayed. 11

Sansthānaka. Yesshir,
Fasht to my head the heated shun-beam clings;
Birds, flying creatures, alsho wingèd things
Resht in the branches of the trees, while men,
People, and pershons shigh and shigh again;
At home they tarry, in their houses shtay,
To bear the heat and burden of the day. 12

Well, shir, that shervant isn't here yet. I'm going to shing shomething to passh the time. (*He sings.*) There, shir, did you hear what I shang?

Courtier. What shall I say? Ah, how melodious!

Sansthānaka. Why *shouldn't* it be malodorous?
Of nut-grass and cumin I make up a pickle,
Of devil's-dung, ginger, and orris, and treacle;
That's the mixture of perfumes I eagerly eat:
Why shouldn't my voice be remarkably shweet? 13

Well, shir, I'm jusht going to shing again. (*He does so.*) There, shir, did you hear what I shang?

Courtier. What shall I say? Ah, how melodious!

Sansthānaka. Why *shouldn't* it be malodorous?
Of the flesh of the cuckoo I make up a chowder,
With devil's-dung added, and black pepper powder;
With oil and with butter I shprinkle the meat:
Why shouldn't my voice be remarkably shweet? 14

But shir, the shervant isn't here yet.

Courtier. Be easy in your mind. He will be here presently.

Enter Vasantasenā *in the bullock-cart, and* Sthāvaraka.

Sthāvaraka. I'm frightened. It is already noon. I hope Sansthānaka, the king's brother-in-law, will not be angry. I must drive faster. Get up, bullocks, get up!

Vasantasenā. Alas! That is not Vardhamānaka's voice. What does it mean? I wonder if Chārudatta was afraid that the bullocks might become weary, and so sent another man with another cart. My right eye twitches. My heart is all a-tremble. There is no one in sight. Everything seems to dance before my eyes.

Sansthānaka (*hearing the sound of wheels*). The cart is here, shir.

Courtier. How do you know?

Sansthānaka. Can't you shee? It shqueaks like an old hog.

Courtier (*perceives the cart*). Quite true. It is here.

Sansthānaka. Sthāvaraka, my little shon, my shlave, are you here?
Sthāvaraka. Yes, sir.
Sansthānaka. Is the cart here?
Sthāvaraka. Yes, sir.
Sansthānaka. Are the bullocks here?
Sthāvaraka. Yes, sir.
Sansthānaka. And are you here?
Sthāvaraka (*laughing*). Yes, master, I am here too.
Sansthānaka. Then drive the cart in.
Sthāvaraka. By which road?
Sansthānaka. Right here, where the wall is tumbling down.
Sthāvaraka. Oh, master, the bullocks will be killed. The cart will go to pieces. And I, your servant, shall be killed.
Sansthānaka. I'm the king's brother-in-law, man. If the bullocks are killed, I'll buy shome more. If the cart goes to pieces, I'll have another one made. If you are killed, there will be another driver.
Sthāvaraka. Everything will be replaced—except me.
Sansthānaka. Let the whole thing go to pieces. Drive in over the wall.
Sthāvaraka. Then break, cart, break with your driver. There will be another cart. I must go and present myself to my master. (*He drives in.*) What! not broken? Master, here is your cart.
Sansthānaka. The bullocks not shplit in two? and the ropes not killed? and you too not killed?
Sthāvaraka. No, sir.
Sansthānaka. Come, shir. Let's look at the cart. You are my teacher, shir, my very besht teacher. You are a man I reshpect, my intimate friend, a man I delight to honor. Do you enter the cart firsht.
Courtier. Very well.

(*He starts to do so.*)

Sansthānaka. Not much! Shtop! Is thish your father's cart, that you should enter it firsht? I own thish cart. I'll enter it firsht.
Courtier. I only did what you said.
Sansthānaka. Even if I do shay sho, you ought to be polite enough to shay, "After you, mashter."
Courtier. After you, then.
Sansthānaka. Now I'll enter. Sthāvaraka, my little shon, my shlave, turn the cart around.
Sthāvaraka (*does so*). Enter, master.

Sansthānaka (enters and looks about, then hastily gets out in terror, and falls on the courtier's *neck*). Oh, oh, oh! You're a dead man! There's a witch,[s] or a thief, that's sitting and living in my bullock-cart. If it's a witch, we'll both be robbed. If it's a thief, we'll both be eaten alive.

Courtier. Don't be frightened. How could a witch travel in a bullock-cart? I hope that the heat of the midday sun has not blinded you, so that you became the victim of an hallucination when you saw the shadow of Sthāvaraka with the smock on it.

Sansthānaka. Sthāvaraka, my little shon, my shlave, are you alive?

Sthāvaraka. Yes, sir.

Sansthānaka. But shir, there's a woman sitting and living in the bullock-cart. Look and shee!

Courtier. A woman?

Then let us bow our heads at once and go,
  Like steers whose eyes the falling raindrops daze;
In public spots my dignity I show;
  On high-born dames I hesitate to gaze. 15

Vasantasenā (in amazement. Aside). Oh, oh! It is that thorn in my eye, the king's brother-in-law. Alas! the danger is great. Poor woman! My coming hither proves as fruitless as the sowing of a handful of seeds on salty soil. What shall I do now?

Sansthānaka. Thish old shervant is afraid and he won't look into the cart. Will you look into the cart, shir?

Courtier. I see no harm in that. Yes, I will do it.

Sansthānaka. Are those things jackals that I shee flying into the air, and are those things crows that walk on all fours? While the witch is chewing him with her eyes, and looking at him with her teeth, I'll make my eshcape.

Courtier (perceives Vasantasenā. *Sadly to himself).* Is it possible? The gazelle follows the tiger. Alas!

Her mate is lovely as the autumn moon,
Who waits for her upon the sandy dune;
And yet the swan will leave him? and will go
To dance attendance on a common crow? 16

(*Aside to* Vasantasenā.) Ah, Vasantasenā! This is neither right, nor worthy of you.

Your pride rejected him before,
  Yet now for gold, and for your mother's will

Vasantasenā. No!

[s] A *rākṣasī* or female demon with cannibalistic tendencies.

She shakes her head.)

ourtier.

Your nature knows your pride no more;
Your honor him, a common woman still. 17

Did I not tell[t] you to "serve the man you love, and him you hate"?

asantasenā. I made a mistake in the cart, and thus I came hither. I throw myself upon your protection.

ourtier. Do not fear. Come, I must deceive him. (*He returns to* Sansthānaka.) Jackass, there is indeed a witch who makes her home in the cart.

ansthānaka. But shir, if a witch is living there, why aren't you robbed? And if it's a thief, why aren't you eaten alive?

ourtier. Why try to determine that? But if we should go back on foot through the gardens until we came to the city, to Ujjayinī, what harm would that do?

ansthānaka. And if we did, what then?

ourtier. Then we should have some exercise, and should avoid tiring the bullocks.

ansthānaka. All right. Sthāvaraka, my shlave, drive on. But no! Shtop, shtop! I go on foot before gods and Brahmans? Not much! I'll go in my cart, sho that people shall shee me a long way off, and shay, "There he goes, our mashter, the king's brother-in-law."

ourtier (*aside*). It is hard to convert poison into medicine. So be it, then. (*Aloud.*) Jackass, this is Vasantasenā, come to visit you.

asantasenā. Heaven forbid!

ansthānaka (*gleefully*). Oh, oh! To visit me, an arishtocrat, a man, a regular Vāsudeva?[u]

ourtier. Yes.

ansthānaka. This is an unheard-of piece of luck. That other time I made her angry, sho now I'll fall at her feet and beg her pardon.

ourtier. Capital!

ansthānaka. I'll fall at her feet myshelf. (*He approaches* Vasantasenā.) Little mother,[v] mamma dear, lishten to my prayer.

I fold my hands and fall before thy feet—
Thine eyes are large, thy teeth are clean and neat,
Thy finger-nails are ten—forgive thy shlave

[t] See Act 1, 31.

[u] Another name for Krishna, the most amorous of the gods.

[v] A term of respect ludicrously out of place here.

What, love-tormented, he offended, shweet. 1[illegible]

Vasantasenā (*angrily*). Leave me! Your words are an insult

(*She spurns him with her foot.*)

Sansthānaka (*wrathfully*).

Thish head that mother and that mamma kissed,
That never bent to worship god, I wist,
Upon thish head she dared to plant her feet,
Like jackals on the carrion they meet. 1[illegible]

Sthāvaraka, you shlave, where did you pick her up?

Sthāvaraka. Master, the highway was blocked by villager[illegible] wagons. So I stopped my cart near Chārudatta's orchard and got out. And while I was helping a villager with hi[illegible] wagon, I suppose she mistook this cart for another, an[illegible] climbed in.

Sansthānaka. Oho! she mishtook my cart for another? an[illegible] didn't come to shee me? Get out of my cart, get out You're going to visit your poor merchant's shon, are you Those are my bullocks you're driving. Get out, get out, yo[illegible] shlave! Get out, get out!

Vasantasenā. Truly, you honor me when you say that came to see Chārudatta. Now what must be, must be.

Sansthānaka. These hands of mine, ten-finger-naily,
These hands sho lotush-leafy,
Are itching-anxious, girl, to dally
With you; and in a jiffy
I'll drag Your Shweetness by the hair
From the cart wherein you ride,
As did Jatāyu Bāli's fair,
The monkey Bāli's bride.[w] 2[illegible]

Courtier. So virtuous ladies may not be
Insulted thus despitefully;
Nor garden creepers may not be
Robbed of their leaves so cruelly. 2

Stand up, man. I will help her to alight. Come, Va[illegible]santasenā!

(Vasantasenā *alights and stands apart.*)

Sansthānaka (*aside*). The flame of wrath was kindled whe[illegible] she despised my proposition, and now it blazes up be[illegible]cause she kicked me. Sho now I'll murder her. Good! This

[w] In the Hindu epic the *Rāmāyana,* Jatāyu was a semi-divin[illegible] vulture who helped the hero Rāma fight the ape-king Bāli.

way. (*Aloud.*) Well, shir, what do you want?

A cloak with fringes hanging down and all,
Tied with a hundred shtrings? or good ragout,
To make you shmack your greedy lips and call
"Chuhoo, chuhoo, chukku, chuhoo, chuhooo"? 22

Courtier. Well?

Sansthānaka. Do me a favor.

Courtier. Certainly. Anything, unless it be a sin.

Sansthānaka. There's not a shmell of a shin in it, shir. Not a perfume!

Courtier. Speak, then.

Sansthānaka. Murder Vasantasenā.

Courtier (*stopping his ears*).

A tender lady, gem of this our city,
A courtezan whose love was stainless ever—
If I should kill her, sinless, without pity,
What boat would bear me on the gloomy river?[x] 23

Sansthānaka. I'll give you a boat. And beshides, in thish deserted garden, who'll shee you murdering her?

Courtier. The regions ten,[y] the forest gods, the sky,
The wind, the moon, the sun whose rays are light,
Virtue, my conscience—these I cannot fly,
Nor earth, that witnesses to wrong and right. 24

Sansthānaka. Well then, put your cloak over her and murder her.

Courtier. You fool! You scoundrel!

Sansthānaka. The old hog is afraid of a shin. Never mind. I'll pershuade Sthāvaraka, my shlave. Sthāvaraka, my little shon, my shlave, I'll give you golden bracelets.

Sthāvaraka. And I'll wear them.

Sansthānaka. I'll have a golden sheat made for you.

Sthāvaraka. And I'll sit on it.

Sansthānaka. I'll give you all my leavings.

Sthāvaraka. And I'll eat them.

Sansthānaka. I'll make you the chief of all my shervants.

Sthāvaraka. Master, I'll be the chief.

Sansthānaka. You only have to attend to what I shay.

Sthāvaraka. Master, I will do anything, unless it be a sin.

Sansthānaka. There's not a shmell of shin in it.

[x] The Vaitaranī, or River of the Underworld, like the Greek Styx. It is both turbulent and fouled with blood and excrement. A Charon-like ferryman carries souls across for a fee.

[y] The four cardinal points of the compass, the four intermediate ones, the zenith, and the nadir. Each of these is guarded by the *āshāpālas* or Gods of the Ends of the Earth.

Sthāvaraka. Then speak, master.
Sansthānaka. Murder Vasantasenā.
Sthāvaraka. Oh, master, be merciful! Unworthy as I am, I brought this worthy lady hither, because she mistook this bullock-cart for another.
Sansthānaka. You shlave, ain't I your mashter?
Sthāvaraka. Master of my body, not of my character. Be merciful, master, be merciful! I am afraid.
Sansthānaka. You're my shlave. Who are you afraid of?
Sthāvaraka. Of the other world, master.[z]
Sansthānaka. Who is thish "other world"?
Sthāvaraka. Master, it is a rewarder of righteousness and sin.
Sansthānaka. What is the reward of righteoushness?
Sthāvaraka. To be like my master, with plenty of golden ornaments.
Sansthānaka. What is the reward of shin?
Sthāvaraka. To be like me, eating another man's bread. That is why I will do no sin.
Sansthānaka. Sho you won't murder her? (*He beats him with all his might.*)
Sthāvaraka. You may beat me, master. You may kill me, master. I will do no sin.

A luckless, lifelong slave am I,
A slave I live, a slave I die;
But further woe I will not buy,
I will not, will not sin. 25

Vasantasenā. Sir, I throw myself upon your protection.
Courtier. Pardon him, jackass! Well done, Sthāvaraka!

Does this poor, miserable slave
Seek virtue's meed beyond the grave?
And is his lord indifferent?
Then why are not such creatures sent
To instant hell, whose sinful store
Grows great, who know not virtue more? 26

And again:

Ah, cruel, cruel is our fate,
And enters through the straitest gate;
Since he is slave, and you are lord,
Since he does not enjoy your hoard,
Since you do not obey his word. 27

Sansthānaka (*aside*). The old jackal is afraid of a shin, and the "lifelong shlave" is afraid of the other world. Who am

[z] Of reincarnation in a lower animal form as a punishment for sin.

I afraid of, I, the king's brother-in-law, an arishtocrat, a man? (*Aloud.*) Well, shervant, you "lifelong shlave," you can go. Go to your room and resht and keep out of my way.

Sthāvaraka. Yes, master. (*To* Vasantasenā.) Madam, I have no further power. (*Exit.*)

Sansthānaka (*girds up his loins*). Wait a minute, Vasantasenā, wait a minute. I want to murder you.

Courtier. You will kill her before my eyes?

(*He seizes him by the throat.*)

Sansthānaka (*falls to the ground*). Shir, you're murdering your mashter.

(*He loses consciousness, but recovers.*)

I always fed him fat with meat,
And gave him butter too, to eat;
Now for the friend in need I search;
Why does he leave me in the lurch? 28

(*After reflection.*) Good! I have an idea. The old jackal gave her a hint by shaking his head at her. Sho I'll shend him away, and then I'll murder Vasantasenā. That's the idea. (*Aloud.*) Shir, I was born in a noble family as great as a wine-glass. How could I do that shin I shpoke about? I jusht shaid it to make her love me.

Courtier. Why should you boast of this your noble birth?
'Tis character that makes the man of worth;
But thorns and weeds grow rank in fertile earth. 29

Sansthānaka. She's ashamed to confessh her love when you're here. Please go. My shervant Sthāvaraka has gone too after getting a beating. He may be running away. Catch him, shir, and come back with him.

Courtier (*aside*).

Vasantasenā is too proud to own,
While I am near, her love for one so crude;
So now I leave her here with him alone;
Love's confidences long for solitude. 30

(*Aloud.*) Very well. I go.

Vasantasenā (*seizing the hem of his garment*). Did I not throw myself upon your protection?

Courtier. Do not fear, Vasantasenā. Jackass, Vasantasenā is a pledge, committed to your hand.

Sansthānaka. All right. Jusht let her be committed to my hand. It's a pledge that I'll execute.

Courtier. Are you honest?
Sansthānaka. Honesht.
Courtier (*takes a few steps*). No! If I go, the wretch might kill her. I will conceal myself for a moment, and see what he intends to do.

(*He stands apart.*)

Sansthānaka. Good! I'll murder her. But no! Perhaps thish tricky trickshter, thish Brahman, thish old jackal, has gone and hidden himshelf; he might raise a howl like the jackal he is. I'll jusht do thish to deceive him. (*He gathers flowers and adorns himself.*) Vasantasenā, my love, my love! Come!
Courtier. Yes, he has turned lover. Good! I am content. I will go. (*Exit.*)
Sansthānaka. I'll give you gold, I'll call you shweet;
My turbaned head adores your feet.
Why not love me, my clean-toothed girl?
Why worship such a pauper churl? 31
Vasantasenā. How can you ask?

(*She bows her head and recites the following verses.*)

O base and vile! O wretch! What more?
Why tempt me now with gold and power?
The honey-loving bees adore
The pure and stainless lotus flower. 32
Though poverty may strike a good man low,
Peculiar honor waits upon his woe;
And 'tis the glory of a courtezan
To set her love upon an honest man. 33
And I, who have loved the mango-tree, I cannot cling to the locust-tree.
Sansthānaka. Wench, you make that poor little Chārudatta into a mango-tree, and me you call a locusht-tree, not even an acacia! That's the way you abuse me, and even yet you remember Chārudatta.
Vasantasenā. Why should I not remember him who dwells in my heart?
Sansthānaka. Thish very minute I'm going to shtrangle "him who dwells in your heart," and you too. Shtand shtill, you poor-merchant-man's lover!
Vasantasenā. Oh speak, oh speak again these words that do me honor!

Sansthānaka. Jusht let poor Chārudatta—the shon of a shlave—reshcue you now!

Vasantasenā. He would rescue me, if he saw me.

Sansthānaka. Is he the king of gods? the royal ape?
Shon of a nymph? or wears a demon's shape?
The kingly deity of wind and rain?
The offshpring of the Pāndu-princes' bane?
A prophet? or a vulture known afar?
A shtatesman? or a beetle? or a shtar? 34

But even if he was, he couldn't reshcue you.

As Sītā [a] in the Bhārata
Was killed by good old Chānakya,
Sho I intend to throttle thee,
As did Jatāyu Draupadī. 35

(*He raises his arm to strike her.*)

Vasantasenā. Mother! where are you? Oh, Chārudatta! my heart's longing is unfulfilled, and now I die! I will scream for help. No! It would bring shame on Vasantasenā, should she scream for help. Heaven bless Chārudatta!

Sansthānaka. Does the wench speak that rashcal's name even yet? (*He seizes her by the throat.*) Remember him, wench, remember him!

Vasantasenā. Heaven bless Chārudatta!

Sansthānaka. Die, wench!

(*He strangles her.* Vasantasenā *loses consciousness, and falls motionless.*)

Sansthānaka (*gleefully*).

Thish bashketful of shin, thish wench,
  Thish foul abode of impudence—
She came to love, she shtayed to blench,
  For Death's embrace took every sense.
But why boasht I of valorous arms and shtout?
She shimply died because her breath gave out.
Like Sītā in the Bhārata, she lies.[b]
Ah, mother mine! how prettily she dies. 36
She would not love me, though I loved the wench;

[a] Sītā was Rāma's wife in the *Rāmāyana* and has nothing to do with Chānakya, an historical character in the *Mahābhārata;* and Jatāyu, the vulture, has nothing to do with Draupadī, the heroine of the *Mahābhārata.*

[b] This mythology is also nonsense.

I shaw the empty garden, set the shnare,
And frightened her, and made the poor girl blench.
My brother! Oh, my father! Thish is where
You misshed the shight of heroism shtout;
Your brother and your shon here blosshomed out
Into a man; like Mother Draupadī,
You were not there, my bravery to shee. 37

Good! The old jackal will be here in a minute. I'll shtep ashide and wait. (*He does so.*)

Enter the courtier, *with* Sthāvaraka.

Courtier. I have persuaded the servant Sthāvaraka to come back, and now I will look for the jackass. (*He walks about and looks around him.*) But see! A tree has fallen by the roadside, and killed a woman in its fall. O cruel! How couldst thou do this deed of shame? And when I see that a woman was slain by thy fatal fall, I too am felled to the earth. Truly, my heart's fear for Vasantasenā was an evil omen. Oh, heaven grant that all may yet be well! (*He approaches* Sansthānaka.) Jackass, I have persuaded your servant Sthāvaraka to return.

Sansthānaka. How do you do, shir? Sthāvaraka, my little shon, my shlave, how do you do?

Sthāvaraka. Well, thank you.

Courtier. Give me my pledge.

Sansthānaka. What pledge?

Courtier. Vasantasenā.

Sansthānaka. She's gone.[c]

Courtier. Where?

Sansthānaka. Right after you.

Courtier (*doubtfully*). No, she did not go in that direction.

Sansthānaka. In what direction did you go?

Courtier. Toward the east.

Sansthānaka. Well, she went shouth.[d]

Courtier. So did I.

Sansthānaka. She went north.

Courtier. This is nonsense. My heart is not satisfied. Speak the truth.

Sansthānaka. I shwear by your head, shir, and my own feet. You may be easy in your heart. I murdered her.

Courtier (*despairingly*). You really killed her?

Sansthānaka. If you don't believe my words, then shee th

[c] "Gone" and "departed," as in English, are synonyms for death

[d] The region of Yama, god of the dead.

firsht heroic deed of Sansthānaka, the king's brother-in-law.

(*He points out the body.*)

Courtier. Alas! Ah, woe is me!

(*He falls in a swoon.*)

Sansthānaka. Hee, hee! The gentleman is calm enough now!

Sthāvaraka. Oh, sir! Come to yourself! I am the first murderer, for I brought the bullock-cart hither without looking into it.

Courtier (*comes to himself. Mournfully*). Alas, Vasantasenā!

The stream of courtesy is dried away,
And happiness to her own land doth flee.
Sweet gem of gems, that knew love's gentle play,
Love's mart and beauty's! Joy of men like me!
Thy mirth-shored stream, that kind and healing river—
Alas! is perished, lost, and gone forever! 38

(*Tearfully.*) Ah, woe is me!

What sin is yet to come, or woe,
Now thou hast done this deed of hate?
Like sin's foul self, hast thou laid low
The sinless goddess of our state. 39

(*Aside.*) Ah! Perhaps the wretch means to lay this sin to my charge. I must go hence. (*He walks about.* Sansthānaka *approaches and holds him back.*) Scoundrel! Touch me not. I have done with you. I go.

Sansthānaka. Aha! Firsht you murder Vasantasenā, then you abuse me, and now where will you run to? And sho a man like me hasn't anybody to protect him.

Courtier. You are an accusèd scoundrel!

Sansth. I'll give you countless wealth, a piece of gold,
A copper, and a cap, to have and hold.
And sho the fame of thish great deed shall be
A common property, and shan't touch me. 40

Courtier. A curse upon you! Yours, and yours only, be the deed.

Sthāvaraka. Heaven avert the omen!

(Sansthānaka *bursts out laughing.*)

Courtier. Be enmity between us! Cease your mirth!

Damned be a friendship that so shames my worth!
Never may I set eyes on one so low!
I fling you off, an unstrung, broken bow. 41

Sansthānaka. Don't be angry. Come, let's go and play in the pond.

Courtier. Unstained my life, and yet it seems to me
Your friendship stains, and mocks my sinlessness.
You woman-murderer! How could I be
A friend to one whom women ever see
With eyes half-closed in apprehension's stress?[e] 42

(*Mournfully.*) Vasantasenā,
When thou, sweet maid, art born again,
Be not a courtezan reborn,
But in a house which sinless men,
And virtuous, and good, adorn. 43

Sansthānaka. Firsht you murder Vasantasenā in my old garden Pushpakaranda, and now where will you run to? Come, defend yourshelf in court before my shishter's husband!

(*He holds him back.*)

Courtier. Enough, you accursèd scoundrel!

(*He draws his sword.*)

Sansthānaka (*recoiling in terror*). Shcared, are you? Go along, then.

Courtier (*aside*). It would be folly to remain here. Well, I will go and join myself to Sharvilaka, Chandanaka, and the rest. (*Exit.*)

Sansthānaka. Go to hell. Well, my little shon Sthāvaraka, what kind of thing is thish that I've done?

Sthāvaraka. Master, you have committed a terrible crime.

Sansthānaka. Shlave! What do you mean by talking about a crime? Well, I'll do it thish way. (*He takes various ornaments from his person.*) Take these gems. I give 'em to you. Whenever I want to wear them, I'll take them back again, but the resht of the time they are yours.

Sthāvaraka. They should be worn only by my master. What have I to do with such things?

[e] Hindu religious tradition acted to preserve women from molestation to a degree that astonished early European visitors. Even a professional criminal would not do this kind of deed.

Sansthānaka. Go along! Take these bullocks, and wait in the tower of my palace until I come.

Sthāvaraka. Yes, master. (*Exit.*)

Sansthānaka. The gentleman has made himshelf invisible. He wanted to save himshelf. And the shlave I'll put in irons in the palace tower, and keep him there. And sho the shecret will be shafe. I'll go along, but firsht I'll take a look at her. Is she dead, or shall I murder her again? (*He looks at* Vasantasenā.) Dead as a doornail! Good! I'll cover her with thish cloak. No, it has my name on it. Shome honesht man might recognize it. Well, here are shome dry leaves that the wind has blown into a heap. I'll cover her with them. (*He does so, then pauses to reflect.*) Good! I'll do it thish way. I'll go to court at once, and there I'll lodge a complaint. I'll shay that the merchant Chārudatta enticed Vasantasenā into my old garden Pushpakaranda, and killed her for her money.

Yesh, Chārudatta musht be shlaughtered now,
  And I'll invent the plan, forgetting pity;
The shacrificing of a sinless cow
  Is cruel in the kindesht-hearted city. 44

Now I'm ready to go. (*He starts to go away, but perceives something that frightens him.*) Goodnessh gracioush me! Wherever I go, this damned monk comes with his yellow robes. I bored a hole in his nose once and drove him around, and he hates me. Perhaps he'll shee me, and will tell people that I murdered her. How shall I eshcape? (*He looks about.*) Aha! I'll jump over the wall where it is half fallen down, and eshcape that way.

I run, I run, I go,
In heaven, on earth below,
  In hell, and in Ceylon,
  Hanūmat's peaks upon—
Like Indra's self, I go. (*Exit.*) 45

Enter hurriedly the Buddhist monk, *ex-shampooer.*

Monk. I've washed these rags of mine. Shall I let them dry on a branch? no, the monkeys would steal them. On the ground? the dust would make them dirty again. Well then, where shall I spread them out to dry? (*He looks about.*) Ah, here is a pile of dry leaves which the wind has blown into a heap. I'll spread them out on that. (*He does so.*) Buddha be praised! (*He sits down.*) Now I will repeat a hymn of the faith.

Who slays the Five Men, and the Female Bane,

By whom protection to the Town is given,
By whom the Outcaste impotent is slain,
He cannot fail to enter into heaven. (2)

After all, what have I to do with heaven, before I have paid my debt to Vasantasenā, my sister in Buddha? She bought my freedom for ten gold-pieces from the gamblers, and since that day I regard myself as her property. (*He looks about.*) What was that? a sigh that arose from the leaves? It cannot be.

The heated breezes heat the leaves,
The wetted garment wets the leaves,
And so, I guess, the scattered leaves
Curl up like any other leaves. 46

(Vasantasenā *begins to recover consciousness, and stretches out her hand.*)

Monk. Ah, there appears a woman's hand, adorned with beautiful gems. What! a second hand? (*He examines it with the greatest care.*) It seems to me, I recognize this hand. Yes, there is no doubt about it. Surely, this is the hand that saved me. But I must see for myself. (*He uncovers the body, looks at it, and recognizes it.*) It *is* my sister in Buddha. (Vasantasenā *pants for water.*) Ah, she seeks water, and the pond is far away. What shall I do? An idea! I will hold this robe over her and let it drip upon her.

(*He does so.* Vasantasenā *recovers consciousness, and raises herself. The* monk *fans her with his garment.*)

Vasantasenā. Who are you, sir?

Monk. Has my sister in Buddha forgotten him whose freedom she bought for ten gold-pieces?

Vasantasenā. I seem to remember, but not just as you say. It were better that I had slept never to waken.

Monk. What happened here, sister in Buddha?

Vasantasenā (*despairingly*). Nothing but what is fitting for a courtezan.

Monk. Sister in Buddha, support yourself by this creeper[1] that clings to the tree, and rise to your feet.

(*He bends down the creeper.* Vasantasenā *takes it in her hand, and rises.*)

[1] A monk may not touch a woman.

Monk. In yonder monastery dwells one who is my sister in the faith. There shall my sister in Buddha be restored before she returns home. You must walk very slowly, sister. (*He walks about and looks around him.*) Make way, good people, make way! This is a young lady, and I am a monk, yet my conduct is above reproach.

The man whose hands, whose lips are free from greed,
Who curbs his senses, he is man indeed.
He little recks, if kingdom fall or stand;
For heaven is in the hollow of his hand. 47

(*Exeunt.*)

ACT IX

The Trial

Enter a beadle.

Beadle.[g] The magistrates said to me, "Come, beadle, go to the court-room, and make ready the seats." So now I am on my way to set the court-room in order. (*He walks about and looks around him.*) Here is the court-room. I will enter. (*He enters, sweeps, and puts a seat in its place.*) There! I have tidied up the court-room and put the seats in readiness, and now I will go and tell the magistrates. (*He walks about and looks around him.*) But see! Here comes that arrant knave, the king's brother-in-law. I will go away without attracting his attention.

(*He stands apart.*)

Enter Sansthānaka, *in gorgeous raiment.*

Sansth. I bathed where water runs and flows and purls;
I shat within a garden, park, and grove
With women, and with females, and with girls,
Whose lovely limbs with grace angelic move. 1
My hair is shometimes done up tight, you shee;
In locks, or curls, it hangs my forehead o'er;
Shometimes 'tis matted, shometimes hanging free;
And then again, I wear a pompadour.
I am a wonder, I'm a wondrous thing,
And the husband of my shister is the king. 2

And beshides, I've found a big hole, like a worm that has

[g] This official is in charge of the court-room and of summoning defendants and witnesses. The court-room is in the king's palace.

crawled into the knot of a lotush-root, and is looking for a hole to creep out at. Now who was I going to accuse of thish wicked deed? (*He recalls something.*) Oh, yesh! I remember. I was going to accuse poor Chārudatta of thish wicked deed. Beshides, he's poor. They'll believe anything about him. Good! I'll go to the court-room and lodge a public complaint against Chārudatta, how he shtrangled Vasantasenā and murdered her. Sho now I'm on my way to the court-room. (*He walks about and looks around him.*) Here is the court-room. I'll go in. (*He enters and looks about.*) Well, here are the sheats, all arranged. While I'm waiting for the magishtrates, I'll jusht sit down a minute on the grass.

(*He does so.*)

Beadle (*walks about in another direction, and looks before him*). Here come the magistrates. I will go to them.

(*He does so.*)

Enter the judge, *accompanied by a* gild-warden, *a* clerk, *and others.* [h]

Judge. Gild-warden and clerk!

Gild-warden and *Clerk.* We await your bidding.

Judge. A trial depends to such an extent upon others that the task of the magistrates—the reading of another's thoughts—is most difficult.

Men often speak of deeds that no man saw,
Matters beyond the province of the law;
Passion so rules the parties that their lies
Hide their offenses from judicial eyes;
This side and that exaggerate a thing,
Until at last it implicates the king;
To sum it up: false blame is easy won,
A true judge little praised, or praised by none. 3

And again:

Men often point to sins that no man saw,
And in their anger scorn the patient law;
In court-rooms even the righteous with their lies
Hide their offenses from judicial eyes;
And those who did the deed are lost to view,

[h] In theory the king was supposed to be in court, and the judge was his representative. Since many cases involved business matters, the warden of the merchants' guild was present in the court.

Who sinned with plaintiff and defendant too;
To sum it up: false blame is easy won,
A true judge little praised, or praised by none. 4

For the judge must be

Learnèd, and skilled in tracing fraud's sly path,
And eloquent, insensible to wrath;
To friend, foe, kinsman showing equal grace,
Reserving judgment till he know the case;
Untouched by avarice, in virtue sound,
The weak he must defend, the knave confound;
An open door to truth, his heart must cling
To others' interests, yet shun each thing
That might awake the anger of the king. 5

Gild-warden and *Clerk*. And do men speak of defects in your virtue? If so, then they speak of darkness in the moonlight.

Judge. My good beadle, conduct me to the court-room.

Beadle. Follow me, Your Honor. (*They walk about*.) Here is the court-room. May the magistrates be pleased to enter.

(*All enter*.)

Judge. My good beadle, do you go outside and learn who desires to present a case.

Beadle. Yes, sir. (*He goes out*.) Gentlemen, the magistrates ask if there is any here who desires to present a case.

Sansthānaka (*gleefully*). The magishtrates are here. (*He struts about*.) I desire to present a cashe, I, an arishtocrat, a man, a Vāsudeva, the royal brother-in-law, the brother-in-law of the king.

Beadle (*in alarm*). Goodness! The king's brother-in-law is the first who desires to present a case. Well! Wait a moment, sir. I will inform the magistrates at once. (*He approaches the magistrates*.) Gentlemen, here is the king's brother-in-law who has come to court, desiring to present a case.

Judge. What! the king's brother-in-law is the first who desires to present a case? Like an eclipse at sunrise, this betokens the ruin of some great man. Beadle, the court will doubtless be very busy to-day. Go forth, my good man, and say "Leave us for to-day. Your suit cannot be considered."

Beadle. Yes, Your Honor. (*He goes out, and approaches Sansthānaka*.) Sir, the magistrates send word that you are to leave them for to-day; that your suit cannot be considered.

Sansthānaka (wrathfully). Confound it! Why can't my shuit be conshidered? If it isn't conshidered, then I'll tell my brother-in-law, King Pālaka, my shister's husband, and I'll tell my shishter and my mother too, and I'll have thish judge removed, and another judge appointed.

(He starts to go away.)

Beadle. Oh, sir! Brother-in-law of the king! Wait a moment. I will inform the magistrates at once. (*He returns to the* judge.) The brother-in-law of the king is angry, and says—

(He repeats Sansthānaka's words.)

Judge. This fool might do anything. My good man, tell him to come hither, that his suit will be considered.

Beadle (approaching Sansthānaka). Sir, the magistrates send word that you are to come in, that your suit will be considered. Pray enter, sir.

Sansthānaka. Firsht they shay it won't be conshidered, then they shay it will be conshidered. The magishtrates are shcared. Whatever I shay, I'll make 'em believe it. Good! I'll enter. (*He enters and approaches the magistrates.*) I am feeling very well, thank you. Whether you feel well or not—that depends on me.

Judge (aside). Well, well! We seem to have a highly cultivated plaintiff. (*Aloud.*) Pray be seated.

Sansthānaka. Well! Thish floor belongs to me. I'll sit down wherever I like. (*To the* gild-warden.) I'll sit here. (*To the* beadle.) Why shouldn't I sit here? (*He lays his hand on the* judge's *head.*) I'll sit here.

(He sits down on the floor.)

Judge. You desire to present a case?

Sansthānaka. Of courshe.

Judge. Then state the case.

Sansthānaka. I'll whishper it. I was born in the great family of a man as glorioush as a wine-glass.

> My father's father of the king—in law;
> The king, he is my daddy's son-in-law;
> And I am brother to the king—in law;
> And the husband of my shishter is the king. 6

Judge. All this we know.

Why should you boast of this your noble birth?
'Tis character that makes the man of worth;
But thorns and weeds grow rank in fertile earth. 7

State your case.

Sansthānaka. I will, but even if I was guilty, he wouldn't do anything to me. Well, my shishter's husband liked me, and gave me the besht garden there is, the old garden Pushpakaranda, to play in and look after. And there I go every day to look at it, to keep it dry, to keep it clean, to keep it blosshoming, to keep it trimmed. But fate decreed that I shaw—or rather, I didn't *shee*—the proshtrate body of a woman.

Judge. Do you know who the unfortunate woman was?

Sansthānaka. Hello, magishtrates! Why shouldn't I know? A woman like that! the pearl of the city! adorned with a hundred golden ornaments! Shomebody's unworthy shon enticed her into the old garden Pushpakaranda when it was empty, and for a mere trifle—for her money!—shtrangled Vasantasenā and killed her. But *I* didn't—

(*He breaks off, and puts his hand over his mouth.*)

Judge. What carelessness on the part of the city police! Gild-warden and clerk, write down the words "I didn't," as the first article in the case.

Clerk. Yes, sir. (*He does so.*) Sir, it is written.

Sansthānaka (*aside*). Goodnessh! Now I've ruined myshelf, like a man that shwallows a cake of rice and milk in a hurry. Well, I'll get out of it thish way. (*Aloud.*) Well, well, maghishtrates! I was jusht remarking that I didn't shee it happen. What are you making thish hullabaloo about?

(*He wipes out the written words with his foot.*)

Judge. How do you know that she was strangled—and for her money?

Sansthānaka. Hello! Why shouldn't I think sho, when her neck was shwollen and bare, and the places where you wear jewels didn't have any gold on them?

Gild-warden and *Clerk.* That seems plausible.

Sansthānaka (*aside*). Thank heaven! I breathe again. Hooray!

Gild-warden and *Clerk.* Upon whom does the conduct of this case depend?

udge. The case has a twofold aspect.

ild-warden and *Clerk.* How so?

udge. We have to consider the allegations, then the facts. Now the investigation of the allegations depends upon plaintiff and defendant. But the investigation of the facts must be carried out by the wisdom of the judge.

ild-warden and *Clerk.* Then the conduct of the case depends upon the presence of Vasantasenā's mother?

udge. Precisely. My good beadle, summon Vasantasenā's mother, without, however, giving her cause for anxiety.

eadle. Yes, Your Honor. (*He goes out, and returns with the mother of the* courtezan.) Follow me, madam.

Mother. My daughter went to the house of a friend to enjoy her youth. But now comes this gentleman—long life to him!—and says, "Come! The judge summons you." I find myself quite bewildered. My heart is palpitating. Sir, will you conduct me to the court-room?

eadle. Follow me, madam. (*They walk about.*) Here is the court-room. Pray enter, madam.

(*They enter.*)

Mother (*approaching*). Happiness be yours, most worthy gentlemen.

Judge. My good woman, you are very welcome. Pray be seated.

Mother. Thank you.

(*She seats herself.*)

Sansthānaka (*abusively*). You're here, are you, you old bawd?

Judge. Tell me. Are you Vasantasenā's mother?

Mother. I am.

Judge. Whither has Vasantasenā gone at this moment?

Mother. To the house of a friend.

Judge. What is the name of her friend?

Mother (*aside*). Dear me! Really, this is very embarrassing. (*Aloud.*) Any one else might ask me this, but not a judge.

Judge. Pray do not be embarrassed. The conduct of the case puts the question.

Gild-warden and *Clerk.* The conduct of the case puts the question. You incur no fault. Speak.

Mother. What! the conduct of the case? If that is so, then listen, worthy gentlemen. There lives in the merchants' quarter the grandson of the merchant Vinayadatta, the son of Sāgaradatta, a man whose name is a good omen in itself—that name is Chārudatta. In his house my daughter enjoys her youth.

Sansthānaka. Did you hear that? Write those words down. My contention is with Chārudatta.

Gild-warden and *Clerk.* It is no sin for Chārudatta to be her friend.

Judge. The conduct of this case demands the presence of Chārudatta.

Gild-warden and *Clerk.* Exactly.

Judge. Dhanadatta, write as the first article in the case "Vasantasenā went to the house of Chārudatta." But must we summon the worthy Chārudatta also? No, the conduct of the case summons him. Go, my good beadle, summon Chārudatta,—but gently, without haste, without giving him cause for anxiety, respectfully, as it were incidentally,—with the words "The judge wishes to see you."

Beadle. Yes, Your Honor. (*He goes out, then returns with* Chārudatta.) Follow me, sir.

Chārudatta (*thoughtfully*).

My character and kin are known
Unto the king who rules our state;
And in this summons there is shown
A doubt begotten of my wretched fate. 8

(*Reflectively. Aside.*)

Ah! Were there those, the man to recognize
Who met me on the road, from bondage freed?
Or did the king, who sees through cunning spies,
Learn that my cart was lent him in his need?
Why should I else be forced to tread the street,
Like one accused of crime, my judge to meet? 9

But why consider thus? I must go to the court-room. My good beadle, conduct me to the court.

Beadle. Follow me, sir.

(*They walk about.*)

Chārudatta (*apprehensively*). And what means this?

Hear how the gloomy raven[1] hoarsely croaks;
The slaves of justice summon me again;
My left eye twitches; these repeated strokes
Of threatened evil frighten me and pain. 10

Beadle. Follow me, sir, gently and without haste.

Chārudatta (*walks about and looks before him*).

[1] The raven or crow is a bird of bad omen, as in the West.

Upon the withered tree, a crow
Turns to the sun;
His left eye falls on me. Ah, woe!
My doubt is done. 11

(*He looks in another direction.*) But see! a snake!
His eye is fixed upon me; and his back
Flashes like antimony's lustrous black;
His long tongue quivers; four white fangs appear;
His belly swells and coils. He slumbered here,
This prince of serpents, till I crossed his path,
And now he darts upon me in his wrath. 12

And more than this:
I slip, although the ground has felt no rain;
My left eye, and my left arm throb again;
Another bird is screaming overhead;
All bodes a cruel death, and hope is fled. 13

Surely, the gods will grant that all may yet be well.

Beadle. Follow me, sir. Here is the court-room. Pray enter.

Chārudatta (*enters and looks about*). How wonderfully splendid is the court-room. For it seems an ocean,
Whose waters are the king's advisers, deep
In thought; as waves and shells it seems to keep
The attorneys; and as sharks and crocodiles
It has its spies that stand in waiting files;
Its elephants and horses [j] represent
The cruel ocean-fish on murder bent;
As if with herons of the sea, it shines
With screaming pettifoggers' numerous lines;
While in the guise of serpents, scribes are creeping
Upon its statecraft-trodden shore: the court
The likeness of an ocean still is keeping,
To which all harmful-cruel beasts resort. 14

Come! (*As he enters, he strikes his head against the door. Reflectively.*) Alas! This also?
My left eye throbs; a raven cries;
A serpent coils athwart my path.
My safey now with heaven lies. 15

But I must enter.

(*He does so.*)

Judge. This is Chārudatta.
A countenance like his, with clear-cut nose,
Whose great, wide-opened eye frank candor shows,

[j] Elephants and war-horses were used to execute criminals.

Is not the home of wantonness;
With elephants, with horses, and with kine,
The outer form is inner habit's sign;
With men no less. 16

Chārudatta. My greetings to the officers of justice. Officials, I salute you.

Judge (*betraying his agitation*). You are very welcome, sir. My good beadle, give the gentleman a seat.

Beadle (*brings a seat*) Here is a seat. Pray be seated, sir.

(Chārudatta *seats himself.*)

Sansthānaka (*angrily*). You're here, are you, you woman-murderer? Well! Thish is a fine trial, thish is a jusht trial, where they give a sheat to thish woman-murderer. (*Haughtily.*) But it's all right. They can give it to him.

Judge. Chārudatta, have you any attachment, or affection, or friendship, with this lady's daughter?

Chārudatta. What lady?

Judge. This lady.

(*He indicates* Vasantasenā's *mother.*)

Chārudatta (*rising*). Madam, I salute you.

Mother. Long life to you, my son! (*Aside.*) So this is Chārudatta. My daughter's youth is in good hands.

Judge. Sir, is the courtezan your friend?

(Chārudatta *betrays his embarrassment.*)

Sansthānaka. He tries to hide the deed he did;
He lies, from shame or fear;
He murdered her, of her got rid
For gold, and thinks the deed is hid;
Not sho his mashter here. 17

Gild-warden and *Clerk.* Speak, Chārudatta. Do not be ashamed. This is a lawsuit.

Chārudatta (*in embarrassment*). Officials, how can I testify that a courtezan is my friend? But at worst, it is youth that bears the blame, not character.

Judge. The case is hard; then banish shame,
Though it oppress your heart;
Speak truth with fortitude, and aim
To set deceit apart. 18

Do not be embarrassed. The conduct of the case puts the question.

Chārudatta. Officer, with whom have I a lawsuit?
Sansthānaka (arrogantly). With me!
Chārudatta. A lawsuit with you is unendurable!
Sansthānaka. Well, well, woman-murderer! You murder a woman like Vasantasenā who used to wear a hundred gems, and now you try deceitful deceivings to hide it!
Chārudatta. You are a fool.
Judge. Enough of him, good Chārudatta. Speak the truth. Is the courtezan your friend?
Chārudatta. She is.
Judge. Sir, where is Vasantasenā?
Chārudatta. She has gone home.
Gild-warden and *Clerk.* How did she go? When did she go? Who accompanied her?
Chārudatta (aside). Shall I say that she went unobserved?
Gild-warden and *Clerk.* Speak, sir.
Chārudatta. She went home. What more shall I say?
Sansthānaka. She was enticed into my old garden Pushpakaranda, and was shtrangled for her money. Now will you shay that she went home?
Chārudatta. Man, you are crazy.

The very clouds of heaven wet not you;
Your lips are like the blue-jay's wing-tip worn,
Yes, full as fickle with their speech untrue,
And like the winter lotus luster-lorn. 19

Judge (aside).

Take the Himalayan hills within your hand,
And swim from ocean strand to ocean strand,
And hold within your grasp the fleeting wind:
Then may you think that Chārudatta sinned. 20

(*Aloud.*) This is the noble Chārudatta. How could he commit this crime?

(*He repeats the verse* "A countenance like his:" *page 249.*)

Sansthānaka. Why thish partiality in a lawshuit?
Judge. Away, you fool!

Illiterate, you gloss the Sacred Law,[k]
And still your tongue uninjured find?
The midday sun with steadfast eye you saw,
And are not straightway stricken blind?
You thrust your hand into the blazing fire,

[k] All law in India in these times being sacred, only a Brahman would be authorized to expound the law.

And draw it forth, unscathed and sound?
Drag Chārudatta's virtue in the mire,
Nor sink beneath this yawning ground? 21

How could the nobel Chārudatta commit a crime?

Of all the riches of the mighty sea
Only the swelling waters now are left,
Because, without consideration, he—
For others' good—himself of all has reft.
And should this high-souled man, this store-house where
All gems of virtue gather and unite,
For lucre's sake, so foul a trespass dare
That in it even his foe could not delight? 22

Mother. You scoundrel! When the golden casket that was left with him as a pledge was stolen by thieves at night, he gave in place of it a pearl necklace that was the pride of the four seas. And he should now, for a mere trifle—for her money!—do this sin? Oh, my child, come back to me, my daughter!

(*She weeps.*)

Judge. Noble Chārudatta, did she go on foot, or in a bullock-cart?

Chārudatta. I did not see her when she went. Therefore I do not know whether she went on foot, or in a bullock-cart.

Enter Vīraka, *in anger.*

Vīraka. My anger was so prodded to the quick
By that dishonoring, insulting kick,
And so I brooded, till at last the night
Unwilling yielded to the dawning light. 23

So now I will go the court-room. (*He enters.*) May happiness be the lot of these honorable gentlemen.

Judge. Ah, it is Vīraka, the captain of the guard. Vīraka, what is the purpose of your coming?

Vīraka. Well! I was looking for Aryaka, in all the excitement about his escape from prison. I had my suspicions about a covered bullock-cart that was coming, and wanted to look in. "You've made one inspection, man, I must make another," said I, and then I was kicked by the highly respectable Chandanaka. You have heard the matter, gentlemen. The rest is your affair.

Judge. My good man, do you know to whom the bullock-cart belonged?

Vīraka. To this gentleman here, Chārudatta. And the driver said that Vasantasenā was in it, and was on her way to have a good time in the old garden Pushpakaranda.

Sansthānaka. Lishten to that, too!

Judge. This moon, alas, though spotless-bright,
Is now eclipsed, and robbed of light;
The bank is fallen; the waves appear
Befouled, that once were bright and clear. 24

Vīraka, we will investigate your case here later. Mount the horse that stands before the court-room door, go to the garden Pushpakaranda, and see whether a woman has perished there or not.

Vīraka. Yes, sir. (*He goes out, then returns.*) I have been there. And I saw the body of a woman, torn by wild beasts.

Gild-warden and *Clerk.* How do you know that it was the body of a woman?

Vīraka. That I perceived from the traces of hair and arms and hands and feet.

Judge. Alas for the difficulties which are caused by the actions of men!

The more one may apply his skill,
The harder is the matter still;
Plain are indeed the law's demands,
Yet judgment insecurely stands
As some poor cow on shifting sands. 25

Chārudatta (*aside*).
As bees, when flowers begin to blow,
Gather to sip the honey, so
When man is marked by adverse fate,
Misfortunes enter every gate. 26

Judge. Noble Chārudatta, speak truth!

Chārudatta. A mean and jealous creature, passion-blind,
Sets all his soul, some fatal means to find
To slay the man he envies; shall his lies
By evil nature prompted, win the prize?
No! he is unregarded by the wise. 27

And more than this:

The creeper's beauty would I never blight,
Nor pluck its flowers; should I not be afraid
To seize her hair so lovely-long, and bright
As wings of bees, and slay a weeping maid? 28

Sansthānaka. Hello, magishtrates! How can you inveshtigate the cashe with such partiality? Why, even now you let thish shcoundrel Chārudatta shtay on his sheat.

Judge. My good beadle, so be it.

(*The* beadle *follows* Sansthānaka*'s suggestion.*)

Charudatta. Consider, magistrates, consider what you are doing!

(*He leaves his seat, and sits on the floor.*)

Sansthānaka (*dancing about gleefully. Aside*). Fine! The shin that I did falls on another man's head. Sho I'll sit where Chārudatta was. (*He does so.*) Look at me, Chārudatta, and confessh that you murdered her.

Chārudatta. Magistrates!

A mean and jealous creature, passion-blind,
Sets all his soul, some fatal means to find
To slay the man he envies; shall his lies,
By evil nature prompted, win the prize?
No! he is unregarded by the wise.

(*Sighing. Aside.*)

My friend Maitreya! Oh, this cruel blow!
My wife, thou issue of a spotless strain!
My Rohasena! Here am I, laid low
By sternest fate; and thou, thou dost not know
That all thy childish games are played in vain.
Thou playest, heedless of another's pain! 29

But Maitreya I sent to Vasantasenā, that he might bring me tidings of her, and might restore the jewels which she gave my child, to buy him a toy cart. Why then does he linger?

Enter Maitreya *with the gems.*

Maitreya. Chārudatta bade me go to Vasantasenā, to return her jewels, and he said to me: "Maitreya, Vasantasenā adorned my dear Rohasena with her own jewels, and sent him thus to his mother. It was fitting that she should give him the jewels, but not that we should receive them. Therefore restore them to her." So now I will go to Vasantasenā's house. (*He walks about and looks around, then speaks to a person behind the scenes.*) Ah, it is Master Rebhila. Oh, Master Rebhila, why do you seem so exceedingly troubled? (*He listens.*) What! do you mean to say that my dear friend Chārudatta has been summoned to court? That can hardly be an insignificant matter. (*He reflects.*) I will go to Vasantasenā's house later, but now I will go to the court-room. (*He walks about and looks around.*) Here is the court-room. I will go in at once. (*He enters.*) May happiness be the lot of the magistrates. Where is my friend?

Judge. Here.

Maitreya. My friend, I wish you happiness.

Chārudatta. It will be mine.

Maitreya. And peace.

Chārudatta. That too will be mine.

Maitreya. My friend, why do you seem so exceedingly troubled? And why were you summoned?

Chārudatta. My friend,

> A scoundrel I, who bear the blame,
> Nor seek in heaven to be blest;
> A maid—or goddess—'tis the same—
> But *he* will say the rest. 30

Maitreya. What? what?

Chārudatta (*whispers*). That is it.

Maitreya. Who says that?

Chārudatta (*indicating* Sansthānaka). This poor fellow is the instrument that fate uses to accuse me.

Maitreya (*aside to* Chārudatta). Why don't you simply say that she went home?

Chārudatta. Though I say it, it is not believed, so unfortunate is my condition.

Maitreya. But gentlemen! He adorned the city of Ujjayinī with mansions, cloisters, parks, temples, pools, and fountains, and he should be mad enough to commit such a crime—and for a mere trifle? (*Wrathfully.*) You offspring of a loose wench, you brother-in-law of the king, Sansthānaka, you libertine, you slanderer, you buffoon, you gilded monkey, say it before me! This friend of mine doesn't even draw a flowering jasmine creeper to himself, to gather the blossoms, for fear that a twig might perhaps be injured. How should he commit a crime like this, which heaven and earth call accursèd? Just wait, you son of a bawd! Wait till I split your head into a hundred pieces with this staff of mine, as crooked as your heart.

Sansthānaka (*angrily*). Lishten to that, gentlemen! I have a quarrel, or a lawshuit, with Chārudatta. What right has a man with a pate that looks like a caret, to shplit my head into a hundred pieces? Not much! You confounded rashcal!

(*Maitreya raises his staff and repeats his words.* Sansthānaka *rises angrily and strikes him.* Maitreya *strikes back. During the scuffle the jewels fall from* Maitreya*'s girdle.*)

Sansthānaka (*picks up the jewels and examines them. Excitedly*). Look, gentlemen, look! These are the poor girl's jewels! (*Pointing to* Chārudatta.) For a trifle like thish he murdered her, and killed her too.

(*The magistrates all bow their heads.*)

Chārudatta (*aside to* Maitreya).

'Tis thus my fate would vent its gall,
That at this moment they should fall,
These gems—and with them, I. 31

Maitreya. But why don't you simply tell the truth?

Chārudatta. My friend,

The king perceives with blinded eye,
Nor on the truth that eye will bend;
Though telling all, I cannot fly
A wretched and inglorious end. 32

Judge. Alas! Alas!

With Mars strives Jupiter, and dies;
Beside them both there seems to rise
A comet-planet[1] in the skies. 33

Gild-warden and *Clerk* (*looking at the casket. To* Vasantasenā's *mother*). Madam, pray examine this golden casket attentively, to see whether it be the same or not.

Mother (*examining the casket*). It is similar, but not the same.

Sansthānaka. Oh, you old bawd! You confessh it with your eyes, and deny it with your lips.

Mother. Away, you scoundrel!

Gild-warden and *Clerk.* Speak carefully. Is it the same or not?

Mother. Sir, the craftsman's skill captivates the eye. But it is not the same.

Judge. My good woman, do you know these jewels?

Mother. No, I said. No! I don't recognize them; but perhaps they were made by the same craftsman.

Judge. Gild-warden, see!

Gems often seem alike in many ways,
When the artist's mind on form and beauty plays;
For craftsmen imitate what they have seen,
And skilful hands remake what once has been. 34

Gild-warden and *Clerk.* Do these jewels belong to Chārudatta?

[1] The fallen jewels.

Chārudatta. Never!

Gild-warden and *Clerk.* To whom then?

Chārudatta. To this lady's daughter.

Gild-warden and *Clerk.* How did she lose them?

Chārudatta. She lost them. Yes, so much is true.

Gild-warden and *Clerk.* Chārudatta, speak the truth in this matter. For you must remember,

Truth brings well-being in its train;
Through speaking truth, no evils rise;
Truth, precious syllable!—Refrain
From hiding truth in lies. 35

Chārudatta. The jewels, the jewels! I do not know. But I do know that they were taken from my house.

Sansthānaka. Firsht you take her into the garden and murder her. And now you hide it by tricky trickinessh.

Judge. Noble Chārudatta, speak the truth!

Merciless lashes[m] wait to smite
This moment on thy tender flesh;
And we—we can but think it right. 36

Chārudatta. Of sinless sires I boast my birth,
And sin in me was never found;
Yet if suspicion taints my worth,
What boots it though my heart be sound? 37

(*Aside.*) And yet I know not what to do with life, so I be robbed of Vasantasenā. (*Aloud.*) Ah, why waste words?

A scoundrel I, who bear the blame,
Nor think of earth, nor heaven blest;
That sweetest maid, in passion's flame—
But *he* will say the rest. 38

Sansthānaka. Killed her! Come, you shay it too. "I killed her."

Chārudatta. You have said it.

Sansthānaka. Lishten, my mashters, lishten! He murdered her! No one but him! Doubt is over. Let punishment be inflicted on the body of thish poor Chārudatta.

Judge. Beadle, we must do as the king's brother-in-law says. Guardsmen, lay hold on this Chārudatta.

(*The guardsmen do so.*)

Mother. Be merciful, good gentlemen, be merciful! (*She repeats what she had said before, beginning* "When the

[m] "Merciless lashes" may be a metaphor for "grievous guilt," because no corporal punishment could be inflicted on a Brahman unless he were degraded out of his caste.

golden casket:" *page 252.*) If my daughter is killed, she is killed. Let him live for me—bless him! And besides, a lawsuit is a matter between plaintiff and defendant. I am the real plaintiff. So let him go free!

Sansthānaka. You shlave, get out of the way! What have you got to shay about him?

Judge. Go, madam. Guardsmen, conduct her forth.

Mother. Oh, my child, my son! (*Exit weeping.*)

Sansthānaka (*aside*). I've done shomething worthy of myshelf. Now I'll go. (*Exit.*)

Judge. Noble Chārudatta, the decision lies with us, but the rest depends on the king. And yet, beadle, let King Pālaka be reminded of this:

The Brahman who has sinned, our laws declare,
May not be slain, but banished from the realm,
And with his wealth entire abroad may fare.[n] 39

Beadle. Yes, Your Honor. (*He goes out, then reenters in tears.*) Oh, sirs, I was with the king. And King Pālaka says: "Inasmuch as he killed Vasantasenā for such a trifle, these same jewels shall be hung about his neck, the drum shall be beaten, he shall be conducted to the southern burying-ground, and there impaled." And whoever else shall commit such a crime, shall be punished with the like dreadful doom.

Chārudatta. Oh, how wanton is this act of King Pālaka! Nevertheless,

Although his counselors may plunge a king
Into injustice' dangers great,
Yet he will reap the woe and suffering;
And 'tis a righteous fate. 40

And more than this:

They who pervert the king's true bent,
The white crow's part who play,
Have slain their thousands innocent,
And slay, and slay, and slay. 41

My friend Maitreya, go, greet the mother of my son in my name for the last time. And keep my son Rohasena free from harm.

Maitreya. When the root is cut away, how can the tree be saved?

Chārudatta. No, not so.

[n] The king and the members of the Brahman caste were exempt from corporal punishment and from the confiscation of their property. Exile was the only possible punishment. A king putting a Brahman to death might be expected to endure twenty-one reincarnations in animal form.

When man departs to worlds above,
In living son yet liveth he;
Bestow on Rohasena love
No less than that thou gavest me. 42

Maitreya. Oh, my friend! I will prove myself your friend by continuing the life that you leave unfinished.

Chārudatta. And let me see Rohasena for a single moment.

Maitreya. I will. It is but fitting.

Judge. My good beadle, remove this man. (*The* beadle *does so.*) Who is there? Let the headsmen receive their orders.

(*The guardsmen loose their hold on* Chārudatta, *and all of them go out.*)

Beadle. Come with me, sir.

Chārudatta. (*mournfully repeats the verse, page 254, beginning* "My friend Maitreya!" *Then, as if speaking to one not present*)

If you had proved my conduct by the fire,
By water, poison, scales, and thus had known
That I deserved that saws should bite my bone,
My Brahman's frame, more could I not desire.
You trust a foeman, slay me thus? 'Tis well.
With sons, and sons' sons, now you plunge to hell! 43

I come! I come! (*Exeunt omnes.*)

ACT X

The End

Enter Chārudatta, *accompanied by two* headsmen.

Headsmen. Then think no longer of the pain;
In just a second you'll be slain.
We understand the fashions new
To fetter you and kill you too.
In chopping heads we never fail,
Nor when the victim we impale. 1

Out of the way, gentlemen, out of the way! This is the noble Chārudatta.

The oleander ° on his brow,
In headsmen's hands you see him now;
Like a lamp whose oil runs nearly dry,
His light fades gently, ere it die. 2

Chārudatta (gloomily).
My body wet by tear-drops falling, falling;
My limbs polluted by the clinging mud;
Flowers from the graveyard torn, my wreath appalling;
For ghastly sacrifice hoarse ravens calling,
And for the fragrant incense of my blood. 3

Headsmen. Out of the way, gentlemen, out of the way!
Why gaze upon the good man so?
The ax of death soon lays him low.
Yet good men once sought shelter free,
Like birds, upon this kindly tree. 4

Come, Chārudatta, come!

Chārudatta. Incalculable are the ways of human destiny, that I am come to such a plight!

Red marks of hands in sandal paste

° A flower usually planted in cemeteries.

O'er all my body have been placed;
The man, with meal and powder strewn,
Is now to beast of offering grown. 5

(*He gazes intently before him.*) Alas for human differences! (*Mournfully.*)

For when they see the fate that I must brave,
With tears for death's poor victim freely given,
The citizens cry "shame," yet cannot save,—
Can only pray that I attain to heaven. 6

Headsmen. Out of the way, gentlemen, out of the way! Why do you gaze upon him?

God Indra moving through the sky,[p]
The calving cow, the falling star,
The good man when he needs must die,—
These four behold not from afar. 7

Goha. Look, Ahīnta! Look, man!

While he, of citizens the best,
Goes to his death at fate's behest,
Does heaven thus weep that he must die?
Does lightning paint the cloudless sky? 8

Ahīnta. Goha, man,

The heaven weeps not that he must die,
Nor lightning paints the cloudless sky;
Yet streams are falling constantly
From many a woman's clouded eye. 9

And again:

While this poor victim to his death is led,
No man nor woman here but sorely weeps;
And so the dust, by countless tear-drops fed,
Thus peacefully upon the highway sleeps. 10

Chārudatta (*gazes intently. Mournfully*).

These women, in their palaces who stay,
From half-shut windows peering, thus lament,
"Alas for Chārudatta! Woe the day!"
And pity-streaming eyes on me are bent. 11

Headsmen. Come, Chārudatta, come! Here is the place of proclamation. Beat the drum and proclaim the sentence.

Listen, good people, listen! This is the noble Chārudatta, son of Sāgaradatta, and grandson of the merchant Vinayadatta. This malefactor enticed the courtezan Vasantasenā into the deserted old garden Pushpakaranda, and for a mere trifle murdered her by strangling. He was taken with the booty, and confessed his guilt. Therefore are we under orders from King Pālaka to execute him. And if

[p] The lightning.

any other commit such a crime, accursèd in this world and the next, him too King Pālaka condemns to the like punishment.

Chārudatta (*despondently. Aside*).

By hundred sacrifices purified,
My radiant name
Was once proclaimed by countless altars' side,
And knew no blame.
Now comes my hour of death, and evil men
Of baser fame
In public spots proclaim it once again,
But linked with shame. 12

(*He looks up and stops his ears.*) Vasantasenā! Oh, my belovèd!

From thy dear lips, that vied with coral's red,
Betraying teeth more bright than moonbeams fair,
My soul with heaven's nectar once was fed.
How can I, helpless, taste that poison dread,
To drink shame's poisoned cup how can I bear? 13

Headsmen. Out of the way, gentlemen, out of the way!

This treasure-house, with pearls of virtue stored,
This bridge for good men o'er misfortune's river,
This gem now robbed of all its golden hoard,
Departs our town to-day, departs forever. 14

And again:

Whom fortune favors, find
That all the world is kind;
Whose happy days are ended,
Are rarely thus befriended. 15

Chārudatta (*looks about him*).

Their faces with their garments' hem now hiding,
They stand afar, whom once I counted friends:
Even foes have smiles for men with Fortune biding;
But friends prove faithless when good fortune ends. 16

Headsmen. They are out of the way. The street is cleared. Lead on the condemned criminal.

Chārudatta (*sighing*).

My friend Maitreya! Oh, this cruel blow!
My wife, thou issue of a spotless strain!
My Rohasena! Here am I, laid low
By sternest fate; and thou, thou dost not know
That all thy childish games are played in vain.
Thou playest, heedless of another's pain! [q]

Voices behind the scenes. My father! Oh, my friend!

[q] See Act IX, 29.

Chārudatta (listens. Mournfully). You are a leader in your own caste. I would beg a favor at your hands.

Headsmen. From *our* hands you would receive a favor?

Chārudatta. Heaven forbid! Yet a headsman is neither so wanton nor so cruel as King Pālaka. That I may be happy in the other world, I ask to see the face of my son.

Headsmen. So be it.

A voice behind the scenes. My father! oh, my father!

(Chārudatta *hears the words, and mournfully repeats his request.*)

Headsmen. Citizens, make way a moment. Let the noble Chārudatta look upon the face of his son. (*Turning to the back of the stage.*) This way, sir! Come on, little boy!

Enter Maitreya, *with* Rohasena.

Maitreya. Make haste, my boy, make haste! Your father is being led to his death.

Rohasena. My father! oh, my father!

Maitreya. Oh, my friend! Where must I behold you now?

Chārudatta (perceives his son and his friend). Alas, my son! Alas, Maitreya! (*Mournfully.*) Ah, woe is me!

Long, too long, shall I thirst in vain
Through all my sojourn dread;
This vessel[r] small will not contain
The water for the dead. 17

What may I give my son? (*He looks at himself, and perceives the sacrificial cord.*) Ah, this at least is mine.

The precious cord[s] that Brahmans hold
Is unadorned with pearls and gold;
Yet, girt therewith, they sacrifice
To gods above and fathers[t] old. 18

(*He gives* Rohasena *the cord.*)

Goha. Come, Chārudatta! Come, man!

Ahīnta. Man, do you name the noble Chārudatta's name, and forget the title? Remember:

[r] Rohasena is himself conceived as the receptacle of the water that a son must pour as a drink-offering to his dead father.

[s] The sacred thread that is a mark of the Brahman caste, given to the young Brahman at a confirmation ceremony. It is always worn in worship.

[t] Respect was due to one's ancestors as well as to the gods.

In happy hours, in death, by night, by day,
Roving as free as a yet unbroken colt,
Fate wanders on her unrestricted way. 19

And again:

Life will depart his body soon;
Shall our reproaches bow his head?
Although eclipse may seize the moon,
We worship while it seems but dead. 20

Rohasena. Oh, headsmen, where are you leading my father?

Chārudatta. My darling,

About my neck I needs must wear
The oleander-wreath;
Upon my shoulder I must bear
The stake, and in my heart the care
Of near-approaching death.
I go to-day to meet a dastard's ending,
A victim, at the fatal altar bending. 21

Goha. My boy,

Not we the headsmen are,
Though born of headsman race;
Thy father's life who mar,
These, these are headsmen base. 22

Rohasena. Then why do you murder my father?

Goha. Bless you, 'tis the king's orders must bear the blame, not we.

Rohasena. Kill me, and let father go free.

Goha. Bless you, may you live long for saying that!

Chārudatta (*tearfully embracing his son*).

This treasure—love—this taste of heaven,
To rich and poor alike is given;
Than sandal better, or than balm,
To soothe the heart and give it calm. 23

About my neck I needs must wear
The oleander-wreath
Upon my shoulder I must bear
The stake, and in my heart the care
Of near-approaching death.
I go to-day to meet a dastard's ending,
A victim, at the fatal altar bending. (21)

(*He looks about. Aside.*)

Their faces with their garments' hem now hiding,
They stand afar, whom once I counted friends:
Even foes have smiles (16)

Maitreya. My good men, let my dear friend Chārudatta go free, and kill me instead.

Chārudatta. Heaven forbid! (*He looks about. Aside.*) Now I understand.

for men with Fortune biding;
But friends prove faithless when good fortune ends. (16)
(*Aloud.*) These women, in their palaces who stay,
From half-shut windows peering, thus lament,
"Alas for Chārudatta! Woe the day!"
And pity-streaming eyes on me are bent. (11)

Goha. Out of the way, gentlemen, out of the way!

Why gaze upon the good man so,
When shame his living hope lays low?
The cord was broken at the well,
And down the golden pitcher fell. 24

Chārudatta (*mournfully*).

From thy dear lips, that vied with coral's red,
Betraying teeth more bright than moonbeams fair,
My soul with heaven's nectar once was fed.
How can I, helpless, taste that poison dread,
To drink shame's poisoned cup how can I bear? (13)

Ahīnta. Proclaim the sentence again, man.

(Goha *does so.*)

Chārud. So lowly fallen! till shame my virtues blur,
Till such an ending seem not loss, but gain!
Yet o'er my heart there creeps a saddening pain,
To hear them cry abroad "*You* murdered *her!*" 25

Enter Sthāvaraka, *fettered, in the palace tower.*

Sthāvaraka (*after listening to the proclamation. In distress*). What! the innocent Chārudatta is being put to death? And my master has thrown me into chains! Well, I must shout to them.—Listen, good gentlemen, listen! It was I, wretch that I am, who carried Vasantasenā to the old garden Pushpakaranda, because she mistook my bullock-cart for another. And then my master, Sansthānaka, found that she would not love him, and it was he, not this gentleman, who murdered her by strangling.—But they are so far away that no one hears me. What shall I do? Shall I cast myself down? (*He reflects.*) If I do, then the noble Chārudatta will not be put to death. Yes, through this broken window I will throw myself down from the palace tower. Better that I should meet my end, than that the noble Chārudatta should perish, this tree of life for noble youths. And if I die in such a cause, I have attained heaven. (*He throws *himself down.*) Wonderful! I did not meet my end, and my fetters are broken. So I will follow the sound of the headsmen's voices. (*He discovers the* headsmen, *and hastens forward.*) Headsmen, headsmen, make way!

Headsmen. For whom shall we make way?

Sthāvaraka. Listen, good gentlemen, listen! It was I, wretch that I am, who carried Vasantasenā to the old garden Pushpakaranda, because she mistook my bullock-cart for another. And then my master, Sansthānaka, found that she would not love him, and it was he, not this gentleman, who murdered her by strangling.

Chārudatta. Thank heaven!

But who thus gladdens this my latest morn,
When in Time's[u] snare I struggle all forlorn,
A streaming cloud above the rainless corn? 26

Listen! do you hear what I say?

Death have I never feared, but blackened fame;
My death were welcome, coming free from shame,
As were a son, new-born to bear my name. 27

And again:

That small, weak fool, whom I have never hated,
Stained me with sin wherewith himself was mated,
An arrow, with most deadly poison baited. 28

Headsmen. Are you telling the truth, Sthāvaraka?

Sthāvaraka. I am. And to keep me from telling anybody, he cast me into chains, and imprisoned me in the tower of his palace.

Enter Sansthānaka.

Sansthānaka (*gleefully*).

I ate a shour and bitter dish
Of meat and herbs and shoup and fish;
I tried at home my tongue to tickle
With rice-cakes plain, and rice with treacle. 29

(*He listens.*) The headsmen's voices! They shound like a broken brass cymbal. I hear the music of the fatal drum and the kettledrums, and sho I shuppose that that poor man, Chārudatta, is being led to the place of execution. I musht go and shee it. It is a great delight to shee my enemy die. Beshides, I've heard that a man who shees his enemy being killed, is sure not to have shore eyes in his next birth. I acted like a worm that had crept into the knot of a lotush-root. I looked for a hole to crawl out at, and

[u] Time (*kāla*) is an epithet for Yama, the god of death.

brought about the death of thish poor man, Chārudatta. Now I'll climb up the tower of my own palace, and have a look at my own heroic deeds. (*He does so and looks about*). Wonderful what a crowd there is, to shee that poor man led to his death! What would it be when an arishtocrat, a big man like me, was being led to his death? (*He gazes.*) Look! There he goes toward the shouth, adorned like a young shteer. But why was the proclamation made near my palace tower, and why was it shtopped? (*He looks about.*) Why, my shlave Sthāvaraka is gone, too. I hope he hasn't run away and betrayed the shecret. I musht go and look for him.

(*He descends and approaches the crowd.*)

Sthāvaraka (*discovers him*). There he comes, good masters!

Headsmen. Give way! Make room! And shut the door!
Be silent, and say nothing more!
Here comes a mad bull through the press,
Whose horns are sharp with wickedness. 30

Sansthānaka. Come, come, make way! (*He approaches.*) Sthāvaraka, my little shon, my shlave, come, let's go home.

Sthāvaraka. You scoundrel! Are you not content with the murder of Vasantasenā? Must you try now to murder the noble Chārudatta, that tree of life [v] to all who loved him?

Sansthānaka. I am beautiful as a pot of jewels. I kill no woman!

Bystanders. Oho! *you* murdered her, not the noble Chārudatta.

Sansthānaka. Who shays that?

Bystanders (*pointing to* Sthāvaraka). This honest man.

Sansthānaka (*fearfully. Aside*). Merciful heavens! Why didn't I chain that shlave Sthāvaraka fasht? Why, he was a witnessh of my crime. (*He reflects.*) I'll do it thish way. (*Aloud.*) Lies, lies, good gentlemen. Why, I caught the shlave shtealing gold, and I pounded him, and murdered him, and put him in chains. He hates me. What he shays can't be true. (*He secretly hands* Sthāvaraka *a bracelet, and whispers.*) Sthāvaraka, my little shon, my shlave, take thish and shay shomething different.

Sthāvaraka (*takes it*). Look, gentlemen, look! Why, he is trying to bribe me with gold.

Sansthānaka (*snatches the bracelet from him*). That's the

[v] In Hindu mythology, an enchanted tree that had the power of producing anything asked of it.

gold that I put him in chains for. (*Angrily.*) Look here, headsmen! I put him in charge of my gold-chest, and when he turned thief, I murdered him and pounded him. If you don't believe it, jusht look at his back.

Headsmen (*doing so*). Yes, yes. When a servant is branded that way, no wonder he tells tales.

Sthāvaraka. A curse on slavery! A slave convinces nobody. (*Mournfully.*) Noble Chārudatta, I have no further power.

(*He falls at* Chārudatta's *feet.*)

Chārudatta (*mournfully*).

Rise, rise! Kind soul to good men fallen on pain!
  Brave friend who lendest such unselfish aid!
Thy greatest toil to save me was in vain,
  For fate would not. Thy duty now is paid. 31

Headsmen. Beat your servant, master, and drive him away.

Sansthānaka. Out of the way, you! (*He drives* Sthāvaraka *away.*) Come, headsmen, what are you waiting for? Kill him.

Headsmen. Kill him yourself, if you are in a hurry.

Rohasena. Oh, headsmen, kill me and let father go free.

Sansthānaka. Yesh, shon *and* father, kill them both.

Chārudatta. This fool might do anything. Go, my son, to your mother.

Rohasena. And what should I do then?

Chārud. Go with thy mother to a hermitage;[w]
    No moment, dear, delay;
  Lest of thy father's fault thou reap the wage,
    And tread the selfsame way. 32

And you, my friend, go with him.

Maitreya. Oh, my friend, have you so known me as to think that I can live without you?

Chārudatta. Not so, my friend. Your life is your own. You may not throw it away.

Maitreya (*aside*). True. And yet I cannot live apart from my friend. And so, when I have taken the boy to his mother, I will follow my friend even in death. (*Aloud.*) Yes, my friend, I will take him to her at once.

(*He embraces* Chārudatta, *then falls at his feet.* Rohasena *does the same, weeping.*)

[w] The forest hermitage is the favorite place of exile for the disgraced, and also for Brahmans in the last stages of their lives.

Sansthānaka. Look here! Didn't I tell you to kill Chārudatta, and his shon, too?

(*At this,* Chārudatta *betrays fear.*)

Headsmen. We haven't any orders from the king to kill Chārudatta, and his son, too. Run away, boy, run away! (*They drive* Rohasena *away.*) Here is the third place of proclamation. Beat the drum!

(*They proclaim the sentence again.*)

Sansthānaka (*aside*). But the citizens don't believe it. (*Aloud.*) Chārudatta, you jackanapes, the citizens don't believe it. Shay it with your own tongue, "I murdered Vasantasenā." (Chārudatta *remains silent.*) Look here, headsmen! The man won't shpeak, the jackanapes Chārudatta. Jusht make him shpeak. Beat him a few times with thish ragged bamboo, or with a chain.

Goha (*raises his arm to strike*). Come, Chārudatta, speak!

Chārudatta (*mournfully*).

Now am I sunk so deep in sorrow's sea,
I know no fear, I know no sadness more;
Yet even now one flame still tortures me,
That men should say I slew whom I adore. 33

(Sansthānaka *repeats his words.*)

Chārudatta. Men of my own city!

A scoundrel I, who bear the blame,
Nor seek in heaven to be blest;
A maid—or goddess—'tis the same—
But *he* will say the rest.[x]

Sansthānaka. Killed her!

Chārudatta. So be it.

Goha. It's your turn to kill him, man.

Ahīnta. No, yours.

Goha. Well, let's reckon it out. (*He does so at great length.*) Well, if it's my turn to kill him, we will just let it wait a minute.

Ahīnta. Why?

Goha. Well, when my father was going to heaven, he said to me, "Son Goha, if it's your turn to kill him, don't kill the sinner too quick."

[x] See Act IX, 30.

Ahīnta. But why?

Goha. "Perhaps," said he, "some good man might give the money to set him free. Perhaps a son might be born to the king, and to celebrate the event, all the prisoners might be set free. Perhaps an elephant might break loose, and the prisoner might escape in the excitement. Perhaps there might be a change of kings, and all the prisoners might be set free." [y]

Sansthānaka. What? What? A change of kings?

Goha. Well, let's reckon it out, whose turn it is.

Sansthānaka. Oh come! Kill Chārudatta at once.

(*He takes* Sthāvaraka, *and withdraws a little.*)

Headsmen. Noble Chārudatta, it is the king's commandment that bears the blame, not we headsmen. Think then of what you needs must think.

Chārudatta. Though slandered by a cruel fate,
And stained by men of high estate,
If that my virtue yet regarded be,
Then she who dwells with gods above
Or wheresoever else—my love—
By her sweet nature wipe the stain from me! 34

Tell me. Whither would you have me go?

Goha (*pointing ahead*). Why, here is the southern burying-ground, and when a criminal sees that, he says good-by to life in a minute. For look!

One half the corpse gaunt jackals rend and shake,
And ply their horrid task;
One half still hangs impaled upon the stake,
Loud laughter's grinning mask. 35

Chārudatta. Alas! Ah, woe is me!

(*In his agitation he sits down.*)

Sansthānaka. I won't go yet. I'll jusht shee Chārudatta killed. (*He walks about, gazing.*) Well, well! He shat down.

Goha. Are you frightened, Chārudatta?

Chārudatta (*rising hastily*). Fool!

Death have I never feared, but blackened fame;
My death were welcome, coming free from shame,
As were a son, new-born to bear my name. (27)

[y] A large fine was often an alternative for the death penalty. Amnesty was often declared on such occasions as the birth of an heir to the king or the ascension to the throne of a new king. The revolution is foreshadowed here.

Goha. Noble Chārudatta, the moon and the sun dwell in the vault of heaven, yet even they are overtaken by disaster. How much more, death-fearing creatures, and men! In this world, one rises only to fall, another falls only to rise again. But from him who has risen and falls, his body drops like a garment. Lay these thoughts to heart, and be strong. (*To* Ahīnta.) Here is the fourth place of proclamation. Let us proclaim the sentence.

(*They do so once again.*)

Chārudatta. Vasantasenā! Oh, my belovèd!
From thy dear lips, that vied with coral's red,
Betraying teeth more bright than moonbeams fair,
My soul with heaven's nectar once was fed.
How can I, helpless, taste that poison dread,
To drink shame's poisoned cup how can I bear? (13)

Enter, in great agitation, Vasantasenā *and the* Buddhist monk.

Monk. Strange! My monkish life did me yeoman service when it proved necessary to comfort Vasantasenā, so untimely wearied, and to lead her on her way. Sister in Buddha, whither shall I lead you?

Vasantasenā. To the noble Chārudatta's house. Revive me with the sight of him, as the night-blooming water-lily is revived by the sight of the moon.

Monk (*aside*). By which road shall I enter? (*He reflects.*) The king's highway—I'll enter by that. Come, sister in Buddha! Here is the king's highway. (*Listening.*) But what is this great tumult that I hear on the king's highway?

Vasantasenā (*looking before her*). Why, there is a great crowd of people before us. Pray find out, sir, what it means. All Ujjayinī tips to one side, as if the earth bore an uneven load.

Goha. And here is the last place of proclamation. Beat the drum! Proclaim the sentence! (*They do so.*) Now, Chārudatta, wait! Don't be frightened. You will be killed very quickly.

Chārudatta. Ye blessèd gods!

Monk (*listens. In terror*). Sister in Buddha, Chārudatta is being led to his death for murdering *you.*

Vasantasenā (*in terror*). Alas! For my wretched sake the noble Chārudatta put to death? Quick, quick! Oh, lead me thither!

Monk. Hasten, oh, hasten, sister in Buddha, to comfort the noble Chārudatta while he yet lives. Make way, gentlemen, make way!

Vasantasenā. Make way, make way!

Goha. Noble Chārudatta, it is the king's commandment that bears the blame. Think then of what you needs must think.

Chārudatta. Why waste words?

Though slandered by a cruel fate,
And stained by men of high estate,
If that my virtue yet regarded be,
Then she who dwells with gods above
Or wheresoever else—my love—
By her sweet nature wipe the stain from me! (34)

Goha (drawing his sword). Noble Chārudatta, lie flat and be quiet. With one stroke we will kill you and send you to heaven.[z] (Chārudatta *does so.* Goha *raises his arm to strike. The sword falls from his hand.*) What is this?

I fiercely grasped within my hand
My thunderbolt-appalling brand;
Why did it fall upon the sand? 36

But since it did, I conclude that the noble Chārudatta is not to die. Have mercy, O mighty goddess of the Sahya hills![a] If only Chārudatta might be saved, then hadst thou shown favor to our headsman caste.

Ahīnta. Let us do as we were ordered.

Goha. Well, let us do it.

(*They make ready to impale* Chārudatta.)

Chārud. Though slandered by a cruel fate,
And stained by men of high estate,
If that my virtue yet regarded be,
Then she who dwells with gods above
Or wheresoever else—my love—
By her sweet nature wipe the stain from me! (34)

Monk and *Vasantasenā (perceiving what is being done).* Good gentlemen! Hold, hold!

Vasantasenā. Good gentlemen! I am the wretch for whose sake he is put to death.

Goha (perceiving her).

[z] They are going to do him a favor by decapitating him before they impale him.

[a] The goddess is Durgā, wife of Shiva and goddess of destruction. She is also called Pārvatī and Kālī. The Sahya hills are now known as the Western Ghats.

Who is the woman with the streaming hair
  That smites her shoulder, loosened from its bands?
She loudly calls upon us to forbear,
  And hastens hither with uplifted hands. 37

Vasantasenā. Oh, Chārudatta! What does it mean?

(*She falls on his breast.*)

Monk. Oh, Chārudatta! What does it mean?

(*He falls at his feet.*)

Goha (*anxiously withdrawing*). Vasantasenā?—At least, we did not kill an innocent man.

Monk (*rising*). Thank heaven! Chārudatta lives.

Goha. And shall live a hundred years!

Vasantasenā (*joyfully*). And I too am brought back to life again.

Goha. The king is at the place of sacrifice. Let us report to him what has taken place.

(*The two* headsmen *start to go away.*)

Sansthānaka (*perceives* Vasantasenā. *In terror*). Goodnessh! who brought the shlave back to life? Thish is the end of me. Good! I'll run away. (*He runs away.*)

Goha (*returning*). Well, didn't we have orders from the king to put the man to death who murdered Vasantasenā? Let us hunt for the king's brother-in-law.

(*Exeunt the two* headsmen.)

Chārudatta (*in amazement*).

Who saves me from the uplifted weapon's scorn,
When in Death's jaws I struggled all forlorn,
A streaming cloud above the rainless corn? 38

(*He gazes at her.*)

Is this Vasantasenā's counterfeit?
  Or she herself, from heaven above descended?
Or do I but in madness see my sweet?
  Or has her precious life not yet been ended? 39

Or again:

Did she return from heaven,
  That I might rescued be?
Was her form to another given?
  Is this that other she? 40

Vasantasenā (*rises tearfully and falls at his feet*). O noble Chārudatta, I am indeed the wretch for whose sake you are fallen upon this unworthy plight.

Voices behind the scenes. A miracle, a miracle! Vasantasenā lives.

(*The bystanders repeat the words.*)

Chārudatta (*listens, then rises suddenly, embraces* Vasantasenā, *and closes his eyes. In a voice trembling with emotion*). My love! You *are* Vasantasenā!

Vasantasenā. That same unhappy woman.

Chārudatta (*gazes upon her. Joyfully*). Can it be? Vasantasenā herself? (*In utter happiness.*)

Her bosom bathed in streaming tears,
When in Death's power I fell,
Whence is she come to slay my fears,
Like heavenly magic's spell? 41

Vasantasenā! Oh, my belovèd!

Unto my body, whence the life was fleeting,
And all for thee, thou knewest life to give.
Oh, magic wonderful in lovers' meeting![b]
What power besides could make the dead man live? 42

But see, my belovèd!

My blood-red garment seems a bridegroom's cloak,
Death's garland seems to me a bridal wreath;
My love is near.
And marriage music seems the fatal stroke
Of drums that heralded my instant death;
For she is here. 43

Vasantasenā. You with your utter kindliness, what can it be that you have done?

Chārudatta. My belovèd, he said that I had killed you.

For ancient hatred's sake, my mighty foe,
Hell's victim now, had almost laid me low. 44

Vasantasenā (*stopping her ears*). Heaven avert the omen! It was he, the king's brother-in-law, who killed me.

Chārudatta (*perceiving the* monk). But who is this?

Vasantasenā. When that unworthy wretch had killed me, this worthy man brought me back to life.

Chārudatta. Who are you, unselfish friend?

Monk. You do not remember me, sir. I am that shampooer, who once was happy to rub your feet. When I fell

[b] In Sanskrit poetry the reunion of lovers was supposed to have almost religious beauty and significance.

into the hands of certain gamblers, this sister in Buddha, upon hearing that I had been your servant, bought my freedom with her jewels. Thereupon I grew tired of the gambler's life, and became a Buddhist monk. Now this lady made a mistake in her bullock-cart, and so came to the old garden Pushpakaranda. But when that unworthy wretch learned that she would not love him, he murdered her by strangling. And I found her there.

Loud voices behind the scenes.

Unending victory to Shiva be,
Who Daksha's [c] offering foiled;
And victory may Kārttikeya see,
Who Krauncha smote and spoiled;
And victory to Aryaka the king—
His mighty foe he kills—
Far over all the earth's expansive ring,
That earth her joyous flag abroad may fling,
The snowy banner of Kailāsa's hills.[d] 45

Enter hurriedly Sharvilaka.

Sharv. Yes, Pālaka, the royal wretch, I slew,
Anointing Aryaka good king and true;
And now, like sacrificial flowers, I wed
The king's commandment to my bended head,
To give sad Chārudatta life anew. 46
The foe whose powers and friends had fled, he slew,
Consoled and comforted his subjects true;
And earth's broad sovereignty has gladly wed
His power, and bent to him her lowly head,
Who toward his foe plays Indra's part anew. 47

(*He looks before him.*) Ah! There he will be found, where the people are thus gathered together. Oh, that this deed of King Aryaka might be crowned with the rescued life of noble Chārudatta! (*He quickens his steps.*) Make way, you rascals! (*He discovers* Chārudatta. *Joyfully.*) Is Chārudatta yet living, and Vasantasenā? Truly, our sovereign's wishes are fulfilled.

Now, thanks to heaven, from sorrow's shoreless sea
I see him saved by her he loved, set free

[c] Daksha, the father-in-law of Shiva, offended both his daughter and the god himself by not inviting them to a sacrifice. In some versions of the myth Shiva had Daksha slain. Kārttikeya, a god of war, split asunder Mount Krauncha in the Himālaya chain.

[d] Mount Kailāsa (today Kailas) is considered by Hindus to be the most sacred spot on earth.

By that sweet bark, that knew her course to steer
With virtue's tackle and with goodness' gear.
He seems the moon, whose light shines clear at last,
When all the sad eclipse is overpast. 48

Yet how shall I approach him, who have so grievously sinned against him? But no! Honesty is always honorable. (*He approaches and folds his hands. Aloud.*) O noble Chārudatta!

Chārudatta. Who are you, sir?

Sharvilaka. I forced your house in manner base,
And stole the gems there left behind;
But though this sin[1] oppress my mind,
I throw myself upon your grace. 49

Chārudatta. Not so, my friend. Thereby you showed your faith in me.

(*He embraces him.*)

Sharvilaka. And one thing more:
The very noble Aryaka,
To save his family and name,
Has slain the wretched Pālaka,
A victim at the altar's flame. 50

Chārudatta. What say you?

Sharvilaka. 'Twas your cart helped him on his way,
Who sought the shelter of your name;
He slew King Pālaka to-day,
A victim at the altar's flame. 51

Chārudatta. Sharvilaka, did you set free that Aryaka, whom Pālaka took from his hamlet, and confined without cause in the tower?

Sharvilaka. I did.

Chārudatta. This is indeed most welcome tidings.

Sharvilaka. Scarcely was your friend Aryaka established in Ujjayinī, when he bestowed upon you the throne of Kushāvatī, on the bank of the Venā. May you graciously receive this first token of his love. (*He turns around.*) Come, lead hither that rascal, that villain, the brother-in-law of the king!

Voices behind the scenes. We will, Sharvilaka.

Sharvilaka. Sir, King Aryaka declares that he won this kingdom through your virtues, and that you are therefore to have some benefit from it.

Chārudatta. The kingdom won through my virtues?

[1] A mortal sin because the jewels were golden and the theft was from a Brahman.

Voices behind the scenes. Come on, brother-in-law of the king, and reap the reward of your insolence.

Enter Sansthānaka, *guarded, with his hands tied behind his back.*

Sansthānaka. Goodnessh gracious!

It came to pass, I ran away
Like any ass, and had my day.
They drag me round, a prishoner,
As if they'd found a naughty cur. 52

(*He looks about him.*) They crowd around me, though I'm a relative of the king's. To whom shall I go for help in my helplesshnessh? (*He reflects.*) Good! I'll go to the man who gives help and shows mercy to the shuppliant. (*He approaches.*) Noble Chārudatta, protect me, protect me!

(*He falls at his feet.*)

Voices behind the scenes. Noble Chārudatta, leave him to us! let us kill him!

Sansthānaka (*to* Chārudatta). O helper of the helplessh, protect me!

Chārudatta (*mercifully*). Yes, yes. He who seeks protection shall be safe.

Sharvilaka (*impatiently*). Confound him! Take him away from Chārudatta! (*To* Chārudatta.) Tell me. What shall be done with the wretch?

Shall he be bound and dragged until he dies?
Shall dogs devour the scoundrel as he lies?
If he should be impaled, 'twould be no blunder,
Nor if we had the rascal sawn asunder. 53

Chārudatta. Will you do as I say?

Sharvilaka. How can you doubt it?

Sansthānaka. Chārudatta! Mashter! I sheek your protection. Protect me, protect me! Do shomething worthy of yourshelf. I'll never do it again!

Voices of citizens behind the scenes. Kill him! Why should the wretch be allowed to live?

(Vasantasenā *takes the garland of death from* Chārudatta's *neck, and throws it upon* Sansthānaka.)

Sansthānaka. You shlave-wench, be merciful, be merciful! I'll never murder you again. Protect me!

Sharvilaka. Come, take him away! Noble Chārudatta, say what shall be done with the wretch.

Chārudatta. Will you do as I say?

Sharvilaka. How can you doubt it?

Chārudatta. Really?

Sharvilaka. Really.

Chārudatta. Then let him be immediately—

Sharvilaka. Killed?

Chārudatta. No, no! Set free.

Sharvilaka. What for?

Chārud. The humble foe who seeks thine aid,
Thou mayst not smite with steely blade—

Sharvilaka. All right. We will have the dogs eat him alive.

Chārudatta. No, no!
Be cruelty with kindness paid. 54–57

Sharvilaka. Wonderful! What shall I do? Tell me, sir.

Chārudatta Why, set him free.

Sharvilaka. It shall be done.

Sansthānaka. Hooray! I breathe again.

(*Exit, with the guards.*)

Sharvilaka. Mistress Vasantasenā, the king is pleased to bestow upon you the title "wedded wife." [f]

Vasantasenā. Sir, I desire no more.

Sharvilaka (*places the veil upon* Vasantasenā. *To* Chārudatta). Sir, what shall be done for this monk?

Chārudatta. Monk, what do you most desire?

Monk. When I see this example of the uncertainty of all things, I am twice content to be a monk.

Chārudatta. His purpose is not to be changed, my friend. Let him be appointed spiritual father over all the monasteries in the land.

Sharvilaka. It shall be done.

Monk. It is all that I desire.

Vasantasenā. Now I am indeed brought back to life. [g]

Sharvilaka. What shall be done for Sthāvaraka?

Chārudatta. Let the good fellow be given his freedom. Let those headsmen be appointed chiefs of all the headsmen. Let Chandanaka be appointed chief of all the police in the land. Let the brother-in-law of the king continue to act exactly as he acted in the past.

[f] As a courtesan, she could not abandon her profession without the king's permission.

[g] Her debt of gratitude to the monk is paid and her wishes are fulfilled.

Sharvilaka. It shall be done. Only *that* man—leave him to me, and I'll kill him.

Chārudatta. He who seeks protection shall be safe.

The humbled foe who seeks thine aid,
Thou mayst not smite with steely blade.
Be cruelty with kindness paid.

Sharvilaka. Then tell me what I may yet do for you.

Chārudatta. Can there be more than this?

I kept unstained my virtue's even worth,
Granted my enemy his abject suit;
Friend Aryaka destroyed his foeman's root,
And rules a king o'er all the steadfast earth.
This dear-loved maiden is at last mine own,
And you united with me as a friend.
And shall I ask for further mercies, shown
To me, who cannot sound these mercies' end? 58

Fate plays with us like buckets at the well,
Where one is filled, and one an empty shell,
Where one is rising, while another falls;
And shows how life is change—now heaven, now hell. 59

Yet may the wishes of our epilogue be fulfilled.

Epilogue

May kine yield streaming milk, the earth her grain,
And may the heaven give never-failing rain,
  The winds waft happiness to all that breathes,
And all that lives, live free from every pain.
In paths of righteousness may Brahmans tread,
And high esteem their high deserving wed;
May kings in justice' ways be ever led,
And earth, submissive, bend her grateful head. 60

(*Exeunt omnes.*)

Part Two

JAPANESE DRAMA

The Nō Play

The Japanese Nō play, at least partly because it is an approach to drama so different from anything in the West, has appealed strongly to certain Western writers and theorists interested in poetic drama. The poet William Butler Yeats was powerfully moved both by the symbolic and evocative force of the Nō and by the simplicity of the stage and of the acting technique. Of the Nō play and of its inspiration to him Yeats said:

> It is natural that I go to Asia for a stage-convention, for more formal faces, for a chorus that has no part in the action and perhaps for those movements of the body copied from the marionette shows of the fourteenth century. A mask will enable me to substitute for the face of some commonplace player, or for that face repainted to suit his own vulgar fancy, the fine invention of a sculptor, and to bring the audience close enough to the play to hear every inflection of the voice. . . . With the help of these plays . . . I have invented a form of drama, distinguished, indirect and symbolic. . . .[1]

Yeats' writings on the Nō and the publication in 1915 of translations by Ernest Fenollosa and Ezra Pound generated a persistent interest in the form among Western thinkers on the drama.

The appeal of the Nō play is various and its limitations from the point of view of the Western dramatic tradition—if one considers them limitations—are obvious. The Nō is

[1] Introduction to *Certain Noble Plays of Japan* by Ezra Pound and Ernest Fenollosa, reprinted in *The Classic Noh Theatre of Japan* (New York: New Directions, 1959), pp. 151, 155.

poetic in the best sense: the style is lofty and subtle rather than dramatic, and the nuance rather than direct statement carries the burden of the literary effect. Echoes of older Japanese poems permeate the texts, as do quotations from Buddhist scriptures. The nature of the Japanese language makes it easy for the poet to create serious puns in the form of homonyms; thus, suggestions of place names emerge with their appropriate historical and legendary connotations. The action of the drama is often in the form of reminiscence of or flashback to the past. The action depicted, that is to say, occurred in the distant past, and either the main character retells it as a memory or a spirit from the past reenacts the incident. No suspense is possible because the outcome of the action is known and has long since been accomplished. A further estrangement of the audience from involvement in the action is accomplished by highly formalized acting techniques. The acting is in the form of a slow-moving and stately dance, with no attempt at realism of any kind, and with a vocabulary of dance steps and gestures to indicate levels of emotional intensity and the kinds of emotions depicted. A Westerner at Nō performances may at first have difficulty in determining just what kind of emotion is depicted and the degree of intensity of it, but study of the plays and regular attendance dissipate this confusion. Relatively little room is given to the individual interpretations of the actor and none to his personality, at least from our Western point of view. As in the Greek drama, masks are used, but usually only by the protagonist, his adversary, and women. Again, as in the Greek drama, there is a chorus.

The Nō stage is small and bare of properties. It is a square, raised platform with a roof, open on two sides, and isolated from the audience by a bare area of small stones or, in the case of the stage at the famous shrine of Itsukushima at Miyajima, by a moat filled with the waters of the sea. To the left and rear of the stage may be found the musicians with their flutes and drums. They enter and leave through a small door at the back of the stage on the right. From the left side of the stage, extending a considerable distance (more than the width of the stage) into the wings, is a runway, the *hashigakari*. The main characters in the drama enter through curtains at the far left of the theater and walk in solemn procession down the *hashigakari* onto the stage proper. This they do in full view of the audience during appropriate lulls in the on-stage action. Since the amount of time necessary for the character to enter in this fashion is considerable, this would seem to be a break in the dramatic action, but actually the entrances engender dramatic tension even though they keep the action at a snail's pace. The stage is constructed of unpainted but beautiful wood, the floor being designed to resound with the footbeats of the dancers. A pine tree is usually painted on the back wall of the stage, but there is no other decoration except the costumes of the actors and a few props.

The costumes of the actors are great works of art, gorgeous and complicated. Occasionally they are used for various kinds of "stage business": in *Aoi no Uye* the beautiful woman, hiding herself in the folds of her gown, switches from the mask of a beautiful woman to the mask of the hideous, horned demon of jealousy on stage. This is done with the assistance of a prop man who is visible but dressed in black and trained to act inconspicuously. In the same play, to represent the body of Lady Aoi, who is on the verge of death from her jealous passion, a folded robe is placed on the stage.

Just as the costumes are among the most elaborate and refined in the world, the Nō masks also are works of art of considerable stature. They do not amplify the voice, as ancient Greek ones presumably did, and are most uncomfortable to wear and to sing through. The actors sing or chant their words in a fashion somewhat like the recitative of Western opera. The music is mostly drums and the flute. It is totally unlike Western music but one becomes used to it and it is quickly apparent how the music heightens the dramatic action. The aesthetics of the Nō, as we shall see, assume a happy marriage of the vocal element and the dance element with each other and with the mood of the audience. Because of their poetic and essentially undramatic nature, the Nō plays have seemed to many Westerners poems with dance accompaniments rather than dramas. The passions exhibited, no matter how strong they may actually be in theory, are muted by formal acting, poetic nuance, and the fact that the action has taken place in the distant past and is being retold long after the event. Buddhist attitudes toward reality, especially the attitude that the world of the flesh is transient and passes like blossoms or drifting smoke, further diminish the dramatic impact of the plots of these plays, though they accentuate the poetic moods. Like the Sanskrit drama, the Japanese Nō drama is essentially the depiction of emotional states rather than the unfolding of a plot. But the Sanskrit drama places much more stress on plot than the Nō drama and the Nō drama is somewhat more restricted in emotional range, though infinitely subtle variations are possible within this range.

Most of the several hundred plays in the Nō repertory date from the fourteenth and fifteenth centuries. The Nō drama seems to have originated in folk dances. An early name for Nō is *sarugaku,* which means "monkey music," a name indicating a relationship of the drama to a lively type of dance about which little is known. Another early source of the form was the religious pageantry connected with certain shrines at festival times. The term for this is *dengaku* or "field music." The *sarugaku* may go back several centuries before the Nō, and the *dengaku* to the thirteenth century. Little is actually known of either of these semi-dramatic dance forms. They were taken by two great dramatists, Kanami Kiyotsugu (1333–1384) and his son Zeami (or Seami) Motokiyo (1363–1443), and elevated to a court drama that became one of the major artistic expressions of Heian Japan. It was probably Kanami and Zeami who brought the powerful influence of early Japanese poetic techniques into the Nō drama. The 5-7-5 syllable arrangement of Japanese verse entered the drama, as did both the rhetorical techniques of the poetry and the plots from early verse and legends. In some cases lines from early poems appear with little change in the plays.

Zeami especially brought the Nō play to its heights with his combination of literary and dramatic talent and extensive speculation on the theory of drama. He left a number of treatises on the various problems of creating and performing plays as well as a large repertoire of plays. He saw the dramatist's problem as a theatrical one, not a literary one, an attitude which has endeared him and the Nō drama to those Westerners who see literary considerations outweighing all others in the Western dramatic tradition to the detriment of theater. Zeami believed that the dramatist must harmonize the literary, the musical, and the dance elements into a whole and must also vary this entity with the mood of the audience, which he saw as being affected by a number of elements such as the time of day, the weather, the presence of nobility at the performance, and the mood of the immediately preceding dramatic construction. Zeami felt that one man—a director, actor, dancer, poet—must weld all of the elements into a whole. Flashes of Zen Buddhist intuition would have to guide this man: a fascinating passage in Zeami describes how the entering actor must instantly analyze the mood of the audience and vary his singing and dancing to fit this mood. The actor, Zeami felt, must dedicate his life to the Nō with the devotion of a religious fanatic.

The Nō plays were formerly presented as a cycle of five plays interspersed with short farces (*kyōgen*) and would take all of an afternoon to perform. The first play in the cycle was a god-play (*kami-* or *waki-nō*) or a religious play celebrating an auspicious religious event. This was followed by a warrior play (*shura-mono*), certainly to us a more interesting group. The warrior in such plays is usually a famous one of the Taira or Minamoto clans, which engaged in constant strife in the twelfth century and are celebrated in the narrative chronicles that are the closest approximation to epic in Japanese literature. Although sometimes battles between two heroes are acted out symbolically in the Nō plays, there is no "blood and thunder" action in the Western sense. The bloody wars are seen through the mists of time as in a dream only partly recalled. Zeami has left us about fourteen of these. The third group of plays was about women, so-called wig plays (*kazura-mono*). These have an air of elegant beauty and have been called the most typical of all Nō plays. A fourth group of plays includes various types, among them "living persons pieces" (*genzai-mono*). *Benkei on the Bridge* (*Hashi-Benkei*) celebrates an incident in the early life of a hero who appears in the Kabuki play *The Subscription List* (p. 393). *The Soga Brothers Attack by Night* (*Yo-uchi Soga*) chronicles an episode in the careers of members of a famous family, also represented later in the Kabuki drama. A most interesting type included in the fourth group is certainly the "madwoman pieces" (*kyōjo-mono*). In these, grief or unrequited love withers away the victim, jealousy becomes a poisonous passion, or, more simply, beauty fades and dies. Perhaps the most appealing plays to Westerners are in this group or in the warrior group. The fifth and final group is labeled "auspicious plays" (*kiri-nō*) and the most interesting ones are concerned with elves, demons, goblins and such minor supernatural creatures. But also in this group are congratulatory pieces which celebrate some important event.

The farces that are interspersed with the Nō plays depend on both verbal and clownish elements for their humor and are frequently slapstick. The Japanese sees no aesthetic problem in moving from the pathos of a serious play to the farce and then quickly back again to the mood of the Nō.

The literary style of the Nō play is complicated. In the first place, it is a high literary style with echoes of quotations from sacred scripture and other written sources. Also,

Japan is a small and homogeneous country and there scarcely exists a site the mention of which does not bring to mind historical allusions. The Japanese language has a large number of words that differ in meaning but are pronounced the same (in the writing system these would be distinguished by different ideographs). The resultant "punning" makes for double entendre with both common and proper nouns, and the mere echoing of a place name gives rise to thoughts of ancient legends or events. Deliberate ambiguities of meaning, including the famous "pivot word," make a transition from one complex of images to another, a device not by any means unknown in the West but carried to greater lengths in Japanese.[2] The audience for the plays must have been highly sophisticated in the days of Zeami. Today, devotees sometimes carry printed texts to which they refer as the plays proceed. The music of the plays, made mostly by the flute and a variety of drums, seems monotonous on records, but is less so in the theater. The tempo varies subtly and adds excitement to the moments of greatest dramatic intensity.

[2] See Donald Keene, *Japanese Literature, An Introduction for Western Readers* (New York: Evergreen, 1955), pp. 3–10, 55–57, for a discussion of "pivot words" and other matters of poetic style.

A Cycle of Nō Plays

From The Nō plays of Japan, *translated by Arthur Waley. London: George Allen and Unwin Ltd., 1921; New York: Grove Press, 1957. Reprinted by permission of George Allen and Unwin Ltd. and Grove Press.*

Haku Rakuten

ZEAMI

Haku Rakuten is a *kami-nō,* a play about the gods, and is therefore in the first group of the five-play cycle. It is about the Chinese poet Po Chü-i (A.D. 722–847),[1] who was known as Haku Rakuten in Japan. Although the Japanese language is not related to Chinese, the Japanese borrowed the ideographic characters they use for writing from the Chinese, absorbed Buddhism from China by way of Korea, and were much influenced by Chinese art and culture. Chinese was occasionally both a language of the court and of literature in early Japan,[2] and among the various Chinese poets admired in Japan, Po Chü-i was a favorite. In the ninth century, Waley tells us, Chinese influence was powerful and "native forms of poetry were for a time threatened with extinction."[3] The play deals with this crisis in literary history. Po Chü-i did not actually visit Japan, but his influence was great, and Zeami quotes him elsewhere.

To the Westerner, the veneration for poetry, which is the cultural heritage of the Chinese and Japanese, is remarkable, and never more than in this play, in which a semi-divine Chinese poet attempts a conquest of Japan and is repulsed by a Japanese god of poetry.

[1] See Arthur Waley, *The Life and Times of Po Chü-i* (London: Allen and Unwin Ltd., 1949).

[2] Some Japanese poetry written in Chinese is translated by Donald Keene in *Anthology of Japanese Literature from the Earliest Era to the Mid-Nineteenth Century* (New York: Grove Press, 1955).

[3] *The Nō Plays of Japan,* Arthur Waley, ed. (New York: Grove Press, 1957). p. 248.

CHARACTERS

RAKUTEN, *a Chinese poet*
AN OLD FISHERMAN, SUMIYOSHI NO KAMI, *who in Act II becomes the God of Japanese poetry*
ANOTHER FISHERMAN
CHORUS OF FISHERMEN

Scene: The coast of Bizen in Japan.

Haku Rakuten

ACT I

Haku. I am Haku Rakuten, a courtier of the Prince of China. There is a land in the East called Nippon.[a] Now, at my master's bidding, I am sent to that land to make proof of the wisdom of its people. I must travel over the paths of the sea.
I will row my boat towards the setting sun,
The setting sun;
And seek the country that lies to the far side
Over the wave-paths of the Eastern Sea.
Far my boat shall go,
My boat shall go,—
With the light of the setting sun in the waves of its wake
And a cloud like a banner shaking the void of the sky.
Now the moon rises, and on the margin of the sea
A mountain I discern.
I am come to the land of Nippon,
The land of Nippon.
So swiftly have I passed over the ways of the ocean that I am come already to the shores of Nippon. I will cast anchor here a little while. I would know what manner of land this may be.

The Two Fishermen (together).
Dawn over the Sea of Tsukushi,
Place of the Unknown Fire.
Only the moonlight—nothing else left!

The Old Fisherman.
The great waters toss and toss;
The grey waves soak the sky.

[a] Haku calls Japan "Nippon," indicating that he is a foreigner. The fishermen, using the same word, pronounce it "Nihon." Both of these forms are in use today.

The Two Fishermen.

So was it when Han Rei left the land of Etsu
And rowed in a little boat
Over the misty waves of the Five Lakes.[b]
How pleasant the sea looks!
From the beach of Matsura
Westward we watch the hill-less dawn.
A cloud, where the moon is setting,
Floats like a boat at sea,
A boat at sea
That would anchor near us in the dawn.
Over the sea from the far side,
From China the journey of a ship's travel
Is a single night's sailing, they say.
And lo! the moon has vanished!

Haku. I have borne with the billows of a thousand miles of sea and come at last to the land of Nippon. Here is a little ship anchored near me. An old fisherman is in it. Can this be indeed an inhabitant of Nippon?

Old Fisherman. Aye, so it is. I am an old fisher of Nihon. And your Honor, I think, is Haku Rakuten of China.

Haku. How strange! No sooner am I come to this land than they call me by my name! How can this be?

Second Fisherman. Although your Honor is a man of China, your name and fame have come before you.

Haku. Even though my name be known, yet that you should know my face is strange surely!

The Two Fishermen. It was said everywhere in the Land of Sunrise that your Honor, Rakuten, would come to make trial of the wisdom of Nihon. And when, as we gazed westwards, we saw a boat coming in from the open sea, the hearts of us all thought in a twinkling, "This is he."

Chorus.

"He has come, he has come."
So we cried when the boat came in
To the shore of Matsura,
The shore of Matsura.
Sailing in from the sea
Openly before us—
A Chinese ship
And a man from China,—

[b] Haku lands in the district of Bizen, on the north shore of the Inland Sea. The fishermen are vaguely groping for the idea of a "Chinaman." They have heard the Chinese legend of Fan Li (Han Rei), sailing from Yüeh (Etsu) in a boat, but they are not yet conscious of the coming arrival of Haku.

How could we fail to know you,
Haku Rakuten?
But your halting words tire us.
Listen as we will, we cannot understand
Your foreign talk.
Come, our fishing-time is precious.
Let us cast our hooks,
Let us cast our hooks!

Haku. Stay! Answer me one question.[c] Bring your boat closer and tell me, Fisherman, what is your pastime now in Nippon?

Fisherman. And in the land of China, pray how do your Honors disport yourselves?

Haku. In China we play at making poetry.

Fisherman. And in Nihon, may it please you, we venture on the sport of making "uta." [d]

Haku. And what are "uta"?

Fisherman. You in China make your poems and odes out of the Scriptures of India; and we have made our "uta" out of the poems and odes of China. Since then our poetry is a blend of three lands, we have named it Yamato,[e] the great Blend, and all our songs "Yamato Uta." But I think you question me only to mock an old man's simplicity.

Haku. No, truly; that was not my purpose. But come, I will sing a Chinese poem about the scene before us.

"Green moss donned like a cloak
Lies on the shoulders of the rocks;
White clouds drawn like a belt
Surround the flanks of the mountains."

How does that song please you?

Fisherman. It is indeed a pleasant verse. In our tongue we should say the poem thus:

Koke-goromo
Kitaru iwao wa
Samonakute,

[c] Haku omits the honorific terms that polite speech demands. He sounds like an ill-bred foreigner. The fishermen speak in elaborately deferential language.

[d] The *uta* is the 31-syllable Japanese stanza, a favorite poetic form.

[e] Yamato is the Japanese heartland: the region from Kyōto south into Ōsaka and Wakayama prefectures.

Kinu kinu yama no
Obi wo suru kana! [f]

Haku. How strange that a poor fisherman should put m verse into a sweet native measure! Who can he be?

Fisherman. A poor man and unknown. But as for the mak ing of "uta," it is not only men that make them. "Fo among things that live there is none that has not the gif of song."

Haku (*taking up the other's words as if hypnotized*) "Among things that have life,—yes, and birds and in sects—"

Fisherman. They have sung Yamato songs.

Haku. In the land of Yamato . . .

Fisherman. . . . many such have been sung.

Chorus.
"The nightingale singing on the bush,
Even the frog that dwells in the pond——"
I know not if it be in your Honor's land,
But in Nihon they sing the stanzas of the "uta."
And so it comes that an old man
Can sing the song you have heard,
A song of great Yamato.

Chorus (*changing the chant*).
And as for the nightingale and the poem it made,—
They say that in the royal reign
Of the Emperor Kōren
In the land of Yamato, in the temple of High Heaven
A priest was dwelling.[g]
Each year at the season of Spring
There came a nightingale
To the plum-tree at his window.
And when he listened to its song
He heard it singing a verse:
"Sho-yō mei-chō rai
Fu-sō gem-bon sei."
And when he wrote down the characters,
Behold, it was an "uta"-song

[f] This is a quotation from the ancient Japanese poetic anthology the *Kokinshū,* compiled in 951 A.D. Waley says, "The fact that Hak continues the quotation shows that he is under a sort of spell an makes it clear for the first time that his interlocuter is not a ordinary mortal. From this point onwards, in fact, the Fisherma gradually becomes a God." (All quotations from Arthur Waley ar from *The Nō Plays of Japan.* New York: Grove Press, 1957. Thi quotation is from p. 253.)

[g] The nightingale is the soul of a boy, the priest's acolyte, wh has died.

Of thirty letters and one.
And the words of the song—

Fisherman.

Hatsu-haru no	Of Spring's beginning
Ashita goto ni wa	At each dawn
Kitaredomo	Though I come,

Chorus.

Awade zo kaeru	Unmet I return
Moto no sumika ni.	To my old nest.

Thus first the nightingale,
And many birds and beasts thereto,
Sing "uta," like the songs of men.
And instances are many;
Many as the myriad pebbles that lie
On the shore of the sea of Ariso.
"For among things that live
There is none that has not the gift of song."

Truly the fisherman has the ways of Yamato in his heart. Truly, this custom is excellent.

Fisherman. If we speak of the sports of Yamato and sing its songs, we should show too what dances we use; for there are many kinds.

Chorus. Yes, there are the dances; but there is no one to dance.

Fisherman. Though there be no dancer, yet even I—

Chorus.
For drums—the beating of the waves.
For flutes—the song of the sea-dragon.
For dancer—this ancient man
Despite his furrowed brow
Standing on the furrowed sea
Floating on the green waves
Shall dance the Sea Green Dance.

Fisherman. And the land of Reeds and Rushes . . .

Chorus. Ten thousand years our land inviolate!

(*The rest of the play is a kind of "ballet"; the words are merely a commentary on the dances.*)

ACT II

Fisherman (*transformed into* Sumiyoshi no Kami, *the God of Poetry*).
Sea that is green with the shadow of the hills in the water!
Sea Green Dance, danced to the beating of the waves.

(*He dances the Sea Green Dance.*)

Out of the wave-lands,
Out of the fields of the Western Sea

Chorus.
He rises before us,
The God of Sumiyoshi,
The God of Sumiyoshi!

The God.
I rise before you
The god—

Chorus.
The God of Sumiyoshi whose strength is such
That he will not let you subdue us, O Rakuten!
So we bid you return to your home,
Swiftly over the waves of the shore!
First the God of Sumiyoshi came.
Now other gods [h] have come—
Of Isé and Iwa-shimizu,
Of Kamo and Kasuga,
Of Ka-shima and Mi-shima,
Of Suwa and Atsu-ta.
And the goddess of the Beautiful Island,
The daughter of Shakāra

[h] These gods do not appear on the stage.

King of the Dragons of the Sea—
Skimming the face of the waves
They have danced the Sea Green Dance.
And the King of the Eight Dragons—
With his Symphony of Eight Musics.
As they hovered over the void of the sea,
Moved in the dance, the sleeves of their dancing-dress
Stirred up a wind, a magic wind
That blew on the Chinese boat
And filled its sails
And sent it back again to the land of Han.[1]
Truly, the God is wondrous;
The God is wondrous, and thou, our Prince,
Mayest thou rule for many, many years
    Our Land Inviolate!

[1] China.

Atsumori at Ikuta

(*IKUTA ATSUMORI*)

Zembō Motoyasu (1453–1532)

Atsumori was a young warrior who fell in the battle of Ichi-no-Tani in 1184. He was a youth of great beauty and his death is depicted as pathetic rather than heroic in the *Tale of Heike* (*Heike monogatari*),[1] which chronicles the bloody wars between the Minamoto (Genji) and the Taira (Heike) clans. Atsumori is also the subject of a play by Zeami.[2]

This is a play of the second group, a *shura-mono* or warrior play, despite the fact that the battle has long since been fought. The clash of arms is described by the chorus in the middle of the play; this is about as much action as the Nō play permits.

Although Yama, the king of Hell, is mentioned, we can imagine Atsumori banished by death, like a Greek hero, to existence in the shades—not to a Christian hell of eternal punishment—and condemned to long for his earthly life and to reenact it until eventually these longings are burned out and rest finally comes.

1 Translated by A. L. Sadler in *The Ten Foot Square Hut and Tales of the Heike* (Sydney: Angus and Robertson, 1928). The death of Atsumori is reprinted in Anderson, *Masterpieces of the Orient* (New York: W. W. Norton & Co., 1961), pp. 331ff. A brief summary of the Genji-Heike wars is in *The Kabuki Handbook* by Halford and Halford (see Bibliography), pp. 418–425.

2 Translated by Arthur Waley in *The Nō Plays of Japan* (New York: Grove Press, 1957).

CHARACTERS

PRIEST, *a follower of Hōnen Shōnin*
ATSUMORI
ATSUMORI'S CHILD
CHORUS

Atsumori at Ikuta

Priest. I am one that serves Hōnen Shōnin[a] of Kurodani; and as for this child here,—once when Hōnen was on a visit to the Temple of Kamo he saw a box lying under a trailing fir-tree; and when he raised the lid, what should he find inside but a lovely man-child one year old! It did not seem to be more than a common foundling, but my master in his compassion took the infant home with him. Ever since then he has had it in his care, doing all that was needful for it; and now the boy is over ten years old.

But it is a hard thing to have no father or mother, so one day after his preaching the Shōnin told the child's story. And sure enough a young woman stepped out from among the hearers and said it was her child. And when he took her aside and questioned her, he found that the child's father was Taira no Atsumori, who had fallen in battle at Ichi-no-Tani years ago. When the boy was told of this, he longed earnestly to see his father's face, were it but in a dream, and the Shōnin bade him go and pray at the shrine of Kamo. He was to go every day for a week, and this is the last day.

That is why I have brought him out with me.
But here we are at the Kamo shrine.
Pray well, boy, pray well!

[a] Hōnen (1133–1212), also known as Genkū, was the founder of the Jōdo or Pure Land school of Buddhism. He lived through the Minamoto-Taira struggle and later retired to the temple of Kurodani on the outskirts of Kyōto.

Boy.
How fills my heart with awe
When I behold the crimson palisade
Of this abode of gods!
Oh may my heart be clean
As the River of Ablution; [b]
And the God's kindness deep
As its unfathomed waters. Show to me,
Though it were but in a dream,
My father's face and form.
Is not my heart so ground away with prayer,
So smooth that it will slip
Unfelt into the favor of the gods?
But thou too, Censor of our prayers,
God of Tadasu,[c] on the gods prevail
That what I crave may be!
How strange! While I was praying I fell half-asleep and had a wonderful dream.

Priest. Tell me your wonderful dream.

Boy. A strange voice spoke to me from within the Treasure Hall, saying, "If you are wanting, though it were but in a dream, to see your father's face, go down from here to the woods of Ikuta in the country of Settsu." That is the marvelous dream I had.

Priest. It is indeed a wonderful message that the God has sent you. And why should I go back at once to Kurodani? I had best take you straight to the forest of Ikuta. Let us be going.

Priest (*describing the journey*).
From the shrine of Kamo,
From under the shadow of the hills,
We set out swiftly;
Past Yamazaki [d] to the fog-bound
Shores of Minasé;
And onward where the gale
Tears travelers' coats and winds about their bones.

[b] The name given to streams that flow through temples. Here perhaps the River Kamo, which flows through Kyōto.

[c] Tadasu is a wood near Kyōto in which the shrine of Kamo was located. There is a pun here: *tadasu* also means "to correct" or "straighten."

[d] Yamazaki is close to southwest Kyōto on the road to present-day Ōsaka. They move westward along the northern shore of the Inland Sea. The Ikuta woods, now a shrine, were near Sannomiya in the heart of modern Kobe.

"Autumn has come to woods where yesterday
We might have plucked the green." [e]
To Settsu, to those woods of Ikuta
Lo! we are come.
We have gone so fast that here we are already at the woods of Ikuta in the country of Settsu. I have heard tell in the Capital of the beauty of these woods and the river that runs through them. But what I see now surpasses all that I have heard.
Look! Those meadows must be the Downs at Ikuta.
Let us go nearer and admire them.
But while we have been going about looking at one view and another, the day has dusked.
I think I see a light over there. There must be a house.
Let us go to it and ask for lodging.

Atsumori (speaking from inside a hut).
Beauty, perception, knowledge, motion, consciousness,—
The Five Attributes of Being,—
All are vain mockery.
How comes it that men prize
So weak a thing as body?
For the soul that guards it from corruption
Suddenly to the night-moon flies,
And the poor naked ghost wails desolate
In the autumn wind.
Oh! I am lonely. I am lonely!

Priest. How strange! Inside that grass-hut I see a young soldier dressed in helmet and breastplate. What can he be doing there?

Atsumori. Oh foolish men, was it not to meet me that you came to this place? I am—oh! I am ashamed to say it,—I am the ghost of what once was . . . Atsumori.

Boy. Atsumori? My father . . .

Chorus.
And lightly he ran,
Plucked at the warrior's sleeve,
And though his tears might seem like the long woe
Of nightingales that weep,
Yet were they tears of meeting-joy,
Of happiness too great for human heart.
So think we, yet oh that we might change
This fragile dream of joy
Into the lasting love of waking life!

[e] Adapted from a poem in the *Shin-kokinshū,* a famous early anthology of Japanese poetry.

Atsumori.

Oh pitiful!
To see this child, born after me,
Darling that should be gay as a flower,
Walking in tattered coat of old black cloth.
Alas!
Child, when your love of me
Led you to Kamo shrine, praying to the God
That, though but in a dream,
You might behold my face,
The God of Kamo, full of pity, came
To Yama, king of Hell.
King Yama listened and ordained for me
A moment's respite, but hereafter, never.

Chorus.

"The moon is sinking.
Come while the night is dark," he said,
"I will tell my tale."

Atsumori.

When the house of Taira was in its pride,
When its glory was young,
Among the flowers we sported,
Among birds, wind and moonlight;
With pipes and strings, with song and verse
We welcomed Springs and Autumns.
Till at last, because our time was come,
Across the bridges of Kiso a host unseen
Swept and devoured us.
Then the whole clan
Our lord leading
Fled from the City of Flowers.
By paths untrodden
To the Western Sea our journey brought us.
Lakes and hills we crossed
Till we ourselves grew to be like wild men.
At last by mountain ways—
We too tossed hither and thither like its waves—
To Suma [f] came we,
To the First Valley and the woods of Ikuta.
And now while all of us,
We children of Taira, were light of heart
Because our homes were near,

[f] Suma is farther along the coast of the Inland Sea, at the western edge of Kobe. A stone pagoda named after Atsumori is at Suma and is believed to mark the spot where he was buried. The battle of Ichi-no-tani was fought nearby.

Suddenly our foes in great strength appeared.

Chorus.

Noriyori, Yoshitsune,—their hosts like clouds,
Like mists of spring.
For a little while we fought them,
But the day of our House was ended,
Our hearts weakened
That had been swift as arrows from the bowstring,
We scattered, scattered; till at last
To the deep waters of the Field of Life[g]
We came, but how we found there Death, not Life,
What profit were it to tell?

Atsumori. Who is that? (*Pointing in terror at a figure which he sees off the stage.*) Can it be Yama's messenger? He comes to tell me that I have outstayed my time. The Lord of Hell is angry: he asks why I am late?

Chorus.

So he spoke. But behold
Suddenly black clouds rise,
Earth and sky resound with the clash of arms;
War-demons[h] innumerable
Flash fierce sparks from brandished spears.

Atsumori.

The Shura foes who night and day
Come thick about me!

Chorus.

He waves his sword and rushes among them,
Hither and thither he runs slashing furiously;
Fire glints upon the steel.
But in a little while
The dark clouds recede;
The demons have vanished,
The moon shines unsullied;
The sky is ready for dawn.

Atsumori.

Oh! I am ashamed. . . .
And the child to see me so. . . .

Chorus.

"To see my misery!
I must go back.
Oh pray for me; pray for me
When I am gone," he said,
And weeping, weeping,

[g] Ikuta means "Field of Life."
[h] A *shura* is a demon–i.e., the warriors are like demons.

Dropped the child's hand.
He has faded; he dwindles
Like the dew from rush-leaves
Of hazy meadows.
His form has vanished.

Early Snow

HATSUYUKI

Zembō Motoyasu (1453-1532)

The third group of plays in the traditional five-play cycle is a *kazura-mono* or "female wig play," but many of the more interesting plays about women belong to the "mad-woman" plays of the fourth group. *Early Snow* is a very simple play. A noble lady keeps a pure white pet bird—presumably a large bird, more like a chicken or a duckling than a songbird—which disappears. At the end of the play, she learns that the bird has been reborn in the Buddhist paradise. Buddhist doctrine does not make the sharp distinction that Christianity makes between man and the other animals of creation, and it is as reasonable for a bird to be reincarnated or translated to paradise as for a man. Moreover, the Japanese immersion in nature makes birds and flowers conventional symbols of various states of transition in life, somewhat more than in the West.

CHARACTERS

EVENING MIST, *a servant girl*
A LADY, *the Abbot's daughter*
TWO NOBLE LADIES
THE SOUL OF THE BIRD HATSUYUKI ("EARLY SNOW")
CHORUS

Scene: The great temple at Izumo

Early Snow

Servant. I am a servant at the Nyoroku Shrine in the Great Temple of Izumo.[a] My name is Evening Mist. You must know that the Lord Abbot has a daughter, a beautiful lady and gentle as can be. And she keeps a tame bird that was given her a year ago, and because it was a lovely white bird she called it Hatsuyuki, Early Snow; and she loves it dearly.
I have not seen the bird to-day. I think I will go to the bird-cage and have a look at it. (*She goes to the cage.*) Mercy on us, the bird is not there! Whatever shall I say to my lady? But I shall have to tell her. I think I'll tell her now. Madam, madam, your dear Snow-bird is not here!

Lady. What is that you say? Early Snow is not there? It cannot be true. (*She goes to the cage.*) It is true. Early Snow has gone! How can that be? How can it be that my pretty one that was so tame should vanish and leave no trace?
Oh bitterness of snows
That melt and disappear!
Now do I understand
The meaning of a midnight dream
That lately broke my rest.
A harbinger it was
Of Hatsuyuki's fate.

(*She bursts into tears.*)

Chorus.
Though for such tears and sighs

[a] The Izumo shrine, the oldest Shintō shrine in Japan, is about twenty-five miles west of Matsue in Shimane prefecture.

There be no cause,
Yet came her grief so suddenly,
Her heart's fire is ablaze;
And all the while
Never a moment are her long sleeves dry.
They say that written letters first were traced
By feet of birds in sand
Yet Hatsuyuki leaves no testament.

(*They mourn.*)

Chorus (*"kuse" chant, irregular verse accompanied by dancing*).
How sad to call to mind
When first it left the breeding-cage
So fair of form
And colored white as snow.
We called it Hatsuyuki, "Year's First Snow."
And where our mistress walked
It followed like the shadow at her side.
But now alas! it is a bird of parting[b]
Though not in Love's dark lane.

Lady. There's no help now.

(*She weeps bitterly.*)

Chorus.
Still there is one way left. Stop weeping, Lady,
And turn your heart to him who vowed to hear.
The Lord Amida, if a prayer be said—
Who knows but he can bring
Even a bird's soul into Paradise
And set it on the Lotus Pedestal?[c]

Lady. Evening Mist, are you not sad that Hatsuyuki has gone? . . . But we must not cry any more. Let us call together the noble ladies of this place and for seven days sit with them praying behind barred doors. Go now and do my bidding.

(Evening Mist *fetches the* Noble Ladies *of the place.*)

Two Noble Ladies (*together*).

[b] Certain birds were known as *wakare no tori*—birds that warn lovers of the approach of day.

[c] That is, turn it into a Buddha, who sits on a pedestal of lotus flowers.

A solemn Mass we sing
A dirge for the Dead;
At this hour of heart-cleansing
We beat on Buddha's gong.

(*They pray.*)

Namu Amida Butsu
Namu Nyorai
Praise to Amida Buddha,
Praise to Mida our Saviour!

(*The prayers and gong-beating last for some time and form the central ballet of the play.*)

Chorus (*the bird's soul appears as a white speck in the sky*).
Look! Look! A cloud in the clear mid-sky!
But it is not a cloud.
With pure white wings beating the air
The Snow-bird comes!
Flying towards our lady
Lovingly he hovers,
Dances before her.

The Bird's Soul. Drawn by the merit of your prayers and songs

Chorus.
Straightway he was reborn in Paradise.
By the pond of Eight Virtues [d] he walks abroad:
With the Phoenix and Fugan his playtime passing.
He lodges in the sevenfold summit of the trees of Heaven.
No hurt shall harm him
For ever and ever.

Now like the tasseled doves we loose
From battlements on holy days
A little while he flutters;
Flutters a little while and then is gone
We know not where.

[d] The eight virtues are: right views, right aims, right speech, right action, right livelihood, right effort, right-mindfulness, and right posture. The Phoenix and Fugan are mythical birds associated with fire and longevity.

Aoi no Uye

Zenchiku Ujinobu (1414–1499?)

The fourth group of plays is a miscellaneous group in which the *kyōjo-mono* or "madwoman" pieces are included. Lady Aoi, the woman killed by jealousy, is a touching figure in Lady Murasaki's great novel, the *Tale of Genji.* Arthur Waley tells the story as follows:

At the age of twelve Prince Genji went through the ceremony of marriage with Aoi no Uye (Princess Hollyhock), the Prime Minister's daughter. She continued to live at her father's house and Genji at his palace. When he was about sixteen he fell in love with Princess Rokujō, the widow of the Emperor's brother; she was about eight years older than himself. He was not long faithful to her. The lady Yūgao next engaged his affections. He carried her one night to a deserted mansion on the outskirts of the City. "The night was far advanced and they had both fallen asleep. Suddenly the figure of a woman appeared at the bedside. 'I have found you!' it cried. 'What stranger is this that lies beside you? What treachery is this that you flaunt before my eyes?' And with these words the apparition stooped over the bed, and made as though to drag away the sleeping girl from Genji's side."

Before dawn Yūgao was dead, stricken by the "living phantom" of Rokujō, embodiment of her baleful jealousy.

Soon after this, Genji became reconciled with his wife Aoi, but continued to visit Rokujō. One day, at the Kamo Festival, Aoi's way was blocked by another carriage. She ordered her attendants to drag it aside.

A scuffle ensued between her servants and those of Rokujō (for she was the occupant of the second carriage) in which Aoi's side prevailed. Rokujō's carriage was broken and Aoi's pushed into the front place. After the festival was over Aoi returned to the Prime Minister's house in high spirits.

Soon afterwards she fell ill, and it is at this point that the play begins.

There is nothing obscure or ambiguous in the situation. Fenollosa seems to have misunderstood the play and read into it complications and confusions which do not exist. He also changes the sex of the Witch, though the Japanese word, *miko,* always has a feminine meaning. The "Romance of Genji" (*Genji Monogatari*) was written by Lady Murasaki Shikibu and was finished in the year 1004 A.D. Of its fifty-four chapters only seventeen have been translated. It furnished the plots of many Nō plays, of which *Suma Genji* (Genji's exile at Suma), *No no Miya* (his visit to Rokujō after she became a nun), *Tamakatsura* (the story of Yūgao's daughter), and *Hajitomi* (in which Yūgao's ghost appears) are the best known.

There is some doubt about the authorship of the play. Seami saw it acted as a Dengaku by his father's contemporary Inuō. He describes Inuō's entry on to the stage in the rôle of Rokujō and quotes the first six lines of her opening speech. These lines correspond exactly with the modern text, and it is probable that the play existed in something like its present form in the middle of the fourteenth century. Kwanze Nagatoshi, the great-grandson of Seami, includes it in a list of Seami's works; while popular tradition ascribes it to Seami's son-in-law Zenchiku.[1]

On the stage, the play generates considerable excitement. The ailing Lady Aoi is represented by a folded robe at the front of the stage, and over this sickbed the saint-priest and the demon of jealousy fight a fearful battle. A considerable shock sweeps the audience as the Lady Rokujō changes her mask from the placid face of a court lady to the hideous countenance of a two-horned devil. This is done on stage, her face hidden by the folds of her robe.

1 Waley, pp. 179–180.

CHARACTERS

OURTIER
ITCH
RINCESS ROKUJŌ
HE SAINT OF YOKAWA
ESSENGER
HORUS

Aoi no Uye

(*A folded cloak laid in front of the stage symbolizes the sick-bed of* Aoi.)

Courtier. I am a courtier in the service of the Emperor Shujaku. You must know that the Prime Minister's daughter, Princess Aoi, has fallen sick. We have sent for abbots and high-priests of the Greater School and of the Secret School, but they could not cure her.
And now, here at my side, stands the witch of Teruhi,[a] a famous diviner with the bow-string. My lord has been told that by twanging her bow-string she can make visible an evil spirit and tell if it be the spirit of a living man or a dead. So he bade me send for her and let her pluck her string. (*Turning to the* Witch, *who has been waiting motionless.*) Come, sorceress, we are ready!

Witch (*comes forward beating a little drum and reciting a mystic formula*).

Ten shōjō; chi shōjō.
Naige shōjō; rokon shōjō.
Pure above; pure below.
Pure without; pure within.
Pure in eyes, ears, heart and tongue.

(*She plucks her bow-string, reciting the spell.*)

You whom I call

[a] A witch (*miko*) named Teruhi is the subject of the play *Sanja Takusen.*

Hold loose the reins
On your grey colt's neck
As you gallop to me
Over the long sands!

(*The living phantasm of* Rokujō *appears at the back of the stage.*)

Rokujō.
In the Three Coaches
That travel on the Road of Law
I drove out of the Burning House . . .[b]
Is there no way to banish the broken coach
That stands at Yūgao's door? [c]
This world
Is like the wheels of the little ox-cart;
Round and round they go . . . till vengeance comes.
The Wheel of Life turns like the wheel of a coach;
There is no escape from the Six Paths and Four Births.[d]
We are brittle as the leaves of the *bashō;*
As fleeting as foam upon the sea.
Yesterday's flower, to-day's dream.
From such a dream were it not wiser to wake?
And when to this is added another's scorn
How can the heart have rest?
So when I heard the twanging of your bow
For a little while, I thought, I will take my pleasure;
And as an angry ghost appeared.
Oh! I am ashamed!

(*She veils her face.*)

[b] "Rokujō has left the 'Burning House,' i.e., her material body. The 'Three Coaches' are those of the famous 'Burning House' parable in the *Hokkekyō*. Some children were in a burning house. Intent on their play, they could not be induced to leave the building; till their father lured them out by the promise that they would find those little toy coaches awaiting them. So Buddha, by partial truth, lures men from the 'burning house' of their material lives. Owing to the episode at the Kamo Festival, Rokujō is obsessed by the idea of 'carriages,' 'wheels' and the like." (Waley, p. 182.)

[c] When Rokujō saw Prince Genji's coach before Yūgao's door, it was "broken" in the sense that he had removed his identifying insignia from it.

[d] Buddhist ways to enlightenment. The "Four Births" are four powers that must be felt in the heart and projected into the world: benevolence, compassion, sympathy, and equanimity.

This time too I have come secretly[e]
In a closed coach.
Though I sat till dawn and watched the moon,
Till dawn and watched,
How could I show myself,
That am no more than the mists that tremble over the fields?
I am come, I am come to the notch of your bow
To tell my sorrow.
Whence came the noise of the bow-string?

Witch. Though she should stand at the wife-door of the mother-house of the square court. . . .[f]

Rokujō. Yet would none come to me, that am not in the flesh.[g]

Witch. How strange! I see a fine lady whom I do not know riding in a broken coach. She clutches at the shafts of another coach from which the oxen have been unyoked. And in the second coach sits one who seems a new wife.[h] The lady of the broken coach is weeping, weeping. It is a piteous sight.
Can this be she?

Courtier. It would not be hard to guess who such a one might be. Come, spirit, tell us your name!

Rokujō.
In this Sahā[i] World where days fly like the lightning's flash
None is worth hating and none worth pitying.
This I knew. Oh when did folly master me?
You would know who I am that have come drawn by the twanging of your bow? I am the angry ghost of Rokujō, Lady of the Chamber.
Long ago I lived in the world.
I sat at flower-feasts among the clouds.[j]
On spring mornings I rode out
In royal retinue and on autumn nights

[e] Rokujō went secretly to the Kamo Festival in a closed carriage.

[f] These words are from an old dance-song.

[g] A play on words: "I am a ghost" but also "I have lost my beauty."

[h] That is, she is pregnant.

[i] A Sanskrit word for the "world of appearances."

[j] That is, at the palace.

Among the red leaves of the Rishis'[k] Cave
I sported with moonbeams,
With colors and perfumes
My senses sated.
I had splendor then;
But now I wither like the Morning Glory
Whose span endures not from dawn to midday.
I have come to clear my hate.

She then quotes the Buddhist saying, "Our sorrows in this world are not caused by others; for even when others wrong us we are suffering the retribution of our own deeds in a previous existence."
'ut while singing these words she turns towards Aoi's *bed; passion again seizes her and she cries*):

I am full of hatred.
I must strike; I must strike.[l]

She creeps towards the bed.)

'*itch.* You, Lady Rokujō, you are a Lady of the Chamber! Would you lay wait and strike as peasant women do? How can this be? Think and forbear!
:okujō. Say what you will, I must strike. I must strike now. (*Describing her own action.*) "And as she said this, she went over to the pillow and struck at it."

She strikes at the head of the bed with her fan.)

'*itch.* She is going to strike again. (*To* Rokujō.) You shall pay for this!
okujō. And this hate too is payment for past hate.
'*itch.* "The flame of anger
okujō. Consumes itself only."[m]
'*itch.* Did you not know?
okujō. Know it then now.
'*horus.*
O Hate, Hate!
Her hate so deep that on her bed

[k] Rishis are semi-divine spirits.

[l] Wives who had been supplanted were according to custom al- wed to strike the new wife to "clear their hate."

[m] From the Buddhist scripture known as the *Sūtrālankāra 'āstra.*

Our lady moans.
Yet, should she live in the world again,[n]
He would call her to him, her Lord
The Shining One, whose light
Is brighter than fire-fly hovering
Over the slime of an inky pool.

Rokujō.

But for me
There is no way back to what I was,
No more than to the heart of a bramble-thicket.
The dew that dries on the bramble-leaf
Comes back again;
But love (and this is worst)
That not even in dream returns,—
That is grown to be an old tale,—
Now, even now waxes,
So that standing at the bright mirror
I tremble and am ashamed.
I am come in my broken coach. (*She throws down her fan and begins to slip off her embroidered robe.*) I will hide you in it and carry you away!

(*She stands right over the bed, then turns away and at the back of the stage throws off her robe, which is held by two attendants in such a way that she cannot be seen. She changes her "deigan" mask for a female demon's mask and now carries a mallet in her hand.*)

(*Meanwhile the* Courtier, *who has been standing near the bed*):

Courtier. Come quickly, some one! Princess Aoi is worse. Every minute she is worse. Go and fetch the Little Saint of Yokawa.[o]

Messenger. I tremble and obey. (*He goes to the wing and speaks to some one off the stage.*) May I come in?

Saint (*speaking from the wing*). Who is it that seeks admittance to a room washed by the moonlight of the Three Mysteries, sprinkled with the holy water of Yoga? Who would draw near to a couch of the Ten Vehicles, a window of the Eight Perceptions?[p]

Messenger. I am come from the Court. Princess Aoi is ill.

[n] The chorus voices the hope that Aoi will recover.

[o] The hero of the "Finding of Ukifune," a later episode in the *Tale of Genji.*

[p] These are all approaches to salvation in Buddhism.

They would have you come to her.

Saint. It happens that at this time I am practicing particular austerities and go nowhere abroad. But if you are a messenger from the Court, I will follow you.

(*He comes on the stage.*)

Courtier. We thank you for coming.
Saint. I wait upon you. Where is the sick person?
Courtier. On the bed here.
Saint. Then I will begin my incantations at once.
Courtier. Pray do so.
Saint.
He said: "I will say my incantations."
Following in the steps of En no Gyōja,[q]
Clad in skirts that have trailed the Peak of the Two
Spheres,[r]
That have brushed the dew of the Seven Precious Trees,
Clad in the cope of endurance
That shields from the world's defilement,
"Sarari, sarari," with such sound
I shake the red wooden beads of my rosary
And say the first spell:
Namaku Samanda Basarada
Namaku Samanda Basarada.[s]

Rokujō (*during the incantation she has cowered at the back of the stage wrapped in her Chinese robe, which she has picked up again*). Go back, Gyōja, go back to your home; do not stay and be vanquished!

Saint. Be you what demon you will, do not hope to overcome the Gyōja's subtle power. I will pray again.

(*He shakes his rosary whilst the* Chorus, *speaking for him, invokes the first of the Five Kings.*) [t]

Chorus. In the east Gō Sanze, Subduer of the Three Worlds.

[q] Founder of a sect of mountain priests (*yamabushi*).

[r] Mount Ōmine is actually a range of mountains climbed by holy people in the Yoshino district, now a national park, which extends from Nara prefecture to Wakayama. Mt. Fuji is occasionally visible from the Ōmine peaks.

[s] Known as the lesser spell of the god Fudō. This consists of corrupt Sanskrit syllables mixed with meaningless magical sounds.

[t] The Myō-o are a group of gods especially sacred to the Shingon sect of Buddhism. The five major ones are listed here beginning with Gō Sanze (or Sensei).

Rokujō (*counter-invoking*). In the south Gundari Yasha.
Chorus. In the west Dai-itoku.
Rokujō. In the north Kongō.
Chorus. Yasha, the Diamond King.
Rokujō. In the center the Great Holy
Chorus.
Fudō Immutable.
Namaku Samanda Basarada
Senda Makaroshana
Sohataya Untaratakarman.
"They that hear my name shall get Great Enlightenment;
They that see my body shall attain to Buddhahood." [u]
Rokujō (*suddenly dropping her mallet and pressing her hands to her ears*). The voice of the Hannya Book! I am afraid. Never again will I come as an angry ghost.
Ghost.
When she heard the sound of Scripture
The demon's raging heart was stilled;
Shapes of Pity and Sufferance,
The Bodhisats [v] descend.
Her soul casts off its bonds,
She walks in Buddha's Way.

[u] From the Buddhist sacred book the *Hannya-kyō*, which was supposed to have a particular influence over female demons, who were called *hannyas*.

[v] Bodhisats or Bodhisattvas are semi-divine mediators between men and the Buddha.

Benkei on the Bridge

(*HASHI-BENKEI*)

Hiyoshi Sa-ami Yasukiyo (15th century?)

Benkei is a favorite hero of the Japanese, and the episode depicted in this *genzai-mono* will remind Western readers of the encounter between Robin Hood and Little John. Benkei, though a monk, became a redoubtable warrior. He is depicted in fiction and drama and in woodblock prints as a large, fierce man, clever and resourceful, and in every way the loyal retainer, the right-hand man of the hero. In this play he meets Ushiwara (Minamoto Yoshitsune) and, after a battle for superiority, becomes his devoted servant. In *The Subscription List* (p. 393) Benkei performs further feats of courage and ingenuity for his noble lord. The encounter in the play takes place on the famous Gojō bridge over the Kamo River in Kyōto.

Benkei on the Bridge is in the fourth group of the traditional cycle.

CHARACTERS

BENKEI
USHIWAKA
FOLLOWER
CHORUS

Benkei on the Bridge

Benkei. I am one who lives near the Western Pagoda. My name is Musashi-bō Benkei. In fulfillment of a certain vow I have been going lately by night at the hour of the Ox[a] to worship at the Gojō Temple.[b] To-night is the last time; I ought soon to be starting.
Hie! Is any one there?

Follower. Here I am.

Benkei. I sent for you to tell you that I shall be going to the Gojō Temple to-night.

Follower. I tremble and listen. But there is a matter that I must bring to your notice. I hear that yesterday there was a boy of twelve or thirteen guarding the Gojō Bridge. They say he was slashing round with his short sword as nimble as a bird or butterfly. I beg that you will not make your pilgrimage to-night. Do not court this peril.

Benkei. That's a strange thing to ask! Why, were he demon or hobgoblin, he could not stand alone against many. We will surround him and you shall soon see him on his knees.

Follower. They have tried surrounding him, but he always escapes as though by magic, and none is able to lay hands on him.

Benkei. When he seems within their grasp

Follower. From before their eyes

Benkei. Suddenly he vanishes.

Chorus.

This strange hobgoblin, elfish apparition,
Into great peril may bring

[a] From 1–3 A.M. The scene is Kyōto.
[b] The Kurama temple.

The reverend limbs of my master.
In all this City none can withstand the prowess
Of this unparalleled monster.

Benkei. If this is as you say, I will not go to-night; and yet. . . . No. It is not to be thought of that such a one as Benkei should be affrighted by a tale. To-night when it is dark I will go to the bridge and humble this arrogant elf.

Chorus.
And while he spoke,
Evening already to the western sky had come;
Soon the night-wind had shattered and dispersed
The shapes of sunset. Cheerless night
Came swiftly, but with step too slow
For him who waits.

(*A comic interlude played by a bow-master is sometimes used here to fill in the time while* Benkei *is arming himself.*)

Ushiwaka. I am Ushiwaka. I must do as my mother told me; "Go up to the Temple at daybreak," she said. But it is still night. I will go to Gojō Bridge and wait there till suddenly
Moonlight mingles with the rising waves;
No twilight closes
The autumn day, but swiftly
The winds of night bring darkness.

Chorus (*speaking for* Ushiwaka).
Oh, beauty of the waves! High beats my heart,
High as their scattered pearls!
Waves white as dewy calabash [c] at dawn,
By Gojō Bridge.
Silently the night passes,
No sound but my own feet upon the wooden planks
Clanking and clanking; still I wait
And still in vain.

Benkei.
The night grows late. Eastward the bells of the Three Pagodas toll.
By the moonlight that gleams through leaves of these thick cedar-trees
I gird my armor on;
I fasten the black thongs of my coat of mail.
I adjust its armored skirts.

[c] The flowers of the *yūgao* or calabash will remind the audience of Lady Yūgao who lived near Gojō Bridge (see p. 317).

By the middle I grasp firmly
My great halberd that I have loved so long.
I lay it across my shoulder; with leisurely step stride forward.
Be he demon or hobgoblin, how shall he stand against me?
Such trust have I in my own prowess. Oh, how I long
For a foeman worthy of my hand!

Ushiwaka.
The river-wind blows keen;
The night is almost spent,
But none has crossed the Bridge.
I am disconsolate and will lie down to rest.

Benkei.
Then Benkei, all unknowing,
Came towards the Bridge where white waves lapped.
Heavily his feet clanked on the boards of the Bridge.

Ushiwaka.
And even before he saw him Ushiwaka gave a whoop of joy.
"Some one has come," he cried, and hitching his cloak over his shoulder
Took his stand at the bridge-side.

Benkei.
Benkei discerned him and would have spoken. . . .
But when he looked, lo! it was a woman's form!
Then, because he had left the World,[d] with troubled mind he hurried on.

Ushiwaka.
Then Ushiwaka said,
"I will make game of him," and as Benkei passed
Kicked at the button of his halberd so that it jerked into the air.

Benkei (*cries out in surprise*). Ah! fool, I will teach you a lesson!

Chorus.
Then Benkei while he retrieved his halberd
Cried out in anger,
"You shall soon feel the strength of my arm," and fell fiercely upon him.
But the boy, not a jot alarmed,
Stood his ground and with one hand pulled aside his cloak,
While with the other he quietly drew his sword from the scabbard

[d] Because he was a priest.

And parried the thrust of the halberd that threatened him.
Again and again he parried the halberd's point.
And so they fought, now closing, now breaking.
What shall Benkei do? For when he thinks that he has conquered,
With his little sword the boy thrusts the blow aside.
Again and again Benkei strikes.
Again and again his blows are parried,
Till at last even he, mighty Benkei,
Can do battle no longer.
Disheartened he steps back the space of a few bridge-beams.
"Monstrous," he cries, "that this stripling . . . No, it cannot be.
He shall not outwit my skill."
And holding out his halberd at full length before him
He rushed forward and dealt a mighty blow.
But Ushiwaka turned and dived swiftly to the left.
Benkei recovered his halberd and slashed at the boy's skirts;
But *he,* unfaltering, instantly leapt from the ground.
And when he thrust at the boy's body,
Then Ushiwaka squirmed with head upon the ground.
Thus a thousand, thousand bouts they fought,
Till the halberd fell from Benkei's weary hands.
He would have wrestled, but the boy's sword flashed before him,
And he could get no hold.
Then at his wits' end, "Oh, marvelous youth!"
Benkei cried, and stood dumbfounded.

Chorus. Who are you that, so young and frail, possess such daring? Tell us your name and state.

Ushiwaka. Why should I conceal it from you? I am Minamoto Ushiwaka.

Chorus. Yoshitomo's son?

Ushiwaka. I am. And your name . . . ?

Chorus (*speaking for* Benkei).
"I am called Musashi Benkei of the Western Pagoda.
And now that we have told our names,
I surrender myself and beg for mercy;
For you are yet a child, and I a priest.
Such are your rank and lineage, such your prowess
That I will gladly serve you.
Too hastily you took me for an enemy; but now begins

A three lives' bond;[e] henceforward
As slave I serve you."
So, while the one made vows of homage, the other girded
up his cloak.
Then Benkei laid his halberd across his shoulder
And together they went on their way
To the Palace of Kujō.[f]

[e] Three incarnations.
[f] The home of Ushiwaka.

The Hatmaker

(*EBOSHI-ORI*)

Miyamasu (16th century?)

The fifth group of Nō plays contains both demon plays and *kiri-nō*, "auspicious pieces," frequently celebrating a deed of a hero. The hero in this play is Ushiwaka, later known as Minamoto Yoshitsune (see p. 393). Here he is a very young man, but circumstances force him to put on manhood rapidly, first in the form of the distinctive hat of his clan and finally by slaying an enemy chief in battle. As the play opens, the fortunes of war have gone against the Minamoto, and the Taira (Heike) are in the ascendancy.

CHARACTERS

KICHIJI HIS BROTHER KICHIROKU	} *gold-merchants*
USHIWAKA	
HATMAKER	
INNKEEPER	
BRIGANDS	
MESSENGER	
HATMAKER'S WIFE	
KUMASAKA	
CHORUS	

The Hatmaker

Kichiji.
We as travelers dressed—
Our weary feet upon the Eastern road
For many days must speed.
I am Sanjō no Kichiji. I have now amassed a great store of treasure and with my brother Kichiroku am going to take it down to the East. Ho! Kichiroku, let us get together our bundles and start now.

Kichiroku. I am ready. Let us start at once.

Ushiwaka. Hie, you travelers! If you are going up-country, please take me with you.

Kichiji. That is a small thing to ask. Certainly we would take you with us . . . , but by the look of you, I fancy you must be an apprentice playing truant from your master. If that is so, I cannot take you.

Ushiwaka. I have neither father nor mother, and my master has turned me adrift. Please let me go with you.

Kichiji. If that is so, I cannot any longer refuse to take you with me. (*Describing his own action.*) Then he offered the boy a broad-brimmed hat.

Ushiwaka. And Ushiwaka eagerly grasped it. To-day, he said, begins our troublous journey's toil.

Chorus (*describing the journey and speaking for* Ushiwaka).
Past the creek of Awata, to Matsusaka,
To the shore of Shinomiya I travel.
Down the road to the barrier of Ōsaka[a] walking behind pack-ponies,

[a] All the places mentioned are in the vicinity of Kyōto, Seta being on Lake Biwa.

How long shall I serve in sadness these hucksters of gold?
Here where once the blind harper[b] lay sorrowing
On a cottage-bed, far away from the City,
Thinking perhaps some such thoughts as I do now.
We have passed the plain of Awazu. Over the long bridge
of Seta
The hoofs of our ponies clank.
We cross the hill of Moru, where the evening dew
Lies thick on country paths and, caught in the slanting
light,
Gleams on the under-leaves till suddenly night
Comes on us and in darkness we approach
The Mirror[c] Inn.

Kichiji. We have traveled so fast that we have already reached the Mirror Inn. Let us rest here for a little while.

Messenger. I am a servant in the Palace of Rokuhara. I have been sent to fetch back young Ushiwaka, Lord Yoshitomo's son, who has escaped from the Temple of Kurama.[d] It is thought that he has taken service with the merchant Kichiji and has gone up-country with him; so they sent me to bring him back. Why, I believe that is he! But perhaps he is not alone. I cannot be sure. I had better go home and fetch help, for if I were one against many how could I hope to take him?

Ushiwaka. I think it is about me that this messenger is speaking. I must not let him know me. I will cut my hair and wear an eboshi,[e] so that people may think I am an Eastern boy. (*He goes to the curtain which separates the green-room from the entrance-passage. This represents for the moment the front of the hatmaker's shop.*) May I come in?

(*The curtain is raised.*)

Hatmaker. Who is it?

Ushiwaka. I have come to order an eboshi.

Hatmaker. An eboshi at this time of night? I will make you one to-morrow, if you like.

Ushiwaka. Please make it now. I am traveling in a hurry and cannot wait.

[b] A legendary musician named Semimaru.

[c] In Japanese mythology, the mirror is sacred, and one of the symbols of royalty.

[d] The Kurama (-dera) temple is on a mountain north of Kyōto.

[e] A tall and conspicuous hat. Hats identified both clans and regions of the country.

Hatmaker. Very well then; I will make it now. What size do you take?

Ushiwaka. Please give me an eboshi of the third size, folded to the left.

Hatmaker. I am afraid I cannot do that. They were worn folded to the left in the time of the Minamotos. But now that the Tairas rule the whole land it would not be possible to wear one folded so.

Ushiwaka. In spite of that I beg of you to make me one. There is a good reason for my asking.

Hatmaker. Well, as you are so young there cannot be much harm in your wearing it. I will make you one. (*He begins to make the hat.*) There is a fine story about these left-folded eboshi and the luck they bring. Shall I tell it you?

Ushiwaka. Yes, pray tell me the story.

Hatmaker. My grandfather lived at Karasu-maru in the Third Ward.[f]

It was the time when Hachimantarō Yoshi-iye,[g] having routed the brothers Sadatō and Munetō,
Came home in triumph to the Capital.
And when he was summoned to the Emperor's Palace, he went first to my grandfather and ordered from him
A left-folded eboshi for the Audience. And when he was come before the Throne
The Emperor welcomed him gladly
And as a token of great favor made him lord
Of the lands of Outer Mutsu.
Even such an eboshi it is that I am making now,
A garment of good omen.
Wear it and when into the world

Chorus.
When into the world you go, who knows but that Fate's turn
May not at last bring you to lordship of lands,
Of Dewa or the country of Michi.[h]
And on that day remember,
Oh deign to remember, him that now with words of good omen
Folds for you this eboshi.

[f] In Kyōto.

[g] The dashing young Minamoto warrior Yoshi-iye in 1062 snatched victory for his clan in a battle in Mutsu, in northernmost Japan. For this he was known as Hachimantarō, the "Firstborn of the God of War."

[h] In northern Japan, near present-day Akita.

Oh that day forget not the gift you owe!
But alas!
These things were, but shall not be again.
The time of the left-folded eboshi was long ago:
When the houses of Gen and Hei [1] were in their pride.
Like the plum-tree and cherry-tree among flowers,
Like Spring and Autumn among the four seasons.
Then, as snow that would outsparkle the moonlight,
Gen strove with Hei; and after the years of Hōgen,
The house of Hei prevailed and the whole land was theirs.
So is it now.
But retribution shall come; time shall bring
Its changes to the world and like the cherry-blossom
This eboshi that knows its season
Shall bloom again. Wait patiently for that time!

Hatmaker. And while they prayed

Chorus.
Lo! The cutting of the eboshi was done.
Then he decked it brightly with ribbons of three colors,
Tied the strings to it and finished it handsomely.
"Pray deign to wear it," he cried, and set it on the boy's head.
Then, stepping back to look,
"Oh admirable skill! Not even the captain of a mighty host
Need scorn to wear this hat!"

Hatmaker. There is not an eboshi in the land that fits so well.

Ushiwaka. You are right; please take this sword in payment for it.

Hatmaker. No, no! I could not take it in return for such a trifle.

Ushiwaka. I beg you to accept it.

Hatmaker. Well, I cannot any longer refuse. How glad my wife will be! (*Calling*.) Are you there?

Wife. What is it?

(*They go aside*.)

Hatmaker. This young lad asked me to make him an eboshi, and when it was made he gave me this sword as a

[1] The Genji (Minamoto) and Heike (Taira). The years of Hōgen are 1156–1159 and are recounted in the *Hōgen monogatari*, translated by E. R. Kellogg in *Transactions of the Asiatic Society of Japan*, XLV (1915).

present. Is it not a noble payment? Here, look at it. (*The* wife *takes the sword and when she has examined it bursts into tears.*) Why, I thought you would treasure it like a gift from Heaven. And here you are shedding tears over it! What is the matter?

Wife. Oh! I am ashamed. When I try to speak, tears come first and choke the words. I am going to tell you something I have never told you before. I am the sister of Kamada Masakiyo who fell at the Battle of Utsumi in the country of Noma.[j] At the time when Tokiwa bore Ushiwaka, her third son, the lord her husband sent her this weapon as a charm-sword, and I was the messenger whom he charged to carry it. Oh were he in the world again;[k] then would our eyes no longer behold such misery. Oh sorrow, sorrow!

Hatmaker. You say that you are the sister of Kamada Masakiyo?

Wife. I am.

Hatmaker. How strange, how strange! I have lived with you all these years and months, and never knew till now. But are you sure that you recognize this weapon?

Wife. Yes; this was the sword they called Konnentō.

Hatmaker. Ah! I have heard that name. Then this must be the young Lord Ushiwaka from Kuruma Temple. Come with me. We must go after him and give him back the sword at once. Why, he is still there! (*To* Ushiwaka.) Sir, this woman tells me she knows the sword; I beg of you to take it back.

Ushiwaka.

Oh! strange adventure; to meet so far from home
With humble folk that show me kindness!

Hatmaker and *Wife.* My Lord, forgive us! We did not know you; but now we see in you Lord Ushiwaka, the nursling of Kurama Temple.

Ushiwaka. I am no other. (*To the* wife.) And you, perhaps, are some kinswoman of Masakiyo?[l]

Wife. You have guessed wisely, sir; I am the Kamada's sister.

Ushiwaka. Lady Akoya?

Wife. I am.

Ushiwaka. Truly I have reason to know. . . . And *I*

Chorus.

[j] In present-day Kobe.

[k] Yoshi-iye, that is.

[l] The conversation between the hatmaker and his wife is an "aside"; Ushiwaka has not heard it.

Am Ushiwaka fallen on profitless days.
Of whom no longer you may speak
As master, but as one sunk in strange servitude.
Dawn is in the east; the pale moon fades from the sky, as he sets forth from the Mirror Inn.

Hatmaker and *Wife*. Oh! it breaks my heart to see him! A boy of noble name walking barefoot with merchants, and nothing on his journey but cloth of Shikama to clothe him. Oh! piteous sight!

Ushiwaka. Change rules the world for ever, and Man but for a little while. What are fine clothes to me, what life itself while foemen flaunt?

Hatmaker. As a journey-present to speed you on the Eastern road . . .

Chorus. So he spoke and pressed the sword into the young lord's hands. And the boy could not any longer refuse, but taking it said, "If ever I come into the World [m] again, I will not forget." And so saying he turned and went on his way in company with the merchants his masters. On they went till at last, weary with travel, they came to the Inn of Akasaka in the country of Mino.[n]

Kichiji (*the merchant*). We have come so fast that here we are at the Inn of Akasaka. (*To his* Brother.) Listen, Kichiroku, you had better take lodging for us here.

Kichiroku. I obey. (*Goes towards the hashigakari or actors' entrance-passage.*) May I come in?

Innkeeper. Who are you? Ah! it is Master Kichiroku. I am glad to see you back again so soon. (*To* Kichiji.) Be on your guard, gentleman. For a desperate gang has got wind of your coming and has sworn to set upon you to-night.

Kichiji. What are we to do?

Kichiroku. I cannot tell.

Ushiwaka (*comes forward*). What are you speaking of?

Kichiji. We have heard that robbers may be coming to-night. We were wondering what we should do. . . .

Ushiwaka. Let them come in what force they will; yet if one stout soldier go to meet them, they will not stand their ground, though they be fifty mounted men.

Kichiji. These are trusty words that you have spoken to us. One and all we look to you. . . .

Ushiwaka. Then arm yourselves and wait. I will go out to meet them.

[m] Into power again, that is.
[n] Near Kyōto; not the Akasaka which is part of Tōkyō.

Chorus. And while he spoke, evening passed to darkness. "Now is the time," he cried, "to show the world those arts of war that for many months and years upon the Mountain of Kurama I have rehearsed."
Then he opened the double-doors and waited there for the slow incoming of the white waves.[o]

Brigands. Loud the noise of assault. The lashing of white waves against the rocks, even such is the din of our battle-cry.

Kumasaka. Ho, my man! Who is there?

Brigand. I stand before you.

Kumasaka. How fared those skirmishers I sent to make a sudden breach? Blew the wind briskly within?

Brigand. Briskly indeed; for some are slain and many grievously wounded.

Kumasaka. How can that be? I thought that none were within but the merchants, Kichiji and his brother. Who else is there?

Brigand. By the light of a rocket[p] I saw a lad of twelve or thirteen years slashing about him with a short-sword; and he was nimble as a butterfly or bird.

Kumasaka. And the brothers Surihari?

Brigand. Stood foster-fathers to the fire-throwers and were the first to enter.
But soon there meets them this child I tell of and with a blow at each whisks off their heads from their necks.

Kumasaka. Ei! Ei! Those two, and the horsemen that were near a hundred strong,—all smitten! The fellow has bewitched them!

Brigand. When Takase saw this, thinking perhaps no good would come of this night-attack, he took some seventy horsemen and galloped away with them.

Kumasaka. Ha! It is not the first time that lout has played me false.
How fared the torch-diviners?

Brigand. The first torch was slashed in pieces; the second was trampled on till it went out; the third they caught and threw back at us, but it too went out. There are none left.

Kumasaka. Then is all lost. For of these torch-diviners they sing that the first torch is the soul of an army, the second

[o] A metaphor for robbers. A band of brigands who troubled China in 184 A.D. took the name "White Waves," and the phrase became general.

[p] Torches were thrown among the enemy to discover their number and defenses.

torch is the wheel of Fate, and the third torch—Life itself. All three are out, and there is no hope left for this night's brigandage.

Brigand. It is as you say. Though we were gods, we could not redeem our plight. Deign to give the word of retreat.

Kumasaka. Why, even brigands must be spared from slaughter. Come, withdraw my men.

Brigand. I obey.

Kumasaka. Stay! Shall Kumasaka Chōhan be worsted in to-night's affray? Never! Where could he then hide his shame? Come, robbers, to the attack!

Chorus. So with mighty voice he called them to him, and they, raising their war-cry, leapt to the assault.

(*Speaking for* Ushiwaka.)

"Hoho! What a to-do! Himself has come, undaunted by the fate of those he sent before him. Now, Hachiman,[q] look down upon me, for no other help is here." So he prayed, and stood waiting at the gap.

(*Speaking for* Kumasaka.)

"Sixty-three years has Kumasaka lived, and to-day shall make his last night-assault." [r] So he spoke and kicking off his iron-shoes in a twinkling he leveled his great battle-sword that measured five foot three, and as he leapt forward like a great bird pouncing on his prey, no god or demon had dared encounter him.

(*Speaking for* Ushiwaka.)

"Ha, bandit! Be not so confident! These slinking night-assaults displease me"; and leaving him no leisure, the boy dashed in to the attack.

Then, Kumasaka, deeply versed in use of the battle-sword, lunged with his left foot and in succession he executed The Ten-Side Cut, The Eight-Side Sweep, The Body Wheel, The Hanyū Turn, The Wind Roll, The Blade Drop, The Gnashing Lion, The Maple-Leaf Double, The Flower Double.

Now fire dances at the sword-points;

Now the sword-backs clash.

[q] The god of war.

[r] He feels that he is too old for the work.

At last even the great battle-sword has spent its art.
Parried by the little belt-sword of Zōshi,[s] it has become no more than a guard-sword.

(*Speaking for* Kumasaka.)

"This sword-play brings me no advantage; I will close with him and try my strength!"
Then he threw down his battle-sword and spreading out his great hands rushed wildly forward. But Ushiwaka dodged him, and as he passed mowed round at his legs.
The robber fell with a crash, and as he struggled to rise
The belt-sword of Ushiwaka smote him clean through the waist.
And Kumasaka that had been one man
Lay cloven in twain.

[s] Another name for Ushiwaka.

Part Three

JAPANESE DRAMA

Kabuki and Jōruri

The predominately aristocratic Nō drama exists to this day and no one in Japan with pretensions to culture could afford to ignore it during any of the centuries of its reign. However, in the sixteenth and seventeenth centuries two new types of drama arose along with two new types of theater. The puppet theater (Jōruri) reached great heights, especially through the efforts of Chikamatsu Monzaemon (1653–1725), and the Kabuki, with live actors, flourished in the same period. The dramas performed on these stages fall roughly into two groups, domestic dramas (*sewamono*), concerned with the merchant class of the large cities of Japan, especially Ōsaka and Tōkyō, and historical dramas (*jidaimono*), which glorify and popularize the Japanese warrior-hero and take their subject matter from history—both early and recent—and legend. In a sense, the *jidaimono* are debased Nō plays in that they popularize some of the material from the Nō and the narrative prose epics that provided sources for the Nō. And, though the aesthetic of a play written for use in the puppet theater is different, as we shall see, from that of a play written for live actors, the more successful puppet plays could be and were used on the Kabuki stage. As the puppet theater declined, adaptations of the plays were performed by live actors on the rival stage. Thus we are concerned with two types of drama and two kinds of theatrical presentation, theoretically at least interchangeable.

That a puppet play can be a major art form comes as a surprise to many or at least reminds the theatrically sophisticated that there have been recurrent defenses of puppets and marionettes by Western dramatists and theorists. Most of these advocates of the puppet play follow lines of argument that conveniently fit the Japanese puppet play and its defense by people like Chikamatsu. Some of the advantages that are argued for the puppet play are also possible in live drama. The use of masks, for instance, depersonalizes the actor—it is not his face that we see, but the face of an idealized character, a face created by a wood-carver or sculptor. If the acting is stylized and the actor's face concealed, it is difficult for him to project his own personality, which in any case the author feels would be an alien note. A similar argument certainly accounts for the use of men in women's roles on both the Western and the Oriental stage. The puppet has all the advantages of not being a physical body and not having any personality beyond his carefully designed exterior and the controlled movements of the puppeteer. The puppet stage, however, has other advantages. The problem of realism, or to be more precise, verisimilitude, arises the moment live actors tread the stage. The real-life actor carries, naturally, a real sword. The doors, tables, writing pens, and sake cups on the stage are real. Unless the playwright or stage manager makes a special point of having these things symbolized rather than real (as in Thornton Wilder's *Our Town,* for example), we are amused and our mood is destroyed if the stage properties seem to be faked—if, for instance, the massive stone walls of the castle shake when the hero leans against them. This means that great difficulties arise in the depiction of large-scale scenes or outdoor scenes on stage (this difficulty is most apparent in opera today or in modern productions of Shakespeare—the Elizabethan age was not so concerned with this problem). When to the problems of scenes too large for the stage are added the problems of the fantastic or impossible, the value of the puppet stage becomes apparent. The live hero may indeed fight with real swords another warrior on the stage with verisimilitude, but he cannot fight a real lion, and the introduction of a man in a lion suit becomes comical unless the action is stylized—made into a kind of dance. In Chikamatsu's great historical drama, *The Battles of Coxinga,* the puppet hero does indeed fight a puppet lion.[1] In the same play the Japanese troops are saved by the god Sumiyoshi, who creates a bridge of clouds for them to escape over. Once the audience achieves its "willing suspension of disbelief"

[1] The reader who can't imagine the encounter between the puppet Coxinga and the puppet tiger can see a photograph of a Kabuki version (with a man dressed in a tiger skin) in *Major Plays of Chikamatsu,* tr. by Donald Keene, facing p. 202 (see Bibliography). The Kabuki, however, does not attempt to be realistic. The battle is a fantastic dance.

at the beginning of the puppet play, all of these elements from the realistic to the fantastic are on the same level and equally acceptable. Finally, in the puppet play, the recitation of the words—the speeches of all of the characters—is done by narrators and under control in the sense that these speeches are not subject to the nuances of the individual actor's voice. Chikamatsu notes, however, that this places a great responsibility on the playwright. His literary text must carry a larger part of the artistic effect than the text would in the live theater.

The Japanese puppets, it should be said here, are not marionettes agitated by overhead strings, but dolls of considerable size that are moved by puppeteers who are visible to the audience, though made inconspicuous by black costumes. That the arm of the puppeteer occasionally reaches around the doll and obscures it sometimes seems artificial to the Western viewer. However, it is a fact that the puppeteer disappears into the background when one becomes used to the convention.

Both the puppet and the Kabuki stages, unlike the Nō stage, are Western-type, proscenium-arch stages. The Kabuki stage, however, is not "set" so much as decorated. It is intended to provide a colorful background for the action, but it is not intended to be realistic. A blue cloth on the stage may indicate water; straw mats of the kind used in Japanese homes may suggest an interior. Even when the setting seems to be quite realistic, as may be the case with modern performances, no particular aesthetic premium is placed on realism. The kind of spectacular realism sometimes attained in Western sets is unknown to the Japanese and would not seem artistic to them.

To understand the artistic conventions of the two kinds of dramas, the domestic and the historical, intended for these two stages, some of the background of seventeenth and eighteenth century Japanese life is necessary. This was a period in Japanese history when a rising merchant class, gaining power through increasing prosperity, began to compete for the good things of life with a feudal, landowning class. Japan was at this time governed by warlords. The affairs of the country were in the hands of powerful barons and their retainers, the knight or samurai class. It was apparent to this class that the political stability of the country, its own political future, and the morals of the people required that the *nouveau riche* commercial class, especially as it concentrated in such cities as Edo (now Tōkyō) and Ōsaka, be contained. Financial containment was possible through taxation. Social containment was accomplished by a rather sharp division of the classes. The samurai class wa pledged to a warrior's code of honor and courage and a Zen Buddhist dedication to austere living. This class hel public office but often found itself financially far below th merchant class. To confine the merchant class, sumptuar laws regulating styles of dress and the decoration of home were passed. In general, it was unhealthy for a merchan to seem to be too wealthy or to be seen living too luxuriously Officialdom had various vindictive methods at its disposal t subdue the middle-class businessman too impressed with hi money and rising social position. One inconspicuous mode o extravagance, however, was the world of entertainment, including the theater. In the tea shops, gambling houses, restaurants, and houses of assignation in the "gay quarter" fortune could easily be dissipated. Conspicuous consumptio here might impress one's business colleagues—as with th expense-account set today—that one was both affluent an convivial; it might also result in amorous intrigues, disastrous both to one's honor and to one's bank account, wit courtesans. This world of the gay quarter is, in general, th subject of the domestic plays done on the puppet an Kabuki stages, and also a favorite of the novelists of th period, including the famous Ihara Saikaku.[2]

The plots of Chikamatsu's domestic plays are frequentl of the type that would be featured in the more scanda minded newspapers of our day, and some plots were in fac developed from actual reports of contemporary events. A favorite theme would be the love of a young man for a cultivated and charming prostitute in the gay quarter. The youn man might be married, as in *The Love Suicides at Amijima* Here the young man neglects his business obligations and h family because of his love for a young courtesan who als sincerely loves him. His devoted wife is willing to help hi buy the girl out of her bondage as much to defeat the hero rival as to redeem the girl. The hero's brother and his fathe in-law are pressures on him for morality and duty, but the argue to no avail, and the play ends with the lovers' suicid Like Chūbei in *The Courier for Hell,* the hero of *The Lov Suicides at Amijima* is foolish but sincere. Fate spreads out net for him (there is a pun here in that *ami* in Amijim means "net"). The heroes of these plays are guileless ar passionate. The seriousness of their emotions is testified to b

[2] See Howard Hibbett, *The Floating World in Japanese Fiction* (New York: Oxford Univ. Press, 1959).

heir deaths, but because of their rashness, the deaths are
nore pathetic than tragic. The appeal of the courtesan of
he gay quarter, who is a frequent figure in Japanese drama
nd literature of this period, is far more complicated than
hat of the Western *femme fatale*. The more educated class
f courtesan, like the later geisha, represented the cultiva-
ion of the arts as much as amorous intrigue. This was a
voman gracious in manner, trained in singing, dancing,
alligraphy, and storytelling, a master of witty conversation,
nd widely experienced in life—all of this in sharp contrast
o the Japanese wife, who was secluded from the world, un-
ducated, with the domestic virtues of loyalty, obedience,
nd self-sacrifice for the family, but in no sense a com-
anion to her husband. In Chikamatsu's plays both the cour-
esan and the wife receive sympathetic treatment, and in
ne play at least, *The Drum of Waves of Horikawa* (*Hori-
awa Nami no Tsuzumi*), it is the samurai's wife who
hrough loneliness and drinking succumbs to temptation.

Of all the writers for the Kabuki and Jōruri stage Chika-
natsu is the acknowledged literary master. His style is end-
essly complex, poetic, filled with multiple allusions and
uns. In general, he is colloquial, unlike the writers of Nō
lays, but he is a great stylistic virtuoso.[3] The domestic
lays give him opportunities for the depiction of various
ypes of characters from middle-class life. This he does with
reat skill, and his servants have the same stamp of his
enius as his heroes. But his domestic plays, though the in-
rigues are frequently resolved with suicide or murder, do
ot rise to the level of great tragedy as we know it in the
Vest. They are limited to a narrower world, even as the
vorld of Romeo and Juliet is narrower than that of Hamlet
r Lear. Nevertheless the domestic plays of Chikamatsu are
ery moving, perhaps because the disaster that occurs usually
omes about not through one false move or fatal flaw on the
art of the hero, but because of a number of false moves,
nost of which could be redeemed but aren't, and because
he hero is all the more human for the warmhearted and un-
hinking nature of his actions. A special feature of many of
he plays augments the pathos of the domestic disaster that
s unfolding before our eyes and permits the writer to com-
nent and moralize on it: toward the end of the plays there is
requently a poignant journey made by the hero and his
oved one. This journey (*michiyuki*) takes the lovers to their

[3] See Keene's *Major Plays*, pp. 26–33, and Shively's *Love Sui-
ides at Amijima*, pp. 42–48 (see Bibliography).

deaths through streets and gardens, over bridges, past temples and well-known historical sites with such detail that the audience could mentally follow their progress and the modern researcher, if he wished, could reconstruct the journey on a map. All the Japanese love for well-known sites and the nuances of places comes into play here, and the journey gives the writer a chance for beautiful descriptions and provides a poetic and tranquil stretch between the intrigues of the beginning and the disasters of the denouement.

Though Chikamatsu's domestic plays and the domestic plays of other writers for Kabuki and Jōruri tend to interest us now more than the *jidaimono* or historical plays, Chikamatsu's most famous play, and a popular one during his lifetime, *The Battles of Coxinga* (*Kokusen'ya Kassen*), was a historical play. The historical hero in this case was not a Japanese warrior of the Minamoto-Heike wars of centuries ago, but a half-Chinese, half-Japanese hero of the fifteenth century, who helped the Chinese Ming dynasty fight the usurping Manchus. *Coxinga* is a fascinating play because of the variety of its scenes—some of them in Japan and some of them in China—and its delineation of character, both male and female, Chinese and Japanese. The essential ingredient in the *jidaimono* is the warrior spirit, with its attendant courage and loyalty and sensitivity to questions of honor. *The Treasurer of Loyal Retainers* (*Kanadehon Chushingura*) by Takeda Izumo (d. 1756) has been one of the most popular of all Kabuki plays and is frequently played today either in its entirety or in the form of selected episodes. It is a complicated tale of samurai with violent tempers, adulterous love, forced suicide (*seppuku,* incorrectly called hara-kiri), and the revenge of the hero's retainers after his unjust death. The loyalty of samurai to their master is a frequent theme in both Japanese literature and Japanese life. The masterless samurai, the *rōnin,* is a familiar character, and the real-life episode of 1840 in which forty-seven *rōnin* carefully avenged their master's death and then committed suicide as a group (to be remembered in the form of a Shinto shrine in Tōkyō) gives immediacy to such tales. *The Subscription List* is a play about the courage and quick-wittedness of a loyal retainer, and is another very popular Kabuki play. Both *Chushingura* and *The Subscription List* depend more, perhaps, on acting than on literary style. The *seppuku* scene in *Chushingura* is immensely effective and the scene in *The Subscription List* in which

enkei beats his master sends a thrill of horror through the
apanese audience.

The acting technique in Kabuki is dignified, and the cos-
ımes are so striking that they have appeared in the wood-
lock prints of some of the great artists of the period. The
ctors deliver their words in a high-pitched falsetto voice
hich is difficult for the Westerner to get used to, but which
:retches out the action, creating suspense and protracting
gonizing moments. Unlike the Nō play, which is today the
roperty of intellectuals and connoisseurs of the culture of
arlier Japan, the Kabuki continues to appeal to a wide au-
ience. The theaters in Tōkyō and Kyōto are always full and
ompanies tour the provinces. And the dignified and intense
cting and posturing of the Japanese warriors in such moon pictures as *Gate of Hell, Rashomon,* and *Ugetsu* owe
ıuch to Kabuki.

ecker beats his master sends a thrill of horror through the apanese audience.

The acting technique in Kabuki is dignified, and the costumes are so striking that they have appeared in the woodblock prints of some of the great artists of the period. The actors deliver their words in a high-pitched falsetto voice which is difficult for the Westerner to get used to, but which stretches out the action, creating suspense and protracting agonizing moments. Unlike the Nō play, which is today the property of intellectuals and connoisseurs, of the culture of earlier Japan, the Kabuki continues to appeal to a wide audience. The theaters in Tōkyō and Kyōto are always full and companies tour the provinces. And the dignified and intense acting and posturing of the Japanese warriors in such movie-pictures as *Gate of Hell*, *Rashomon*, and *Ugetsu* owe much to Kabuki.

The Courier for Hell

(*MEIDO NO HIKYAKU*)

by Chikamatsu Monzaemon

m Major Plays of Chikamatsu, *translated by Donald ne. New York: Columbia University Press, 1961. Re-ited by permission of Columbia University Press.*

The Courier for Hell

(*MEIDO NO HIYEKU*)

Chickamatsu Monzaemon

The play was first performed on April 22, 1711. It is presumed that the source was an actual event.

The most remarkable feature of the *Courier for Hell* is the recklessness of the hero Chūbei. It is a characteristic of many of the domestic plays that the hero is impetuous and Chūbei's motivation—to not lose face before the courtesans of the gay quarter—also motivates other heroes, but Chūbei's foolishness is striking. It is not his home and wealth that he jeopardizes by his breaking the seal on the packet of gold, but the wealth of others, given to him as a trust. His redeeming feature to the Japanese audience is his utter sincerity. Chūbei rises to heights that he—an ordinary businessman—could not possibly reach during the routine of his regular life both in business and with his family. He disregards reason with something of the quick temper of the Renaissance hothead, too quick with his sword and with the same lack of hope for any gain from his rashness except saving his honor. His dubious moral position—he is jeopardizing his family honor, his business, and his friends for the affection of a prostitute—might make one think that he would not have the sympathy of the audience. But he emerges a much more warm and human figure than the wiser and better people of the play, Hachiemon especially. Powerful emotions drive him to do what he has done; he acts without hope of personal gain.

In the last lines of Act II the hero and heroine begin a final lovers' journey. This journey, the *michiyuki,* a much discussed feature of Chikamatsu's plays, is not as elaborate here as it is in other plays such as the *Love Suicides at Amijima.* The journey begins with a pun on "thousand days" (p. 378). It takes the lovers out into the countryside around

Ōsaka, to a shrine, and past familiar scenes. It has been argued that Chikamatsu employed the *michiyuki* largely to demonstrate his verbal ingenuity, and the Japanese love for wordplay based on place-names is certainly a factor in the enjoyment of these journeys. But the *michiyuki* is also a tranquil period after the tumult of the action during which the hero and heroine, partially purged of their passions and conscious of the imminence of death, meditate on their love amid familiar surroundings. If there is to be a popular religious or philosophical overtone, the *michiyuki* is an ideal place for it. In this play, the narrator says of Chūbei and Umegawa: "For them purple passion is a thing of the past; today they are truly husband and wife." And further: "All that they begrudge is their remembrance of this world." The last especially is a typical Buddhist sentiment. One can accept the fact that the material world, "the world of dew," is transitory—here today and gone tomorrow, as we say—but its beauties and pleasures are poignant, if fleeting, and one is not easily purged of a longing for them. Chūbei's character takes on new dimensions in these last scenes as he calms the fears of and gives courage to Umegawa.

The translator has skillfully imitated where it is possible to do so Chikamatsu's versatile and at times dazzling stylistic effects. The richness of his language is a great source of his appeal, and a considerable amount of it comes through in the following translation.

CHARACTERS

CHUBEI, *aged 24, proprietor of the Kame-ya, a courier service*
HACHIEMON, *his friend*
KATSUGI MAGOEMON, *Chūbei's father*
CHUZABURO, *a friend of Chūbei in Ninokuchi Village*
JINNAI, *a samurai*
IHEI, *a clerk*
GOHEI, *a servant*
CLERKS, MESSENGERS, APPRENTICES, POLICE
UMEGAWA, *aged 22, a courtesan of low rank*
MYOKAN, *Chūbei's foster mother*
KIYO, *proprietress of the Echigo House*
WIFE OF CHUZABURO
MAN, *a maid*
TOYOKAWA, *a prostitute*
TAKASE, *a prostitute*
PROSTITUTES, MAIDS

The Courier for Hell

ACT I

Scene: The shop of the Kame-ya, a courier service in Ōsak

Time: Late in the eleventh moon (of 1710?)

Narrator. In Naniwa of water-markers, in Naniwa wher bloom these flowers,[a] three are the streets in the Quarte of Flowers, Sado and Echigo and Hyōtan in between. To them from Awaji Street "visited by shore birds" comes Chūbei, a frequent visitor, heir to the Kame-ya a youth barely turned four and twenty, arrived fror Yamato four years ago as an adopted son with a dowry He is clever in business, at assigning packloads, and a managing the thrice-monthly couriers to Edo. Adept i the tea ceremony, poetry, chess, and backgammon, h writes an elegant hand. When it comes to saké, he ca manage three, four, or at most five cups, and he wear with the proper assurance a heavy silk cloak with fiv crests. His plain sword guard, so cunningly inlaid on would never suspect it was of country workmanship, i rare as Chūbei among country lads. Knowing in the way of love, familiar of the Quarter, he does not wait fo evening to race thither on flying feet.

[a] The water-marker (*miotsukushi*) was used as an epithet fc Naniwa (Ōsaka). It is today the emblem of the city. "Where bloor these flowers" is a quotation from an old song about Naniwa; th flower in question is the plum blossom, and may be an allusion t Umegawa, whose name contains the word "plum" (*ume*).

[b] Three streets in Shimmachi licensed quarter of Ōsaka.

[c] Allusion to the poem by Minamoto no Kanemasa, no. 288 c *Kinyōshū* (A.D. 1128): "Guardian of the barrier of Suma, ho many nights have you awakened to the crying of the shore bird that visit the Isle of Awaji?"

In his absence the courier shop, busy with packing and unpacking, is crowded front and back with clerks scratching in the ledgers and clicking their abacuses. The ease with which they handle tens of thousands of *ryō* and transact business with distant Kyushu and Edo without stirring from the shop makes you think the gold and silver pieces came with wings.

The collector has returned from his rounds of the city and begins to enter the commissions in the register, when a voice is heard at the door.

innai. Could you tell me, is Chūbei at home?

Narrator. The visitor is a samurai from a daimyo household, a regular customer of the shop. The clerk answers politely.

hei. Ah, it's you, sir, Mr. Jinnai. Chūbei is out, but if you have anything to send to Edo, I am at your service. Boy, bring some tea!

Narrator. He speaks deferentially.

innai. No, I have no commissions for you. A letter has come from the young master in Edo. Listen to what he writes.

Narrator. He unfolds a letter.

innai. "I shall send you 300 *ryō* in gold with the courier leaving on the second of next month. Please collect this sum on the ninth or the tenth from Chūbei of the Kameya in Ōsaka, and settle the business which I have discussed with you. I enclose herewith the receipt from the courier service. Surrender it to Chūbei on delivery of the remittance."

These are his orders. Important business arrangements have been disrupted by the failure of the remittance to arrive by today. What is the explanation for this disgraceful negligence?

Narrator. He utters the words with a scowl.

hei. I don't wonder that you're upset, sir, but with all the rain we've been having lately, the rivers are swollen and it takes longer than usual to make the journey. The slowness of your remittance hasn't been our only problem. We've sustained considerable losses. But there's nothing for you to worry about. Even supposing the courier were set upon by robbers or cutthroats, or himself yielded to sudden temptation on the way, the eighteen courier houses would compensate you in full, regardless of the sum of money. You wouldn't suffer the loss of so much as a mustard seed.

Narrator. Jinnai interrupts.

Jinnai. That goes without saying. Chūbei's head would fl
if my master suffered any loss. Any further delay with th
remittance will seriously hamper my master's business
That is why I've come here today to investigate. Send
courier to meet the one from Edo, and see to it that th
money is brought immediately.

Narrator. Foot soldier and stripling that he is, he bran
dishes with authority his sword, silvery-looking, thoug
probably leaden as his heavy dialect. He departs, only t
be followed by another visitor.

Messenger. Excuse me, please. I've been sent by Hachiemo
of the Tamba-ya in Nakanoshima. He says that he's re
ceived notice of a remittance from a rice wholesaler i
Kofuna Street in Edo, and he'd like to know why th
money hasn't reached him yet. He wrote you a lette
about it the other day, but hasn't had any answer, an
when he sent a messenger, you gave him the runaroun
He wonders when you intend to deliver the money. Any
way, my master says that you should turn over the mone
to me and send me back with an escort. I'll return you
receipt. Well, I'm ready to collect the money now.

Narrator. He stands legs astraddle in the doorway, makin
a clamor. The clerk, Ihei, devoted to his master, answers i
unruffled tones.

Ihei. Indeed? I can't believe that a gentleman like Hachie
mon would order us around in such a high-handed mar
ner. Your company's business is not the only concern c
the Kame-ya. This house is entrusted with five or eve
seven thousand *ryō* of people's money at a time, an
our couriers range at will the 130 leagues between Ed
and Ōsaka. It would be strange if deliveries weren't de
layed once in a while. The master is expected back at an
moment. When he returns, I'm sure he'll send a reply. I'
thank you not to make such a commotion over what, afte
all, is less than fifty *ryō*.

Narrator. The messenger, taken aback by his asperity
leaves quietly.
Chūbei's mother, Myōkan, who scarcely ever quit
the *kotatsu*,[d] emerges from the back room.

Myōkan. What was the meaning of that? I'm sure that th
money for the Tamba-ya arrived at least ten days ago
Why hasn't Chūbei delivered it? All morning long I'v
been hearing customer after customer demanding hi

[d] A low table covered with a quilt which reaches the floor; un
derneath the table is a small charcoal fire. A normal type of heatin
even today in a Japanese house.

money. Never since the days of my husband has the house received a demand for even a single piece of silver. We've yet to cause the guild the least trouble. In fact, the Kameya has always been considered the model among the eighteen courier houses. But haven't you noticed? Lately Chūbei's behavior has been very peculiar. Those of you who are recent employees may not know it, but Chūbei is actually not my son. He was the only son of a prosperous farmer from Ninokuchi Village in Yamato named Katsugi Magoemon. His mother died, and his father, afraid that desperation at being under a stepmother might make Chūbei turn to vicious pleasures, suggested that I take him here as successor to the business. I've had no fault to find with Chūbei's running of the household and the business, but of late he's seemed restless and unable to keep his mind on his work. I've wanted to admonish him about his behavior, but I was afraid that he might think that his foster mother is just as bad as a stepmother. Rather than complain, I've preferred to shame him by my silence. I've pretended not to notice, but I've followed everything deserving of my attention. He's become so extravagant. Why, he uses two or three sheets of fine quality tissue, whatever he happens to lay his hand on, just to blow his nose! My late husband always used to say, "Never trust a man who uses one paper handkerchief after another!" Chūbei takes three packs with him whenever he leaves the house. I wonder how he can blow his nose so often—he never has a single sheet left when he returns. He's young and healthy, but if he goes on blowing his nose that way, he's sure to come down with some sickness.

Narrator. Still murmuring complaints, she leaves. The apprentices and errand boys feel sorry for her.

Apprentice. I wish he would please hurry home.

Narrator. While they have been waiting, the sun has journeyed back to the west, and it is time to shut the shop gates.

Love for Umegawa, a bird in a cage, has turned Chūbei into a swallow,[e] ever winging to the Quarter, but now he trudges the streets, his thoughts tangled like a spider's web with schemes for raising money and fears of what may happen at home. He sees the ten-penny harlots emerging at the street corners, and realizes in dismay that day has drawn to a close. He hurries home now, so precipitously

[e] The cry of the swallow *"chū, chū"* leads into mention of Chūbei.

that his feet barely touch the ground. He arrives at th shop entrance, but hesitates, worried about what may hav happened during his absence. Perhaps there have bee dunning messengers from his customers, and Myōkan ha heard their complaints. If only someone would come out so that he could learn the situation before he entered This is his own house, but the threshold seems too hig for him to cross. He peeps inside and sees the cook, Man apparently preparing to visit the saké shop. She is a sul len, sharp-tongued [f] creature, unlikely to reveal anythin free of charge. "I'll pretend I'm in love and trick her int talking," he thinks, when suddenly she appears. He firml grips her hand that holds a saké cask. She cries out.

Man. Master, is that you?

Chūbei. Don't make such an uproar! You know too muc about love for that!—I'm head over heels in love with you They say that when there's love inside, it's bound to shov on the outside. Have you seen the look in my eyes? Wh do you torture me so with that adorable face of yours You'd be kinder if you killed me.

Narrator. He takes her in his arms.

Man. I can tell you're fibbing. I've seen how you go of every single day to Shimmachi, and how you use two o three packs of tissue at a time. When you have such lovely nose to blow, why should you want to wipe it o the likes of me? You're lying!

Narrator. She shakes herself free, but he takes her in hi arms again.

Chūbei. What purpose could I have in lying? It's th truth!

Man. If you really mean it, will you come to my bed to night?

Chūbei. Of course. How happy you've made me! Bu there's something I'd like to ask while I'm at it.

Man. Ask me when we're snug in bed together! You won' fool me, will you? Promise, and I'll take a hot bath be fore you come!

Narrator. She breaks off the conversation and, freeing her self, runs off. Chūbei is irritated, though he is not sur at whom. He looks up.

Chūbei. I wonder who's that swaggering this way fron the north block? Oh—it's Hachiemon. It'd be a nuisanc meeting him.

[f] The expression *ki de hana mogu* means "to treat disagreeably," but literally is "to wipe one's nose with a piece of wood."

Narrator. He starts off to the east, hoping to dodge Hachiemon.

Hachiemon. Chūbei! Don't try to avoid me!

Chūbei. Hachiemon—you're a stranger in these parts! Yesterday, then today too, and come to think of it, the day before yesterday, I planned to send somebody to your place, but what with one thing and another, I put it off. —It's turned decidedly cold. How's your father's rheumatism and your mother's toothache? Oh—you positively reek of saké! You shouldn't overdo it, you know. I'll send someone tomorrow morning first thing. Oh yes, ee-shay [g] sent a message. She says she'd like to see you one of these days.

Narrator. He chatters on, hoping to humor Hachiemon.

Hachiemon. Drop it. I'm not a man to dance to your tune. Am I mistaken in thinking you run a courier service? Why hasn't the remittance of fifty *ryō* from Edo reached me yet? I wouldn't mind waiting four or five days, but it's been over ten days and you still haven't delivered my money. Friendship and business are two different matters. After all, you charge me high enough rates, and the business must be valuable to you. Today I sent a messenger to your shop and your damned clerk gave him a surly answer. I can't believe you treat other customers that way. Are you amusing yourself at my expense? Remember, in Kitahama, Utsubo, Nakanoshima and even in the Temma greengrocers' market they call Hachiemon "The Boss." [h] Make fun of me all you like, but today I get my money. Or must I report you to the messenger guild? First, I'll have a word with your mother.

Narrator. Chūbei stops him from going inside. He whispers.

Chūbei. I'm sorry. I've bungled things. Here, I'm begging you on bended knees—please listen to just one word. I beseech you.

Hachiemon. What, again! You seem to think you can settle anything with your clever tongue. If you try the same tricks on me you've used on Umegawa, you'll find that a man's quite a different proposition. You've something to tell me? Very well, I'm listening.

Narrator. He rebukes him bitterly.

[g] The word *sore* for "she" is given as *reso,* reversing the syllables as in pig Latin.

[h] Kitahama was a section of rich merchants, Utsubo of fish markets, Nakanoshima of samurai residences and storehouses—all in Ōsaka.

Chūbei. If my mother should hear you, nothing, not even my death, would restore my reputation. I beg you, as the supreme act of kindness of a lifetime, keep your voice down.—Ah, I feel so disgusted with myself!

Narrator. He weeps bitterly.

Chūbei. Why should I hide the truth from you? Your money arrived from Edo two weeks ago. As you know Umegawa's customer from the country has been using his money to outbid me. I've been at a complete disadvantage with only the miserable sums, two or three hundred *me* that I've managed to pilfer when my mother and the clerks weren't looking. I was feeling bad enough—more dead than alive—when I learned that her ransom had been decided on, and all that was left was the final striking of hands. Umegawa was heartbroken, and my honor at stake. We should have killed ourselves already. One night we even went so far as to touch the cold steel of our daggers to each other's throats but—perhaps it wasn't yet time for us to die—obstacles of one sort and another interfered, and that night we parted in tears. The following morning—it was the twelfth of this month—the money for you from Edo arrived unexpectedly. I slipped it into my kimono, hardly realizing what I did, and fairly flew to Shimmachi, I have no recollection how. Then, with much effort, I persuaded the owner of the house to break the contract with Umegawa's country customer. He agreed to ransom her to me. I managed to save Umegawa by turning over your fifty *ryō* as earnest money. Every morning and night since then I've faced north [1] and worshiped you, telling myself that saving her was possible only because I have a friend in Hachiemon. Yet I knew that no matter how close we are, it is one thing using the money after first getting your permission—that's the same as borrowing—but quite another asking for it later on. While I was wondering what to do, you began to demand your money. One lie led to another, and now that my earlier excuses have proven false, I don't suppose that anything I can say will seem true to you. But other money ought to be coming from Edo in the next four or five days at the latest. Somehow I'll manage to send it to you. I promise you won't lose a penny. It will only make you angry if you think of me as a human being. Consider instead that you've saved a dog's life and

[1] Hachiemon's house in Nakanoshima was north of Chūbei's place in Awaji-machi.

forgive me, I beg you.—I see now why there are always people being executed for crimes. I have no choice from now on but to steal. Do you think it's easy for a man to confess such things? Try to imagine what it's like! Nothing could be as painful as this, not even if I had to cough up a sword from my throat.

Narrator. He weeps tears of anguish. Hachiemon, a man ready to tackle even demons, also sheds tears.

Hachiemon. I admire you for making such a painful confession. I'm a man—I forgive you and I'll wait. Work out your problem as best you can.

Narrator. Chūbei touches his forehead to the ground.

Chūbei. Thank you. I've had five parents—two fathers and three mothers[j]—but it'd be harder to forget your kindness, Hachiemon, than theirs.

Narrator. Tears interrupt his words.

Hachiemon. I am satisfied, if those are your feelings. Well—somebody may be watching. I'll see you soon.

Narrator. He is about to leave when Chūbei's mother calls from inside.

Myōkan. Is that Hachiemon? Chūbei, invite him in.

Narrator. Chūbei has no choice; hesitantly he leads Hachiemon inside. The mother is incorruptible honesty itself.

Myōkan. You sent a messenger a while ago and now you've come yourself. I can see why you'd be impatient. Chūbei, you know his money arrived ten days ago. Why have you delayed delivering it? Stop and think for a moment. What use is a courier service if money is delivered late? Remember the nature of your business. Give Hachiemon the money at once.

Narrator. But Chūbei has no money to give him. Hachiemon guesses Chūbei's thoughts.

Hachiemon. It may sound as if I'm boasting, ma'am, but I'm not in any desperate need for fifty or seventy *ryō.*—I must leave now for Nagabori. Tomorrow will do just as well.

Narrator. He is about to go.

Myōkan. No, no. I won't be able to sleep at night for worry as long as we are holding your precious money. Chūbei, give Hachiemon the money immediately.

Narrator. Thus urged, Chūbei answers "Yes" and goes into the back room. He looks round blankly, but there is no sign of money. He goes through with the pretense of unlocking the cupboard, though he knows it is empty; even

[j] His real parents, his stepmother, and his foster parents.

the squeaking of the key embarrasses him. Wild with anxiety, he prays in his heart that the gods will grant their help.

Chūbei. Thank heavens! There's a pomade jar [k] in this hairdressing kit. Thank you, god of my ancestors!

Narrator. He lifts the jar thrice to his brow in gratitude, then wraps it in paper as though it were a packet of gold pieces, and quickly inscribes in bold black characters "Fifty *Ryō* in Gold." How shameless his deceit—passing off a worthless pot for fifty *ryō* and tricking his mother too!

Chūbei. Here you are, Hachiemon. As you know, I'm under no obligation to deliver this money now, but I'm giving it to you anyway, to relieve my mother's worries and to show my respect for you as a gentleman. Please accept it without further ado and reassure my mother. I'm sure you won't need to undo the packet. You can tell merely by the feel that it contains fifty *ryō*. Have you any objections?

Narrator. He offers the packet. Hachiemon takes it in his hand.

Hachiemon. Why, who do you take me for? I'm Hachiemon of the Tamba-ya, and as long as I get my money, I certainly won't raise any objections. There you are, ma'am. I acknowledge receipt of the remittance from Edo. I'll be expecting you on your visit to the Fudō Temple.[1]

Narrator. He is about to leave when Myōkan, apparently convinced by their deception, calls out.

Myōkan. Chūbei, it's customary when a remittance has been paid to claim the receipt for it. If Hachiemon hasn't the receipt with him, you should ask him please to write a few words. One has to be careful about everything.

Chūbei (*whispers to* Hachiemon). Mother is illiterate—she can't read a word. Please write something, for form's sake.

Narrator. He holds out a writing set and winks.

Hachiemon. That's no problem. I'll be delighted. Here, Chūbei, see what I write!

Narrator. He scrawls a note as his fancy dictates: "Item. I

[k] *Bimmizuire* is a jar used in dressing the sidelocks (*bin*) in a man's coiffure. It was of an oval shape, about an inch thick, and therefore was roughly the dimensions of a packet of gold coins (*koban*).

[1] A temple in the north of Ōsaka; to go there from Chūbei's house would normally take one by way of Nakanoshima, Hachiemon's place.

am not in receipt of fifty *ryō* in gold. The above is positive guarantee that this evening, as previously promised, I will go drinking in the Quarter, and will accompany you as your clown. I engage always to be present whenever there is merrymaking. In witness whereof, I accept this pomade jar as token of my intention to appear on all festive days." [m]

He dashes off this stream of nonsense.

Hachiemon. I'll be leaving now.

Narrator. As soon as he steps outside Myōkan speaks.

Myōkan. Get everything in writing—a written document always carries weight.

Narrator. Chūbei's mother, deceived again, is honest-hearted as the Buddha, but like the Buddha, she will grow angry if rubbed the wrong way once too often.[n] The night spent waiting for word of the thrice-monthly courier from Edo has deepened when outside there is a jingling of horse bells and the loud cry, "The pack horses have come! Open the inside gates!" Men swarm in, shouldering wicker trunks. Chūbei and his mother are overjoyed.

Chūbei. Good luck has returned, and next year will be lucky too! [o] Saké and tobacco for the drivers!

Narrator. The shop is in a turmoil as the clerks, inkstones at their elbows, frantically jot entries in the ledger. Ihei, the chief clerk, still wears a sour expression.

Idei. Mr. Jinnai, a samurai, was here a while ago from the mansion in Dōjima. He said that notice of the expected arrival of three hundred *ryō* of gold on the ninth had reached him, and he couldn't understand why it was so late. He left in a huff. What was the trouble?

Narrator. The supervisor empties his money belt.

Supervisor. Yes, I know about his three hundred *ryō*. The money's urgently needed. Please deliver it tonight.

Narrator. Eight hundred *ryō* in gold, remittances for various clients, are plopped down. Chūbei grows all the more elated.

Chūbei. Put the silver in the inner storehouse, and the

[m] The terminology of this note is a parody of stereotyped phrases normally found in pledges.

[n] From an old proverb, "Even Buddha will get angry if you rub his face three times."

[o] Chūbei thinks of next year because it is already the end of the eleventh moon. The phrase *shiawaseuma* (good-luck horse) refers to the fact that it was customary to write the words "good luck" on the horse's saddle girth.

gold in the safe. Mother, I'll take these three hundred *ryō* to the daimyo's mansion at once. (*To servants.*) Remember, we're entrusted with other people's money. Keep watch on the gate and shut the doors soon. Be particularly careful about fire. I may be a little late returning, but I'll be traveling in a palanquin, so there's nothing to worry about. Finish your dinners and get to bed early.

Narrator. He puts the money into his kimono and ties the strings of his cloak. Frost is gathering this night on the gate as he steps outside. Though he fully intends to go north, his feet follow their accustomed path to the south.[p] Absent-mindedly he crosses West Yoko Canal, so absorbed in thoughts of the prostitute that he reaches Rice Merchants' Street before he realizes it.

Chūbei. What's this? I'm supposed to be on my way to the mansion in Dōjima. Have I been bewitched by a fox? Good heavens!

Narrator. He retraces a few steps, only to stop.

Chūbei. Perhaps the reason why I've come here without meaning to is that Umegawa needs me, and my protecting god is guiding me to her. I'll stop by her place a moment and look in on her.

Narrator. He turns back again.

Chūbei. No, this is disastrous. With this money on me, I'll surely want to spend it. Shall I stop while I can? Shall I go to her?—I'll go and have done with it!

Narrator. His first thought was sensible, his second insensate, his third sends him as a courier back and forth six times a month on the Six Roads, a courier for hell.[q]

[p] North would take him to Dōjima, south to the Shimmachi Quarter.

[q] The courier service went three times a month in both directions between Osaka and Edo, for a total of six trips. The Six Roads refer to the six ways before the soul when it reaches the afterworld.

ACT II

Scene: The Echigo House in the Shimmachi Quarter

Time: Later the same evening

Narrator.

"*Ei-ei!*" cry the crows, the crows,
The wanton crows,
On moonlit nights and in the dark,
Looking for their chance;
"Let's meet!" they cry, "let's meet!"[r]
Green customers are ripened each day, till evening comes and charcoal fires glow, by the love of courtesans of their choice: the love and sympathy these women give, regardless of rank, is in essence one.[s] The Plum blossoms are fragrant and the Pines are lofty, but leaving rank aside,[t] teahouse girls have the deepest affections. Here comes one now, guided by a maid in a cotton print kimono to Echigo House in Sadoya Street—"Oh for a bridge between Echigo and Sado!" the song goes. The owner here is a woman; no doubt this is the reason why the girls who call feel so at home and open their hearts' deepest secrets of love. Umegawa thinks of the Echigo House as her refuge in sorrow, and neglects her duties elsewhere to come here,

[r] The cry of the crows, "*aō, aō,*" is interpreted as the future of the verb *au* (to meet).

[s] Literally, "green wicker hats turn [the color of] scarlet leaves. . . ." Men visiting the Quarter concealed their faces with basket-like wicker hats. Some commentators take the passage to mean that the men stay on until their green hats are reddened by the glow of charcoal fires.

[t] Pines (*matsu*) were the highest rank of courtesan, and Plum blossoms (*ume*) came next. Umegawa belongs to the humble class of *mise jorō*, prostitutes who call to customers from their shops.

hiding a while from the Island House—"island hiding," as Kakinomoto said.[u]

Umegawa (*to* proprietress). Kiyo, that blockhead of a country bumpkin has been bothering me all day and my head is splitting. Hasn't Chūbei showed up yet? I sneaked away from my customer, hoping at least to see you, my only connection with Chūbei.

Narrator. She slides open the *shōji* door as she enters, even as she will slide it tomorrow at dawning.

Kiyo. I'm glad you've come. There's a crowd of girls upstairs relaxing. They're drinking and playing ken[v] to pass the time until their customers call. Why don't you join them in a game of ken and have a cup of saké? It'll cheer you up. Some of your friends are there.

Narrator. Umegawa goes upstairs. The room is draughty and the women—no men are present—are drinking saké warmed over a *hibachi,* their hands tired from the gestures of the game. *"Romase!" "Sai!" "Tōrai!"*[w] "A tie!" Takase of the high-pitched voice takes on Toyokawa, and her fingers flash. *"Hama!" "San!" "Kyū!" "Gō!" "Ryū!" "Sumui!"*

Toyokawa. I win! You must drink another cup! You can manage one, can't you, Narutose?

Takase. Look, Umegawa's here. (*To* Umegawa.) You couldn't have come at a better time. You're so good at *ken.* Chiyotose's been beating us all evening long, and we're furious. Do take her on. Oh, I'll get another bottle of saké for you.

Umegawa. I hate saké and I'm in no mood for *ken.* What I would like from you is a few tears of sympathy. My customer from the country intends to ransom me. Why, just today at the Island House he was trying to badger me into consent. I lost my temper, I hate him so. All the same, he spoke first. Chūbei asked later on, and it took all the master's efforts to get Chūbei permission to put down the earnest money. The master even extended the deadline when Chūbei failed to pay the balance as he promised. We've managed to stay together so far but, after all, Chūbei has responsibilities. He must think of

[u] Kakinomoto no Hitomaro, the great poet of the early eighth century. The phrase occurs in poem No. 409 of the *Kokinshū.*

[v] A game of Chinese origin. Each player holds out none to five fingers; the one who guesses the total held out by both wins.

[w] Approximations of the Chinese pronunciations with various suffixes: *romase* is "six," *sai,* "seven," and *tōrai,* "ten." The numbers later in the passage are, respectively, eight, three, nine, five, six, and four.

his foster mother, and he runs an important business between here and Edo, with commissions from the daimyo granaries and all the leading merchants. Anything at all might ruin our plans.

If I allow myself be redeemed by that oaf, I could kill myself afterwards and still people would say, since I'm not a high-class courtesan, "Her head was turned by filthy lucre. What contemptible creatures those teahouse girls are!" I must think of my reputation and the feelings of my friend Kamon and the other girls of my class. Oh, I wish I could be together with Chūbei, as we've always planned, and free myself from this endless gossip!

Narrator. Her sleeve is soaked with tears as she speaks. Her listeners, the other prostitutes, compare their lot to hers, and nodding, share in her tears.

Prostitute. I feel terribly depressed. Why don't we cheer ourselves with a little music? Will one of you maids run down and ask Takemoto Tanomo to come here? [x]

Umegawa. Don't bother—I was buying some hair oil at his shop a few minutes ago and I happened to hear that he went directly from the theater to the Fan House in Echigo Street.[y] But I am a pupil of Tanomo's. I'll show you how well I can imitate him! A samisen, please.

Narrator. She begins to play a piece about Yūgiri, using this old example to tell of the courtesan's fate today.

Umegawa. There's no truth in courtesans, people say, but they are deceived, and their words but confessions of ignorance in love. Truth and falsehood are essentially one. Consider the courtesan, so faithful to her lover that she is ready to throw away her life for him—when no word comes from the man and he steadily grows more distant, brood over it as she may, a woman of this profession cannot control her fate. She may be ransomed instead by a man she does not love, and the vows she has pledged become falsehoods. But sometimes it happens that a man favored by a courtesan from the start with merely the false smiles of her trade may, when constant meetings have deepened their love, become her lifelong partner; then all her first falsehoods have proved to be truth. In short, there is neither falsehood nor truth in love. All that we can say for certain is that fate brings people to-

[x] A leading *jōruri* chanter of his day. He owned a hair-oil shop in the Shimmachi Quarter.

[y] The Fan House (Ōgi-ya) was famous as the scene of the loves of Yūgiri, the great courtesan, and Izaemon. The selection about Yūgiri which Umegawa sings is quoted from an early work by Chikamatsu, *Sanzesō* (1686).

gether. The very courtesan who lies awake, sleepless night with longing for the lover she cannot meet, may b cursed by him for her cruelty, if he knows not her grie If that country fellow curses me, let him. I can't hel loving Chūbei, that's my sickness. I wonder if all wom of our profession have the same chronic complaint?

Narrator. The story of one who all for love abandon the world induces melancholy reveries, and even the effec of the saké wear off. Hachiemon of Nakanoshima, a proaching from Nine House Street, hears the singing.

Hachiemon. Ah-ha! I recognize the voices of those whore Is the madam there?

Narrator. He charges in. He picks up a long-handled broo and, holding it by the sweeping end, bangs loudly on th ceiling with the handle.

Hachiemon. You give yourselves away, girls! I've been li tening to you down here. What kind of man do you mi so much? If it makes you lonely being without a ma there's one available here, though I don't suppose he's your taste. How would you like him?

Narrator. He shouts up through the floor. Umegawa do not recognize him.

Umegawa. Of course I want to see my sweetheart! If it wrong for me to say so, come up and beat me! (*To* Kiyo. Who is that downstairs, Kiyo?

Kiyo. Nobody to worry about. It's Hachi from Nakan shima.

Narrator. Umegawa is alarmed.

Umegawa. Oh, dear, I don't want to see him. Please, a of you, go downstairs and don't let on, whatever you d that I'm here.

Prostitute. We'll be the souls of discretion.

Narrator. They nod and file downstairs.

Hachiemon. Well, well—Chiyotose, Narutose, quite a dis tinguished gathering! They told me at the Island Hous that Umegawa left her room early this evening and wer off somewhere, but Chūbei doesn't seem to have showe up here yet. Madam, come closer. You too, girls, an the maids also. I have something to tell about Chūbei, fo your ears only. Gather round.

Narrator. He whispers confidentially.

Prostitute. What can it be? You have us worried.

Narrator. They are all anxious lest Umegawa upstairs hea some unfortunate rumor. Just at this moment Chūbe furtively runs up to the Echigo House, his body chille by the night and the icy weight of the three hundre *ryō* on his heart. He peeps inside and sees Hachiemon sitting in the place of honor, spreading rumors about himself. Astonished, Chubei eavesdrops, while upstairs Umegawa is listening with rapt attention. The walls have ears: Hachiemon's words heard through them are the source of the disasters that follow, though he does not suspect it.

Hachiemon. You may imagine from what I am going to say that I'm jealous of Chūbei, but—Heaven strike me down if I lie!—I feel sorry when I think of how he's going to end his days. Yes, it's true that he sometimes shelters under his roof for a time a thousand or even two thousand *ryō* of other people's money, but his own fortune, throwing in his house, property, and furniture, doesn't amount to fifteen or twenty *kamme* [z] at most. They say his father in Yamato is a rich man but, after all, he's a farmer, and you can imagine the size of his fortune if he had to send Chūbei as an adopted son to the Kame-ya. I'm a young man myself, and like any other young man, I have to visit the teahouses every so often, though it costs me ten or twenty *ryō* a year. But Chūbei is so mad about Umegawa that he's bought her for himself most of the time since last June in competition with another customer at the Island House, though he can ill afford it. I gather that her ransom was recently arranged and Chūbei gave as his deposit fifty of the 160 *ryō* required. That's why the money he should have delivered to various customers hasn't been paid, and he's had to resort to outright lies in order to stave them off. He's caught in a terrible fix. Just supposing he decided to ransom Umegawa as of this minute—she must have her debts, and he could weep his head off, and the bill would still come to 250 *ryō*. Does he think the money will fall from heaven or gush up out of the ground? His only way to raise it is to steal. Where do you suppose the fifty *ryō* he gave for the deposit came from? He intercepted a remittance of mine from Edo and that's what he used. I suspected nothing of this, and when I went to claim my money, there was his foster mother, poor woman. She knew that the money had arrived from Edo and she urged Chūbei to deliver it immediately. Shall I show you the gold pieces Chūbei paid me?

Narrator. He takes out a packet.

Hachiemon. See—it looks like fifty *ryō* on the outside,

[z] Fifteen *kamme* would make about 250 *ryō* and twenty *kamme* over 333 *ryō*. Twenty *kamme* would be worth about $10,000.

but I'll reveal what's actually inside. This is why Chūb
will end up on the block!

Narrator. He cuts open the packet and empties it: o
drops a pottery pomade jar. The proprietress and all th
prostitutes shrink back with cries of alarm. Upstair
Umegawa, her face pressed against the *tatami*, weep
stifling her sobs. Chūbei, whose short temper is his u
doing, fumes.

Chūbei. Telling something to a prostitute is proclaiming
to the world. Such arrogance and insults on my manhoo
all because he advanced me a paltry fifty *ryō!* I'm su
that if Umegawa hears of this she'll want to kill hersel
I'll draw fifty *ryō* from the 300 in my wallet, thro
them in his face, and tell him exactly what I think of hin
It'll save my honor and wipe out the insult to Umegaw
—But this money belongs to a samurai, and besides, it
urgently needed. I must be patient.

Narrator. His hand goes to his wallet again and again a
he disconsolately debates which way to turn, at cros
purposes with himself like the crossbill's beak. Inevitabl
he fails to understand Hachiemon's intent.

Hachiemon holds up the pomade jar.

Hachiemon. You can buy one of these for eighteen copper
Gold may be cheap, but never since the days of Jimmu
has fifty *ryō* in gold gone for eighteen coppers. If this
the way he treats even a friend, you can imagine how h
must cheat strangers. From now on you'll see how h
goes step by step from cutpurse to cutthroat and finall
to the block where his own head gets cut off. It's
shame. When a man is that corrupted, nothing can cur
him—not the threat of disinheritance by his parents c
master, nor the admonitions of Shaka or Daruma, nc
even a personal lecture delivered by Prince Shōtoku him
self.[b] I'd like you to spread this story throughout th
Quarter and see to it that Chūbei isn't permitted her
again. I wish you'd also persuade Umegawa to break wit
him and gracefully allow herself to be ransomed by he
country customer at the Island House. Rascals like Chūbe
never come to a good end. They either get involved in
love suicide or else they wind up stealing some prostitute'
clothes. They're sure to bring disgrace on their friends b
being exposed in the stocks at the Main Gate with on

[a] The legendary first emperor of Japan.

[b] Shōtoku Taishi, one of the chief figures in the establishmer
of Buddhism in Japan (573–621?).

sidelock shaven.[c] That's what is meant by being outside the pale of human society. If you care for Chūbei, don't let him in here again.

arrator. Umegawa, hearing his words, is torn by mingled grief and pity and a feeling of helplessness. Silent tears rack her breast.

megawa. I wish I had a knife or even a pair of scissors so I could cut out my tongue and die.

arrator. The women downstairs can guess the agony she undergoes.

rostitute. Umegawa must be miserable. What an unlucky girl! Poor Umegawa, I feel sorriest for her!

arrator. The servants, the cooks, and even the young maids wring their sleeves for the tears.

Chūbei, always hot-tempered, is unable to endure more. He bursts into the room and plops himself down almost in Hachiemon's lap.

hūbei. Well, Mr. Hachiemon of the Tamba-ya. Just as eloquent as ever, I see. Ah, there's a man for you, a prince! A gathering of three is a public meeting, they say —how kind of you to make an inventory of my possessions before this assemblage!—Look here! This jar was an understanding between friends. I handed it to you only after first asking indirectly if you'd accept it in order to reassure my mother. You agreed. But are you so worried now you might lose the fifty *ryō* you lent me that you must blab it all over the Quarter and ruin my reputation? Or have you taken a bribe from that customer at the Island House to win over Umegawa and deliver her to him? I've had enough of your nonsense! You've nothing to worry about. Chūbei's not a man to cause a friend to lose fifty or a hundred *ryō*. My esteemed Mr. Hachiemon—damn you, Hachiemon! Here's your money! Give me back the pledge!

arrator. He pulls out the money and is about to untie the packet when Hachiemon stops him.

achiemon. Chūbei—wait! Don't let your foolishness get the better of you. I know your character well enough to realize you'd never listen to any advice from me. I hoped that if I could persuade the people of the Quarter to keep you at a distance, you might pull yourself together and become a normal human being again. I acted out of kindness to a friend and for no other reason. If I had been

[c] A punishment imposed by the authorities of the Quarter on ustomers who transgressed its regulations.

afraid for my fifty *ryō,* I'd have said so before yo mother. Why, I even wrote out a crazy receipt to hum your mother, though she can't read. And have I still n been considerate enough?—That packet you've got the looks like 300 *ryō.* I don't suppose it belongs to yc No doubt it's money you'll have to account for. If y tamper with it, you won't find another Hachiemon to set for a pomade jar! But perhaps you intend to give yo head in exchange? I suggest that instead of flying off t handle you deliver the money to its owner. You unsettl lunatic!

Narrator. He roundly upbraids Chūbei, point for point.

Chūbei. Stop trying to act the part of the disinterest friend! What makes you so sure that this money belon to somebody else? Do you think I haven't three hundr *ryō* of my own? Now that you've called my fortune in question before all these women, my honor demands the more that I return your money.

Narrator. Unfastening the packet, he scoops out ten, twent thirty, forty, and then—the final step to disaster—fif *ryō.* He quickly wraps the coins in paper.

Chūbei. Here's proof that nobody loses any money on a count of Chūbei of the Kame-ya! Take your money!

Narrator. He flings it down.

Hachiemon. What kind of insult is this? Say "thank yo politely and offer it again.

Narrator. He throws back the money.

Chūbei. What thanks do I owe you?

Narrator. Again he throws the money at Hachiemon, wh throws it back. They roll up their sleeves and grapp Umegawa, overcome by tears, runs downstairs.

Umegawa. I've heard everything. Hachiemon is entire right. Hachiemon, please forgive Chūbei, for my sake.

Narrator. She raises her voice and weeps.

Umegawa. Shame on you, Chūbei! How can you lose yo head that way? Men who come to the Quarter, even mi lionaires, are frequently pressed for money. A disgra here is no disgrace at all. What do you hope to achie by breaking the seal on someone else's money and scatte ing it around? Would you like to get arrested and dragg off to prison with a rope around you? Would you pref such a disgrace to your present trouble? It wouldn't only a matter of disgrace for you—what would happ to me? Calm yourself at once and apologize to Hachiemo Then wrap up the money and deliver it as quickly as yc can to its owner. I know you don't want to give me up another man. I feel the same. I have plans all worked out in my mind if I should have to sacrifice myself. My contract still has two years to run. Then, even if I have to sell myself to some country brothel—Miyajima, who knows?—or become a streetwalker on the Ōsaka docks, I'll look after you. I'll never let my man suffer. So calm yourself. You're acting shamefully.—But whose fault is it? Mine. And knowing it's entirely my fault, I feel grateful and sorry for you at the same time. Try to imagine what I am going through.

Narrator. She pleads with him, and her tears, falling on the pieces of gold, are like the dew settling on the primroses of Idé.

Chūbei, utterly carried away, has recourse to a desperate last resort; he remembers the money he brought with him as an adopted son.

Chūbei. Be quiet! Do you take me for such a fool? Don't worry about the money. Hachiemon himself knows that I brought it from Yamato when I came here as an adopted son. It was left in someone's keeping, but I've claimed it now in order to ransom you. Madam, come here!

Narrator. He summons her.

Chūbei. The other day I gave you a deposit of fifty *ryō*. Here are 110 *ryō* more. That makes a total of 160 *ryō*, the money needed to ransom Umegawa. These forty-five *ryō* are what I owe you on account—you worked it out the other day. Five *ryō* are for the Chaser.[d] I believe that Umegawa's fees since October come to about fifteen *ryō* altogether, but I can't be bothered with petty calculations. Here're twenty *ryō*, and now please clear my account. These ten *ryō* are a present for you, by way of thanks for your trouble. One *ryō* each goes to Rin, Tama, and Gohei. Come get it!

Narrator. He showers gold and silver in the momentary glory of the dream of Kantan.[e]

Chūbei. Please arrange the ransom at once so that Umegawa can leave this evening.

Narrator. His words stir the proprietress into sudden animation.

Kiyo. It's a strange thing with money—when you haven't

[d] A teahouse employee who served as both a procuress and a guardian of the courtesans.

[e] Reference to the Nō play *Kantan* (originally based on a Chinese legend) which tells of Rosei, a man who slept on a magic pillow in Kantan and dreamed a lifetime of glory. He awoke to discover that scarcely an hour had passed since he went to sleep.

got it, you haven't got it, but when it comes, it comes i a flood. There's nothing more to worry about. I hop you're happy, Umegawa. I'll take this precious money t the owner. Rin and Tama—come along.

Narrator. They hurry out together. Hachiemon looks ur convinced.

Hachiemon (to himself). I don't believe he's telling th truth, but it's money he owes me anyway, and it'd be fool ish reticence to refuse (*To* Chūbei.) Yes, I acknowledg receipt of the fifty *ryō*. Here's your note!

Narrator. He throws it at Chūbei.

Hachiemon. Umegawa, you're lucky to have such a fin man. Enjoy yourselves, girls.

Narrator. He departs, stuffing the money into his wallet

Prostitutes. We should be going too. Congratulations, Ume gawa.

Narrator. They leave for their respective houses. Chū bei is impatient.

Chūbei. Why is the madam taking so long? Gohei, go tel her to hurry.

Narrator. He urges the man frantically.

Gohei. I'm sorry, sir, but when a woman is ransomed th owner's permission is necessary. Then the elders of th Quarter cancel the seals on her contract. Finally the man ager of the Quarter for the current month has to issue a pass or she can't go out the Main Gate. It'll take a bi longer.

Chūbei. Here, this is to speed them.

Narrator. He throws another gold piece.

Gohei. Leave it to me, sir!

Narrator. He races off nimbly: a piece of gold is mor effective in building strong legs than a moxa cure.[f]

Chūbei (to Umegawa). You get ready in the meanwhile You look a mess. Here, tighten your sash.

Narrator. He speaks with desperate urgency.

Umegawa. Why are you so excited? This is the most won derful occasion of my life. I'd like to offer the other girl a drink and say good-by properly. Please give me mor time before I leave.

Narrator. Her face is flushed with innocent high spirits Chūbei bursts into tears.

Chūbei. My poor dear! Didn't you realize that somethin was wrong? That money was an urgent remittance for

[f] The burning of the herb *mogusa* (moxa) at various places o the skin is still believed to strengthen different parts of the body

samurai residence in Dōjima. I knew that once I touched the money my life was ended. I tried very hard to restrain myself, but I could tell how mortified you were to see your lover humiliated before your friends. I wanted so badly to cheer you that my hand went unconsciously to the money. Once a man goes that far, he can't back away. Please try to think of our troubles as the workings of fate. —Hachiemon is on his way now to tell my mother—it was written all over his face. People will be here any moment from the eighteen courier houses to question me. We are now one foot over the brink of hell. Run away with me!

arrator. He clings to her and weeps. Umegawa moans and begins to tremble. Her voice shakes into tears.

megawa. There—isn't this what I've always predicted? Why should we cling any longer to life? To die together is all we can ask. I would gladly die this very moment. Calm yourself, please, and think.

hūbei. Could I have committed such a terrible crime if I had planned to go on living? But let us stay alive and together as long as we can, though we are resolved that sooner or later we must kill ourselves.

megawa. Yes, we'll stay together in this world as long as it's possible. But someone may come at any moment. Hide here.

arrator. She pushes him behind a screen.

megawa. Oh, I left my good-luck amulet in the chest of drawers in my room. I wish I had it.

hūbei. How could we escape punishment for our crime, no matter how powerful your amulet may be? Make up your mind to it—we are doomed to die. I will offer prayers for your repose. Please offer them for mine.

arrator. He raises his head above the screen.

megawa. Ugh—how horrible! Please don't do that—you look too much like something I can't bear.[g]

arrator. She throws her arms around the screen and chokes with tears.

The proprietress of the Echigo House and her servants return.

iyo. Everything's been settled. I've had your pass sent round to the West Gate. That's the shortest way for you.

arrator. She speaks words of good cheer, but the hus-

[g] His head appearing over the screen looks like the severed head f a criminal exposed on a wall.

band and wife are trembling, and their voices shake as they repeat, "Good-by, good-by."

Kiyo. You sound as if you're cold. How about a drink?

Chūbei. The saké wouldn't get down my throat.

Kiyo. I don't know whether to congratulate you or to tell you how sorry I am to see you go. I could chatter on a thousand days and still not run out of things to say.

Chūbei. I wish you hadn't mentioned "Thousand Days." [h]

Narrator. They take their farewells as the cock is crowing. His extravagance has been with others' money; now all is scattered like sand. They pass Sand Bank,[i] and let their feet guide them, come fields or come mountains, along the road to Yamato.

[h] Sennichi (Thousand Days) was an execution ground in Ōsaka.

[i] Sunaba (Sand Bank) was just outside the West Gate of the Quarter.

ACT III

Scene One: The road to Ninokuchi Village in Yamato

Time: The next day and the following three weeks

Narrator.
The green curtains, the crimson bedding,
The chamber where once, under familiar coverlets,
They ranged pillows all night through
And heard the drum sound the Gate's closing—
All has now vanished, comes not again even in dreams.

Umegawa.
Yes, though my lover promised without fail
He'd ransom me before autumn, I waited in vain.[j]
I trusted the fickle world, I trusted people,
But now my ties with the world and people are broken.
Though once we shared midnight trysts at the Gate,
Now we are kept apart by the barrier of men's eyes.
His hair is uncombed since yesterday;
When I take my comb to smooth his twisted locks,
My fingers are frozen with tears.
We press our chilled limbs to each other's thighs,
Making a double *kotatsu*.
The bearers pause, a moment's breathing spell—
How strange that we still breathe, that our lives go on!

Narrator.
They weep at Spillway Gate.[k]
There's still a while before the dawn, they think,
And lift the blinds of their palanquin.
Their knees remain entwined; they remember
Meetings at night in her little room—so alike,

[j] Most of the above description is taken almost word for word from the Nō play *Hanjo,* though the phrases acquire a somewhat different meaning in this context.

[k] Kobore-guchi, the gate leading to Hirano.

But when did charcoal ashes turn to morning frost?
When summoned by the night winds,
Only the maid-pines[l] of the fields respond,
Recalling nights gone by, a source of tears.

Chūbei. Why are you so distraught? This is our foretaste of rebirth on one lotus.[m]

Narrator. He comforts Umegawa and takes comfort himself in smoking a double pipe with her.[n] The thin smoke and the morning fog melt and clear; the wind blows wild through the wheat sprouts. Ashamed to be seen by the early-rising farmers or by some field watchman who might ask them for a light, they stop their palanquin and dismiss the bearers. They do not begrudge the bearers' fees nor even their uncertain lives, much less the hardship of walking barefoot. All that they begrudge is their remembrance of this world.

Never before has she worn an old woman's wadded hat.

Umegawa. Here, please warm yourself with this. It's more important than that I hide my face.

Narrator. She offers her purple kerchief to protect him from the wind, but for them purple passion is a thing of the past; today they are truly husband and wife.

They worship at the Kōshin Shrine[o] where prayers are answered. They turn back and see some boy actors praying for popularity before the Aizen of the Shōman Temple amid offerings from the Dōtombori players and the women of the familiar houses of the Quarter. Among the lanterns marked with crests she knows, she notices one—oh painful memories!—from the Tsuchi-ya, her own house.

Umegawa. Look, here is your crest, the muskmelon, and next to it mine, the double pine cone. When we offered this lantern, we prayed for the pine's thousand years, but our vows were ill-fated.

Chūbei. Tonight, as the lanterns of our existence flicker

[l] *Kaburomatsu* are low, thick-growing pines. *Kaburo* (or *kamuro*) is the name of a courtesan's maid; here the contrast is made between the gay quarters where *kaburo* answered when summoned and the windswept fields where only the *kaburomatsu* reply.

[m] In Pure Land Buddhism, saved souls are reborn on lotuses in the Western Paradise. Lovers hope to be reunited on the same lotus, in the manner that Chūbei and Umegawa now share one palanquin.

[n] A pipe with two stems leading to a single bowl, smoked by lovers.

[o] A shrine south of the South Gate of the Tennō-ji. Shōman Temple is northwest of the same group of buildings. The Guardian King Aizen was popular with courtesans, boy actors, and others who depended on *ai* (love).

out, let us consider the crested robes we wear are our mourning shrouds, and journey hand in hand to hell.

Umegawa. Yes, I will be led by you.

Narrator. Again they take each other's hands; the tears they shed glaze the ice on their sleeves.

Though no one bars their way, they advance slowly, asking directions at every turn. Umegawa is still in this morning's attire;[p] her frozen sandals stick to her bare feet. A bank of clouds in the sky threatens sleet, and leaves flutter in a wind mixed with hail. They have reached Hirano.[q]

Chūbei. Many people know me here. Come this way.

Narrator. They cover their faces with their sleeves and twist their way through the back streets of the town and over rice field paths till they reach Wisteria Well Temple.[r]

Chūbei. Look—you see, even the remotest village belongs to the world of love!

Narrator. A girl of seventeen or so, picking vegetables behind her house, is singing:

"You, standing by the gate,
Are you my secret lover?
The field winds will do you harm,
Please come inside the house."

They envy others' words of tenderness.

Chūbei. Do you remember? When was it—that morning of the first snow when the early customers were arriving and you walked back with me, still in your night clothes, through the thin snow by the Great Gate? The snow today is no different, but our hopes have entirely changed. You poor dear—it was because of me that you were first made to suffer, step by step the white cloth was dyed deeper, from blue to indigo. If divine punishment should strike for the vows we wrote, the Hachiman of Konda as our witness, may it spare you!

Narrator. He weeps.

Though for a while I may escape
The prying eyes of men. . . .

Umegawa. I'm as much to blame as you!

Narrator. Her words dissolve in endless tears that soak her folded handkerchiefs. Her skirts are torn by the dun-

[p] She wears a courtesan's robes, conspicuous outside the Quarter. Courtesans do not wear *tabi* (linen socks).

[q] About five miles south of Ōsaka; today part of the city.

[r] *Fujii-dera.* Twisting streets are associated with the twisting of

colored weeds. In the frost-withered fields the wind crackles through the desolate stretches of pampas grass.

Chūbei. Was that rustling the sound of people coming after us?

Narrator. He stands over Umegawa, concealing her, but when he glances up, he realizes that the sounds were not of men.

Chūbei. For what crime are we being punished that we should be frightened by the flapping of pheasants' wings?

Narrator. Flocks of crows over the forest of Tonka harshly scold, weeping—or laughing?—to see the lovers attempt to comfort each other, unwilling to allow them even one untroubled night. At Takama Mountain—shades of the god of Katsuragi [s]—they hesitate to travel by daylight on their furtive road, their road of love, their road through a world made narrow by themselves. At Within-the-Bamboos Pass their sleeves are soaked. Next they journey the stony road called Cavern Crossing. They struggle on, across fields, mountains, and villages, all for love.

The laws of a well-governed land are strict; pursuers have been despatched to the home provinces in search of the guilty pair. Yamato especially, as Chūbei's birthplace, is canvassed by men from the seventeen courier houses, some disguised as pilgrims, others as dealers in old clothes or itinerant performers. They peep into the houses and with peep shows and sweets beguile the children into furnishing clues. Umegawa and Chūbei are like birds in a snare or fish in a weir: they are doomed not to escape. Unfortunate Chūbei!—it is hard enough to conceal himself alone, but impossible to keep Umegawa's appearance from attracting attention. They spend days in hired sedan chairs, five nights at an inn in Nara, and three nights at a teahouse in Miwa. In a little over twenty days they have spent forty *ryō*, and only half a *ryō* remains of the money. They pass by without stopping at Hatsuse Mountain —how misty the sound of its bell—and finally reach Ninokuchi Village, his father's home.

Scene Two: Ninokuchi Village, outside the hut of Chūzaburō

Time: The end of the twelfth moon

[s] The god of Katsuragi was so ashamed of his ugliness that he appeared only at night.

'hūbei. O-ume,[t] this is the town where I was born and grew up. I spent my first twenty years here, but I can never remember having seen so many beggars and peddlers of every description at the end of the year, nor even at New Year, for that matter. Look—do you see those men standing there? There were a couple of others at the edge of the fields. I'm beginning to feel nervous. Another four or five hundred yards farther on and we'll be at my real father's—Magoemon's—house, but I daren't go there. I haven't heard from my father since I went away and, besides, there's my stepmother. This thatch-covered hut belongs to Chūzaburō, a tenant farmer with an allotment from my family. He's been a close friend ever since I was a boy, and I know I can trust him. Let's call on him.

Varrator. He leads her inside the hut.

'hūbei. Chūzaburō, are you at home? I haven't seen you in ages.

Varrator. He goes boldly in. A woman, apparently Chūzaburō's wife, meets him.

Vife. Who is it, please? My husband's been at the headman's house since this morning, and he's still not come back.

'hūbei. Chūzaburō never used to have a wife. Who might you be, please?

Vife. I came here as his bride three years ago, and I don't know any of my husband's old friends. Excuse me, but I wonder if you folks wouldn't happen to be from Ōsaka? People have been talking about our landlord Magoemon's stepson[u]—Chūbei's his name. He went to Ōsaka as an adopted son and took up with a prostitute. They say he stole some money and ran off with her. The magistrate's investigating now. Magoemon disowned his son long ago, and he says that whatever may happen to Chūbei is no concern of his, but all the same, they're father and son, and it must be hard on a man of his age. My husband's an old friend of Chūbei, and he has the idea that Chūbei may be wandering in this neighborhood. He'd be sorry to see him get caught, and he's been keeping watch everywhere. Today the village headman sent for my husband. What with meetings and papers to seal, the whole village is in an uproar—now, at the end of the year!—all

[t] Umegawa's real name, presumably. Umegawa was her name as a ourtesan.

[u] Possibly called "stepson" because he is not the child of Aagoemon's present wife.

on account of that prostitute. She's certainly causing a l
of trouble.

Narrator. The woman babbles unrestrainedly. Chūbei
stunned.

Chūbei. Yes, rumors about Chūbei are going around Osak
too. My wife and I are on our way to Ise for an end o
the year retreat at the shrine. I stopped by for old time
sake, happening to be in the neighborhood. Would yo
please ask Chūzaburō to come here a moment? I'd lik
to see him before I leave, even if there isn't time to s
down. But please don't tell him we've come from Osaka.

Wife. Are you in such a big hurry? I'll go fetch him a
once. But you know, there's a priest from Kyoto who
been giving sermons every day at the temple in Kamad
Village. My husband may have gone there directly fro
the headman's house. Please keep the fire going under th
soup while I'm away.

Narrator. She rolls up her sleeves and runs out. Umegaw
shuts the back gate and fastens the latch.

Umegawa. We're really in the midst of the enemy here. D
you think we'll be all right?

Chūbei. Chūzaburō has an unusually chivalrous natur
for a farmer. I'll ask him to put us up for the night. I
I'm to die, it's best that it be here, where my bod
will become the earth of my native soil. I'd like to b
buried in the same grave with my real mother so that i
the future world I can present to her my bride.

Narrator. His eyes grow heavy with tears.

Umegawa. How happy that would make me! My ow
mother lives at Rokujō in Kyōto. I'm sure that the au
thorities have gone to question her during these past day
She's always suffered from dizzy spells, and I wonder how
she's taken the news. I'd like to go to Kyōto and see m
mother again before I die.

Chūbei. I'm sure you would. I'd like to meet your mothe
too, and tell her I'm her son.

Narrator. They embrace, for no one can see. The rain o
tears is too much for their sleeves to hold; a driving show
er beats against the windows.

Chūbei. It seems to have started raining.

Narrator. He opens the patched paper *shōji* a crack
Through the lattice window facing west, he looks out on
windswept road across the fields. Worshipers are hurryin
towards the temple, their umbrellas tilted to protect ther
from the rain slanting from behind.

Chūbei. I know them all—they're people of the villag
The man in front is Sukezaburō from Taruibata, a lead

ing man in the village. And that old woman is Den's mother, Den the humpbacked porter. What a tea drinker she is! That man over there with his head almost completely shaved used to be the poorest man in town. He had so much trouble paying his taxes that he sold his daughter to Shimabara Quarter in Kyōto. A rich paper merchant ransomed her and made her his wife. Now, thanks to his son-in-law, the old man is a property holder—five *chō* of ricelands and storehouses in two places. I've ransomed a courtesan too, just as the paper merchant did, but it breaks my heart to think of the unhappiness I've brought your mother.—That old man is Tōjibei the Leveler.[v] At eighty-eight he ate a quart and a half of rice and didn't leave a grain. This year he's turned ninety-five. That priest coming up after him is Dōan the needle-doctor.[w] He killed my mother with his needle. He's my mother's enemy, now that I think of it.

Narrator. His bitterness comes from grief.

Chūbei. Look! That's my father! You can see him now.

Umegawa. The man in the hemp jacket?[x] Yes, his eyes are just like yours.

Chūbei. To think that a father and son who look so much alike cannot even exchange a few words! This must be my father's punishment!—He's grown old. How unsteady his legs are! Farewell, father, for this life!

Narrator. He joins his hands in prayer.

Umegawa. I see you for the first and last time. I am your son's wife. My husband and I are doomed not to know even our next moments, but I hope that when you have passed your hundred years we shall meet again in the future life.

Narrator. She murmurs the words to herself. The two join hands and, in voices choked with tears, lament.
Magoemon passes by their door, pausing again and again to rest his aged limbs. He slips on the ice of the ditch at the edge of the fields and, when he checks himself, the thong of his high *geta* snaps. He falls heavily on his side into the muddy field. Chūbei cries out in dismay. He writhes in anguish and alarm but, fugitive that he is, he dares not leave the house.

[v] Tōjibei was asked, in deference to his auspicious old age, to make leveling rods for rice measures. The eighty-eighth birthday is called the "rice anniversary" (*beiju*) because of the calligraphic pun on the character.

[w] Acupuncture is still a branch of traditional Japanese medicine.

[x] A sleeveless jacket worn by believers in Pure Land Buddhism when they went to worship.

Umegawa rushes out. She lifts the old man in her arms and wrings the muddy water from the skirt of hi kimono.

Umegawa. You haven't hurt yourself anywhere, have you What a dreadful thing to happen to an old gentleman! I'l wash your feet and mend the thong. Please don't feel th least embarrassed with me.

Narrator. She comforts him, massaging his back and knees Magoemon raises himself.

Magoemon. Thank you, whoever you are. No, I haven' hurt myself. What a kind young lady! You've shown me solicitude not even a daughter-in-law could match, merel because of my years. Some people go to the temple for th sermons, but if they are cruel here, in their hearts, the might just as well not go. Your kindness is an act of tru piety. Please wash your hands now. Luckily there's som straw here. I'll use it to mend the thong myself.

Narrator. He takes some coarse paper from his wallet.

Umegawa. I have some good paper. I'll twist it into a cor for you.

Narrator. Magoemon is surprised to see how skillfully sh tears the soft paper into strips.

Magoemon. You know, I don't recall ever having seen yo before in this neighborhood. Who are you, and why ar you so kind to me?

Narrator. He closely examines her face. Umegawa's breas feels all the more constricted.

Umegawa. I'm traveling through. I have a father-in-law just your age, and he looks exactly like you. I don't fee in the least as if I'm helping a stranger. It's a daughter in-law's duty, after all, to serve and comfort her age father when he is stricken. You can't imagine how happ it makes me to be of help! I'm sure that, if he could, m husband would all but fly to your side, taking you for hi father. Please give me your paper in exchange for mine I'll ask my husband to keep it next to his skin as a keep sake for an old gentleman who looks like his father.

Narrator. She tucks the coarse paper in her sleeve. Hid the tears as she will, her emotion betrays itself in her face Magoemon guesses everything from one word and an other, and he cannot suppress his fatherly love. His age eyes are blinded with tears.

Magoemon. You say you show me such devotion becaus I look like your father-in-law? That makes me happy an furious at the same time. I have a grown son with whom I broke off relations for certain reasons. I sent him t

Ōsaka as an adopted son, but some devil got into him, and he laid his hands on a good deal of money belonging to other people. The upshot was that he ran away, and now the search for him has extended to this village. If you want to know who's to blame, it's all my daughter-in-law's fault. It's a foolish thing, I know, but just as in the old proverb this is a case of not hating the son who steals but resenting instead the people who involved him in the crime. Now that I've broken with him, I suppose I should feel utterly indifferent whether he comes to good or ill. But you can imagine how happy it used to make me, even when people said Magoemon was a fool, an idiot, to have disinherited a son so clever, intelligent and well-behaved that he'd made a fortune since going to Ōsaka as an adopted son. Now, when he is hunted and soon to be dragged off a prisoner, you can imagine my grief even when people praise my foresight and good luck in having disinherited him in good time. I shudder to think what will happen. I'm on my way now to worship before Amida and the Founder,[y] and to pray that I may die at least one day ahead of my son. I do not lie to the Buddha.

arrator. He falls prostrate on the ground and weeps aloud. Umegawa sobs and Chūbei holds his hands out through the *shōji,* bowing in worship before his father. His body is shaken by grief.

Magoemon again brushes away the tears.

agoemon. There's no disputing blood. A child, even one disinherited for all eternity, is always dearer to his parent than the closest friend.—Why didn't he take me into his confidence before he embarked on his stealing and swindling? If he had sent me word privately that he was in love with such and such a courtesan and needed money, for whatever purpose it was, I would, of course, have come to his help. Trouble brings a family together, they say, and we are father and son. And he's a motherless son at that. I'd have sold the fields I've saved to support me in my old age to keep him from the jailer's rope. Instead, he has become notorious. He's brought hardship to Myōkan, his foster mother, and caused other losses and suffering. Could I still say, "You're Magoemon's son," and harbor him? Could I even offer him shelter for a single night?

It's all his own doing. He's suffering now, and society

[y] Shinran Shōnin (1173–1262), founder of the Shin Sect of re Land Buddhism.

is too small to hold him. He's brought misery on his wif
and he must slink through the wide world hiding from h
dearest friends, his acquaintances, and even his kin.
didn't bring him into the world so that he might die a di
graceful death! He's a scoundrel, I know, but I love hir

Narrator. He falls into uncontrollable weeping. How hard
is for those who share the same blood! Still weeping, h
takes a piece of silver from his purse.

Magoemon. I happen to have this coin with me. I had i
tended to offer it for the building fund of the Naniw
Temple. I do not give you this money because I take yo
for my daughter-in-law, but by way of thanks for yo
kindness a while ago.—But if you wander about th
neighborhood, people will notice your resemblance to th
fugitive woman. They'll arrest you, and they'll certain
arrest your husband. Use this money for your journe
Take the Gosé Road and leave this place as fast as yo
can. I'd like a glimpse of your husband's face. No—th
would be shirking my duty to society. Send me goo
news soon, that you're safe.

Narrator. He takes two or three steps, then turns back.

Magoemon. What do you think? Would there be any har
in my seeing him?

Umegawa. Who will ever know? Please go to him.

Magoemon. No, I won't neglect my duty to his fami
in Ōsaka.—Urge him, I beg you, not to violate nature b
making a father mourn his son.

Narrator. He chokes with emotion. They part at last, tur
ing back again and again. Then the husband and wife co
lapse in tears and, forgetting that others might see, th
abandon themselves to their grief. How pathetic the ti
between this father and son!

Chūzaburō's wife returns, drenched with rain.

Wife. I'm sorry to have kept you waiting. My husband we
straight from the headman's house to the temple, and
couldn't get to see him. The rain is beginning to let u
I'm sure he'll be coming back soon.

Narrator. At that moment Chūzaburō runs up, all out
breath.

Chūzaburō. Chūbei—your father's told me everythir
Police agents have come to the village from Ōsaka to a
rest you, and the magistrate is conducting a search. Yo
luck has run out. You're surrounded by swords in bro
daylight. Somebody must've recognized you. They've su
denly started a top to bottom, house to house searc
They're at your father's place now, and my house w

be next. Your poor father—he was out of his mind with grief. He begged me to help you to get away quickly. You're in the jaws of the crocodile now. Hurry, make your escape. Take the road back of the house to the Gosé Highway and head for the mountains.

Narrator. Chūbei and Umegawa are at their wits' ends. Chūzaburō's wife does not realize what is going on.

Wife. Shall I run away with them?

Chūzaburō. Don't be a fool.

Narrator. Pushing her aside, he helps Chūbei and Umegawa into old straw raincoats and rainhats. Their hearts and footsteps are agitated like reeds in a driving rain, but this kindness will not be forgotten even though they die; profoundly touched, they secretly creep out.
Hardly has Chūzaburō breathed a sigh of relief than two parties of raiding constables from the magistrate's office, led by the headman and a village official, simultaneously break into Chūzaburō's house from front and back gates. They roll up the mats, break through the flooring, turn over cabinets, rice chests, and dustbins in their search. The hut is so small that there is nowhere for anyone to hide.

Officer. This house is all right. Search the roads through the fields.

Narrator. The men hunt for the couple among the tea bushes in the field. Magoemon rushes up, barefooted.

Magoemon. What's happened, Chūzaburō? Tell me—they're all right, aren't they?

Chūzaburō. They're all right. There's nothing to worry about. They've both managed to escape.

Magoemon. Thank you. I'm grateful to you. I owe this to Amida's grace. I must go to the temple again immediately and offer my thanks to the Founder. How happy and grateful I am!

Narrator. The two start off together.

Voice. Chūbei of the Kame-ya and Umegawa of the Tsuchi-ya have been apprehended!

Narrator. A crowd mills north of the village. Soon the constables lead in the husband and wife, tightly bound. Magoemon loses consciousness and seems about to expire. Umegawa, seeing Magoemon, weeps till her eyes dim over, to think that she and her husband, bound prisoners, are powerless to help. Chūbei shouts.

Chūbei. I am guilty of the crime and I am ready for my punishment! I know that I cannot escape death. I humbly request you to pray for my repose. But the sight of

my father's anguish will prove an obstacle to my salva
tion. Please, as a kindness, cover my face.

Narrator. An officer takes the towel at Chūbei's waist an
tightly binds his eyes, as though for blindman's buff. Ume
gawa weeps, a sanderling by a river whose flow is un
certain as human fate.

They leave behind in Naniwa the name of two wh
gave their lives for love.

The Subscription List

(KANJINCHŌ)

by Namiki Gohei III

From Kanjincho, a Japanese Kabuki Play, *by A. C. Scott. Tokyo: Hokuseido Press, 1953. Reprinted by permission of A. C. Scott and the Hokuseido Press.*

The Subscription List

This is one of the most popular Kabuki plays ever written. It is an adaptation of a Nō play called *Ataka*[1] by Namiki Gohei III (1789–1855), and was first performed in 1840. It is one of the *juhachiban* or "Eighteen Great Plays." The hero Benkei, a warrior-monk, is depicted both in the drama and in woodblock prints as a large and ferocious, but sensitive, retainer—the epitome of the right-hand man of a nobleman. He appears in other Nō and Kabuki plays (see p. 323).[2]

The Subscription List is a great play for the actor. It is not poetry or beauty we seek here, but action, and even today one feels that the play would make a good film. The situation is a simple, heroic one. The young warrior Yoshitsune is fleeing to the north to seek aid against the persecutions of his older brother. He and his followers are stopped by frontier guards at the barrier in Kaga, and through the courage and cleverness of his chief lieutenant, Benkei, Yoshitsune passes through the barrier to freedom.

Various incidents, guaranteed to win the Japanese audience, give the actor playing Benkei's part a chance to excel. There is a battle of wits between two dignified and powerful opponents, a debate on strategy—shall we try to trick them or fight?—an amusing drinking scene, and an almost unpardonable breach of conduct on Benkei's part which wins the victory. This last episode, in which Benkei beats his disguised master to maintain the deception that he is just a servant, is a heinous breach of the samurai code and certainly brought shudders to the Japanese audience. Benkei's remorse after this episode is acute, and he could quite rea-

[1] Translated by Sir George Sansom in *Transactions of the Asiatic Society of Japan*, XXXVIII, Pt. 3 (1911).

[2] *Benkei in the Boat* (*Funa-Benkei*) is translated in *The Noh Drama, Ten Plays from the Japanese*, translated by the Special Noh Committee (Rutland, Vt.: Charles E. Tuttle Co., 1960), and also by Sansom, above.

sonably commit suicide, but this would spoil the mood o
the play. The end of the play reflects credit on the enemy
Both sides have satisfied the rules of honor.

The action of the play is heightened by virtuoso dances
The version presented here is one close to that used on the
contemporary Kabuki stage.

CHARACTERS

TOGASHI SAEMON, *chief of the warlord Yoritomo's guards at the frontier barrier at Kaga*

GUNNAI, GENNAI, HEINAI — *soldiers of Togashi*

A PAGE TO TOGASHI

YOSHITSUNE, *famous swordsman and younger brother of Yoritomo*

BENKEI, *formerly a monk, and now loyal retainer to Yoshitsune*

KAMEI, KATAOKA, SURUGA — *retainers of Yoshitsune*

The Subscription List

Before the play commences, the notes of flute and drum are heard for several minutes. When the curtain is pulled aside to the sound of the wooden clappers, the nagauta *orchestra* (debayashi) *is revealed at the rear of the stage. Twelve samisen players and eight singers are seated in a row on a long dais* (yamadai) *covered with a scarlet drape and stretching the whole length of the stage. In front of the* yamadai *are seated two stick drummers, three hand drummers, and a single flute player. The two stick drummers sit sideways to the audience, the others face it. The curtain* (age maku) *at the right of the stage is pulled upwards and* Togashi *strides on. He is followed by a small page* (tachimochi) *bearing his sword, and three soldiers. He walks in a slow and stately manner to the front of the stage and faces the audience, the* tachimochi *stands behind, and the three soldiers seat themselves at his right in a single row.* Togashi *then speaks.*

Togashi. I am Saemon Togashi of Kaga[a] province. Now that Yoritomo is estranged from his brother, Yoshitsune and his retainers are said to be fleeing from the capital,[b] disguised as *yamabushi*.[c] Yoritomo, knowing this, has built a new barrier in each province to enable every traveler to be examined. I am the guardian of this barrier. I want you to be careful that no *yamabushi* pass through without being questioned.

[a] Kaga province is in present-day Ishikawa Prefecture on the west coast of Japan opposite Korea. The coastal plain here is still called the Kaga plain and there is today a small city of Kaga.

[b] Kyōto.

[c] Religious mendicants. *Yamabushi* means literally "mountain priest."

Gunnai (first soldier). The other day we killed some suspicious looking *yamabushi* and placed their heads on *kyobokus*.[d]

Gennai (second soldier). If any *yamabushi* comes along we will tie him with ropes and kill him.

Heinai (third soldier). We have been very careful, from now on any *yamabushi* will be held and brought before you.

Gunnai. Each of us is prepared! (*The three join in chorus.*)

Togashi. I am pleased to hear it, you are to be praised for your diligence. If any *yamabushi* appear I will take them by ruse, and Yoritomo's mind will be at rest. I hope you will continue to be on your guard.

Three soldiers together. Your order will be obeyed, sir!

Togashi *then walks over to the left and seats himself on a cylindrical, lacquer tub* (katsura oke). *The soldiers sit at his right and the* tachimochi *to the left rear. The* debayashi *commences a song.*

Song: We set out on a journey wearing suzukake.[e] Because *our expedition is a sad one our sleeves are wet with tears as well as the dew. We left the capital in the moonlight on the night of February the tenth, crossing Mount Ōsaka, and looking back we regretted we could not see Kyōto because of the spring mist. Having crossed Lake Biwa by ship we arrived at Kaizu.*[f]

While this song is being played, Yoshitsune *comes down the* hanamichi *carrying a stave and a large circular hat with the* oizuru [g] *strapped on his back. He turns and poses dramatically, left foot forward, hat held in front of him, his head is raised and he leans back on the stave held in his right hand. He then turns to face the right of the* hanamichi *down which come four of his retainers in single file. They pass beyond him and stand in a row facing left, and assume a kneeling position as* Benkei *makes his entry. He takes a position next to* Yoshitsune, *standing diagonally across the* hanamichi. *While this action is going on* Togashi *and his men re-*

[d] High wooden stands on which captives' heads were placed in former times.

[e] Two large white pompons on the back and two on the front.

[f] They go by ship to the northern end of Lake Biwa.

[g] A box containing an image of the god Fudomyo-O which priests carry on their backs.

main motionless in their positions on the stage. When Benkei *has taken up his stand* Yoshitsune *speaks for the first time.*

Yoshitsune. Now Benkei, we have said on the way here that we shall be unable to reach Michinoku[h] if we are compelled to pass through a series of barriers. It is shameful to be killed by nameless men and I am prepared to die by my own hand first. I cannot ignore my retainer's loyalty however, and on your advice I have disguised myself as a *gōriki.*[i] Have you a good plan to enable us to pass through this barrier?

Kamei (first retainer). Sir, why do we wear these swords? If we do not use them now we shall never do so. It is a critical moment for our master.

Kataoka (second retainer). We must be ready to kill the barrier guards and pass through.

Suruga (third retainer). We have to repay our master's kindness over long years.

All four (rising and speaking in unison). Let us brave this barrier today.

Benkei (facing them). Stop! wait a little. This is a critical moment, we must think carefully. If we meet with the same difficulties at every barrier beyond this one, we are bringing trouble on ourselves by using violence now, it will be still harder to reach Michinoku. That is why I asked my master to take off his *kesa* and *tokin*[j] and disguise himself as a *gōriki* carrying an *oizuru* on his shoulders. Leave everything to me. I sympathize with you, my master. Pull your hat well down over your eyes and act as though you are weary, enter the barrier some distance behind us. If you do this they will pay less attention to you so please enter some distance behind.

The four retainers have knelt again while Benkei *is speaking and slow taps of the drum are heard from the* debayashi, *seeming to emphasize a pending crisis.*

Yoshitsune. I depend on you. I ask every one of my retainers to follow the orders of Benkei.

Four retainers together. We will obey!

Benkei. Go ahead all of you.

[h] The area north of Kaga, in present-day Noto peninsula. A wild area that sheltered the Heike during the earlier Genji-Heike wars.

[i] A person collecting alms or a subscription collector for a temple.

[j] The *kesa* is a kind of surplice; the *tokin,* a small, black pill-box hat set on the front of the head.

The debayashi *commences a song.*

Song: They agree to pass the barrier and now they are before it.

Yoshitsune *faces right on the* hanamichi *and commences to fasten on his hat.* Benkei *walks past him on to the stage, followed by the others.* Yoshitsune *brings up the rear.* Togashi *rises from his seat and comes towards the center of the stage and* Benkei *walks up to him.* Yoshitsune *has seated himself to the right of the stage, his head is bent and hidden by his large hat, both hands are clasped on the stave which rests over his right shoulder. The four retainers sit in a row behind him. The drum beats out slow taps as* Benkei *speaks to* Togashi.

Benkei. We are *yamabushi* and wish to pass this barrier.
Gunnai. What! *yamabushi* at the barrier.
Togashi and his men together. Have they come?
Togashi. What! *yamabushi* attempting to pass the barrier. I am ready for them! (*To* Benkei.) Now you priests, this is one of your barriers.
Benkei. I have heard of it. Many priests have been sent out to all the provinces to collect funds for the restoration of the Todai temple at Nara.[k] I am responsible for the provinces of Hokurohodo[l] district and we are on our way there.
Togashi. I appreciate your efforts in these times, but this barrier is especially forbidden to *yamabushi.*
Benkei. You speak strange words. For what reason?

(Togashi *and* Benkei *turn to face the audience.*)

Togashi. It is as follows. Since Yoritomo is estranged from his brother, Yoshitsune and his retainers are said to be on their way to Michinoku disguised as *yamabushi,* to ask for Hidehira's help. Yoritomo, knowing this, has ordered

[k] The Todaiji is one of the great temples of the holy city of Nara, near Kyōto. It was destroyed in the religious wars of the previous period.

[l] Northwest Japan, from the bend in the coastline near present-day Tsuruga northward.

every *yamabushi* to be strictly examined. I am the keeper of this barrier.[m]

Gunnai. We have been ordered to question all *yamabushi* and we are on our guard.

Heinai. As there are so many of you—

Gennai. Not one of you may pass this barrier.

All three together. You cannot pass!

Benkei. I see why, but I think you have been ordered to stop disguised *yamabushi* not real ones.

Gunnai. As we killed three yesterday—

Heinai. No matter if you are real ones.

Gennai. If you wish to pass through you do so at the risk of your lives.

All three together. At the risk of your lives!

Benkei. Was Yoshitsune among the *yamabushi* you beheaded?

Togashi. I cannot discuss that question with you, *yamabushi* may not pass!

Three soldiers. May not pass!

(Benkei *faces* Togashi *with opened fan,* Togashi *turns and goes back to his seat.*)

Benkei. What an abominable way to speak. I did not expect to meet with such sacrilege. There is nothing more we can do, we must perform our last rites and resign ourselves to death. (*Turning to his party.*) Come closer all of you.

Four together. Yes sir!

Benkei. Let us perform the last rites.

The drums and samisens are now playing and Benkei *goes to the rear of the stage with his back to the audience. The four retainers kneel in the center of the stage in a square, facing outwards.* Yoshitsune *remains where he is.* Benkei *turns and comes into the center of the square holding a* juzu;[n] *the retainers rise and they do a slow dance, each one rolling a* juzu *between his palms. The four then resume a kneeling position once more, hands clasped as though in prayer.* Benkei *stands in the midst*

[m] The exact location of the barrier-gate is not known. The ancient coast is now under a half-mile of water. The barrier-gate is supposed to have been at the rear of the Sumiyoshi Shrine on the Ataka River about three miles from present-day Komatsu, south of Kanazawa. Hidehira Fujiwara, a great warlord, did protect Yoshitsune during his lifetime.

[n] A form of Buddhist rosary.

of them. While this action is taking place the debayashi *is playing a song.*

ong: Yamabushi *follow the teaching of* Enno Shokaku, *as they are his disciples they represent Buddha himself while they live.* Myō-o [o] *will guard our destiny, if you kill us here we cannot tell what he may do but* Kumano Gongen *will punish you instantly. We pray to them for help.*

o saying Benkei *rolled his* juzu.

ogashi. I admire your brave preparations for death. You said you were soliciting subscriptions for the Todai temple at Nara. If that is so you must carry a subscription scroll. Read it please, let me hear you.

enkei. What! Do you wish me to read the subscription scroll?

ogashi (ironically). That is what I mean!

enkei. Um—all right.

he debayashi *plays.*

ong: Of course he has no kanjincho *but taking out a scroll from his box pretends to read loudly.*

enkei *goes to the rear of the stage and returns with a scroll which he slowly unrolls and commences to read. His party have returned to their original position.* Togashi, *who is sitting upright and motionless, rises slowly and dramatically and begins to move deliberately towards* Benkei *with uplifted fan. Each movement is considered as part of a formal design which seems to lay emphasis on the mounting tension. The audience waits expectantly, the atmosphere of the theater is hushed.* Togashi *stops, he is leaning forward in an attitude of suspicious enquiry; suddenly he starts forward, glances at the scroll in* Benkei's *hands, then draws back quickly. He says nothing but his face indicates his innermost thoughts.* Benkei *turns aside clutching the false* kanjincho *to him and assumes a rigid pose.*

he scene is a triumph of that subtle play upon facial ex-

[o] The Myō-o are a group of gods of the Shingon sect of Buddhism.

pression which forms such an important part of th Kabuki actor's technique. Togashi *is a man whos suspicions have been confirmed but who at the sam time has decided to ignore his duty in deference t deeper feelings.* Benkei *realizes the moment is a cruci one but is prepared to see it out to the end, and matc his mental skill against that of his adversary. It is ope to the master actor to place a more delicate emphas one way or the other on his interpretation of parts suc as these, which require the great artists of the Kabuk stage to bring to them the finesse they require.*

After this incident Benkei *faces* Togashi *and commences t read again while the guardian of the barrier stands lis tening.*

Benkei. Let me explain. Since Gatama[p] died there ha been no one to succor people from the perplexities of lif and death. In the mediaeval age there was an Empero who was a sincere believer and took pity on the people One night he had a dream and divine revelation came t him. He was so impressed that he built a temple for th peace of the world as well as for his own people. How ever, it was destroyed by fire in the Jisho era, and it wa regrettable that after its destruction people no longer ob served the traditions of their faith in that place. Now priest named Shun bo Chōgen[q] has received an Im perial Mandate and wishes to rebuild the temple. He ha sent many of us out to different provinces. Those wh contribute even a piece of paper or a small coin, will ob tain the highest happiness on this earth and find peac in the next world. My words are heard by Buddha.

(Benkei *rolls up the scroll sharply as he finishes reading.*)

The debayashi *plays.*

Song: He read so loudly that it echoed in the heavens

Togashi *half turns to face the audience.*

Togashi. As I have heard you read the subscription scrol there is no room for further suspicion. However, let m

[p] Gatama is another name for Buddha.

[q] Shun bo Chōgen made a pilgrimage to China in 1167–8 an was commissioned by the emperor to rebuild the Todaiji templ which had been burned by the Taira clan.

avail myself of the opportunity to ask a few more questions. The costumes of priests differ but only the dress of the *yamabushi* has an intimidating appearance. I do not understand why such clothing is necessary to pious men, Is there a reason for it?

Benkei *faces the audience then turns to* Togashi.)

enkei. That is easily answered. *Yamabushi* must climb high mountains where others dare not pass, and kill wild beasts and poisonous snakes. We take compassion on ordinary men and practice religious austerities over long years, we try to persuade lost souls to achieve the true state of Buddha, and evil spirits too. We make our prayer for the peace of the world. So, although *yamabushi* are peaceful men beneath, outwardly they must appear fierce. This *juzu* symbolizes the virtues of Buddhism in overcoming the evils of the world.

'ogashi. You wear a *kesa* like an ordinary priest, but why do you wear a *tokin* on your head?

enkei. Tokin and *suzu kake* are comparable to the helmet and armor of a warrior. We carry stout swords blessed by Amitābha Buddha, and *kongozue* [r] blessed by Gotohama. We strike the ground with our *kongozue* and we can cross high mountains and steep places.

ogashi. The temple priest carries a palmer's staff only, why do you defend yourselves with *kongozue?*

enkei. It is very easily explained. The *kongozue* is a divine staff because it was used by Arara, who lived on Dantoku mountain in India. When Gotohama [s] was called Kudonsami, he practiced austerities under Arara, who admired his piety and changed his name to Shofubiku.

'ogashi. And how was the *kongozue* introduced into your religion?

enkei. Enoshokaku, the founder of our religion, carried this staff when crossing fields and mountains, from him it was handed down from generation to generation. As it originally came from Arara it is a divine staff.

ogashi. You are a priest yet you wear a sword. Is it for appearance or do you really use it?

enkei. It may seem like the bow and arrow carried by

[r] Amitābha Buddha (also Amida), the Buddha of Pure Bliss. The *›ngozue* is an iron-tipped staff.

[s] Japanese Buddhism derived from India via China. These are stortions of Indian Buddhist legends.

a scarecrow but we do not wear it just for effect. Besid wild beasts and poisonous snakes we kill any evil ma who brings harm to the world, or goes against the law o Buddha and the Imperial Realm. We can dispatch hi instantly. If we save many by killing the one we are in th right.

Togashi. You can kill visible things but suppose invisib evils attack the Imperial Realm, how do you destroy them

Benkei. We have no difficulty, we use spiritual weapons an pray to Buddha.

Togashi. What does the costume of the *yamabushi* sym bolize?

Benkei. It represents the shape of Fudomyo-O.[t]

Togashi. What is the meaning of your *tokin?*

Benkei. It is a coronet which symbolizes the five wisdom

Togashi. What about your *kesa?*

Benkei. It symbolizes the Kuemandara.[u]

Togashi. What meaning have your leggings?

Benkei. They represent the darkness of the inner world.

Togashi. What about your eight straw sandals?

Benkei. We wear them to symbolize treading on the eig petals of the lotus flower.[v]

Togashi. What meaning is there when you draw breath?

Benkei. It represents ah—un. Ah is the voice with an ope mouth and un when the mouth is shut. It stands fo the beginning and end of all things.

Togashi. What about Kujinoshington?[w] Let me avail myse of an answer to that question. Answer me quickly.

Benkei. The meaning is very subtle and hard to explai but I will tell you to allay your suspicions. When yo wish to make this prayer you must stand erect and strik your teeth thirty-six times with the thumb of your rig hand, draw five vertical lines and four horizontal lin after that, then pray "kiu kiu go ritsurei."[x] All kin of evils as well as heretics may be instantly destroyed. is like pouring hot water on frost and acts as an invisib weapon more powerful than the sword made by Bakuya

[t] Deity of the Yamabushi sect.

[u] A Buddhist scroll illustrating enlightenment (*nirvana*).

[v] The Buddhist symbol for purification. Buddha is represented seated on a lotus leaf.

[w] A prayer containing the nine sacred characters of the Shingo sect.

[x] He invokes the sacred law.

[y] A famous swordmaker of ancient China.

If you have any further questions about our religion I will answer them for you. Its virtues are great and boundless. Remember this and keep it to yourself. I vow these words before all the Gods[z] in Great Japan, as well as Buddha. We speak with reverence in our minds.

ogashi. I was wrong to suspect so reverent a priest even for a moment. Now I will be a contributor to your subscription fund. (*To his men.*) Bring my offerings here.

hree soldiers. Yes sir!

he debayashi *plays.*

ong: The retainers bearing a ceremonial costume in white, silks from Kaga province and other things, place them in position on three wooden stands.

ogashi. I am afraid these are poor gifts but I ask you to accept them in good faith.

Benkei *faces* Togashi *and blesses the gifts with his rosary, then bends to pick them up and hand them to one of his party who rises and returns to his place with them.)*

enkei. Thank you, I am grateful to you, you are a generous donator. I am sure you will be happy in this life and in the next world. I have another favor to ask you. I must travel round the provinces soliciting contributions and I shall return here about mid-April. Until then these gifts will be a burden to us and I would like you to keep them for us. Now all of you, go ahead!

our together. Yes sir!

enkei. Now we must hurry on our way.

our together. We are ready.

he debayashi *plays.*

ong: The yamabushi *stood up and went on their way quietly rejoicing.*

he four followers rise and troop round to follow Benkei, Yoshitsune *well in the rear.* Benkei *has reached the middle of the* hanamichi *when one of* Togashi's *men points to* Yoshitsune *who is still on the stage.* Togashi

[z] There are gods of various places and minor gods, some of them f the Shinto faith.

immediately calls upon him to stop, posing threatening with his hand on his sword. It is the prelude to t climax towards which the action has been leading.

Togashi. Hey you *gōriki,* wait a minute!

The debayashi *plays.*

Song: They suspect my master. It is a critical moment, a the yamabushi *step back in anxious suspense.*

At Togashi's *shout* Benkei *and the others all run back o to the stage hurriedly. The four retainers return to the original position, kneeling with backs to the audienc* Yoshitsune *is kneeling in the center of the stage, h head lowered.* Benkei *faces* Togashi *across* Yoshitsune.

Benkei. Aiya! Wait a minute, don't be too hasty in you actions. You *gōriki,* why don't you move along?

Togashi. I stopped him.

Benkei. For what reason?

Togashi. Someone informs me he resembles a certain pe son, that is why I stopped him.

Benkei. It is not unusual for someone to resemble anothe but who is he like?

Togashi. I am told that he resembles Yoshitsune, so stopped him to make sure of his identity.

Benkei (*ironically*). What! It will be a never forgotten da in his life that he has been mistaken for Yoshitsune. It exasperating. (*Angrily.*) We hope to reach Noto provin by sundown if possible, but this *gōriki* carrying only small burden on his back lags behind. (Benkei's *feign anger rises.*) That is why he brings suspicion on us. (*T* Yoshitsune.) What a useless fellow you are! You shall pa dearly for it! Because you were incompetent in your tas you were mistaken for Yoshitsune.

Benkei *then seizes the stave from his disguised master hand, raises it aloft for a moment, and commences beat* Yoshitsune *across the shoulders with it. The act does not actually touch his victim of course; the bea ing is a piece of graphic symbolism and dextrous mani ulation done to a coordinated rhythm.*

Benkei (finishing the beating). Now go ahead!

Yoshitsune *rises hurriedly and goes off to the right corner of the stage. In the meantime a short song has been played.*

Song: With his kongozue *he gave* Yoshitsune *a good beating.*

Togashi. No matter what you say we cannot let him pass.
Three soldiers in chorus. We cannot let him pass.
Benkei. Why do you keep an eye on that *oizuru.* Is he a thief?

The debayashi *plays.*

Song: Why do you all try to draw your swords to fight for such a gōriki.

Benkei. Kore!

Then follows a scene which is full of great power and superb stagecraft. Benkei's *four followers rush to him forming a square, and press forward threateningly; he holds them back with his stave.* Togashi, *his sword half drawn, and* Benkei, *grasping the stave in both hands, perform a characteristic movement; with bent knees they slowly shuffle round to face each other at bay. Then a slow dance is performed in time to the rhythm of the music.* Togashi *and his men with slow and measured paces press* Benkei *and his followers backwards; the position is then reversed and* Benkei *and his party surge forwards against* Togashi *and his soldiers who recede to their original starting point. The whole action forms a pattern of threatening movement which is vivid in its appeal to the eye. At the conclusion the entire group remains posed in tableaux.* Benkei *raises the stave above his men's heads and speaks.*

Benkei. If you are still suspicious I will leave the *gōriki* in your charge with the gifts. Treat him as you like, or shall I beat him to death on the spot?
Togashi. Your actions are violent. It is wrong for a priestly leader.
Benkei. Then why did you suspect him?

Togashi. Because one of my retainers informed me.

Benkei (raising his staff on high). I will beat him to deat to allay your suspicions.

Togashi (restraining Benkei *with an anguished gesture).* D not be rash. Just because my retainers were suspicious an needlessly mistook the man for Yoshitsune you beat hir like that. My suspicions are now allayed, you may tak him and go on your hasty way.

Benkei. But for our generous contributor's words I woul have beaten him to death and abandoned him here. (*T* Yoshitsune.) What a lucky fellow you are! Be more care ful from now on!

Togashi. We will be on our guard yet more strictly. Ha

The debayashi *plays.*

Song: The keeper of the barrier accompanied by his re tainers enters the gate.

Togashi's *men have reverted to their former position, sit ting in a row.* Benkei's *men go to the far right of th stage.* Togashi *next turns with a deliberate movemen and strides slowly to the left followed by his men, th whole party disappearing through the small trap.* Benke *stands and watches them go and turns as they vanish* Yoshitsune *rises and walks slowly from the far corner* Benkei *passes him with lowered head at the extrem right.* Yoshitsune *seats himself at the left whilst th four followers rise and sit in a row at the rear cente of the stage.* Benkei *turns and comes over, bows, an kneels to the right of the group. The scene that follow contains a pathos which is touching in its reserved dig nity to the Japanese playgoer.*

Yoshitsune. You have acted with great presence of min today. No man can compete with you. You saved my lif by beating me like an inferior menial and ignoring To gashi. I am deeply indebted to you. It was by the protec tion of Heaven and the divine will of the gods of Genji.

(*While he is speaking there is slow samisen music and th intermittent taps of the drum.*)

[a] The gods of the Genji (Minamoto) and of Yoshitsune's an cestors, despite the fact that his quarrel is with his brother.

Hitachibo (first follower). We thought it was a critical moment when our master was stopped by the barrier guard.

Suruga (second follower). It is a sign that the gods of Genji protect our master. We can now proceed to Michinoku more easily than we hoped.

Kataoka (third follower). We owe everything to the wit of Benkei. Without him we would have been lost.

Kamei (fourth retainer). We cannot compete with him.

Hitachibo. Hoho!

Four together. We are impressed.

Benkei. Although we live in a world of increasing corruptness the sun and the moon are still in heaven. We are happy that you were saved. Although I beat my master as a ruse I thought I should incur divine punishment. I can lift a thousand pounds weight but at that moment my arm seemed numb. How irreverent I was!

Benkei *bows his head; a slow song is played.*

Song: Benkei *had never wept before but at this moment he weeps. It is touching and* Yoshitsune *takes his hand.*

Benkei *moves forward on his knees towards* Yoshitsune, *with his hand before his eyes.* Yoshitsune *moves forward and extends his hand;* Benkei *starts back with arms outstretched.* Yoshitsune *then turns sadly aside, his hand before his eyes;* Benkei *bows his head to the ground and* Yoshitsune *speaks.*

Yoshitsune. I was born of a samurai family but I do not know why I am not favored with the fortunes of war. I was prepared to give my life for my brother Yoritomo, and leave my corpse floating in the sea.

Benkei *and his master then move to face each other and there is a quick passage of music.*

Song: We slept on mountains, in fields, and by the sea coast. Whenever we slept we were in armor, and in constant danger of attack our sleep was fitful. Aboard a ship our fates were once at the mercy of the waves, once high in the mountains we met a snowstorm which covered our horses to their knees. For three years we helped Yoritomo *to become powerful, but in spite of this you are unfortunate; I sympathize with you.*

Benkei's *look was as a thistle beaten down by frost and rain.*

Benkei, *still kneeling, gestures with his fan and concludes with a pose in which one arm is raised and supported on his knee. The others rise to their feet.*

Hitachibo. Hurry, hurry.
Four together. Let us go quickly.

Benkei *hastily ushers them to the right of the stage as* Togashi *reappears through the curtain.*

The debayashi *plays.*

Song: Urging one another they were about to leave when—

Togashi. Wait, wait!

(Togashi *followed by his page and the soldiers bearing saké go to their position on the left, except that this time* Togashi *seats himself on the ground. A soldier places a stand in front of him and pours out a small bowl of saké.* Togashi *drinks.)*

Togashi. As I was so impolite to you I have brought some saké. Now let us drink. Take this cup.
Benkei. Thank you generous contributor, we will drink.

The soldier takes the stand with the saké and places it in front of Benkei, *who is seated facing the audience. The two other soldiers come over and kneel on either side of* Benkei, *each holding a flask of saké. The left-hand soldier carefully pours out a measure;* Benkei *pauses, then drinks. He beckons the third soldier to bring the lid of the lacquer tub. The small stand is removed and the two soldiers pour saké into the lid.* Benkei *raises it aloft and quaffs it; the others watch with astonished expressions on their faces.*

The debayashi *plays.*

Song: He knows how to accept both the saké and hospitality of others.
Because of a girl I met long ago in my past I had to face the

barrier of public criticism. It is an old story and embarrasses me to speak of it.
Once again I am in trouble and face another barrier.
In this transient world you are fortunate or unfortunate by a mere chance.
It is interesting to float a cup in a mountain stream and dance, letting my sleeves touch the winding waters.

While this song is proceeding Benkei *has put the lid down and commences to point his finger through the air slowly. The soldiers follow his movements with a fixed gaze until* Benkei *suddenly claps them both heartily on the back, causing them to lose their balance. He gives a prolonged laugh and his lid is filled again for him to drink it off at one draught.* Benkei *then asks the soldiers for their flasks but they shake their heads disapprovingly at him in turn; he thereupon seizes the flasks from the startled men, empties them into the lid and casts them away upon the ground. The soldiers pick them up and ruefully shake them,* Benkei *drinks again, and the others return to their places.*
After drinking Benkei *places the lid on his head and sits for a few moments.*
This scene introduces a lighter touch into the play as a relief to the tension of the preceding action. Benkei *at first hesitates to drink freely, then mellowed by the wine indulges in some humorous byplay. He reminisces on a romantic episode in his past and uses it as an example to philosophize on his present situation. Finally he rises and dances the game of the winding stream, an ancient pastime which originated in China. In this game wine cups are set afloat on a winding stream some distance between each other. The players sit on the banks and have to compose one short poem between the passing of the cups in front of them. The best poem at the end gains a prize.* Benkei *opens his fan, pretends it is a cup and casts it away from him, as though on the stream. It is the beginning of a final dance in which* Benkei *expresses varying moods and emotions after the experience they have gone through.*

After taking the lid from his head Benkei *rises unsteadily and throws his fan from him, later retrieving it with staggering steps. He then goes down on outstretched legs and posing turns towards* Togashi *and speaks.*

Benkei. Let me offer you a cup of saké on behalf of us all.
Togashi. Dance for us please.

(Benkei *turns on his knees to face front.*)

Benkei. I hope you enjoy long life like the turtle living on a large rock.[b]

The music and singing is by this time increasing in tempo and rhythm.

Song: (Benkei *was originally skillful in the dance, particularly the Ennen dance, a sacred dance.) The mountain stream echoes in the hills as it falls from rock to rock. The echo comes from the waterfall. Though the sun shines the water never dries up.*
Now let us depart quickly, be careful of the various barrier guards, now this is our good bye. They took the oizuru *and slung it over their shoulders as if they were treading on the tail of a tiger or escaping from the fangs of a poisonous serpent. They departed on the way to Michinoku, they departed on their way to Michinoku.*

All this time Benkei *is dancing; after the winding stream prelude he dances with fan closed and outstretched before him. He moves towards the right then back to* Togashi, *and finally stands with open fan and outstretched arms. He turns around several times and dances again, finishing by kneeling in the center of the stage. Next he takes his* juzu *and dances, holding it together with his fan; suddenly he flicks his arm sideways, signaling to his party to leave. They rise to their feet quickly,* Yoshitsune *leading, and swiftly leave the stage by way of the* hanamichi. Benkei *takes the* oizuru *previously worn by* Yoshitsune *and strapping it on to his back seizes the stave and runs towards the* hanamichi *with erratic steps, as though physically overcome with relief at his party's escape.* Togashi *strides forward and takes a striking pose mid stage, one arm upraised on high and his men in a row behind him. The curtain is pulled across and* Benkei *is left standing at the foot of the* hanamichi, *stave in hand and head lowered. He turns and faces down the* hanamichi *and his face breaks into a slow smile. The wooden clappers are heard and his right arm is raised as*

[b] The turtle is a symbol of longevity in Japan.

he does a mie. *He makes his exit down the* hanamichi *with a special movement known as* tobiroppo. *Beginning slowly it increases in tempo as the actor makes his way to the* hanamichi *exit. It may best be described as a form of hopping step, the right arm being thrust forward beyond the actor, whose whole body inclines forward on one leg, the arm being flung back in a wide arc behind his head as he changes to the other foot. Performed to the beating of a drum it constitutes a stirring and dramatic finish to the play.*

Selected Bibliography

In addition to the works listed here, the reader shoul consult the volumes from which the translations were take They contain much valuable material.

Indian Drama

Dhanamjaya. *The Daśarupa.* Translated and with an In troduction by George C. O. Haas. New York: Columb University Press, 1912.

Great Sanskrit Plays in Modern Translation. In new En lish transcreations by P. Lal. New York: New Direction 1964.

Kālidāsa's Abhijñāna-śakuntalā. Translated from the Benga Recension by M. B. Emeneau. Berkeley: University California Press, 1962.

Mṛcchakaṭikā. The Little Clay Cart, a Drama in Ten Act attributed to King Sudraka. Translated by Revilo Oliver. Urbana: University of Illinois Press, 1938. good translation with excellent Introduction and notes

Sacontalá; or the Fatal Ring. Translated by Sir Willia Jones. Calcutta, 1789; London, 1790. The first Englis translation. An elegant one still worth reading.

Shakuntala and Other Writings by Kalidasa. Londo Dent, 1912 (Everyman's Library). Reprinted 1959 (Ne York: Dutton Everyman Paperback) with Preface G. L. Anderson. An excellent translation of th devanagari version; includes Kalidasa's other plays.

Sources of Indian Tradition. Edited by William Theodo de Bary and others. New York: Columbia Universi Press, 1958.

Basham, Arthur L. *The Wonder That was India.* New Yor Grove Press, 1959. A general introduction to India culture.

Keith, Arthur Berriedale. *The Sanskrit Drama.* Oxford: Cla endon Press, 1924.

Iitchell, John D. "The Theater of India and Southeast Asia." *Asia and the Humanities*, edited by Horst Frenz. Bloomington: Indiana University Press, 1959, pp. 146–155.

———. "A Sanskrit Classic: Shakuntala." *Approaches to the Oriental Classics*, edited by William Theodore de Bary. New York: Columbia University Press, 1959, pp. 119–131.

Vells, Henry W. "Sanskrit Drama and the World Theater." *Yearbook of Comparative and General Literature*, XI (1962), pp. 172–176.

Japanese Drama

Genyadana, A Japanese Kabuki Play. Translated by A. C. Scott. Tōkyō: Hokuseido Press, 1953.

apanese Folk-Plays: The Ink-Smeared Lady and Other Kyogen. Translated by Shio Sakanishi. Rutland, Vermont: Charles E. Tuttle Co., 1960. Farces of the type given as interludes between Nō Plays.

apanese Plays: Nō, Kyōgen, Kabuki. Translated by A. L. Sadler. Sydney: Angus & Robertson, 1943. Contains translations of four Kabuki plays.

Major Plays of Chikamatsu. Translated by Donald Keene. New York: Columbia University Press, 1961. Eleven plays, best available translation. Four of these are included in *Four Major Plays of Chikamatsu.* New York: Columbia University Press, 1964.

Sources of Japanese Tradition. Edited by Ryusaku Tsunoda and others. New York: Columbia University Press, 1958.

The Battles of Coxinga. Translated by Donald Keene. London: Taylor's Foreign Press, 1951. Detailed study and earlier translation of a play that appears in *Major Plays,* above.

The Love Suicide at Amijima: A Study of a Domestic Tragedy by Chikamatsu Monzaemon. Translated by Donald H. Shively. Cambridge, Mass.: Harvard University Press, 1953. This translation and full-length study, along with the translation in Keene's *Major Plays* (above), provides very elaborate commentary on this play.

The Old Pine Tree and Other Noh Plays. Translated by Makoto Ueda. Lincoln: University of Nebraska Press, 1962. A cycle of plays.

Ernst, Earle. *The Kabuki Theatre*. New York: Grove Press 1959. Especially valuable on the physical stage, acting audience, etc.

———. *Three Japanese Plays from the Traditional Theatre* New York: Grove Press, 1960.

Halford, Aubrey S. and Giovanna M. *The Kabuki Handbook*. Rutland, Vermont: Charles E. Tuttle Co., 1956 Synopses of a large number of plays.

Hamamura, Yonezo and others. *Kabuki*. Tōkyō: Kenkyusha, 1956. On the actors and theater rather than the dramas.

Hozumi, Ikan. "Chikamatsu on the Art of the Puppet Stage." Translated by Donald Keene in his *Anthology of Japanese Literature from the Earliest Era to the Mid-Nineteenth Century*. New York: Grove Press, 1960 pp. 386–390.

Keene, Donald. "The Japanese Theater" in his *Japanese Literature, an Introduction*. New York: Grove Press 1955, pp. 47–66.

Nippon Gakujutsu Shinkōkai (Japan Society for the Promotion of Science), tr. *Japanese Noh Drama*. Tōkyō: NGS 1955–1960, 3 vols. Volume I reprinted Rutland, Vermont: Charles E. Tuttle Co., 1960, as *The Noh Drama Ten Plays from the Japanese*. Good modern translations

O'Neill, P. G. *A Guide to Nō*. Tōkyō: Hinoki Shoten, n.d Brief summaries of a great many plays.

(Zeami). Seami Motokiyo. "The One Mind Linking All Powers" and "On Attaining the Stage of Yugen." Translated by Donald Keene in his *Anthology of Japanese Literature from the Earliest Era to the Mid-Nineteenth Century*. New York: Grove Press, 1960, pp. 258–262

(Zeami). McKinnon, Richard N. "The No and Zeami." *Far Eastern Quarterly*, XI (1952), pp. 355–361. Excellent introduction to Zeami's art.

(Zeami). ———. "Zeami on the Art of Training." *Harvard Journal of Asiatic Studies,* XVI (1953), pp 200–225.

(Zeami). Ueda, Makoto. "Zeami on Art: A Chapter for the History of Japanese Aesthetics." *Journal of Aesthetics and Art Criticism,* XX (1961), pp. 73–79.

(Zeami). "*Seami juroku bushu,* Seami's Sixteen Treatises." Translated by W. Whitehouse and M. Shidehara. *Monumenta Nipponica* (Tōkyō), IV (1941), pp. 530–565. Translation of a major work by Zeami on the art of acting and the philosophy of the Nō.